Law and Literature

Based on the texts of traditional Chinese dramas such as *The Orphan of Zhao*, *Liang Shangbo and Zhu Yingtai*, *The Injustice to Dou E*, and *The Fifteen Strings of Cash*, the book aims to broaden the scope of law and literature in China.

Adopting a comprehensive and interdisciplinary approach of legal theory, literature, sociology, economics, and political science, the author analyzes some theoretical issues that are of the law or relevant to law in these literary playscripts, which breaks the Chinese tradition of moral reading and integrates literary study or humanitarian studies into the study of social sciences. In addition, the book discusses the history, status quo, and prospects of law and literature research in China and reflects on its value and methodology.

The book will appeal to scholars and postgraduate students of legal theory, Chinese literature, and legal history.

Zhu Suli is a chair professor at Peking University, China. His research interests are jurisprudence, sociology of law, and law and literature.

China Perspectives

The *China Perspectives* series focuses on translating and publishing works by leading Chinese scholars, writing about both global topics and China-related themes. It covers Humanities & Social Sciences, Education, Media and Psychology, as well as many interdisciplinary themes.

This is the first time any of these books have been published in English for international readers. The series aims to put forward a Chinese perspective, give insights into cutting-edge academic thinking in China, and inspire researchers globally.

To submit proposals, please contact the Taylor & Francis Publisher for China Publishing Programme, Lian Sun (Lian.Sun@informa.com)

Titles in law currently include:

The Crisis of Distribution (Set: The Crisis of Distribution and the Regulation of Economic Law)
Theoretical Analysis from Economic Law
Shouwen Zhang

Distributive Institutions (Set: The Crisis of Distribution and the Regulation of Economic Law)
The View of Economic Law
Shouwen Zhang

Chinese Law of Personality Rights I
Theory and Practice
Edited by Wang Liming and Shi Jiayou

Chinese Law of Personality Rights II
Codification Experience
Edited by Wang Liming and Shi Jiayou

Law and Literature
A Study Based on Traditional Chinese Drama
Zhu Suli

For more information, please visit www.routledge.com/China-Perspectives/book-series/CPH

Law and Literature

A Study Based on Traditional Chinese Drama

Zhu Suli

LONDON AND NEW YORK

This book is published with financial support from Chinese Fund for the Humanities and Social Sciences.

First published in English 2025
by Routledge
4 Park Square, Milton Park, Abingdon, Oxon OX14 4RN

and by Routledge
605 Third Avenue, New York, NY 10158

Routledge is an imprint of the Taylor & Francis Group, an informa business

English Version by permission of SDX Joint Publishing Company.

British Library Cataloguing-in-Publication Data
A catalogue record for this book is available from the British Library

ISBN: 978-1-041-00944-3 (hbk)
ISBN: 978-1-041-01604-5 (pbk)
ISBN: 978-1-003-61560-6 (ebk)

DOI: 10.4324/9781003615606

Typeset in Times New Roman
by Apex CoVantage, LLC

Contents

Tables

Introduction

The Consideration of Law and Literature in China

This book attempts to expand the scope of law and literature, a new sphere of theoretical research on legal science in contemporary China. I will mainly choose some traditional Chinese drama as source material and analyze some theoretical issues that are of the law or relevant to law.

This means the basic pursuit of this book is not to apply literary material with historical significance to substantiate the history of law, and not even to utilize literary material to annotate or go so far as to propagate some contemporary legal concepts. However, the book strives to investigate some legal, especially Chinese legal, theoretical issues that might be of general significance in a detached way within concrete contexts constructed by literary texts and the historical contexts that construct these texts. I hope this work will make some contributions to the study and comprehension of general legal theoretical issues. Although source material applied in this study is literary, historical, and therefore local, my fundamental concern is of contemporality, reality, and consequently generality. This concern is manifested in the following aspects: first, I try to expound the relevance between these issues and the formation of law and order in the China of today from the theoretical logics instead of the traditional "allegory," or suggestion or insinuation; second, in this effort, I hope to foster the possibility of setting the research on law and literature in China as a branch of theoretical study in legal science and more commonly foster the possibility of considering our theoretical issues that are currently of general significance in China, which is consistent with my previous efforts. The former is concerned with legal institutions, while the latter is concerned with legal theories.

Since the theoretical study will first touch on construction or reconstruction of issues, this study then is not commonly concerned with the literary sphere, but is expected to bring forth some new stimulations and create some new possibilities to ancient Chinese literature, especially dramatic studies as well. The study endeavors to show that the literary study, or humanitarian studies in a more general sense, might, or even should, be integrated into the study of social sciences, and it shouldn't be restricted by tradition; thereby, it will provide insights that only law or only literature can't provide into the understanding of Chinese society and the development of other academic disciplines in the transition period of Chinese society and knowledge. Only the interdisciplinary study in this sense could be the research of knowledge increasement, not the "peripheral study" as the academic decoration.

DOI: 10.4324/9781003615606-1

Even though this study is on law and literature, its basic theoretical framework, point, and method mainly originate from social sciences, primarily referring to social theories, economics, anthropology, sociology, politics, and social biology. I will do my utmost to avoid or reduce academic jargon and to exhibit the powerful interpretive competence of modern social scientific theories through the language that will be understandable to common readers. Theoretical thinking and innovation are not necessarily linked with abstruse terms and obscure expressions. It could, and absolutely should – although it is not easy – be dissolved in our feeling and thinking of quotidian life experiences or familiar source material and be understood by more common readers.

As an introduction, this article will lay emphasis on the analysis of some relevant issues with law and literature as the theoretical study of legal science, including its current situation, issues, and significance, with the premise of reviewing and analyzing the status quo of the study on law and literature at home and abroad. In the meanwhile, there will be a brief introduction and discussion concerning the source material, method, and structure of this book.

Status Quo and Review

It is not a new thing to study law from a literary perspective (the literature here is in a broad sense, but mainly refers to narrative literature). In China, at least from the 1990s onwards, some scholars in the community of legal science[1] have touched on the sphere of law and literature in different ways. In my opinion, some relatively meaningful efforts among them include the following achievements. He Weifang's article, "The Style and Spirit of Judicial Verdicts in Ancient China: A Study with the Song Dynasty as the Research Basis and the Comparison with Britain,"[2] was involved in the literary color of verdict writing of ancient officials in "the administration of justice," especially those "fancy verdicts" that were characterized with the obvious literary pursuit, or even the suspicious "dallying with literature." Liang Zhiping's book *Legal Intent and Human Feeling*[3] compared the differences between Chinese and Western legal cultures with notes, essays, and stories of ancient scholars as source material and, simplistically raised, explicated some questions concerning law. Liu Xing first published a series of Western legal stories in *Southern Weekly* using Yi Zheng as his pen name, which were compiled to be published later.[4] The analyses of these stories were rather meticulous with powerful reasoning

---

1 Actually, some literary scholars deal with law and literature as well, for instance, studies on *gong'an* plays (dramas of clever magistrates settling complicated cases of crime), dramas concerning the honest official Bao Zheng (999–1062), and other honest officials in the Yuan Dynasty. But the basic method of their study is predicated on literature or historical materials. For this reason, the book will not elaborate on it for the time being. As for the related legal study in dramas of the Yuan Dynasty, please consult with the related articles in Zhang, Yuezhong, chief ed. 张月中. *Yuanqu tongrong shang* 元曲通融上 (Taiyuan: Shanxi Ancient Books, 1999), 687.

2 He, Weifang 贺卫方. "Zhongguo gudai sifa panjue de fengge yu jingsheng yi songdai wei jiben yiju jianyu yingguo bijiao" 中国古代司法判决的风格与精神 – 以宋代为基本依据兼与英国比较. In *Zhongguo shehui kexue* 中国社会科学, no. 6 (1990), 203–219.

3 Liang, Zhiping 梁治平. *Fayi yu renqing* 法意与人情 (Shenzhen: Haitian, 1992).

4 Liu, Xing 刘星. *Xichuang fayu* 西窗法语 (Guangzhou: Huacheng, 1998).

and concise wording, which were quite popular among readers. Xu Zhongming, the colleague of Liu Xing, has been following the path of Chinese historians' motto "to substantiate history with literature" and "the mutual testimony between poetry and history" for years. He delved into literary works of ancient China and studied the historical material of legal institutions of ancient China. He has made consistent efforts in the study on law and literature in China.[5] With a similar train of academic thoughts to Xu's but using different applied material, Wang Shirong's work analyzed traditional Chinese legal institutions from verdicts of ancient China, including those in literary works.[6] Moreover, Qiang Shigong's article that tackled feminism was not only related to the female image in three classic literary works at home and abroad but also was characterized by the strong color of legal comparison between China and foreign countries.[7] In addition, in recent years, there are other scholars such as Yu Zongqi,[8] Ling Bing,[9] Yu Xiaoming,[10] Zhao Xiaoli,[11]

5   For example, the series papers of Xu, Zhongming 徐忠明. "Cong xuepan dasi zhangsan mingan kan qingdai xingshi susong zhidu" 从薛蟠打死张三命案看清代刑事诉讼制度. In *Faxue wenji 4* 法学文集4, *Zhongshan daxue xuebao congshu* 中山大学学报丛书, 1992; "Cong qiaotaishou luandian yuanyangpu kan zhongguo gudai sifa wenhua de tedian" 从乔太守乱点鸳鸯谱看中国古代司法文化的特点. In *Lishi daguanyuan* 历史大观园, no. 9 (1994); "Wusong mingan yu songdai xingshi susong zhidu qiantan" 武松命案与宋代刑事诉讼制度浅谈. In *Lishi daguanyuan* 历史大观园, no. 11 (1994); "Huo diyu yu wanqing zhouxian sifa yanjiu" 活地狱与晚清州县司法研究. In *Bijiaofa yanjiu* 比较法研究, no. 3 (1995); "Cong mingqing xiaoshuo kan zhongguoren de susong guannian" 从明清小说看中国人的诉讼观念. In *Zhongshan daxue xuebao shehui kexueban* 中山大学学报社会科学版, no. 4 (1996); "Dou e yuan yu yuandai fazhi de ruogan wenti shixi" 窦娥冤与元代法制的若干问题试析. In *Zhongshan daxue xuebao zengkan* 中山大学学报增刊, 1996; "Baogong zaju yu yuandai falv wenhua de chubu yanjiu shang" 包公杂剧与元代法律文化的初步研究上. In *Nanjing daxue falv pinglun* 南京大学法律评论 (Autumn 1996). All these and other articles are compiled as Xu, Zhongming 徐忠明. *Faxue yu wenxue zhijian* 法学与文学之间 (Beijing: China University of Political Science and Law Press, viz. CUPL Press, 2000). Another study concerning law and literature is Xu, Zhongming 徐忠明. *Baogong gushi yige kaocha zhongguo falv wenhua de shijiao* 包公故事: 一个考察中国法律文化的视角 (Beijing: CUPL Press, 2002).
6   Wang, Shirong 汪世荣. *Zhongguo gudai panci yanjiu* 中国古代判词研究 (Beijing: CUPL Press, 1997).
7   Qiang, Shigong Shigong, Qiang 强世功. "Wenxue zhong de falv anti genie dou e yu baoxiya nvxing zhuyi de falv shijiao ji jiantao" 文学中的法律: 安提戈涅、窦娥与鲍西亚 – 女性主义的法律视角及检讨. In *Bijiaofa yanjiu* 比较法研究, no. 2 (1995).
8   The series of researches of Yu, Zongqi 余宗其. *Falv yu wenxue de jiaochadi* 法律与文学的交叉地 (Shenyang: Chunfeng, 1995); "Liangwei meiguo faxuejia de wenxue lunju de deyushi falixue wenti he meiguo falvshi guankui" 两位美国法学家的文学论据的得与失 – 法理学问题和美国法律史管窥. In *Guowai shehui kexue* 国外社会科学, no. 4 (1998); *Falv yu wenxue manhua* 法律与文学漫话 (Beijing: Huayi, 2001); *Zhongguo wenxue yu zhongguo falv* 中国文学与中国法律 (Beijing: CUPL Press, 2002) and *Waiguo wenxue yu waiguo falv* 外国文学与外国法律 (Beijing: CUPL Press, 2003).
9   Ling, Bin 凌斌. "Pufa famang yu fazhi" 普法、法盲与法治. In *Fazhi yu shehui fazhan* 法制与社会发展, no. 2 (2004).
10 Yu, Xiaoming 余晓明. "Wenxue yu falv zhijian yi baimaonv de wenben yanti weili" 文学与法律之间 – 以白毛女的文本演替为例. In *Nanjing shifan daxue wenxueyuan xuebao* 南京师范大学文学院学报, no. 1 (2004).
11 Zhao, Xiaoli 赵晓力. "Yaoming de difang qiuju da guansi zai jiedu" 要命的地方: 秋菊打官司再解读. In *Beida falv pinglun* 北大法律评论 (Beijing: Law Press, Spring 2005).

and Chen Hongguo[12] who have done the research on law and literature to varying degrees. As a whole, the discussion on legal issues on the basis of literary works is on a steady rise.

In retrospect, namely, to reconstruct and explicate these works or articles from the perspective of today, they have touched on all the major aspects of the law and literature sphere that was initially created and defined by American scholars. He Weifang's article actually discussed "law as literature" but with the emphasis on the texts of judicial verdicts. Liu Xing's work was also generally classified as "law as literature" but with the broader scope than He's. Liu stressed the effort of considering all of the legal events recorded in the history as the research subject with a relatively complete story (text). Liang Zhiping's work and Qiang Shigong's article were more concerned with "law in literature" but with a slight emphasis on theoretical issues. Being classified as the research of "law in literature" as well, Xu Zhongming's research was oriented toward the legal history with attention to the excavation of the information in literary works that might be used as research on the legal history. Wang Shirong's study on court verdicts was involved in "law in literature" and "law as literature" in the meantime.

Although these works and articles, including my own article concerning the film *The Story of Qiuju*,[13] have touched on law and literature to varying degrees, all of them lack the theoretical consciousness of law and literature in general. Qiang's article might be considered a possible exception. For example, Liang's work availed itself with notes and stories of ancient China that could be listed as the literary texts to some extent, but the author's short comments usually flowed as random thoughts and caprices with the focus on the discussion concerning legal culture, and it only kept law at arm's length in a usual way. Liu's work was rather adept at raising questions with jurisprudential significance in legal stories and was endowed with the summarization power of theoretical thinking. But because of the length limit in a special column of a newspaper, the issues weren't probed further. He's article was related to "law as literature," but its focus was not on it, which naturally passed over some questions that might be implied. It was the same case with Wang's study. Xu's article attached the greatest attention to law and literature, but because of the influence of his professional path, he entered the sphere of law and literature even more from the perspective of traditional historiography. What he cared for was to open up the material concerning the study of legal history, and he hadn't theoretically investigated this sphere and failed to raise questions of legal theories. The theoretical thinking in Qiang's article drifted away between feminism and law and literature, two branches of theoretical studies in legal science with an emphasis on the feminist investigation.[14]

---

12 Chen, Hongguo 谌洪果. *Falv ren de jiushu* 法律人的救赎 (Beijing: China Democratic and Legal Press, 2011).

13 Zhu, Suli 朱苏力. "Xiandai fazhi de helixing he juxianxing" 现代法律的合理性和局限性. In *Dongfang* 东方, no. 3 (1996).

14 My views here are not the comprehensive academic criticism on these research fruits, but only the analytical criticism concerning their theoretical contribution to the study of law and literature.

In this period, the most noteworthy Chinese author in law and literature might be Feng Xiang, who then taught at the Faculty of Law at the University of Hong Kong. Because of his academic training background that spanned two specialties and his literary love in his youth,[15] each one of his works exhibited the mastery of profound legal and literary theories, susceptible art feelings, and adroit narrative skills at the same time. For instance, his article "Unswerving Persistence of Good Things in Life"[16] discussed the frontiers of literary art and advertisements, and even touched on the ideological issues concerning literature and advertisements from the perspective of intellectual property that was his legal expertise. Another example was the article "Qiuju's Puzzles and the Vega Civilization,"[17] in which the author discerned a question of a major principle from minor issues. He made a further analysis on the social formation of "Qiuju's" puzzles (why Qiuju failed to win the understanding of villagers) and the related historical formation (how Qiuju became the person ignorant of the law in the modern discourse of ruling by law). He incisively pointed out the ideological features of modern capitalist discourse of ruling by law and the implied paradox. Moreover, he was proficient in connecting Qiuju with the American film *Contact* (1997) through the means of montage and created the connectivity of meanings out of the irrelevance in time and space, which ushered in a rather unique reading effect and presented a mode of narrative and demonstration that was not seen in standard law articles of contemporary China. In Feng's other articles and books such as *Ynis Gutrin: King Arthur from Camelot to China* (2003) and *Notes on Politics and Laws* (2004),[18] he was skilled in the application of this mode of narrative as well. In this sense, Feng Xiang has actually touched on another issue of contemporary law and literature, namely the issue of narrative, or "law through literature." At least one portion of his own specialty, intellectual property, was "law of literature." Feng Xiang's long article "Law and Literature"[19] first introduced several issues of the American law and literature movement in a systematic, summary, and complete way in China. The article further put forth a series of his views on law and literature that were relatively systematic and characterized with theoretical potentials yet failed to set off the demonstration. His broad and incisive vision, his mode of narrative, and demonstration were even beyond the frontiers outlined by the American law and literature movement today.

15 See "Resume of the Author," in Feng, Xiang 冯象. *Mutui zhengyi* 木腿正义 (Guangzhou: The Sun Yat-ten University Press, 1999).
16 Feng, Xiang 冯象. "Shenghuo zhong de meihao shiwu yongcun buyi" 生活中的美好事物永存不移. In *Dushu* 读书, no. 2 (1997).
17 Originally published as Feng, Xiang 冯象. "Qiuju de kunhuo" 秋菊的困惑. In *Dushu* 读书, no. 1 (1998).
18 Feng, Xiang 冯象. *Bolidao yase yu wo sanqiannian* 玻璃岛: 亚瑟与我三千年 (Beijing: SDX Joint Publishing Company, 2003); Feng, Xiang 冯象. *Zhengfa biji* 政法笔记 (Nanjing: Jiangsu People's Press, 2004).
19 Feng, Xiang 冯象. "Falv yu wenxue" 法律与文学. In *Beida falv pinglun* 北大法律评论, vol. 2, no. 2 (Beijing: Law Press, 2000), 687–711.

But the most important contribution of Feng Xiang actually didn't lie in the aspects of depth and "skill" of these analyses. Through the analysis of the transformation of political and legal strategies, Feng Xiang made the contribution that defined the frontiers and therefore were pioneering – he himself might not be aware of it – to the law and literature movement in two aspects. First, he actually put forward the literary moralizing function of "law as literature" that served as a part of a social control system and was mutually complementary to the "official" legal institutions, which were mainly based on the experiences of China, especially the experiences of the Cultural Revolution from 1966 to 1976. Second, he greatly expanded, or actually might have reconstructed, the sphere of "law through literature" that was defined by the research of American scholars at the moment, which were based on the experiences of China as well, but the experiences concerning the disputes of intellectual property since the reform and opening-up in the 1980s. In *Notes on Politics and Laws* and his articles, especially "Persons Ignorant of the Law and the Copyright," he made careful analysis of how the "modern rule of law" entered modern Chinese society by virtue of the recollecting of copyright and portrait right and completed or was implementing the transition of political and legal strategies in the whole society. This is law through literature that was more meaningful, which had the fundamental changes with more academic significance in comparison with the one that only stressed narratives. Both propositions have pioneered a new research space for the law and literature movement.

Since the American law and literature movement has been mentioned, a few more words need to be uttered. There has been a topic of law and literature in the American community of legal science for years,[20] but as a movement or sphere or school of legal science, it was developed mainly within the circle of law schools in America since the 1970s. At present, all major law schools in America open the course of law and literature, which reflects the extensive influence of this movement. As for this movement, Dr. Feng Xiang has made a good summary, which saved my efforts in elaborating on it. Here, I only want to explain the influence of this movement on me and the relationship between the movement and this book.

Today, the American law and literature movement might have four branches in the meticulous classification, mentioned earlier. The first is law as literature, namely, to consider legal texts or even judicial practices as literary texts for study. Viewed from this way, law is nothing but another form of stories that need to be explained and comprehended.[21] Therefore, it might be possible to apply all sorts

---

20 The early example is Cardozo, the famous American jurist who published the article entitled "Law and Literature" in 1925, but he discussed the issues of literary style and rhetoric of judicial papers. See Cardozo, Benjamin N. "Law and Literature," in *Selected Writings of Benjamin Nathan Cardozo*, ed. Margaret E. Hall (New York: Fallon Publications, 1947); Another example is Curiae Amicus, ed. *Law in Action, an Anthology of the Law in Literature* (New York: Crown Publishers, 1947), in which Ezra Pound wrote the introduction.

21 Cf. Levinson, Sanford. "Law as Literature," in *Texas Law Review*, vol. 60 (1982), 373ff.; Farber, Daniel A.; Sherry, Suzanna. "Telling Stories Out of School: An Essay on Legal Narratives," in *Stanford Law Review*, vol. 45 (1993), 807.

of literary theories, including interpretation theories, to study all kinds of legal texts and practices. The second is law in literature, namely, to study the law that is reflected and exhibited in literary works and to mull over the theories and practical issues of legal science.[22] The third is law of literature, namely, to study all kinds of law that regulate literary and art products including copyright, freedom of the press, the punishment on obscene literary books and journals, and the infringement on others' reputation by literary works. The fourth is law through literature, which is on the rise after the 1990s. Noticing the literary appeal, some authors try to narrate, discuss, and elucidate the legal issues through literary means.[23] But generally speaking, the first branch is usually bracketed with the fourth branch as one category by the academic community, because if it is discussed as the theoretical issue, the legal expression in literary style can still be classified as law as literature. There is not much difference between the third branch and traditional legal study, and it is just concerned with the issues of freedom of speech and tort law in literature. Accordingly, it can be said that in the law and literature movement, what are relatively interesting in a true sense are mainly two branches, namely, law as literature (works and theories) and law in literature.[24] Both aspects exerted influences on the current study to some extent; the former's influence on me was much earlier, while the latter inspired me more.

Let's begin with the former. Like many youths of the 1970s, I used to be a lover of literature. Literature is a compensation for the life that is impossible to be possessed in a certain sense, and it helped me to understand the people and the lives that I couldn't enter and understand then, or even ever. But in the middle of the 1980s, my love for theoretical reasoning was on the rise because of the limitation of specialization. Since I pursued my study in America and was far away from a literary environment in Chinese, I gradually gave up the dream of my youth. During the period of studying in America, I was first engaged in professional legal training. Although I didn't like its excessive technicality, the down-to-earth, and anti–grand narrative thinking and technical training in American law schools exerted great influences on me. In retrospect, the case-based teaching that was popular in American law schools was the elucidation around the stories and legal texts to some extent. This training enabled me to surmount traditional legal frontiers and observe legal and social issues that I cared for. But my ensuing judgment was that literature and law were diametrically different and hard to be compatible with each other.

---

22 For example, Wesberg, Richard H. *The Failure of the World: The Lawyer as Protagonist in Modern Fiction* (New Haven: Yale University Press, 1984).

23 For example, Williams, Patricia J. *The Alchemy of Race and Rights* (Cambridge, MA: Harvard University Press, 1991). Since the author is a feminist and belongs to a minor ethnicity, this book is considered a monograph with features of feminism and ethnic criticism.

24 See Posner, Richard A. *Law and Literature*, 2nd ed. (Cambridge, MA: Harvard University Press, 1998); Brooks, Peter; Gewirtz, Paul. *Law's Stories, Narrative and Rhetoric in the Law* (New Haven: Yale University Press, 1996), 3; Minda, Gary. *Post-Modern Legal Movements, Law and Jurisprudence at Century's End* (New York: New York University Press, 1995), 150. Feng Xiang has done the same work in his articles of law and literature; please check Note 19.

One of the influences that changed me was from law as literature, especially the related interpretation theories. In the mid-to-late 1980s, I was very interested in the American Constitution and judicial institution, especially judicial verdicts and interpretations of the Supreme Court of the United States. But I was puzzled as well from time to time – the interpretations concerning the American Constitution by the Supreme Court were always elusive for me. At that time, as a person who had received traditional training of Chinese education of legal science that laid emphasis on legal articles and concepts, I couldn't fully understand the tradition of American case law and tended to consider law as text; I couldn't understand that the relationship between the practice of the American Constitution and the original text of Constitution was actually not as close and tight as people had imagined; I couldn't understand that what dominated theoretical discourse of the Constitution was mainly the practice of legal discourse of the specific society, and the meaning of the constitutional text therefore was formed in its incessant absorption of political and ethic judgments from society in American judicial practices; I couldn't understand the social standard meaning of words that were not from dictionaries, but from social practices. At that time, American communities of legal science and judiciary were engaged in a large-scale debate about what were the original or substantial meanings of constitutional texts. This debate was actually a contest among political powers,[25] but it was unfolded in the name of learning, and all the concerned parties had mobilized lots of academic resources. As an outsider who was not familiar with the real political procedure of America, I treated this academic debate with a political background, or a political battle wrapped in the package of learning, as a pure academic issue and tried to seek a certain answer in terms of theories.

It was in this process of pursuit that I encountered law as literature. One of the core views of this branch at that time was more or less like this: The interpretation method of literary works could be of help for legal interpretations, such as the original meaning of the authors of literary works, the recreation of readers, social conditions of readers' recreation, issues of language, etc. It was in this process of pursuit and study as well that I gradually touched on new criticism, philosophical hermeneutics, analytical philosophy, and interpretative methods of sociological and anthropological understanding that were related to hermeneutics.

But by 1992 when I returned to China, I had already basically given up the naïve thought of finding an interpretative method or hermeneutics to ensure the unification and correction of legal interpretations. It didn't mean that the scholars of "law as literature" failed to put forward some meaningful propositions which could be used as guidelines or even principles for individuals to comprehend texts, but it did mean that these methods were basically useless among groups with different political interests, among scholars with different political leanings, or even among

---

25 See Levinson, Sanford; Mailloux, Steven, eds. *Interpreting Law and Literature, a Hermeneutic Reader* (Chicago: Northwestern University Press, 1988), especially "Part 1 Political and Interpretative Theories."

individuals with different judgments because of other reasons. Even if there were such principles or guidelines, their applications would be up to users who knew where the shoe pinched, and there wouldn't be "objective" standards that could be tested repeatedly. Especially when textual interpretations were involved in the conflict of fundamental interests, you would never demand or even force two parties concerned in the conflict to conclude the consensus. Legal interpretations therefore are more like a battlefield for the rivalry between interests, not the standard to demarcate interests. The ideal status of interpretation demands all the interpreters be honest and impartial, but it fails to provide the measure to check whether there is impartiality or not; it also demands the uniformity between human intelligence and their knowledge, but it is impossible to set this premise in reality. Moreover, if human beings did possess both conditions like these, would we be in need of justices to settle lawsuits? At least there would be no need for lawyers. Therefore, after the 1990s, the hermeneutics movement around the American Constitution basically came to an end. The superficial reason, or one aspect of reasons, was both parties in the debate came to find that the interpretative method of literature wasn't of any help to legal interpretations. But the more important reason was the liberal-minded associate justices of the Supreme Court reached the venerable age and retired one by one starting in the late 1980s, and the newly elected associate justices tended to be conservative in general, who were no longer in need of making an issue around "interpretation." The debate on "interpretation" had already lost its "practical significance." After all, the power of theories is limited. Many issues are not solved by theories, but solved by time and the reshuffle of personnel, by natural power.

Though my illusion of acquiring the correct interpretative method through literary interpretation theories, and even hermeneutics or analytic philosophy of language, had been burst, this kind of academic experience, including the experience of disillusion, still brought great benefits to my study. All in all, I toured some related spheres, although it was a cursory journey. Hermeneutics enables me to notice various possibilities of interpretation, the important role of readers in interpretation, biases of readers (not in the derogatory sense), and the historicity of these biases; it enables me not only to see words, legal articles, and books but also to see more of the "text" and its historical, social, and political formation. Analytic philosophy enables me to lay more emphasis on the usage and function of language and the contexts of words and phrases used. I learned to reject the "correct" words and definitions and came to understand the communion and complementarity between words and other symbols. Foucault's discourse theory enables me to observe the sign function of language, the relationship between power and knowledge, and the historical formation of academic discourse and proposition from another aspect. But the most important thing is, in this experience, these theories are no longer just concepts and propositions for me, nor the academic decoration of words, but have become a kind of reminder to my own reading and comprehension experiences. They have more or less merged into my academic study, urged me to be more considerate in understanding issues, and enabled me to be more sensitive – and more tolerant while more demanding – to facts, events, power, contexts, and texts than before. The acquisition of this competence greatly expands my world.

I mainly owe the change of my views on law and literature in a fundamental way to the research of famous American jurist and justice Richard A. Posner, especially his study on law in literature. It mainly occurred in 1992 when I came back to China. Starting in 1993, I began to translate Justice Posner's *The Problems of Jurisprudence* (1990)[26]; one section of this book was especially on law and literature, and another section discussed some literary works with the coverage of the feminism as well. He made the analysis of some Western literary classics from the perspective of law and put forward very practical problems of law and theories of legal science from ordinary or even nonlegal stories, which broadened my horizon. His other important monographs also made meticulous analyses of literary works. In addition to the monograph entitled *Law and Literature* (1988), in the book *The Economics of Justice* (1981), he analyzed political and legal institutions of ancient Greek society, with Homer's *Iliad* and *Odyssey* as source material, and analyzed some other legal or paralegal institutions of ancient traditional society. In *Overcoming Law* (1995), he analyzed law and literature from time to time as well.[27] In 1997, in order to compile the Chinese version of *Collected Works of Posner*,[28] I translated parts of his *Law and Literature* (1988) and read the whole book in a more careful way. The reading had an important influence on me. I gradually sensed the significance of literary works in terms of the comprehension of theoretical problems of legal science and the comprehension of problems of legal institutions in specific eras.

Posner is one of the core figures of the American law and literature movement, a figure who couldn't be bypassed.[29] But strictly speaking, Posner is not the initiator of law and literature. On the contrary, he is a critic in some sense. The subtitle of the first version of *Law and Literature* was "A Misunderstood Relation." The second version deleted this assertion, but he still holds strongly critical attitudes toward many scholars and basic propositions concerning law and literature. However, Posner's criticism is not the opposition in a general sense. He doesn't groundlessly reject them while standing on the outside, nor does he apply the legal economics that is his other expertise to attack others' study of law and literature (this type of

---

26 Posner, Richard A. *The Problems of Jurisprudence* (Cambridge, MA: Harvard University Press, 1990).

27 Posner, Richard A. *Law and Literature, A Misunderstood Relation* (Cambridge, MA: Harvard University Press, 1988). Ten years later, the book was revised and expanded with the deletion of the subtitle. See also Posner, Richard A. *The Economics of Justice* (Cambridge, MA: Harvard University Press, 1981); Posner, Richard A. *Overcoming Law* (Cambridge, MA: Harvard University Press, 1995).

28 I compiled *Collected Works of Richard A. Posner* with 12 volumes, which were published by CUPL Press from 2001 to 2005.

29 Posner's *Law and Literature* is consistently one of the textbooks that are mostly chosen in law schools since the publication of the first version in 1998. It is also one of the monographs that are mostly cited in the law and literature movement. In 1998, the second revised version of this book was issued, and the advertisement on the back cover stated "Richard A. Posner's *Law and Literature* has handily lived up to the Washington Post's prediction that the book would 'remain essential reading for many years to come.'"

criticism does occur frequently in the academic community, not just in China). He holds the engaged, participating opposition and criticism. He has made full use of his familiarity and sensitivity of Western literary classics (in the second version of *Law and Literature*, he even discussed some contemporary popular literary works of America) and Western literary criticisms (Posner himself completed a bachelor's degree at the Department of English Literature, Yale University, and was the best graduate student). In the meanwhile, he fully mobilizes his training, knowledge, intuition, and insight as a jurist, justice, economist, and sociologist to analyze lots of literary works and puts forward his comprehension and interpretation of these works. He lets his own interpretation vie with others' in "the market of learning and thinking." Posner's way holds the greatest influence on me, this study, and the writing of this book.

Posner is well known in the community of legal science as a classic libertarian economist. But in the study of law and literature, law, and other disciplines,[30] the basic way he analyzes problems – in my view – is actually consistent or compatible with Marx's historical materialism to some extent. He always puts the stories of literary works or his other research subjects into the specific social and historical conditions for the investigation. He attaches great importance to the restriction of real conditions of social material life on the actions of institutions and individuals. The terms used in his works merely are more susceptible to the traditional influences of contemporary new institutional economics. Besides, because of the rigor of economic training and sensitivity of literary training, and because of his great attention to academic achievements and technologies of modern social sciences as well, Posner's analysis is more meticulous, rigorous, and careful than the analysis of Marxist political economics. In my opinion, Posner's means of analysis can really be an improvement and refinement of the means of Marxist research not only in the aspect of literary analysis but also in the study of other social basic institutions. However, Posner is opposite to Marxism in political ideology.

In a nutshell, the inspiration that this study has received from Posner is listed in two aspects. The first is the frontier of law and literature outlined by Posner. He lets me reconsider the relationship between law and literature and find a new sphere and some source materials for the study of certain theories in legal science. The second is the way he handles law and literature and his attention to institutions, concrete social and historical contexts, and the full investigation of the restrictions by historical and social conditions.

---

30 Posner is a true polymath, who is the founder of the legal economics movement, namely law and economics, and the expert on antitrust issues. His versatility is demonstrated in the titles of other monographs written by him alone, such as *The Problems of Jurisprudence* (1990), *Sex and Reason* (1992), *Overcoming Law* (1995), *Aging and Old Age* (1995), *The Federal Courts* (1988, 1998), *The Problems of Moral and Legal Theory* (1999), *An Affair of State: The Investigation, Impeachment, and Trial of President Clinton* (1999), *Frontiers of Legal Theory* (2001), *Antitrust Law* (2001), *Law, Pragmatism, and Democracy* (2004), and *Catastrophe: Risk and Response* (2005). Because of his well-rounded talent, the *New York Times* claimed that he was "a one-man think tank" several years ago.

Significance

The understanding of American law and literature enables me to see a sphere that waits to be developed, but it doesn't require me to inevitably enter this sphere. In modern China, there are so many spheres that wait to be developed, especially in the transition period. Moreover, knowledge is not necessarily power; at least "knowing" itself will not empower people with action. On the contrary, knowing too much sometimes might deprive people of the power of action, such as "doubting" brought by knowing, "seeing-through" brought by knowing, etc. The power of action must be beyond "knowing" and originate from valuable things that actors believe in, or to be frank and straightforward, from actors' evaluation and pursuit of personal interests, although individual interests can coincide with public interests. Therefore, the question turns out to be what interests drove me to enter this sphere and write this monograph.

First, it is my unquenchable curiosity for new knowledge, new spheres and new disciplines, academic creativity of desiring to challenge myself, and the pleasure of transcending myself. It even includes this possibility, although I don't expect it to happen one day, that Chinese and Western scholars will gather to discuss only Western law and *Western* literature, or more bizarrely, Western scholars discuss Chinese law and Chinese literature. Although it is not far from an impossibility, however many years later, people might ask, where were Chinese jurists at that time?

The more direct motive is my dissatisfaction with the current situation of contemporary Chinese theoretical studies and education in legal science. The study of law and literature might possibly expand the sphere of contemporary Chinese theoretical studies in legal science and change the mode of research from one flank. Theories of legal science should not be just what they look like on the present textbooks of jurisprudence. No one could stipulate that theories of legal science must discuss issues such as the substance of law, sociality, origins, classification, rights, and duties in terms of concepts or must apply the present mode or concepts to utter words. Theories of legal science should be livelier and have more intellectual challenges. They should draw on modern social life and academic fruits to put forward new propositions and concepts; they should have a more close and direct relationship with the legal branch and lives of ordinary people; they even should point out some new research spheres for legal science and present basic questions; they should be interesting; they should be in the words of contemporary Chinese instead of foreigners – and not like the Chinese spoken by foreigners, but the modern Chinese spoken by the ancient people. "There must be a use for my tant since it is Heaven that has endowed me with it." I don't believe that all the basic or main theoretical issues of legal science have been observed by our ancestors or foreigners, while our mission is just to chew steamed buns again that had been chewed by them, only to chew buns in a more refined or smoother way.

Law and literature provides a possibility. It can enable people to shake off abstract thinking that most Chinese are not quite familiar with and accustomed to in general and enable people to comprehend general issues of law by virtue of concrete stories. The totality of stories might help people more easily grasp and comprehend legal and social issues in whole, observe the mutual connection and influence be-tween law and society, and force people not just to attach attention to abstract single articles and institutional stipulations. In this sense, the world presented in stories will be even more true and real than the world exhibited in diffuse, abstract legal ar-ticles. It demands readers enter one and another concrete context and be confronted with concrete problems, while legal principles might be in conflict as for these prob-lems, or even it is impossible to provide the perfect justice promised by legal books. Readers must ponder answers to these questions in a comprehensive, balanced, and concrete way, which can't be evaded by adopting some eternally correct principles or big words. Even readers sometimes must make decisions that might be wrong. Besides, it can cultivate people's sensitivity to the real world, facts, and human beings and enable people to be familiar with the issue of how law operates in life. Through concrete stories, it can show the deficiency of concepts, propositions, and theories, just as Qiuju's story shows us the problem of "the strict enforcement of law" (although the strict enforcement of law is not necessarily denied as a result). It can help us to think twice before do things with a one-track mind.

Law and literature doesn't mean to deny abstract theoretical thinking. On the contrary, it can help people understand how these abstract concepts and proposi-tions are bred in concrete situations of life. What kind of bitter experiences and lessons are condensed in these propositions? What conditions have gone through changes in contemporary Chinese society, such that a certain old problem is no longer a problem, or has become a false problem, a meaningless problem? How can we put forward new theoretical propositions from concrete cases and events? Consequently, the combination of law and literature can make theories of legal sci-ence livelier and more true and help to integrate "sense and sensibility" and dispel "pride and prejudice" caused by the familiarity with some eternally big words.

This development is not only more useful for Chinese society of today but also can improve the internal and external living standards of our community of legal science. As for the internal, how many jurists or jurisprudents consider the study of legal articles itself as an enjoyment (and therefore not a relief of a heavy burden upon the completion of research or the professional promotion and contribution fee brought forth by the publication of papers)? As for the external, it can improve the repulsive image of legal professionals in literary works and society at home and abroad, such as "official pettifogger," "legal pettifogger," "legal immaturity," and "The first thing we do, let's kill all the lawyers" (Shakespeare, *Henry VI*).

As always, I nurture a desire, which is to excavate the theoretical problems of legal science in the life of our nation that are more directly connected with our pre-sent life. In the meanwhile, I believe that there is no contradiction between the lo-cality of where the product is produced and the universality of where the product is used, as I have indicated in other articles.[31] I hope this study sufficiently proves that

---

31 Zhu, Suli 朱苏力. "Daolun yanjiu zhongguo jiceng sifa" 导论: 研究中国基层司法. In *Songfa xi-axiang* 送法下乡 (Beijing: CUPL Press, 2000).

even in our traditional society or drama, in those insignificant or almost worn-out stories, there are actually many complex and highly intellectually challenging theoretical problems in a general sense, which even might make some contributions to the academic progress in the world.

As a course, law and literature can compensate for some deficiencies in China at the moment, especially the education of legal science for undergraduate students. The education of legal science has lagged behind for a long time in China, which not only lacks the academic tradition and is excessively affected by political ideology but also definitely lacks the vitality as a result of the long-term absence of a market of legal practice and of the stimulation from practices in legal science. Scholars only make the conceptual deduction and the interpretation of legal articles at their own studies. From the 1990s onwards, owing to the squeezing of the market, the legal professional circle came into being and began to accumulate professional legal knowledge and skills, but it is still not sufficient. Besides, most faculty fellows of law schools – I am a typical person in this case – attach too much importance to the utterable "knowledge," they don't have or have a few experiences of legal practice, or they just have relatively simple experiences of legal affairs, or lack the theoretical summarization and generalization of these experiences, or they despise theories of legal science because of their experiences of legal practice, or treat the education of legal science as a sideline because of their excessive devotion into legal practice. All in all, the education of legal science is still basically prioritized on legal concepts and articles. The knowledge with practical reason that is accumulated by the legal profession still fails to enter the education of legal science sufficiently. Legal theories, principles, and rules that students have learned are usually non-contextual and are generally defined by academic tradition, or even "private experiences" of teachers or students themselves, instead of being defined in the tradition of legal practice. This situation hampers the research development of legal science and education in the long run. And it is very difficult for our current case-based teaching to change this situation.

As for the target of education, especially undergraduate students, they are too young, and nearly all just graduated from senior secondary schools. The overwhelming majority of them don't have or only have a few social experiences. The education of senior secondary school is basically inculcated in one direction, while the university entrance examination is more focused on the examination score. Students are filled with passions and relatively simple-minded, who tend to use simplistic concepts such as the good and the bad to classify people and things. Many of them might know the complexity of society as interpersonal relations but don't comprehend the complexity of society as the cluster of institutions. They are young and living – they have the full reason to live – in the future. They are idealists and full of vim and vigor, who are always in the hope of changing society and others overnight and accustomed to changing the world with hope. Because of the lack of social experiences, they even don't know themselves.

It is appropriate to set the undergraduate education of legal science in China as the quality-oriented education, which is targeted at the previously mentioned situation. But the issue is, the education of today is no longer completely dominated by teaching plans, but will be affected or even dominated by the market. The market demands more specialized and professionalized lawyers, which has been changing the education of legal science. The pressure of employment and the unified judicial examination have forced the education of some law schools to have the actual shifting and are changing students' study behaviors.

This phenomenon can be understandable, but it will have disturbing consequences over the long haul. If there isn't a good quality-oriented education and the education is only dictated by the current market, it will be very difficult to imagine that excellent justices, lawyers, and jurists can be cultivated, and it will be very difficult to adapt to demands of Chinese society and the market ten years or twenty years later. If we don't expect the education of legal science to completely degenerate into the training for the bar examination, we must appropriately integrate humanistic education into the education of legal science while ensuring the quality of the latter. The cultivation of this basic or comprehensive quality will not only be beneficial for their cause or study but more beneficial for the progress of Chinese society and legal science in the long run. As for the top-notch law schools such as the one of Peking University, they should especially provide better professional and comprehensive education for their students and urge the education of legal science and educational products in the whole society to have the further division of labor and differentiation.

In this circumstance, the involvement of law and literature might *slightly* compensate for this inadequacy. First, all the good literary works generally reflect the complexity of social life and human characters. To read these works can make up for the deficiency of social life experiences of young students. Second, to read and comprehend literary works itself might enhance the humanistic quality of students and cultivate their sensibilities to words, details, textual contexts, contexts of the events, and their sensibilities to the people and things described by these words. Third, it will be helpful to cultivate students' competence of distilling theoretical propositions and thinking out of concrete stories and to revise the academic means of studying legal articles and concepts in a literal way. Fourth, because of the openness of interpretations of literary works without the ultimate correct explication, it can foster students' creative thinking and their active participation. Therefore, fifth, it might change the course of legal science, especially the dull, terse, monotonous trend of current theoretical courses.

Thorny Problems

Although there are benefits and potential significances, as mentioned earlier, and the American law and literature movement provides lines of thinking, methods, and patterns, law and literature has its own weaknesses as well. One important weakness might lie in the fact that it is of thinking and interpretation, instead of operation and practice, while "the point" – just as Karl Marx said – "is to change it."[32] It is of vital importance for law. Law demands action and judgment, while law and literature can't provide such a policymaking assistance, nor the power of action. What it can provide is even more understanding, which is the requisite quality of legal professionals. Consequently, we shouldn't have the impractical expectation on the study and course of law and literature, which only slightly compensates for the deficiency of the education of legal science right now.

It might not be the most principal weakness. The more important weakness lies in that because of its own distinction, law and literature finds difficulty in being introduced into China like other schools of jurisprudence. Actually, this issue is also concerned with the legal sociology and the legal anthropology, which needs to be addressed further.

Since modern times, when scholars introduce Western academic fruits of legal science into China, they usually present the background of the related Western scholars and their monographs, then summarize, generalize, or induce their theoretical views and conclusions into several points in addition to the introducers' likely irrelevant comments (regardless of praises and criticism), and that is all – the research comes to an end. This kind of introduction is by no means meaningless; however, it is roughly a knowledge-based introduction. There isn't too much connection with Chinese legal science or legal practice, or even just the conceptual connection. Readers usually can't sense the connection between these introduced doctrines and themselves and their living situations. In the past two decades, the effort of introducing American critical legal studies, legal economics, feminism and some schools, and figures of the legal sociology into China basically remains at this level, just with a few exceptions. It can be said that this type of "transplantation" in legal science is dead from the very beginning. This effort didn't exert substantial influence on the progress of the rule of law, society, and the research of legal science in China except for the addition of one or two unknown names to the academic community, some new terminologies, some sensational new propositions, or even some new labels that could be readily stuck as "criticism" to the opponents. We can just find the proof in cases of the legal economics and the critical legal studies, including the research of postmodernism in *the community of legal science*.[33]

However, some leading scholars of the legal economics and critical legal studies have some relatively systematic and complete theories after all, and their

---

32 The original sentence is as follows: "The philosophers have only interpreted the world in various ways; the point is to *change* it." in "Theses on Feuerbach," Marx, Karl; Engels, Frederick. *Collected Works*, vol. 5, trans. Clemens Dutt, W. Lough and C. P. Magill (New York: International Publishers Co, 1976), 5.

33 The study of legal economics in the community of legal science basically stops at the introduction or comments at theoretical level with few exceptions. For example, Zhao, Xiaoli 赵晓力. "Zhongguo jindai nongcun tudi jiaoyi zhong de qiyue xiguan yu guojiafa" 中国近代农村土地交易中的契约、习惯与国家法. In *Beida falv pinglun* 北大法律评论, vol. 1, no. 2 (Beijing: Law Press, 1999). As of today, the relatively meaningful academic fruits of legal economics all come from Chinese economists, especially in the aspect of the institutional economic study.

representative monographs are written in the more generalized conceptual terms and expressive modes with which Chinese scholars are familiar. Therefore, the related translating, editing, retelling, and summarizing are comparatively easy,[34] although mistakes of various types consequently occur as well. In comparison, the "transplantation" of law and literature is much more difficult (it is a similar case with legal sociology and legal anthropology; these disciplines lay more emphasis on the study of concrete issues). The literary texts discussed by American law and literature scholars are generally Western classics, such as the works of Homer, Dante, William Shakespeare, Charles Dickens, Fyodor Dostoevsky, Leo Tolstoy, Franz Kafka, Robert Frost, and James Joyce. To most Chinese legal professionals, they might know the names of these authors but don't read much of these works. Besides, because of the contexts of literary works and habits of literary appreciation, Chinese readers usually focus on the story lines of works and might not pay attention to the effort of understanding and grasping the problems raised in them. Some readers are even not familiar with authors.[35] This fact makes it hard for law and literature to set foot in China. When the case happens here or now, even those jurists who consistently advocate for "the following of international practice" in the spirit of political correctness will pick up another set of politically correct phrases and believe that "the actual conditions of China should be taken into consideration." But this discourse is very hypocritical. It doesn't only mean that the new research is rejected, but this discourse can disguise the ignorance or incompetence of the speaker as the farsightedness of "a sophisticated person, who holds that there is nothing new under the sun" and the confidence of bearing a well-thought-out plan in mind. It seems that he or she has already specifically investigated the actual conditions of China and other countries and reached this conclusion.

However, this discourse does indirectly reflect a highly realistic and inevitable problem, namely, in a society that is strange to Western literary classics, you will find it very hard to introduce the law and literature movement that happened in America and let it take root in China, or even it can be described as the impossible mission. After all, you are not expected to initially popularize Western literature in China or the Chinese community of legal science before the introduction of law and literature.[36] Moreover, being quite different from the legal economics and the legal critical studies, law and literature doesn't have, or hasn't had up until now – a solid core of theory. It is hard to assert that it is the same case in the future – it is

---

34 But it may not be so. At present, the critical legal studies in China are mainly focused on Roberto Unger, while there are few discussions on Duncan Kennedy, the leading scholar of the critical legal studies. The key reason is that the major academic fruits of Kennedy are articles. These articles are usually not written in the generalized language and the expressive mode that seems to be detached from the concrete contexts and texts for comprehension with which Chinese scholars are familiar. In my opinion, it is the fundamental reason why Kennedy's thoughts (not his name) have been neglected in China for a long time.

35 I cite a true example. The law school library of a university classified *Crime and Punishment*, the long novel of Dostoevsky, in the category of criminal law books.

36 But if literature comprises film and TV series, the power of this question might be greatly weakened.

just a sphere and hasn't its own stable theoretical system and method. Its research is mainly based on the discussion on concrete literary texts or the application of concrete literary criticism. Under this circumstance, if the discussion of "law in literature" is unfolded, the first involved issue is in *which* literature the discussion of law is engaged. To expound the contract in literary works shouldn't always start with Sherlock's contract in China! Many readers don't know who Sherlock is and might not know what *The Merchant of Venice* is about. Just like the operation of any discourse, law and literature is also in need of a unified or reformatted operation space.[37] It is very hard to discuss *Hamlet*, *Great Expectations*, *Odyssey*, or *Divine Comedy* with contemporary Chinese, even those senior intellectuals. The locality of knowledge and theoretical practice is portrayed in such a prominent way in literature. In my opinion, it is the fully fundamental reason that the law and literature movement clinging to literary texts of Western classics has failed to enter China in a real sense for a long time.

Comparatively speaking, the introduction of "law as literature" seems to be more difficult because it not only demands the comprehension of Western literary works and the related Western legal texts but also the understanding of a whole set of Western literary critical theories. If Western literary classics could be read as stories at least, or have a smattering of value of understanding as a sign of a certain learning and status to those "who know something," these literary criticisms and interpretation theories will be nearly meaningless to those general nonliterary professionals. In the eyes of some of the community of legal science, some of them are even somewhat absurd, such as Roland Barthes's "the death of the author." These theories are highly abstract and a mystery of mysteries.

It is true that many literary critics describe these theories as "a game," but it might be just so only for those who are free from anxieties of food and clothing and willing to participate in it. To contemporary Chinese jurists or even jurisprudents, this game is undoubtedly a torture, let alone the fact that it usually demands them to give up some costs of opportunities or a certain portion of money or nonmonetary profits. If to read some Western literary works occasionally will be considered acceptable, to understand and apply Western literary criticisms and interpretation theories of various types or some specific types and to regard law as literature to be appreciated and analyzed doesn't really arouse great interest. Even if there are some capable ones who have interest, there isn't such a market demand as of now. Without the demand, the output will be hard to come by. Actually, even belles-lettres is not so far away from the market, at least not *so* far away as many persons have imagined.

Even if the factor of market is cast aside, on the basis of the previously mentioned analyses, we can observe that the so-called theoretical research itself is more of a practical problem and a problem of how to earnestly practice what one advocates. It is not enough if we just know the current situation and theories of the American law and literature movement, or even understand some related propositions and

---

37 See Zhu 朱苏力. *Songfa xiaxiang* 送法下乡, Chapter 6.

terms. It is more like coaches or many ardent fans with the mastery of theories – no matter how great enthusiasm they have and no matter how clear and logical their theories, strategies, and tactics are, it is impossible for them to replace the China Men's National Football Team to storm out of Asia. To know theories and to be capable of doing things are not exactly the same thing. It is destined that except for brief and necessary introductions, if law and literature wants to set foot in China in a real sense – actually it is the same case with any academic theory and theoretical school – *it must be creative and practicable at the beginning*. If it is to study "law as literature," Chinese law must be studied.

However, there are many problems.

First, China is a country of statutory law; therefore, there are not so many judicial cases that can serve as stories and *attract the consensual and long-term attention of the legal community*. There are not remarkable judicial opinions that *attract long-term and consensual attention* and can serve as literary works for reading as well. I need to elaborate more on the stressed words. Although the comprehension of all the literary texts is concerned with interpretation, and there will be different interpretations, the texts that have applied or need to apply various interpretations or literary critical theories are usually the ones that have been labeled as "classics" because of various reasons. In Jorge Luis Borges's words, "A classic book is that which a nation or a group of nations – or time itself in its length – has decided to read as if everything in its pages were deliberate, fatidic, as profound as the cosmos, and capable of endless interpretations." However, he added, "A classic book is not a book (I repeat) which necessarily possesses these or some other qualities; it is a book which generations of men, driven by various reasons, read with that same initial fervor and that same mysterious loyalty."[38] Only in these texts that draw the wide attention will be manifested the dispute of various literary critical theories. As for those texts to which a few or the minority of people pay attention, you can make any interpretation you like, and there will be no one who has interest in arguing with you. While different persons apply various theories to analyze diverse texts, we can't find any significance of theories at all. In this sense, classic texts are not only composed of the words themselves in these texts but also readers and many other social factors that can't be enumerated one by one and even are unaccountable.

Actually, it is the same case with legal texts that need to be interpreted. In British and American society that follows the tradition of case law, because of the principle of abiding by the precedents, justices and other legal professionals, including students of law schools, have to pay long-term attention to some important judicial cases and the judicial opinions at retrials on appeal. To abide by the precedents, such a principle and institutional request constructs these interpretation texts that attract long-term attention from the legal community. On this basis, legal professionals or talents are motivated and can apply different literary critical theories to

---

38 Luis Borges, Jorge. "Sobre los clásicos," in *Obras Completas 1923–1972* (Buenos Aires: Emecé Editores, 1974), 773.

these cases and judicial opinions. But in the area of statutory law, there doesn't exist the institutional factor of constructing the classic legal texts. Although people sometimes pay attention to some cases and judicial verdicts in a certain period, there isn't an institution to fix some legal precedents. Legal precedents and problems with which people are concerned must be fluid as a result. It is not necessary and, in fact, useless for people to pay concentrated attention to a case and judicial verdict in the long term. Generally speaking, in countries of statutory law, except for the code, there aren't classic legal texts like the ones in British and American law that are used for interpretation, and then there aren't legal texts that can serve as the premise of effectively applying different literary interpretations and critical theories.

Maybe, someone will say, the American Constitution isn't statue law? Isn't it the first written constitution since modern times? Why do American interpretation theories just revolve round the American Constitution? How do you know legal professionals in China will not resort to literary interpretation and critical theories revolving round Chinese statutory law? But I still believe that up till now, the statutory law in China doesn't have serious interpretation problems that are in urgent need of assistance from literary interpretation and critical theories just like those of American Constitution, and it will not be likely in the future as well. It doesn't mean that the statutory law in China is free of the interpretation problems, nor do I underestimate the legal interpretation issues in China. Nevertheless, it means that the judicial significance of legal interpretation issues in China isn't as great as the one in the American Constitution because of various institutional conditions. The American Constitution makes few amendments, while society is consistently changing. As for the effort of applying a text with a long-term fixation to cope with the new cases that keep popping up all along, interpretation naturally becomes a fundamental problem, a problem with all the concerned parties' interests at stake. In comparison, the longest history of statutory law in contemporary China is just more than two decades, and the legislative body revises law relatively frequently and conveniently; therefore, the legal interpretation problems can't be so prominent and necessary. Second, although Chinese justices or courts "interpret" law as well, to be more exact, they usually apply power to directly "stipulate" or "substantiate" the legal meaning. It is not the "interpretation" in its original sense.[39] Third, the texts that need to be interpreted in the American Constitution are very general words or phrases, such as "interstate trade," "due process," and "equal protection." Because of their general feature, these words and phrases are highly inclusive. Yet in countries with a tradition of statutory law, especially the contemporary Chinese judiciary, there aren't these problems of judicial practices. Fourth, the meaning of

---

39 "Judicial interpretation" in China is basically presented in the form of general rules, which are actually the legal rules and regulations in detail. Consequently, some scholars call it "judicial law." The verdict interpretation delivered by judges in specific cases generally haven't the legal power as rules do.

legal words and phrases will blur and be in need of more interpretations in a country with diverse cultures.[40] In China, a society with relatively high homogeneity, the task of legal interpretations will not be so arduous. Owing to these conditions, the law might not be much likely to turn out classic texts in Chinese society – even today.

Besides, even if possible, it might not be necessary as a whole. It is from the pragmatic viewpoint that we reach this judgment. The fundamental function of legal interpretations is not a pure intellectual activity, not the interpretation for the sake of interpretation, but is the fulfillment of a social function of law. As a result, if a society has the appropriate mechanism to ensure that law fulfills this function, then legal interpretations will not be so developed. For example, in European countries, including Britain, that follow the tradition of common law, since parliamentary legislation including legislation, amendment, and abolition, is more active and less restricted than the American Congress,[41] we can find that verdicts by justices and courts of European countries aren't more like American ones; the latter are characterized with such literary grace and individuality and have the stories and likelihood of becoming the texts of law as literature. As a whole, legal interpretation theories and practices in European countries are far less colorful than America's, although the original place of legal interpretation theories used by American scholars is usually Europe. The current institution of legislative and judicial division of labor in China is more like the European one; in my opinion, it is very hard to generate law as literature in this institution.

Henceforth, the double swords of the American law and literature movement haven't been drawn out; one sword of "law as literature" gets turned in China, while the other sword of "law in literature" is left. Perhaps it will be a relatively easy scenario? After all, China is a country with a long literary tradition! But our eyes shouldn't be dazzled by words and phrases, and we should still carefully investigate it. Truly, China has a long-term literary tradition; however, it doesn't naturally mean that it will be easy to study law in Chinese literature. The first question is: What is literature?

If we compare Chinese literature with Western literature, the mainstream of the former is characterized with emotional conveyance over a long period of time. Lyric poetry is the main body of Chinese literature, while the created narrative literature is a latecomer with a relatively smaller portion in comparison. Lyric poetry can definitely become the source material of law in literature, especially the source

---

40 Posner. *The Problems of Jurisprudence*, 1990.

41 As for the positive research of the relationship between the British judiciary and legislative body, see Atiyah, Patrick S. "Judicial-Legislative Relations in England," in *Judges and Legislators: Toward Institutional Comity*, ed. Robert A. Katzmann (Washington, DC: Brookings Institution, 1988), 129; Jordan III, William S. "Legislative History and Statutory Interpretation: The Relevance of English Practice," in *29 University of San Francisco Law Review*, vol. 1 (1994). As for the similarity between Britain and European countries, see Posner, Richard A. *Law and Legal Theory in England and America* (Oxford: Oxford University Press, 1996).

material that serves as "the mutual testimony between poetry and history," and the legal history can sometimes be used as the research material of the legal culture. However, when using lyric poetry – if in comparison with narrative literature – as the source material of law and literature, its inadequacy is obvious. Lyric poetry mainly expresses poets' personal thoughts and feelings with relatively strong subjectivity; therefore, it has great inadequacy in terms of the reflection of law in society and the reflection of a social relationship and character relationship in a specific intricate legal event.

Thus, law and literature in China must mainly rely on Chinese narrative literature. But the literary works with novels, scripts for storytelling, and dramas as representatives came into being in a relatively late period. It was until the Tang Dynasty that scripts for storytelling began to appear in China, and dramas began to gradually develop with the Song, Jin, and Yuan dynasties, while there were the relatively conscious efforts of writing novels in the Ming and Qing dynasties. Certainly, there are other types of narrative works in China, but they are usually mixed with the history, such as *Shi Ji* (*The Grand Scribe's Records*), *Han Shu* (*Chronicles of the Han Dynasty*), and the earlier works *Zuo Zhuan* (*The Commentary of Zuo*) and *Zhan Guo Ce* (*Strategies of the Warring States*). These "impure" works actually have very strong literary features as well; some of them are even just a literary creation.[42] Law and literature can choose these works as source material. Surely, contemporary narrative literature in China provides the wide resources as well, yet it needs time to define which ones are "classic" texts.

Moreover, the study of law and literature can be multiple-faceted, as mentioned. Except for law in literature and law as literature, even the legal intellectual property protection of literary works, reputation lawsuits caused by literary works, and even issues concerning the illicit publication of pornographic literary books can be classified into the category of law and literature.[43] Using literary works to study the authenticity of ancient legal institutions, namely, to testify history by literature, is totally a research pattern of law and literature. After all, law and literature is a sphere, not a theory.

Domain of Discourse

However, this monograph doesn't intend to discuss law and literature in a general sense, but strives to distill the issues with the theoretical significances of legal science out of ancient Chinese literary works and to extend the theoretical research of legal science to a new sphere. In other words, although the source materials for study are historical and literary, the orientation of my research yet is for the

---

42 "In ancient China, literature and history were undoubtedly unseparated from each other, and the distinction between history and novel was not easy to come by. It was after Sima Qian that novel and history were separated." Tang, Degang 唐德刚. *Shixue yu wenxue* 史学与文学 (Shanghai: East China Normal University Press, 1999).

43 See Posner. *Law and Literature*, 1998, Part 4.

contemporary age and the future. Since the reading and appreciation of literary works are a kind of empirical activity in which readers or audiences participate and even hold a dominant position,[44] I might apply the distance advantage possessed by the latecomers and the specific information advantage as a jurist to distill some generalized issues that can be understood today out of the texts that will not be outmoded forever. Because of this type of generalization, these issues might be related to the contemporary age and the future as well. Actually, in this study, despite the fact that what I have studied are the issues of ancient society, I consistently try to put these events, figures, and issues into their epochal or even specific placements, but what I care for is consistently contemporary issues. What I aim for is not the reconstruction of historical reality or details, but the foci on the theoretical issues presented in these traditional Chinese drama stories. To start with this concern, I believe there is the possibility of undertaking the law and literature research within three main sub-spheres in order to make up for the inadequacy of former research on legal theories.

First, the historical institutional transformation. The major institutional transformation is a relatively rare phenomenon in human history, which usually needs to take quite a long time, one hundred, or even hundreds of, years to be accomplished. In this regard, even individuals who are present on the scene usually fail to have absolute certainty and thorough understanding. It is not that life is too short for this transformation, but more importantly, the person who is living in this transformation finds it very hard to investigate this transformation as an observer who keeps a distance and holds the panoramic and detached views. Although the latecomer hasn't the direct and personal feelings, which is his weak points, yet he possesses the strong points that the person concerned didn't possess. That is the distance between him and history, and he has become the observer of those historical events and figures, who therefore is relatively less swayed by direct emotions or interests. Or generally speaking, he might get access to more related knowledge and information through other channels. To master such historical changes originally is the work of historians. But what this mastery actually needs is the construction of history more than the historical materials. A "great view of history" is needed. To construct such a great history by reading historical materials requires social theories, which is not only very difficult and subject to the queries of traditional historiology, but also very easy to criticize. On the contrary, because of their condensed and symbolic features, literary works or historical stories can instead provide a means for understanding and mastering history in a macroscopic way, and a traditional historiology that is *centered on historical materials* finds it hard to replace this path. In the process of this change, the fates of some individuals, or a historical event might concentratedly reflect lots of historical information along with institutional transformation, and consequently possess prominent theatrical features, which easily become the source materials of literature. Therefore, they usually possess very strong theatrical features, which easily become the source materials of

---

44 Fish, Stanley. *Is There a Text in This Class?* (Cambridge, MA: Harvard University Press, 1980).

literature. This situation might be more prominent in premodern literary works. To deliberately investigate and comprehend these works, we have the chance to observe and analyze a series of issues related to the institutional transformation.

Second, we can study basic frameworks of some concrete legal institutions, or even some details through literature, and comprehend conventional social issues targeted by these concrete institutions, the rationality (and irrationality) of their contextualized existence. This point is particularly important for the contemporary community of legal science in China. Because the legal science of traditional China is not advanced, the explications concerning the legitimacy and rationality of some institutions in the contemporary community of legal science in China usually come from books, which normally repeat Western discourses. Just as Lu You, a Chinese poet (1125–1210) said, "The knowledge gained from books is always not enough." Some of these explications have relevance to the reality of China, while some are the complete deduction of a conceptual system or the fragmentary comparison of institutional outlooks. The latter proves to be a failure of understanding the issues that traditional Chinese society needed to solve and the basic restrictive conditions in which institutions were generated. Or they indicate the thorough unwillingness of explicators to understand these things.[45] Since literary works link the legal system with some concrete and typical cases, they then might help us walk out of the dilemma of conceptually legal science and legalism and gain personal understanding of some concrete ancient institutions.

Third, we can investigate "literature as law" as well. It just investigates the interdependence between general literature and social political laws and their basic layouts and proceeds to investigate the role of literature as a social control in different types of society. As mentioned earlier, this domain was first advanced by Feng Xiang and hasn't been observed in the American law and literature movement at present.[46] The reason lies in this fact. In the modern West, because of the tradition of rule by law and social division of labor, law is *defined* as self-sufficient, which can cover everything, while literature is just in the margins and is the entertainment and social recreation – literature for literature's sake. The competence of literature is only no more than "the reflection of reality" and "the criticism towards reality." Feng Xiang points out that the function of "literature" actually is far from being limited thus. Poet Percy B. Shelley once emphasized that "poets are the unacknowledged legislators of the world." Literature in a broad sense actually possesses the consistent function of molding people's behaviors and thoughts; otherwise, why are there so many forbidden books in Western countries as well? Why is there the film rating system? This function might be exaggerated in traditional Chinese society.

---

45 The exception with the typical significance is, Zhang, Weiying; Deng, Feng 张维迎、邓峰. "Xinxi jili yu liandai Zeren dui zhongguo gudai lianzuo baojia zhidu de fa he jingjixue jieshi" 信息、激励与连带责任－对中国古代连坐、保甲制度的法和经济学解释. In *Zhongguo shehui kexue* 中国社会科学, no. 3 (2003).

46 Feng. 冯象. *Mutui zhengyi* 木腿正义, 24.

But it is this "exaggeration" that enables this function of "literature" to be excessively prominent in traditional Chinese society and to be carried on today. Literature not only carries "the culture" with which we customarily endow the positive and neutral significance but also actually carries the function of disseminating and integrating important orthodox ideologies all along. Literature possesses a certain function of social control. It is in this sense that Feng Xiang believes, at least in the period from 1949 to 1978, that the most important "legal" document in Chinese society was not the constitution, or even the executive orders from the government, but the texts such as Mao Zedong's *Talks at the Yan'an Conference on Literature and Art*, *Serve the People*, *In Memory of Norman Bethune*, and *Foolish Old Man Who Removed the Mountains* and various literary and art works that were produced to "educate people, attack enemies" under the guidance of these thoughts.[47] All of those who went through the Cultural Revolution have personal experiences. Only since the reform and opening-up, with the development of Chinese modernization and the increasing competence of state and legal governance, does the political and legal function of art seem to be gradually on the decline, and art is increasingly becoming an entertainment. All of society will be no longer excited at a novel or a film. Perhaps it is in this modernized layout of history that the literary discourse is on the decline, while the discourse of rule by law stands out and becomes the mainstream discourse. This change is inevitably connected with changed policies of the ruling party to a large extent, but it isn't mainly the random choice of governance strategy, but the new layout of politics, law, and literature that is generated in a new historical condition.

In comparison with Chinese society, this issue has already been present in Western society. The literature has been marginalized, and the jurists only toe the line, these are not the questions that really exist for Western jurists of today. Naturally, they then fail to pose this question, or even might not want to pose this question, because to pose this question not only threatens the myth of "rule by law," but realistically speaking, it will not push the front of law and literature forward in the positional warfare with its major rival, the legal economics. Consequently, in the research sphere of law and literature in America, this aspect is basically blank.

In this sense, Chinese jurists or literary scholars in the period of historical transition occupy a superb position. They can personally experience and observe the historical changes that will not last for a long time. Through their own creativity and intellectual efforts, they can not only comprehend the legal "culture" of China by investigating the transformation of legal and literary layouts and develop a kind of institutional explication for culture but also change the frontier of this sphere basically defined by the research fruits of American law and literature at present and expand the research border through their own research achievements.

---

47 Feng. 冯象. *Mutui zhengyi* 木腿正义, 24.

The Further Discussion of Significance

The study of law and literature can not only expand the research of legal science, especially jurisprudence, legal sociology, and legal history, but also make the contribution to other disciplines and provide research lines of thought and related achievements for the development of other disciplines. As a result, it might possess a positive externality.

It is not a mere fantasy. First, the current system of knowledge in the world is not born like this, but is the layout exhibited in a historical accretion. The frontier of each discipline knowledge actually is not clear, but an artificial demarcation. If this argument is valid, then there will be no reason to argue that legal science could only "import" knowledge of other disciplines and has no ability to "export" some of its own products to other disciplines. Certainly, the metaphor of importing and exporting has the implication of consolidating the frontier of disciplines. Considering the consistently insufficient study of institutional law (not the organizational structure and legal articles) and its actual function and utility in traditional Chinese scholarship, it is rather inadequate to present the so-called traditional Chinese culture in such a scholastic tradition. Although the legal science of contemporary China lacks such competence at present, it should totally provide an institutional path for cultural research, namely the analysis of Chinese cultural forms from the perspective of the institution.

Professor Ge Zhaoguang once pointed out that the general history of ideas should be studied.[48] Other scholars also indicated that we should pay attention to the small tradition within the great tradition.[49] But it is difficult to accomplish this pursuit only through the access of the history of ideas itself; the research contributions of other disciplines must be involved. The study of law and literature might provide some research fruits. For example, my analysis of traditional drama in Chapter 5 of this book shows that the people at that time longed for honest officials in the intellectual sense; another instance in Chapter 7 analyzes how the narrative forms and dramatic space of traditional Chinese drama mold the justice value of audiences. Although these conclusions are open for discussion, they might give some inspirations for other scholars, which might be of help for the study on the general history of ideas and the understanding of small traditions.

Even the study of law and literature might inspire literature as well. To some extent, the jurist is a novice in the literary study, but sometimes "a novice can defeat the skilled master by using no strategy at all," just as this Chinese saying goes. Because of the legal training of a jurist and his concern with institutions, his knowledge might bring new perspectives to the literary study, for everyone has his strong and weak points. For example, in this book, I analyze why the story of Zhao the Orphan in *The Grand Scribe's Records* is more moving and genuine than *The*

---

48 Ge, Zhaoguang 葛兆光. "Yiban zhishi sixiang yu Xinyang shijie de lishi sixiangshi de xiefa zhiyi" 一般知识、思想与信仰世界的历史 – 思想史的写法之一. In *Dushu* 读书, no. 1 (1998).

49 For example, Liang, Zhiping 梁治平. *Guojia yu shehui qingdai xiguanfa* 国家与社会: 清代习惯法 (Beijing: CUPL Press, 1996).

Orphan of Zhao, the miscellaneous comedy (*zaju* 杂剧) of the Yuan Dynasty and why the story of the filial daughter-in-law of Donghai in *Chronicles of the Han Dynasty* is more touching than *The Injustice to Dou E*.

In his paper on translation, Professor Gu Zhengkun once analyzed that the tragedy of ancient China was a bitter tragedy, which was different from the tragedy in the Western sense.[50] His analysis is rather meticulous and very persuasive. But on the other hand, I can't completely agree with his viewpoint. Because we now know that literary works are not just created by their authors but also by their readers, and they are the outcome of the tradition of art appreciation.[51] If we make an entry through this path and reflect, we inevitably reach such a conclusion that the bitter tragedy of China might be created by Chinese readers or audiences in accordance with a certain pattern of thinking and appreciation. If we change to another means of art appreciation, these bitter tragedies of Chinese tradition might completely possess the relevant features. The path adopted in this book strives to reconstruct the comprehension of features of some bitter tragedies.[52] Analyses of both *Liang Shanbo and Zhu Yingtai* and *The Injustice to Dou E* prove that the connectivity between these plays and Western tragedies exists in which individuals fight against the almost inevitable "fates." Unlike the traditional comprehension, these tragedies are not caused by one or two mean characters and villains, nor by a good-hearted person who does wrong things. Besides, this type of tragedy will befall others as well if it doesn't befall the protagonists of plays. If this effort is meaningful, then the saying that China hasn't the tragedy in the Western classical sense might be changed through our re-reading. Is the play a tragedy, bitter tragedy, or romantic work (such as *Liang Shanbo and Zhu Yingtai*)? It not only has the factor of work but also the factors of readers, audiences, and even art performers. The *excessive* emphasis on the certainty of the text itself somewhat smacks of authorial or textual determinism, or essentialism. It should be noted that this is not a criticism of Professor Gu Zhengkun; I hope to turn our attention to another aspect of the formation of art works through this analysis. The book makes such an effort.

Material, Means, and Method

The main materials analyzed and used in this book are mainly from traditional Chinese drama. The reason why the drama is used as source material is not only

---

50 Gu, Zhengkun 辜正坤. "Wailai shuyu fanyi yu zhongguo xueshu wenti" 外来术语翻译与中国学术问题. In *Beijing daxue xuebao shehui kexueban* 北京大学学报社会科学版, no. 4 (1998).

51 Fish, Stanley 斯坦利·费什. *Duzhe fanying piping lilun yu shijian* 读者反应批评: 理论与实践, trans. Wen Chuan 文楚安 (Beijing: Chinese Social Sciences, 1998).

52 However, perhaps someone might wonder: What is the point of my effort? Does it only prove the communication and compatibility between Chinese bitter tragedy and Western tragedy? Or the universality of the Western tragic factor? No. From the perspective of literary works, my purpose only aims to deepen the richness of the meaning of our literary texts, expand the space of reading comprehension, and broaden our vision. Perhaps such an effort might facilitate improvement of the capability of our art appreciation.

because it is the component of literature in a broad sense and is the narrative literature but also some other reasons.

First, there are always quite a number of detective plays in traditional Chinese drama, which constitute a special genre unseen in Western drama but familiar to Chinese readers and audiences. To start with the classification with which people are familiar, it will be convenient to initiate the study of law and literature.

Second, since drama is a performing art, theoretically speaking, it might be closer to ordinary people than narrative literary works (even scripts for storytelling). It is such a case at least in a traditional society with low literacy. On the other hand, since drama must rely on, or even cater to, audiences to survive and develop, it might be more susceptible to the influences of audiences. Consequently, at least from the theoretical perspective, drama might more reflect folk culture than the stories in historical books or literary works created by artists, not just the elite culture in the Chinese orthodox cultural tradition dominated by lyric literature.[53]

Third, dramatic works have wider circulation than many textual works and are more familiar to people because of their performative features and the mobile features of their public performances by "running the prefectures and knocking around the provinces." Actually, we can get the point only by comparing Feng Menglong's vernacular short stories and Yuan's plays in terms of familiarity among the masses. Readers are familiar with the works; it will create a better premise condition for the analysis of law and literature. At least sometimes I don't need to make the rather detailed introduction to the outline of story and can proceed to the analysis.

Fourth, for the sake of future development of law and literature research, I feel that the definition of literature shouldn't be overly restrictive at the very beginning. Literature must be a wider category. If possible, it should include art as far as possible. For instance, since drama is a performing art, the research should not only take dramatic stories but also dramatic performances, characters, audiences, stages, or even types of facial makeup into consideration. In one word, we must break through the concept of concrete literary text and fully comprehend the "text" as the category of philosophical hermeneutics. This dramatic feature demands that we understand and reconstruct the historical and art context in which the play takes place. The training of this competence is very important for the disciplinary (law, literature, and history) research with the text in the restrictive sense as the center. What is more, the similarity between drama and modern film, television, and dance is more than the similarity between drama and novels or poetry. The experience and lesson from the drama analysis could more easily extend to the analysis of performing art works such as film, etc.[54]

---

53 For this point, see Liao, Ben 廖奔. "Chongzhou zhuangfu cong washe goulan dao miaohui xitai yuan zaju huodong fangshi kaocha" 冲州撞府: 从瓦舍勾栏到庙会戏台 – 元杂剧活动方式考察. In *Yuanqu tongrong* shang 元曲通融上, 912; Zhu, Guangrong 朱光荣. "Lun yuan zaju fanrong de yuanyin" 论元杂剧繁荣的原因. In *Yuanqu tongrong shang* 元曲通融上, 383.

54 An American scholar has expanded this research sphere to film. See Bergman, Paul; Asimow, Michael. *Reel Justice: The Courtroom Goes to the Movies* (New York: Andrews McMeel Publishing, 2006).

Fifth, convenience. This factor actually might be the most important one that urges me to make a choice, although many researchers might neglect it. In terms of Yuan plays, we have *Selected Plays from the Yuan Dynasty* and *Supplement to Selected Plays from the Yuan Dynasty*, which are respectively edited by ancient and modern authors.[55] Both works have compiled the main plays of the Yuan Dynasty that have been handed down to this very day. The work done by past authors can easily define the purview of my source materials, which saves me the trouble of arguing why these plays are chosen and not others. To use the materials compiled by past authors and others is also another type of division of labor in academic research. The division of labor can avoid the biased conclusion caused by the subjective randomness of personal choice.

Actually, I can't analyze all the traditional plays, which is beyond my capability, and it is not necessary as well, because my purpose doesn't aim for law in the plays of a certain period, but strives to find some legal issues with theoretical significance in plays. It is for the efficient reliance on my present accumulated knowledge, and only thus, that it is possible to push forward the theoretical research of legal science while making a cursory study of law and literature, not to abandon the previous work in order to enter a new sphere. We leave some things undone in order to do other things. Therefore, I must make a choice on the plays.

My first selection standard is the plays must have theoretical issues concerning legal science in accordance with my opinion. The second is that they should be familiar to ordinary Chinese audiences as much as possible. For example, *Liang Shanbo and Zhu Yingtai*, *The Injustice to Dou E*, *Fifteen Strings of Cash*, and *The Orphan of Zhao* all fit two standards. The first standard strives for a certain generality of issues implied in plays. It might not be possible to arouse the interest of contemporary readers in the issues without generality, and it is very hard to undertake theoretical discrimination and have theoretical power. In light of this standard, *Liang Shanbo and Zhu Yingtai*, the play that is usually believed to have no relevance to law, enters this list, while *Qin Xiangliang*, the play that is usually believed to be the legal play, fails. It doesn't mean that *Qin Xiangliang* has no theoretical issue of legal science, but in my opinion, the importance of its issue far lags behind the play chosen by me. If the issues of jurisprudence raised in two plays are basically similar, I will choose one of them for discussion and only mention the other. It aims to save the time of readers, since it is unnecessary to repeat the same argument. The enlightened readers themselves can analyze other plays. For example, both *The Injustice to Dou E* and *Fifteen Strings of Cash* put forward the issues of evidence and the limitation of adjudicators, but I chose *The Injustice to Dou E* to discuss this issue and *Fifteen Strings of Cash* for other issues. Yet I will indicate the mutual reference between them.

55 Zang, Jinshu compiled 臧晋叔. *Yuanqu xuan* 元曲选 (Beijing: Zhonghua Book Company, 1958); Sui, Shusen, ed. 隋树森. *Yuanqu xuan waibian* 元曲选外编 (Beijing: Zhonghua Book Company, 1959).

I attach importance to the plays with which ordinary people are familiar, because it will save my own and readers' "trading fees" in order to win over more readers. In modern society, the opportunity cost of each individual is very high. Not many people have the patience to hear out a story that is totally unknown to them and is seemingly unnecessary for them to know. Authors must respect readers and shouldn't always believe their stories are marvelous. Actually, the outside world is marvelous as well. Consequently, to apply the present drama knowledge of readers, it might be convenient to introduce the story, and it will be easy for readers to understand this as well. More importantly, since most readers themselves will not read the texts mentioned by analysts, the best thing is to use the texts with which readers are quite familiar in order to guarantee the textual openness and prevent the discursive hegemony of analysts. In this way, readers can fully use their own knowledge, experiences, and even common sense to develop their own explanations on the texts that analysts try to explicate. They can compare their experiences and the analyses undertaken by analysts, which enables the text to be a living text as a result. It will be helpful for the development of law and literature.

Both of them are the most basic standards, but are not the only standards. I also chose other texts that might be relatively unfamiliar to readers. The main reason is that these texts embody some jurisprudential issues that other plays have not mentioned but I find them very important, such as *The Chalk Circle* and *The Moheluo Doll*.

What have been mainly analyzed in this study are these six playscripts. But in order to explicate some issues concerned and prevent excessive and farfetched explanations, I have consulted other Yuan plays, other plays of later ages, or modern plays (such as the revenge issue in *Red Detachment of Women* and *The White-Haired Girl*) that reflect similar issues. In order to expound upon some transformations of drama stories, I also have cited some nondramatic narrative texts (such as the story of Zhao the Orphan, the story of the filial daughter-in-law of Donghai, and the story of Huang Ba trying the case) and the different versions of plays (such as *Fifteen Strings of Cash*) and endeavor to present how social life molds the text and theme by virtue of genealogy. For the sake of comparison, I even have analyzed a small portion of Western plays such as *Hamlet* and *Antigone* that are necessary for the issue of evaluation and explication.

Although Yuan plays are the main source materials, the book doesn't study the law in Yuan plays, but studies some theoretical issues concerning law in traditional Chinese society through traditional drama. Otherwise, readers have every reason to question my textual application: Namely isn't it rather arbitrary to use playscripts and other texts regardless of historical period? It isn't a problem, because my analytical unit is one social phenomenon of traditional Chinese society reflected in playscripts, not a certain text, nor a playscript of a certain dynasty. It is only for the sake of convenience for the book to mainly use Yuan plays.

The conventional method of literary history research is to use the time duration as a natural framework that constructs and restricts source materials and topics. But to use the era as the vessel of literature doesn't have the rationality; on the contrary, this rationality itself needs to be evaluated. As for the plays written by the same person in the late Yuan Dynasty and the early Ming Dynasty, how different are they? Does the difference come from dynasties, themes, or other art tastes after all? What is the point of this difference to my analysis? Unless we believe that there is a mysterious essence shared by the literature of a specific dynasty in the concepts such as Song, Yuan, and Ming, we have no reason to use eras or dynasties as the basic analytical units. Many research fruits prove that scripts of many Yuan plays didn't come from one author, but were the concerted product of a series of authors, which went through different forms of adaption. Undoubtedly, Wilt Idema questioned, "Why You Never Have Read a Yuan Drama" and believed that "when we are reading these late texts of Yuan plays, we are reading the perfect authorless text. Julien and Bazin may have been more correct than they ever expected when they studied Yuan drama more as a reflection of *Chinese culture* as such than as the reflection of a specific mind and a specific age."[56] Consequently, although I usually use one playscript as the analytical source material of one chapter, my true concern is more mainly on phenomena related to law in the dramatic literature of traditional Chinese society, such as revenge, marriage, injustice, the legal profession, honest officials, morality and law, dramatic narratives, etc., not one simple play or one dynastical play and law.

As mentioned earlier, the present law and literature is a sphere, not a discipline; therefore, it hasn't had its own unique theoretical path like today. However, it is impossible for the theoretical research to lack a basic path.

In terms of the basic framework of social theories, I mainly rely on Karl Marx's historical materialism in this study; namely, I strive to investigate the issues of legal institutions reflected in literary works on a social productivity level, economic basis, and social structure and investigate the relation layout of law and literature in society. But the framework of historical materialism is too grand and its explanatory power is insufficient sometimes when it is applied to concrete issues. To make up for this defect, I resort to some economic theories from the 1960s onwards, such as the basic theoretical knowledge of institutional economics and information economics. I also consult some findings and the framework of social biology that are connected with the theory of institutional economics. Although in the eyes of some scholars, historical materialism and modern Western economics have different political orientations, in my opinion, the previously mentioned theories have one thing in common, namely, the emphasis that people and institutions are restricted by social material resources and conditions; henceforth, people and institutions have historic features. These theories don't excessively emphasize the utility of concepts, morality, and personal integrity. Although they don't deny this utility, they believe that all these subjective factors have no likelihood of falling from the sky, but play their roles in concrete social environments. In this sense, these theories can be compatible; many of them even reach the same conclusion.

In analyzing issues, I basically adopt the path of analytical philosophy and care for the actual effect of the character and event mentioned by words, not the literal

---

56 Idema, Wilt. "Why You Never Have Read a Yuan Drama: The Transformation of *Zaju* at the Ming Court," in *Studi in onore di Lanciello Lanciotti*, ed. S. M. Carletti, M. Sacchetti and P. Santangelo (Napoli: Istituto Universiatorio Orientale, Dipartimento di Studi Asiatici, 1996), 789.

expressions. I don't make the abstract analysis, but go all out to put words, concepts, and propositions into concrete environments for investigation and observe how they manage to work. In this sense, I adhere to the attitude of pragmatism.

In analyzing source materials, I adopt the method of close reading and contextualization. I strive to distinguish playwrights and speakers in the play and try my best to sympathetically understand the words uttered by speakers and playwrights. I regard the words of playscripts as one part of drama and consider the story that the drama itself wants to present and deem words and deeds of characters in plays as outcomes of concrete environments. I am against the following views: Dramatic characters are deemed as the mouthpiece of playwrights; words and deeds of characters in the works are directly linked with the great era in which they live; dramatic characters and their words and deeds are considered the symbols of a certain idea or a certain character type in social life; and words and deeds of characters in the works simply amount to the playwright's analysis of social issues. I do my utmost to enter through a specific angle, construct the issues with generality reflected in dramatic stories, and endeavor to transcend specific persons and events. I seek for a general explication (theory), not an explanation concerning special cases. I go all out to start with common sense and hold in hand the complex relations between characters in the plays, the general characters, and more basic social powers (economic life conditions, social structure, the development level of science and technology, and institutions). I acknowledge the human weakness and don't further get to the root of personal motives and morality, but care for institutions. I even more consider words and deeds of people as a rational choice (although it might not be a conscious choice) in specifically restrictive conditions. I seek to find the contradiction between people's words and deeds and find the contradiction between the popular comments on these literary works and their characters and the concrete representation of dramatic figures in order to excavate the possible significance within. But I aim to be fair and just and bear no carping in mind; I try to find its inherent unity in the contradiction as far as possible.

The Structure

Finally, I want to expand on the structure of this book. I have mentioned three contributions that law and literature can make to theories of legal science in the earlier passages; these three aspects form three parts of this study.

Two chapters of Part 1 are centered on the discussion of the institutional transformation issue. Chapter 1 discusses the historical conditions in which the revenge system occurs, the utility of the revenge system in traditional society, the related institutional requirements (including ideological requirements), and its weakness in order to probe into the historical necessity and logic of institutional transformation. Chapter 2 applies *Liang Shanbo and Zhu Yingtai* to probe into the insignificant and precious power of individuals in the historical changes of institutions. I carefully analyze the historical rationality of the marriage system composed of arranged marriages and the words of matchmakers and analyze the rationality of the personal will of Liang Shanbo and Zhu Yingtai as well. In the collision of two rationalities, we observe a historical tragedy. I don't simply attribute it to the fault of institutions, but through my analysis, I point out that even Liang and Zhu themselves rationally supported this institution, which must be stable. We hereby notice the conflict between the institution and the passions, the contradiction between the institutional transformation and stability; because of information, a new institution can't be perfectly designed beforehand, and institutional innovation can only be accomplished through people's efforts of breaking through social norms.

Three chapters of Part 2 are centered on the discussion of the system of "administrating justice." In view of the fact that it is very difficult to use the current judicial concepts with the specified meaning to summarize the case trials of the grassroots government in traditional Chinese society, I hereby add quotation marks to the concept of justice. In many places, I also use the concept of "trial" or "adjudication" to replace the concept of "the administration of justice" that is a more customary application for people. In these three chapters, I extend the criticism toward the moralist research on the legal system and the analytical path, which have been implied in Part 1 but haven't been fully unfolded. The criticism is mainly centered on three aspects, namely, science and technology, institutional competence and role, and the limitation of honest officials.

In Chapter 3, I reconstruct the comprehension of *The Injustice to Dou E* and point out that the tragedy of Dou E mainly lies in the information deficiency caused by the inadequacy of science and technology. I try to prove that a capable and efficient judicial system first must have the support of science and technology; without science, any procedure and any good persons can't solve the problem of correct judgment; therefore, the tragedy is inevitable.

In Chapter 4, I mainly analyze the defect of the ancient trial institution, the integration of judiciary and administration, the deficiency of professional division of labor, and the judge's deficiency of trial skills and competences. My analysis advances the theory of comparative institutional competence and the adjudicator's comparative institutional role, and I believe it is the demonstration of supporting judicial independence in a more convincing way. I also analyze why ancient adjudicators lacked the professional technical trial knowledge.

In Chapter 5, I first distinguish two types of plays concerning honest officials; then, from two aspects of wisdom and diligent governance of these officials, I analyze why two factors are insufficient to guarantee the correct and effective trial. Under the restriction of traditional social conditions, the emphasis on these factors can only be conducive to the system of "administrating justice" with the accent on the rule by man. Because of the emphasis on personal responsibility, this system can theoretically encourage officials to be incorruptible, but in the restrictive condition of traditional society whose information costs are extremely high, the operation of this system brings forth the actual outcome that might encourage officials to be lazy or even corrupt.

Since morality is insufficient to guarantee the efficient and fair operation of institutions, why does ancient society still emphasize the rule by virtue and morality given priority over penalty? Why does this layout occur? These are the themes of Part 3. In Chapter 6, I start with the phenomenon that drama makes great efforts to publicize morality and point out that in traditional society, because of the limitation of national finance, human labor, resources, and information, the state can't effectively exercise the national governance by law and must have a political and legal ideology as the assistant institution to guarantee national governance. As a result, morality became the dominant political and legal ideology at that time and ushered in the traditional political and legal ideology of "morality given priority over penalty" and formed the institution of politics and law. Drama, the medium of art dissemination with relative popularization, carries the governance function of a legal system. Literature henceforth becomes the law in a broad sense. Accordingly, we can observe that the rule by virtue is not a cultural choice, but the fact of being chosen under specific restrictions.

Chapter 7 attentively discusses some art representation forms of traditional Chinese drama and tries to explore the compatibility between drama and the institution of morality given priority over penalty and their mutual reinforcement. I point out that traditional drama tends to mold the justice value with the dominance of substantive justice. These research studies are also connected with those on social norms or informal institutions in recent years.[57]

---

57 For example, Ellickson, Robert C. *Order without Law: How Neighbors Settle Disputes* (Cambridge, MA: Harvard University Press, 1991); Posner, Eric A. *Law and Social Norms* (Cambridge, MA: Harvard University Press, 2002); Zhang, Weiying 张维迎. "Falv yu shehui guifan" 法律与社会规范. In *Bijiao* 比较, vol. 11 (Beijing: CITIC, 2004).

Part I
Historical Change

1 Revenge and Law

The Case of *The Orphan of Zhao*

Questions, Academic Background, and Materials

In human history, revenge once had a universal and long-term existence in each society. Although it has been forbidden by law in many countries today, the story with revenge as the subject matter or the theme has invariably moved audiences for generations, and it is a theme that never fails to be repeated. In Western society, from *Antigone* and *Agamemnon* of ancient Greece to Shakespeare's *Hamlet*, or even to modern novels of Alexandre Dumas's *The Count of Monte Cristo* and Erich Maria Remarque's *Arch of Triumph*, they all reflect or are involved in the theme of revenge. Many modern art works involving judicial proceedings are usually motivated by revenge. In China, although all the most soul-stirring revenge stories seemingly happened before the Qin Dynasty (the famous stories including Wu Zixu's whipping the corpse of King of Chu, Prince Yue's sleeping on firewood and tasting gall, Jing Ke's attempt on the life of King of Qin, and Zhao the Orphan),[1] the stories of later ages such as Wu Song's killing Pan Jinlian with the bloodstained blade of a knife to avenge the death of his brother are also consistently widespread among people. Even some modern and contemporary authors try to write articles with a radically different view from time to time under the guidance of so-called new ideas,[2] but it is almost useless for the broad masses, and Wu Song is still a hero of gigantic stature among the people. More astonishingly, with the passage of time, even the most celebrated ballet plays in the Cultural Revolution, namely *Red Detachment of Women* and *The White-Haired Girl*, and other "model plays"

---

1 The stories are, respectively, recorded in "Wu Tzu Hsu, Memoir," in *The Grand Scribe's Records*, Revised vol. 7 (Bloomington: Indiana University Press, 2021); in "Prince Yue, the Hereditary House 11," in *The Grand Scribe's Records*, vol. 5.2 (Bloomington: Indiana University Press, forthcoming); in "The Assassin-Retainers, Memoir," in *The Grand Scribe's Records*, Revised vol. 7 (Bloomington: Indiana University Press, 2021).
2 For example, Wei, Minglun 魏明伦. *Pan jinlian juben he juping* 潘金莲:剧本和剧评 (Beijing: SDX Joint Publishing Company, 1988). But in the 1920s, in the edited playscript of *Pan Jinlian* and its performance, Ouyang Yuqian once attempted to reverse the verdict for Pan Jinlian. See Ouyang, Yuqian 欧阳予倩. "Pan jinlian zixu" 潘金莲自序. In *Ouyang yuqian yanjiu ziliao* 欧阳予倩研究资料, ed. Su Guanxin 苏关鑫 (Beijing: China Theater Press, 1989).

DOI: 10.4324/9781003615606-3

reflecting the class struggle, have revenge as the main thread in retrospect if their modern revolutionary color is discarded.

Revenge has been represented in such a wide and ever-lasting way in literary works, it must have a solid foundation in humanity and complex social origins. If there isn't the firm foundation of humanity, but the social reason, revenge will not appear continuously in various societies, and even the long-term draconian law set by rulers in each country will find it hard to radically forbid it; nor does the lasting ideological publicity as well. Actually, even today, the basic motive of the judicial system is the human revenge instinct: If victims or their relatives have no revenge consciousness, it will be very difficult to initiate the judicial trial, and the whole judicial procedure will be totally different; even it is initiated because of the intervention of the state, victims or their relatives are more willing than other ordinary people to assist the police in investigating criminals regardless of payment; they are more voluntary than ordinary witnesses to testify at the court and even they ask the court to pass severe punishments. Accordingly, in terms of this aspect, the judicial system seems to be very much the same in each country today.[3] If revenge is allegedly less today, it doesn't mean that such wills become less and weakened, but people can thereby take revenge more efficiently through the judicial system.

It also points out the social factor of revenge forms. If there is only the human factor, no social factor, it will be impossible for revenge to assume so many rich and varied forms whether in reality or in literary works. We will find it hard to explain why ancient revenge stories no matter at home or abroad always seem to be more exciting, respectable, and thought-provoking.

This chapter doesn't intend to discuss the revenge issue in a general way, but tries to consider revenge as a legal issue, or to be more accurate (?), as an issue of jurisprudential theory for discussion.

Such an effort of mine might be immediately resisted by the community of legal science in China. In the contemporary society of China, especially in the eyes of city residents, particularly in the eyes of legal professionals who have received modern legal training, revenge tends to be considered a violation of law, and it is an extralegal punishment. In contemporary jurisprudential theories, law is usually defined as universal social norms that will be assuredly implemented with the coercive force of the state, and it allegedly represents, or at least it should represent, social justice. Revenge is usually considered an individual behavior, and it only represents justice in the heart of avenger himself at most. Under the influence of such a social/individual discourse and ideology implied in this set of discourses, revenge is simply treated. Especially in the present days with the emphasis on "rule of law," the discussion on revenge seems to be more inappropriate. However, this chapter will show the following arguments through the analysis: Although revenge is usually outside the nationally statutory law, its significance and function are social, including the case that victims themselves or those who have intimate

---

3 Posner, Richard A. "Retribution and Related Concepts of Punishment," in *Economics of Justice* (Cambridge, MA: Harvard University Press, 1981), 213.

relations with victims (usually their relatives, but we will soon observe that it might not be always this case in ancient China at least) consciously inflict the postponed punishments on infringers before the appearance of the constitution – what has been satisfied is the emotional needs of victims or their relatives; revenge actually is a social system and a social punitive system or a control system executed in a highly dispersed way. If we don't identify law with the legitimate political violence utilized in a centralized way – a modern idea – but emphasize its characteristics of universal norms and functions of maintaining social order, we can fully regard revenge as a part of legal system in a broad sense.

Or, even we insist on the connection between law and state power, we can still understand the origin of law in a renewed way by investigating revenge, not just the origin of criminal law, although many jurists are more accustomed to linking criminal law with revenge.[4]

In this sense, many core elements of the revenge system are still what *traditional* laws[5] must possess in practice. Unlike what many people of today, including the overwhelming majority of jurists, believe, revenge is the outcome of human barbarity and uncivilization; on the contrary, revenge, especially institutionalized revenge, is actually the result of civilization and reason. My analysis proves that in a historical period with a very long duration, the actual situation is that the more advanced the human civilization and reason, the crueler the revenge. The perfecting degree of revenge reflects the advanced degree of civilization at a certain level. Although revenge has been greatly reduced today, this change has no relevance to civilization in a narrow sense, nor to benevolence, kindness, morality, humanity, rationality, enlightenment, civil rights, or culture in a narrow sense. It is mostly attributed to the structural change of social economics and political conditions. Because of this change, revenge loses its universally and importantly social function that it originally possessed and loses its compatibility with modern society.

In any sense, all these discussions concerning the revenge issue will have the significance of jurisprudential theory. On the occasion that the rule of law in China of today is about to see the great transformation because of social change, if we lack the in-depth understanding of the revenge issue and excessively adhere to some so-called "advanced" ideas, we might not have the possibility of reinforcing the rule of law, but might weaken it on the contrary. Therefore, this study has important and practical significance as well.

The theoretical framework of research in this chapter mainly comes from Judge Posner's two important research fruits on the revenge system and the theoretical

---

4 In particular, Holmes believes that all the tort laws, including the tort in civil law, are based on revenge. See Holmes, Oliver Wendell, Jr., *The Common Law* (New York: Little, Brown, and Company, 1948), Lecture 1, 2, 4.

5 They are mainly criminal law and civil law; the constitution, administrative law, economic rules, and procedural law are not included. The latter is mainly connected with the centralized implementation of power; therefore, it is another category in ancient Rome. In Hayek's opinion, it more likely belongs to the category of legislation. See Hayek, Friedrich A. *Law, Legislation, and Liberty*, vol. 1 (Chicago: University of Chicago Press, 1973).

framework of institutional economics[6]; even the effort of studying revenge and law through literary works is also inspired by Posner. But this chapter is not the "replication" or reiteration of Posner's revenge study. It not only uses the source materials from China (although theoretically speaking, it doesn't matter much), but more importantly, it tries to exhibit the historical logic of the decline of the revenge system in China and its rise in the politically centralized power; it analyzes and investigates the change of a series of microscopic institutions and ideologies connected with this systematic change. I believe that many jurisprudential issues are intercultural, but the methods or institutions to solve these issues might vary greatly in accordance with different social conditions. The study of this chapter finds that in comparison with theoretical logic exhibited by Posner through ancient Greek tragedies,[7] the revenge system in the context of traditional Chinese society does present some features, while the social background against which revenge declines in China is also unique.

I mainly resort to *The Orphan of Zhao*,[8] a famous revenge play in the Yuan Dynasty of China, and the related story prototype and background material. The story goes roughly as follows.

Tu'an Gu, the minister of the Jin state, staged the palace coup and murdered another important minister, Zhao Dun: "exterminate all three hundred relatives, noble and base, who filled Zhao Dun's gate" (75). Zhao Shuo, as the royal son-in-law and the son of Zhao Dun, was forced to commit suicide. Before the death, he told the princess wife in pregnancy, "If it is a girl, there is nothing to be said, but if it is a little boy. . . . When he is fully grown, let him cleanse this injustice and take revenge for my father and mother" (75). The princess bore a boy, as expected, and named him Zhao the Orphan. Upon hearing this news, Tu'an Gu plotted to "stamp out the source of trouble." Cheng Ying, the hanger-on of Zhao Dun, stealthily stowed the newborn baby out of the palace and hid them. When Tu'an Gu heard of it, he demanded to kill all the babies whose age ranged from one month to six months

6 See Posner. "Retribution and Related Concepts of Punishment," in *Economics of Justice*, and also see Chapter 6, 7; Posner, Richard A. "Revenge as Legal Prototype and Literary Genre," in *Law and Literature*, rev. & enlarged ed. (Cambridge, MA: Harvard University Press, 1998).

7 According to Posner's analysis of *Oresteia*, the trilogy of *Agamemnon*, *The Libation Bearers*, and *The Eumenides*, in ancient Greece, the abolition of revenge mainly owed to the fact that the logic of strict revenge for one's relatives sometimes led to the revenge on the person himself. Agamemnon sacrificed his daughter for the Trojan War; his wife murdered him to avenge the daughter's death. Their son Orestes killed his mother to take vengeance for his father. According to the rule of revenge, Orestes was finally duty-bound to take vengeance on himself for his mother. The strict liability of revenge therefore ushered in the inextricable dilemma. In the end, the court was established under the presidency of Athena in Athens – which means the birth of public power – to try this case, in which Orestes was declared innocent. For the world of revenge, it was the complete subversion, and all the established laws were overturned. See Posner. *Law and Literature*, 61.

8 Junxiang, Ji. "The Orphan of Zhao Greatly Wreaks Vengeance," in *The Orphan of Zhao and Other Yuan Plays*, trans. Stephen H. West and Wilt L. Idema (New York: Columbia University Press, 2015) (hereafter cited parenthetically in the text). Another famous revenge Yuan play is, *Shuo zhuanzhu wuyuan chuixiao* 说专诸伍员吹箫. In *Yuanqu xuan* 元曲选, 647–667.

within the Jin state. Cheng Ying and Gongsun Chujiu, the former prime minister and the old friend of Zhao Dun, discussed protecting Zhao the Orphan. Cheng Ying passed on his own newborn son as Zhao the Orphan and assigned him to the care of Gongsun Chujiu. Then, Cheng Ying went to Tu'an Gu and pretended to inform against Gongsun. The son of Cheng Ying and Gongsun Chujiu died accordingly. The real Zhao the Orphan was adopted by Tu'an Gu as his son and lived safely along with Cheng Ying. Twenty years later, Zhao the Orphan grew up to be an adult, to whom Cheng Ying painfully poured out the past events. With the order of the duke, Zhao the Orphan staged the mutiny, and likewise wiped out the whole family of Tu'an Gu. The family of Zhao was restored to its original social status.

The play draws materials from a palace coup that occurred in the Jin state in the Spring and Autumn Period.[9] Today, it has gone through various literary and art representations and received many comments. Therefore, the evolution of this story itself also provides the possibility of investigating law and literature from another perspective, namely how authors of different texts recount this story. To investigate related comprehensions, presentations, and comments on this story, we can observe the subtle change of social ideology that is connected with the change of the revenge system. But this chapter is centered on the discussion concerning the change of the revenge system and is only occasionally involved in the related ideology in order to keep the focus on the theme. I will leave more analyses from the ideological perspective to Chapter 6. Besides, this chapter will occasionally discuss other related revenge stories and events in passing out of necessity.

Retaliation and Revenge

In order to understand the characteristics of revenge, we first examine the retaliation in a general sense. In this chapter, I will define retaliation as the fight and counterattack of a biological individual victim toward the infringer out of the biological instinct. Without close examination, we can find that retaliation has a universal existence in social life. When a person is infringed on,[10] no matter if what has been infringed is his body, life, property (daily necessities), sex partner, descendent, or other small or even imagined interests (for example, a disdainful gesture, even if unintentional), he will naturally have the subconscious response. In addition to the anger exhibited in his emotions, he will punish the infringer in actions. The slightest punishment is to cut down the contact, and he refuses to give the assistance demanded by the infringer; or he informs others not to associate with the infringer, which is actually "the exile" within the community. The severe punishment is to

---

9 Legge, James, trans. *The Chinese Classics, vol. V: The Ch'un Ts'ew with the Tso Chuen* (Hong Kong: Hong Kong University Press, 1960), 290, 366–367.

10 Here, "infringement" in my words is in the broad sense and is behavioralist. See Wilson, Edward O. *Sociobiology, the New Synthesis*, 25th Anniversary ed. (Cambridge, MA: Harvard University Press, 2000), esp. Chapter 11. The concept of "aggression" used by Wilson includes the ruler controlling the organization's members, the male animals pursuing and forcing the female animals, and "parents" disciplining children.

fight against the infringer with his possible power (therefore, it is usually called self-defense) and bring pain, hurt, or even death to the infringer. Such a human passion is so strong that sometimes, even if the victim knows the insufficiency of his power and the total invalidity of his counterattack, he will still do his utmost to "attempt" (this term has a strong rational color, which seems to be an oxymoron when it is used here) to inflict pain or hurt on the infringer. Even the bystander might say this person "has lost his reason," but the infringer who seems to be strong might usually flinch as a result.

The retaliation response is a normal phenomenon in biology and is the basic need and instinct of any living thing in the survival competition of nature. If a species doesn't possess this instinct, it will be eliminated by nature. If any individual of a species doesn't have this instinct and lets other individuals plunder all types of resources vital to its own survival and its procreation of offspring, it either dies or has no descendants. All in all, its genes can't be passed on. The genes of those individuals possessing this instinct cannot only be carried on but will be relatively or absolutely multiplied as a result. In the end, with the declining number of individuals without this instinct or the complete elimination, this species is also actually changed. In fact, among all the animals, we can observe this phenomenon. There is a folk saying, "the worm turns." In the eyes of human beings, although these fights are indeed just the quarrel between snail horns,[11] yet for the snail, this "quarrel" means life or death. It can be described as the instinct preserved by any biological living individual because of the long-term natural selection, which keeps the individual surviving. Likewise, humans carry this instinct. Due to different reasons, our instinctive response *might* have been weakened today or deliberately played down and cracked down. We seem to scarcely "encounter passions."

Revenge is another type of retaliation, although I foresee that there will be someone who protests my ascribing self-defense and revenge to the category of retaliation. Self-defense and revenge do have a fundamental difference. The former is generally "passive," while the latter is usually "active"; self-defense has the main purpose of preserving oneself, while revenge deliberately intends to hurt others (although they are infringers). I acknowledge these differences and accept that these differences are vitally important in some systems of discursive analysis such as "the justifiable defense" in modern criminal law. However, if viewed from the perspective of functionalism and from the analytical discursive system based on biology, these differences are not very important. They are the same response of human beings when they are infringed. All their actual effects are to strike infringers and inflict a certain pain on infringers, which force them to dare not to continue the offending or desist it in order to actualize self-preservation consequently. In the terms of the game theory, it is the response fitting rationality of one player in the game toward those who don't cooperate.

11　Watson, Burton, trans. *The Complete Works of Zhuangzi* (New York: Columbia University Press, 2013), 218.

In comparison with self-defense as a general concept, the most prominent *external* feature of revenge is diachronic, namely the non-immediate connection in time between the prior offending act and the late revenging act. From the widespread popularity of the saying, "it is never too late to take one's revenge," we can even observe that people seem to deliberately emphasize and delay the time lag feature of the revenge act.

Why is there a time lag? It is mainly because of rational involvement. If only being motivated by the biological drive, then revenge will be immediate and simultaneous, which will be only represented as self-defense. This response might not be necessarily in need of rational involvement, or it might not be mainly the outcome of rational calculation, although this instinctive response still fits the reason of purpose or measure. However, when we observe the avenger like Zhao the Orphan or when we say that someone has "a strong sense of retaliation" (it usually doesn't refer to his severe retaliation act, but more to his characteristics of remembering the infringement forever and being calculating all the time), what we describe is not just the biologically instinctive response. In the end, this retaliation is still motivated by the biological instinct, which yet has quite a large portion of "cultural" factor within it. That is to say, it is reason that works. Besides, generally speaking, the longer the time lag, the deeper the rational involvement. Under some circumstances, it is impossible for people to use the time interval, long or short, to measure more or less rational involvement.

Another feature of revenge is it is deliberately done by the avenger, who usually makes a meticulous calculation and arrangement, although it is not a necessary scenario. If one person kills his enemy unintentionally and it is not known by others, it is not classified as a perfect or typical revenge. People even more regard it as a "punitive justice" – God wills it. An ideal type of revenge must "let you or me know what it is about," which has been represented in many dramas and films. It means that although there is a time interval, revenge still must be the response to the prior offending act of infringers, at least *in the eyes of the avenger*. It actually has the implied meaning in two aspects. First, the *original* revenge is out of personal liking (the later analysis will revert to this issue), not morality or justice at least, although it might fit popular morality or the concept of justice. In my opinion, more probably, morality or justice is just the retroactive recognition of a concept or ideology of such a human revenge instinct. Second, revenge must possess the corresponding and symmetrical features. The symmetry of acts might not be necessarily the symmetry of severe degrees. Otherwise, this act is no longer revenge, but is regarded as a new infringement. Both features of revenge become the fundamentally basic and core element or principle of morality and law (corrective justice, judicial fairness, fair trade) that are accepted by later societies.

These analyses are sufficient to show that revenge doesn't simply have the biological factors working and is not the barbarian act on the whim of animal instincts (the term "barbarian" here is more like a rhetoric, an ideological discourse); it is a mainly humanistic factor (reason) that works. Because generally speaking, the impulse on the basis of biological instinct of individuals only occurs immediately; even human beings have memory, but time will erode it; revenge passion always

gradually weakens with the passage of time, until it completely disappears. Therefore, as time goes by, grudge vanishes when foes greet each other with a smile,
although some infringements, even some intolerable infringements, once existed.
The typical example is Han Xin, the commanding general who didn't wreak revenge on the person forcing him to crawl between legs. When a son's revenge for
his victim father or revenge like Cheng Ying's in *The Orphan of Zhao* appears,
since the infringement suffered by an individual can't be directly passed to others
through physical contact, the revenge psychology and passion of a specific individual stimulated by a specific infringement can't be inherited as well – what can
be inherited is just the general human retaliation instinct. Therefore, it is obvious
that "culture" works more. Were it not for Cheng Ying who painfully poured out
the family history of Zhao the Orphan and aroused the latter's retaliation instinct, it
would be very difficult for us to imagine the revenge of Zhao the Orphan. Actually,
without Cheng Ying's recounting, Zhao the Orphan would be utterly unaware of
his family background.

Zhao the Orphan killed the whole family of Tu'an Gu, which likewise shows the
cultural factor working in revenge. Obviously, it can't be thoroughly explicated by
the revenge instinct, the biological factor,[12] because the overwhelming majority of
those he killed hadn't hurt him or his family members. Such a cruelty is inevitably
involved with the cultural factor.

From Retaliation to Revenge: The Development of Civilization

The last sentence of the previous passage needs to be defined. The involvement
of cultural factors not only refers to Cheng Ying's bitter recounting the family
history in the revenge of Zhao the Orphan but also refers to, or even *mainly* refers
to, that revenge has a special function and meets with some social demands in the
society lacking any efficient public power to prevent and punish offending acts.
In other words, revenge has a certain active function in maintaining the order in
such a society. In this sense, not only revenge itself is a cultural phenomenon but
also revenge – I presume social security and order as public goods worthy of being
pursued – holds the positive and active significance for civilization's progress in
the broadly social sense. Actually, even revenge motivated by the purely biological drive also has such a social function. It is because of such a function that the
revenge instinct can be preserved in biological competition through the survival of
the fittest. I will start with such a social function of revenge and retaliation.

"Heaven and Earth are not kind: The ten thousand things are straw dogs to
them."[13] Nature is neither morality bounded forever nor related to morality.

---

12 It is just incomplete. There still might be the biological factor, namely, to destroy the genes of a
group, so it could be more beneficial to pass on its own genes to later generations.

13 Lao-Tzu. *Tao Te Ching*, trans. Stephen Addiss and Stanley Lombardo (New York: Hackett Publishing Company, 1993), 7. See Holmes's views: "I have no grounds for assuming that my can't helps
are cosmic can't helps and some reasons for thinking otherwise"; "when one thinks coldly I see no
reason for attributing to man a significance different in kind from that which belongs to a baboon

From the perspective of biology, within any species, the competition is always held among individuals for survival and reproduction. The competition doesn't necessarily mean the cannibalism, but the conflicts of interest, infringements, or imagined infringements are inevitable because of the fight for living space and goods. Since foods have important significance for the survival of individuals, just like the spouse for the biological inheritance, living things, including human beings – especially the male (certainly, in the primitive age, it might be the outcome of natural selection) – will instinctively exercise self-defense or retaliation against the invaders to protect their foods or spouses in order to ensure the possibility of keeping their own lives and life genes. Consequently, the counterattack or fight of any living things on the basis of such an instinct has significance beyond the existence of individuals and has "social" significance. It resists the extinction of living things, maintains the diversity and multiplicity of living species, and creates a potential possibility for later evolution and progress of any living things, including human beings.

It is just the beginning for the social function of revenge, not the end. Once all the survived individuals have such a retaliation instinct, it actually creates a possibility of peace at least among human beings, the living species. Out of the fear of retaliation and its ensuing pains, injuries, and/or death, any individual then will not dare or at least greatly reduce the chance of offending others if there is any other possibility (opportunity cost). The subsequent possibility of achieving the partial or temporary peace creates a relatively stable social living environment. Since retaliation elevates the cost of acquiring daily necessities or spouses through infringement (death or injuries; in the primitive living condition, injuries always meant death as well), it also forces the individual to have to choose other methods of acquiring foods, property, or spouses at the lower risks, namely the lower costs. It also means that people must strive to pursue peaceful development and mutual competition in other aspects of social life. As a result, although retaliation itself is barbarian and biological, it is with such a barbarity as the prop that people can possibly actualize the cooperation (nonaggression) in the sense of game theory, which forces people to live in the way of making the pie bigger instead of unceasingly cutting it. Human beings can enter "civilization" then. The civilization here not only refers to peace but also includes the human activities of competitively creating material and spiritual wealth and creating production and subsistence materials. In this sense, human peace and civilization are supported by violence in the end, and their birth, existence, and development are accompanied by violence all along.

With the further development of human reason and culture, once the infringement act occurs, revenge (perhaps inevitably) derives from the retaliation instinct. That is the retaliation with the features of prearrangement, the occurrence with time lag, and the more successful chances usually. Especially when the following

---

or to a grain of sand." Posner, Richard A., ed. *The Essential Holmes, Selections from the Letters, Speeches, Judicial Opinions, and Other Writings of Oliver Wendell Holmes, Jr.* (Chicago: University of Chicago Press, 1992), 107, 108.

point is taken into consideration, the derivation will more likely and more necessarily occur. That is, in daily life, there isn't the ideal and indiscriminate individual implicitly presumed in the previously mentioned discussion. There is a diametrical difference between individuals of real life in terms of age, sex, physical strength, and intelligence. In the face of infringement from others, an underage child has the biological retaliation instinct likewise; but if the opponent is strong, his resistance sometimes is almost to no avail. In this circumstance, regarding the biological instinct, his first choice might be more likely to seek survival, run away, and abandon the smattering of foods that were possibly his painstaking acquisition.

It might not be a big deal if he didn't resist this time. The question is: Is it impossible for this child to adopt the policy of nonresistance all along, which will surely bring more infringements? The strong middle-aged man will still follow suit or even make insatiable demands. Other men who are not as strong as the man, or even any man, might make infringements because the child is an easy target. The final result is that the child can't make a living. Under this circumstance, he must retaliate if he wants to survive with a sense of security. Besides, because of his weakness, he must exercise effective retaliation. To this end, some individuals will endure temporary plunder and humiliation, "the curving of the looper aims for the stretching," and make full preparations for the retaliation when the time is right. Calculation and reason are hereby introduced into retaliation, and revenge, the deliberately postponed retaliation, occurs. In this sense, revenge is the product processed by reason. If we don't *identify* culture with literary pursuits but regard it as the product of spiritual activities of people for the assurance of their existence or better existence, we have full reason to say that revenge itself *is* a culture.

Rational involvement and cultural progress can't necessarily make retaliation civilized. On the contrary, retaliation might be more miserable and crueler. The effective retaliation doesn't only mean that the opponent will be chased away but also usually means to destroy the opponent's ability to thwart the retaliation. In other words, the child must deal a deathly blow to that strong man only once, leaving the opponent no chance of implementing any counterattack or having a breathing spell. For human beings, this "knowledge" is gradually acquired through countless miserable lessons, and it likewise goes through the biological selection of survival of the fittest. That is to say, those who have this instinct and potential, or can understand this point earlier, or are more "cunning" with crueler retaliation, they usually have more possibilities to survive and pass on this experience through culture or pass on this instinct through the biological gene to their offspring.[14] For the individual, if it is acquired later, then this choice must have rational involvement.

However, from another perspective, it is because revenge derives from the instinctive retaliation that the frequency of sharp conflicts between people might

---

14 "Those that employed it (warfare) best became – tragically – the most successful." See Wilson, Edward O. *On Human Nature* (Cambridge, MA: Harvard University Press, 1978), 116–117. It should be noted that Wilson discusses societies; although there is a difference in the analytical unit, the reason is the same.

be also lowered. The reason is just like the earlier-mentioned analysis – the fear for retaliation, especially the fear for revenge, occurring with cultural progress. Because when rationality is involved in retaliation, physical strength is no longer the only or even major element of ensuring success. The weak with elaborate plots defeats the absent-minded strong opponent; this possibility is augmented instead. Being threatened by this revenge, even the strong must be reasonable and cautious; they mind self-restrictions, try to contain impulses, don't infringe on the rights of others as far as possible (otherwise, it means their own death), or care to "fight no battle unprepared, fight no battle they are not sure of winning." Henceforth, human beings will become "polite" and civilized on many occasions at least.

Once reason becomes an important factor of the survival competition and is exploited, people will still be actively engaged in the competitive exploitation in this aspect and will surely bring forth many unexpected by-products. To win the hearts of the opposite sex, they might not resort to arms any more. It is entirely possible for them to outshine others in the competition of production, or in singing, or horse racing contests. In this sense, and only in this sense, rationality and reason become the positive driving force of civilization in our words of today. But even so, we shall not forget that this civilization actually is still propped up by retaliation. Without the threats of retaliation and revenge, there won't be the civilization of such an act and the development of civilization, including the development of art.

The Escalation of Cruelty: A Group Issue

The analysis mentioned earlier is actually simplified and must have some appropriate variables, which will enable us to see through revenge, especially the large-scale revenge such as Zhao the Orphan. One simplified factor is the group – the previous analysis considers all human activities as the individual activity.

In real life, humans always and must live in a large or small group. A person's growth must be cared for by his parents, or at least his mother or others, for years; afterward, he can live independently. An individual, no matter male or female, needs to reproduce and raise posterity and inevitably forms a small group gradually. Humans never grow up by themselves, especially in ancient times; they were basically born and grew up in the group of relatives with shared genes. (Adoption is the exception. But in the case of inconvenient communications of ancient society, adoption was rare, provided it even existed.) Since the same gene is shared, according to the research of social biologists, humans will subconsciously develop limited altruism – inclusive altruism and reciprocal altruism – for the reason of the survival of the fittest.[15] An individual can not only protect himself but also protect those who share his gene (for example, the parental protection of children, the

---

15 See Wilson. *On Human Nature*, Chapter 7; Mayr, Ernest. *This Is Biology, the Science of the Living World* (Cambridge, MA: Harvard University Press, 1997), esp. Chapter 12; and Ridley, Matt. *The Origins of Virtue: Human Instincts and the Evolution of Cooperation* (London: Penguin Books, 1998).

mutual help among siblings) and assist in disseminating genes (for example, the male's protection of his wife) and others who are relatively close in terms of gene and blood relations. The sharing of gene or blood relations can be described as an important, but not the only, cornerstone for primitive humans to form groups.[16] Because of the existence of a group, the further social division of labor also occurs within the group, which will promote the development of society as well.

The existence of a group makes the revenge issue more complicated. The survival competition among humans doesn't rest with the individuals any more, but usually happens among the groups. Since culture can only be inherited in group life, revenge receives more cultural nourishment as a result. The existence of groups also means that the blood relations of humans are the differentiating factor. As for people with different blood relations, the revenge instinct will have divergence in terms of intensity. Consequently, this instinct becomes less reliable, and revenge is in need of institutionalization. Group life also makes this institutionalization possible. Once such a series of factors is involved, on the one hand, if invasion or revenge happens, its scale, cruelty, and time duration will be escalated.

On the other hand, it also means that the necessity and possibility of peaceful coexistence is further augmented. Because under this circumstance, even if a stronger and cleverer individual can escape from the revenge implemented by the victim himself, or even kill the victim before he takes vengeance in ordinary cases, there are several points that enable the individual in the group to be more easily hurt than the individual outside the group.

First, if I hurt someone, then the avenger whom I face now is no longer the individual per se, but a group consisting of the victim and his relatives. In the revenge plot undertaken by many persons, even if an individual has more power and higher intelligence, it is impossible for him to have constantly effective self-protection everywhere.

Second, I now have family members and relatives with whom I am concerned. At least some of them are easily hurt. Others in my group or clan might be retaliated against premeditatedly because I have infringed on the rights of others. Or even the avenger only seeks to lay hands on the weak and young family members I most care for in order to avoid direct engagement with me for the sake of security and safety, or even only to amplify my pains. They know that to kill my child might make me suffer more than to kill me.

Third, even if the population of my clan is relatively large and the opponent knows no way to make a move, my family members and I have received good protection for a certain period as a result. But because of the involvement of culture and rationality, it will make me and my family members *feel* more unsafe. Because, owing to the group, the unfulfilled revenge desire of the victim and his relatives might be more likely passed on to the next generation, and it is the posterity who

16 Kuper, Adam. *The Chosen Primate, Human Nature and Cultural Diversity* (Cambridge, MA: Harvard University Press, 1994), 209–210. The anthropologists find that another major cornerstone of social organization is the territory.

takes revenge. Just like Zhao the Orphan, it took 20 years for him to wreak vengeance. At this moment, even though Tu'an Gu knew the existence of Zhao the Orphan and cared to prevent the revenge, it was impossible for him to constantly keep the high vigilance everywhere in 20 years and protect himself and his family members well.

Fourth, because of the involvement of such cultural and rational factors, it actually creates another new punishment. If Tu'an Gu knew the existence of Zhao the Orphan, then he would be fidgety every day in these 20 years. It is not the corporeal punishment to humans in a traditional sense, but the spiritual or psychological punishment that can't be avoided. We once again observe that the rational and cultural factors participate in the punishment and *reinforce* it. Accordingly, we can also notice that the more rational a person is, the graver threat he feels.[17]

In the face of the group, the infringer still has two basic countermoves. The first is to enlarge the scale of infringement, which is represented as to "exterminate all three hundred relatives, noble and base, who filled Zhao Dun's gate" in *The Orphan of Zhao*; even the newborn Zhao the Orphan was not allowed to be alive. It is the common saying, "stamping out the source of trouble." It must be noticed that even if Tu'an Gu's "stamping out the source of trouble" in the play might be ascribed to his cruelty and evilness, in terms of theoretical analysis, whether a person adopts this strategy or not has absolutely nothing to do with whether he is cruel and evil or not. This is another criticism of the moralized explication. To eliminate all is a rational operation strategy that is developed mainly with the group as the target, and the group is represented as the clan family system, the universally social organization system in ancient China. Its fundamental purpose is not to kill more persons, but to completely and efficiently deprive the opponent of the revenge capability. Actually, in many criminal cases of today, it is also represented in various forms: The common saying is "killing the person concerned including the eyewitness," and its purpose is not to kill someone, but to deprive the victim of the capability of resorting to the law for revenge.

In the face of enlarged infringement and augmented cruelty, the avenger party correspondingly also puts on fiercer responses, or even inevitably has a fiercer response by adopting the revenge of exterminating the whole extended family. That is the reason why Zhao the Orphan "will return the favor by butchering nine generations of his" (106). Some modern scholars might believe that the revenge of Zhao the Orphan went too far.[18] Its implication is that it was only Tu'an Gu who victimized the whole family of Zhao, and Zhao the Orphan should punish Tu'an Gu only.

17 This point is also manifested in many cases of today and is usually applied. A criminal claimed he was on tenterhooks at the siren of a police car. At least some criminals themselves first collapse under such a huge spiritual pressure and willingly accept the legal punishment in order to escape from this net of Heaven, which has a large mesh but lets nothing through.

18 This is one of the reasons that the play was not collected in the book compiled by Gu Xuejie in 1956. See, Gu, Xuejie 顾学颉. "Qianyan"前言. In *Yuanren zaju xuan* 元人杂剧选 (Beijing: People's Literature, 1998), 11.

Even if my intuition could accept this opinion, we must be clear that such intuition and opinion are the product of our present social life and cultural condition and the product of modern cultural disciplining. If it is analyzed carefully, three factors at least demand or force Zhao the Orphan to exterminate the whole extended family of Tu'an Gu. Likewise, it has nothing to do with whether he is kind and merciful or cruel and evil.

The first factor is the revenge wish and capability of the Tu'an family. In the Yuan play *The Orphan of Zhao*, Tu'an Gu was the treacherous courtier, and audiences would easily hold Tu'an accountable for the punishment. But observed from *The Grand Scribe's Records*, the conflict between Tu'an and Zhao families is more like a power struggle, behind which there is even the shadow of Duke Jing of the Jin state – in *The Orphan of Zhao*, it is Duke Ling – the ruler aiming to exterminate the important courtier with a borrowed knife to maintain his own sovereignty. Sima Qian basically held a neutral attitude toward the records of grievance between two families and made no definite criticism of them. What he conveyed under his writing brush was the respect for Gongsun Chujiu and Cheng Ying even more. If the slaughter of the Zhao and Tu'an families was the power struggle or Tu'an Gu executed the whole family of Zhao under the order of Duke Jing, then, after Zhao the Orphan successfully carried out his vengeance, the Tu'an family had full reason to seek revenge again in terms of morality and justice.

Even if it doesn't matter (it only slightly matters to me and the audiences I want to persuade), because even Tu'an Gu is a truly vicious villain, we will still ask the question: To *whom* is he a villain? To his wife, children, and clan, Tu'an Gu might be a great person of gigantic stature; after all, he once brought safety and all the benefits of wealth and power to the family members. Once Tu'an Gu was killed, all of these would be gone.

We must firmly remember what has been stated; that is, retaliation is more motivated by biological features, not "morality" or "justice." There is a Chinese saying, "to kill one's father, it is the absolutely irreconcilable hatred." In this saying, the foundation for revenge completely doesn't lie in whether the father is the symbol of social justice or morality; what it refers to and emphasizes is only such a biological blood relation.

Just for the consideration of this biological revenge instinct, Zhao the Orphan should and could fully foresee that there might not impossibly be another "Tu'an the Orphan" in the clan family after only Tu'an Gu was killed. This orphan would avenge Zhao the Orphan and his family again one day. Even if it is not the passionate impulse but rational thinking, Zhao the Orphan must face reality as an ordinary person – he must exterminate the whole extended family of Tu'an for his security and that of his family members. The analysis here doesn't try to defend anyone or any cruel act; what I only want to say is that in investigating historical figures, my or current moral standards shouldn't be applied first to judge whether their acts were good or wrong. The first thing should be to understand why they acted thus.

There is another factor as to why revenge must be sufficiently cruel. Punishment will have the deterrent with the condign force; otherwise, the punishment of revenge will have no social utility. If a person stole 500 RMB and were only fined 50 RMB, this punishment would have no deterrent force, not for the stealer himself or other potential stealers in society.

Many contemporary jurists might feel this analogy is inappropriately applied here, because Zhao the Orphan's revenge had implicated innocent persons. But this inappropriate sense has become the indubitable axiom when we consider the punishment issue because of the individualist principle of bearing liability solely for one's own crime since modern times. But it is not the universally applicable axiom. In history, and among ordinary people of each country, the liability system of familism or collectivism has been adopted for quite a long time. Individualism and the corresponding judicial liability system are the by-product of capitalist economics and society to a large extent. What on earth is the appropriate basic unit that should assume the liability and account for the wrongdoings? It is not a natural, physical concept (a person), but always is the cultural construction that occurs on the basis of human needs in a certain social and historical condition.[19] If the revenge of Zhao the Orphan were not sufficiently strong and only Tu'an Gu himself were punished, it would probably be "humanity" in our opinion, but for the clan family of Tu'an, it actually had the significance of "sacrificing one person to save many persons." It would exert a very bad influence on other families and clan families in society. This revenge has neither warning significance nor the deterrent of preventing the occurrence of similar tragedies and protecting family members and relatives as well.

The third factor as for why revenge must be cruel is the institutionalization of revenge. Once the group revenge act became the justifiable act acknowledged by society at that time, it acquired legitimacy and became the institution that demanded people to strictly abide by it (I will discuss it in the next section); then, Zhao the Orphan must abide by it. Otherwise, his act would lose legitimacy, because he didn't act with rule or law – he violated "law."

The involvement of the group factor might undoubtedly upgrade the cruelty and scale of infringement and revenge, but it is still not the only choice. Another choice

---

19 Among the people, even today, there is always a saying that the retribution befalls descendants is to pay the sins made by their parents. In the symbolic sense, it also implies the acknowledgement of the family as the liability unit to a certain degree at least. Even the official liability theory in many modern countries is individualist, if we only observe the reality, the reality of the group sharing of joint liability still universally exists, no matter at home or abroad, no matter in criminal law (corporate crime, organized crime) or the tort law (joint liability), even in some statutory laws (antitrust), and even in international law (international sanction). Actually, there exists the factor of joint liability to a certain extent. For example, the father is imprisoned as a criminal, the family income is reduced, and the living standard of his wife and children is actually lowered, which is also the indirect punishment. On the other hand, one physical individual who commits the crime might not be punished as the individual, for instance, the pregnant woman. Even if it is just a fertilized egg, once being discovered, it will be considered the innocent in modern society at least and be separated from its mother.

is still peace. It is not just because in the face of cruel consequences, people have to be more reasonable and seek peace and cooperation of the lowest degree with competitors, namely nonaggression and peaceful coexistence. Generally speaking, the probability of intense conflict among groups will be lowered along with the enlargement of the group, which runs counter to people's intuition. Individuals within the group still have their selfish calculations; there is a centrifugal force, and the organization cost of collective action is high.[20] As Wang Shuo or Jiang Wen has observed, while sometimes looking for allies, the parties in conflict might find the same batch of persons or the same person, who will make great efforts to mediate for their or his self-interests as well.[21] At this moment, if there were no ringleader, it would be very hard to organize the collective operation. We should notice that the infringement and revenge acts of Zhao and Tu'an families in the play were all initiated by their "heads."

Group leaders might not be willing to witness the large-scale conflict as well. In order to prevent the conflict caused by the accidental event, leaders usually implement the strict disciplines and rules within the group and prevent any individual from kicking up a row and making trouble outside or acting absentmindedly with the tough collective punishment as the prop. Because any individual harms the members of other groups, it might possibly bring forth the tragic revenge between groups, clan families, or tribes, or even blood vendetta for generations. Therefore, even if the organization hasn't reduced the conflicts between groups, it at least has greatly reduced the outbursts of group conflicts or controlled the scales. Certainly, even if the group makes such an effort within, sometimes the accident inevitably occurs. At this moment, in order to avoid the large-scale revenge and the implication of the innocents within the group, the group to which perpetrator belongs even takes the initiative by turning the perpetrator over to the victim or his relatives for punishment, or to oust the perpetrator from the group (exile him), or forces the perpetrator to make amends when society begins to have a wealth surplus and the victim is willing to accept it. The punishment discipline within henceforth joins hands with the external revenge intimidation to facilitate the wider peace.

From such an organization discipline within the group, we have seen the shadow of the earliest public power in human society, which can even be described as the prototype of the earliest administrative and judicial system. I will give a more elaborate analysis of it later. I hereby only want to point out that the analysis shows that the political and legal system is also not the product of rational design; it is civilized, but comes out of the social life filled with blood ties. The justice that people ask for is just another way of saying human retaliation instinct.

---

20 Olson, Mancur. *The Logic of Collective Action* (Cambridge, MA: Harvard University Press, 1971).
21 Jiang, Wen et al. 姜文. "Yangguang canlan de rizi wancheng taiben" 阳光灿烂的日子完成台本. In *Dansheng* 诞生 (Beijing: Huayi, 1997), 358.

Institutionalized Revenge: A Refined Culture

No matter the reality of social history or the research of modern game theory, they all show that the only and the most efficient tactic for the player is tit for tat, which inflicts the resolute punishment on any noncooperation but doesn't augment the punishment under the premise of multiple games in order to ensure cooperation from the opponent without the illusion of opportunism and escaping from punishment.[22] In Confucius's words, "Repay hatred with uprightness"[23]; the sayings in *The Holy Bible* and *The Holy Qur'an* is "an eye for an eye, and a tooth for a tooth."[24] In the modern legal language of today, they are "the punishment suitable to the crime" and "protection against double jeopardy." In terms of the prior prevention or safeguarding peace, the only strategy that can be chosen in this game to truly and effectively desist and prevent infringement is the potential victim must let the potential infringer firmly believe that if he dares to offend, the victim will spare no efforts to retaliate, and the infringer must receive the punishment with the same severity. If the infringer thinks that he can escape from the retaliation through a certain method just like what Tu'an Gu did to the whole family of Zhao, or believes so, the retaliation might not be so severe; henceforth for the infringer, the total gains are larger than the total costs, and the infringer might be more likely to choose to do the same thing again. Consequently, the fundamental condition of keeping peace in the words of the ancient people is, "Even if Chu has but three households left, it will be Chu that destroys Qin"[25]; in Mao Zedong's words, "we will not attack unless attacked." That is tit for tat. Actually, many scholars point out, why did the United States and USSR, two hegemony states, keep the peace that lasted for 40 years in the Cold War? The most important reason was that both parties knew their counterpart had the ability to undertake nuclear retaliation at any cost.[26]

---

22 As for the famous research of game theory on this issue, see Axelrod, Robert M. *The Evolution of Cooperation* (New York: Penguin Books, 1990); Schelling, Thomas C. *The Strategy of Conflict* (Cambridge, MA: Harvard University Press, 1980).

23 Watson, Burton, trans. *The Analects of Confucius* (New York: Columbia University Press, 2007), 101. It should be noted that Confucius didn't advocate for "the hatred for the hatred." In my opinion, the reason is hatred is emotional, and revenge might more likely exceed the necessary limits under the promotion of "the hatred for the hatred." It is because of this reason that Confucius maintained, "Repay hatred with uprightness." His proposition is not only the correct summarization of long-term revenge experiences of humans but also is consistent with the conclusion of modern research on game theory. Besides, it also exhibits that revenge as the institution (social norms) is the rational decision.

24 Maulwi Sher Ali, *The Holy Bible* (King James Version) (New York: Ivy Books, 1991), Matthew 5:38, "An eye for an eye, and a tooth for a tooth"; Exodus 21:24–25, "Eye for eye, tooth for tooth, hand for hand, foot for foot, Buring for burning, wound for wound, stripe for stripe"; Deuteronomy 19:21, "And thine eye shall not pity; but life shall go for life, eye for eye, tooth for tooth, hand for hand, foot for foot." "And therein We prescribed for them: A life for a life, and an eye for an eye, and a nose for a nose, and an ear for an ear, and a tooth for a tooth, and for other injuries equitable retaliation." Maulwi Sher Ali, *The Holy Qur'an* (Surrey: Islam International Publications Ltd., 2021), 157.

25 Ch'en, Ssu-ma. *The Grand Scribe's Records*, vol. 1, ed. William H. Nienhauser Jr. (Bloomington: Indiana University Press, 1994), 183.

26 For example, Posner. *Law and Literature*, 51.

As our analysis goes so far, we can observe in the historical condition such as the Spring and Autumn Period that there wasn't a unified and strong public power to maintain social peace and order, or in a certain concrete social environment such as the gangdom where law is to no avail, and the remote areas where law and government are far from here, revenge actually has become the basic system of maintaining peace in such a society. Here, people not only autonomously act out of the revenge instinct but also must reinforce this revenge system in order to ensure peace and order within the society. The so-called system means that the rule is not allowed to be broken apart from extreme cases. Even Zhao the Orphan himself didn't want to kill the whole family of Tu'an Gu out of his mercy or for other reasons; it was impossible for society to acknowledge his choice.

Group life puts forward the demand for institutions. But human biological instinct itself, whether love or hatred, is not sufficient to establish the institution. As mentioned earlier, the passion of revenge will fade out with the passage of time, and it is impossible for anyone to live in the blazing revenge passion for decades. Otherwise, is it a life? I also mention that after the appearance of revenge as a culture and institution, revenge itself is a certain type of limitation and restriction of the retaliation instinct.

Besides, the retaliation instinct stimulated by injuries is usually limited to the injured biological individual, which can't be inherited, and it can only be extended to some closest relatives through the cultural method at most. Therefore, when the population of a group is on the rise, on the one hand, the individuals within will be inevitably safer because of the enlargement of the group; on the other hand, internal blood relations and even inclusive altruism are on the decline as a result. The revenge impulse for others within the group is greatly weakened, and people will have more selfish calculations and reckon the interests of their own or their family members. It means that only reliance on the biological revenge instinct can't guarantee that the individuals within the group have the will and determination to take vengeance for others, and it further means that social peace and security ensured with the definite revenge are in impending danger. Revenge needs institutionalization, which will turn revenge into a common obligation for people.

In order to meet such an institutional demand, a series of assisting practices, institutions, and ideologies is derived in ancient Chinese society to reinforce, encourage, and regulate the revenge impulse of people. For example, the story of Prince Yue, if it is put in such an analytical framework, is the method of arousing the memory of physical pains to prevent the revenge passion from fading out with the passage of time by constantly and self-determinedly stimulating the physical senses. Certainly, the body technology (in Foucault's words) proves not to be always effective in practices and is actually abandoned soon later as a result.[27]

---

27 The proof is that the practice of Prince Yue is seldom implemented for later generations. This story or this saying is actually transformed to be the ideology concerning revenge; or it becomes totally irrelevant to revenge and is just the synonym of "making determined efforts to better oneself."

Another institution and system related to revenge is the strict liability. Typical expressions include "a life for a life," "to kill one's father", and "it is the absolutely irreconcilable hatred."[28] It should be noted that these expressions are universal statements without restriction, neither demanding nor including the concepts such as "crimes," "wrongs," etc., although such a limitation is gradually added through explanations by later generations, and some special cases evolve out of them. The reason why we emphasize the strict liability is first because of the factors that science and technology at that time were not advanced, the information cost of verifying "crimes" or (intentional or accidental) "faults" was high, and there wasn't a neutral and professional agency due to the issue of financial expenses. But the most important is still to ensure that revenge be completely implemented as a system. The simplest measure is to remove crimes and faults, the essentials of modern punishment, which thereby facilitates the initiation of revenge. Therefore, human society has practiced the strict liability for a long time,[29] which is continued in modern times. The victim is obliged to or resorts to public power and other social mechanisms to avenge the infringer, no matter if it is negligent or intentional infringement. If the infringer fails to prove that his action is the negligent offense with convincing evidence, his action will be presumed to be intentional. The infringer must be punished accordingly.

Therefore, the social ideology commending and encouraging revenge is implied in the concept of strict liability, in the saying of "even ten years isn't a long time for a gentleman to seek vengeance"[30] and in the great admiration and commendations reserved for avengers in the public opinion and even among administrative and judicial officials.[31] In view of social function, it is a set of institutions that complements the revenge practice.[32] It rewards and guides social behaviors of humans, and its basic function is to dispel or reduce the instability of

---

28 "With the enemy who has slain his father, one should not live under the same heaven." Legge, James, trans. *The Sacred Book Books of China: The Texts of Confucianism*, Part III, *The Li Ki* (Oxford: Clarendon Press, 1885), 92. "One who doesn't avenge the murder of his father is not qualified to be the son." *Chunqiu gongyang zhuan* 春秋公羊传 (Shenyang: Liaoning Education, 1997), 8.

29 See Holmes. *The Common Law*. The saying "a murder must pay with his life" was emphasized in ancient China, which was reflected in Yuan plays. Only in this historical condition, we can understand why many jurists believe that it is a huge historical progress for *Code civil des Français* to adopt the principle of fault liability.

30 There was a discussion for how many generations could revenge in the fourth year of Duke Zhuang. It was believed that "hundred generations can revenge." In *Chunqiu gongyang zhuan* 春秋公羊传, 21. In the early period of Greece, there were similar expressions. "The Fates triform and the unforgetting Furies" in Aeschylus, *Prometheus Bound*, trans. Paul E. More in Oates, Whitney J.; O'Neill, Eugene, eds. *The Complete Greek Drama* (New York: Random, 1938), 141; ". . . mindful of our solemn vengeance," "Ancient of days and wisdom," in Aeschylus, *The Eumenides*, trans. E. D. A. Morshead in *The Complete Greek Drama*, 284, 300.

31 Qu, Tongzu 瞿同祖. *Zhongguo falv yu zhongguo shehui* 中国法律与中国社会 (Beijing: Zhonghua Book Company, 1984), 77.

32 For the ideology as the system, see North, Douglass C. *Structure and Change in Economic History* (New York: W. W. Norton, 1981).

the biological revenge factor as far as possible in order to prevent the avenger's opportunism. Henceforth, we might understand why *The Grand Scribe's Records* adapted the historical story of Zhao the Orphan[33] and fully exhibited and praised the charismas of Cheng Ying and Gongsun Chujiu, who were loyal, righteous, and heroic and faced death unflinchingly. For example, when the family of Zhao were slaughtered, Gongsun Chujiu asked Cheng Ying why Cheng didn't commit suicide. Cheng answered, "I want to see whether the Princess will give birth to a boy or a girl. If it were a girl, it would not be too late to take my own life." When they secretly plotted to protect Zhao the Orphan from the search organized by Tu'an Gu, Gongsun Chujiu asked Cheng Ying if to die or to take vengeance for the family of Zhao would be more difficult. Cheng Ying said the latter would be more difficult. Then Gongsun continued, "Let me do the easy thing, and let you assume the more arduous task." Gongsun faced death awe inspiringly. After the revenge and the status of the Zhao family was restored, Cheng Ying was determined to commit suicide and said, "The reason I die later is because the family of Zhao and Gongsun Chujiu believed I could accomplish this mission. If I didn't die, they would think I hadn't accomplished the mission." Soon, Cheng Ying ended his life resolutely. What is more, a series of other stories with revenge as the center in *The Grand Scribe's Records*, such as Prince Yue, Wu Zixu, Jing Ke, Gao Jianli, Fan Yuqi, Nie Zheng, and his elder sister Nie Ying all had the soul-stirring martyr style,[34] in which the personality of the determined avengers was praised. They all revealed the ideologies (of the legal system) concerning revenge in society at that time, which further reinforced and guaranteed the revenge system in turn.

In all these propping up or assisting institutions of revenge, the institution of retainer and hanger-on might be the most distinctive feature of China, which was reflected in Cheng Ying and Gongsun Chujiu in the story. According to *The Grand Scribe's Records*, Gongsun Chujiu was not the former courtier; he and Cheng Ying were the friends or hangers-on of Zhao Shuo, the father of Zhao the Orphan. It was because they had no blood relations to the family of Zhao Dun, when the whole family of Zhao Shuo were exterminated by Tu'an Gu, that they got free. In the so-called "*The Orphan of Zhao* greatly wreaks vengeance," the key figures who truly plotted, facilitated, and implemented this revenge are Cheng Ying and Gongsun Chujiu (including Han Jue to a certain extent); Zhao the Orphan is just a revenge instrument in this process and a sign that legitimates this revenge. The earlier-mentioned stories of Jing Ke and Nie Zheng, etc., share the same feature as well; all of them didn't exact *revenge for themselves or their family members, but revenge for others in the capacity of friends.*

---

33 In the *Commentary of Zuo*, the massacre of the family of Zhao was caused by the conflict between the sovereign and courtiers and the internal strife within the family and Tu'an Gu, Gongsun Chujiu and Cheng Ying didn't exist. In his "creation," Sima Qian obviously emphasized the revenge.

34 "The Assassin-Retainers, Memoir," in *The Grand Scribe's Records*, Revised vol. 7.

In the limited number of Western literary works I have read, this type of figure is seldom seen and it seldom appears in historical and literary works after the Qin and Han dynasties. Only in the works of the pre-Qin Dynasty did this type of figure recur. In view of the analytical framework presented in this chapter, this phenomenon is actually a component of the elaborate revenge system in those days.

We can still cite the story of Zhao the Orphan as an example. When a society heavily relies on the blood relations to take self-defense and vengeance, when the infringer makes the offense, he will pay particular attention to stamp out the source of trouble as the counterattack, just as mentioned earlier, and divest the opponent of the revenge capability at the very beginning. In order to deal with the strategy of "stamping out," and in order to guarantee the effective fulfilment of the revenge strategy, some princes, dukes, aristocrats, and influential officials paid special attention to keeping retainers if their personal finances allowed for this. They looked for heroic men, men of firm resolve, and capable men as their aides. In the Spring and Autumn Period, there was the so-called phenomenon of "asking for the help from retainers in dire straits."[35] There are many outstanding showcases recorded in historical books.

By keeping retainers, on the one hand, they established a wider social connection, formed a greater group of interests, and enlarged political power, which enabled them to march and make an attack, or retreat and make a defense in the political power contest filled with crises. It was beneficial for the protection of themselves, clan families, and groups. Especially when they were in distress and needed revenge, only one or two figures like Cheng Ying and Gongsun Chujiu among these retainers and hangers-on could help them to get away from the distress or help their clan families to accomplish the mission of revenge. It has not been the strategy of enlarging their own revenge capabilities in a general sense, but a strategy of efficiently hiding their revenge capabilities as well. Under this circumstance, the potential infringer can't stamp out the source of trouble by virtue of the blood relations that used to be easily recognized. To completely destroy such a revenge possibility, information and execution costs paid by the infringer will be so high that the strategy of stamping out can't be fulfilled. It is another type of strategy ("a wily hare has three burrows"), a strategic reserve of revenge.

Until the Warring States Period, this strategy reached the apex among some hereditary houses.[36] Four famous lords at that time, namely Lord Mengchang, Lord Pingyuan, Lord Xinling, and Lord Chunsheng, were aristocratic sons in power, respectively, in the states of Qi, Zhao, Wei, and Chu. Each of them had thousands of retainers and hangers-on; among them there were a few gallant men who were thoughtful and farsighted, loyal and devoted, and didn't hesitate to honor the words

---

35 "The disaster must befall you, immediately ask for the help from the retainers." *Guoyu jinyu wss* 语·晋语五.

36 "The knights and assassins in the Spring and Autumn Period were only reserved for the nobility . . . in the Warring States Period . . . it was a fashion for high-ranking officials and ministers to keep retainers." Qi, Sihe 齐思和. "Zhanguo zhidu kao"战国制度考. In *Zhongguo shi tanyan* 中国史探研 (Shijiazhuang: Hebei Education, 2000), 219, 220.

"a knight will die for the one who recognizes his worth, a woman will make herself beautiful for the one who delights in her."[37] There is a series of moving stories so widespread and well-known to each household in China.

As for this phenomenon, some scholars present their explication that the common practice of keeping retainers is "a life style of the nobility."[38] There is no denying that this explication is reasonable because human behaviors do exert mutual influences to a certain extent. But if the causality is investigated, this explication is invalid, which only rests on the phenomenal description and is a circular argument. It doesn't answer why this practice only specially flourished in this period. If in view of some accompanying historical stories, the institution of retainers and hangers-on is more likely the aggressive or self-protection measure of the nobility, if only in view of revenge, this institution is actually the extremely meticulous and refined revenge system.[39] The story of Zhao the Orphan is such a successful showcase.

The Weakness and Decline of the Revenge System

However, man proposes, God disposes. When revenge evolves to be such a refined system and forms such a culture, it has already reached or nearly reached the end no matter in terms of analytical logic or the historical facts.

First, the institution of retainers and hangers-on has some fatal weaknesses. For the host who keeps retainers and hangers-on, the implementation of this institution needs the financial competence to support them, which is not suitable for everyone. There are many other questions. Not all of those willing to be retainers and hangers-on are the heroic warriors with loyalty and righteousness who honor their solemn promises. The host yet doesn't know who is truly loyal and capable and lacks the reliable mechanism to make this evaluation. We shall remember the poor performance of Qin Wuyang, who accompanied Jing Ke to assassinate the king of Qin. Therefore, the host has to keep a large number of retainers and hangers-on in the hope of "extensive cultivation and low harvest," which surely further aggravates the financial burden of the host. Besides, the institution of retainers and hangers-on itself has a paradox. Retainers and hangers-on exchange their loyalty to the host for ample food and clothing, but this exchange relation precisely means that they have the possibility of selling this loyalty to others in principle if only

---

37 Ch'en. *The Grand Scribe's Records*, Revised vol. 7, 598.

38 For example, Qi 齐思和. "Zhanguo zhidu kao" 战国制度考; Wang, Qi 王齐. *Zhongguo gudai de youxia* 中国古代的游侠 (Beijing: The Commercial Press International, 1997), 8–9. Chen, Shan 陈山. *Zhongguo wuxia shi* 中国武侠史 (Shanghai: Sanlian Book, 1992), 19.

39 It should be noted that I don't think that the emergence of the institution of retainers and hangers-on is only because of revenge, but I mean there is this factor. Or viewed from the functional perspective, this point should not be ignored. Certainly, it is only one "presumption," which needs further demonstration and argument. Qi Sihe once mentioned the relationship between the institution of retainers and hangers-on and revenge, which "might be used to revenge." See Qi 齐思和. "Zhanguo zhidu kao" 战国制度考, 219.

there are more temptations. Therefore, they are not truly trusted by those even possessing such a financial competence in turn.

But these weaknesses might not affect the intimidating effect of the institution of retainers and hangers-on. This institution still upsets the infringer, because he can't completely exterminate the possibility of revenge from the opponent. Even so, the infringer might not be sure of it. Even if all the retainers and hangers-on are only present for their personal gain and disperse when their host falls from power, none of them will sacrifice himself to take vengeance for the host; the infringer himself can't know it and can't be further sure of it. Second, along with other institutionalized factors of revenge in the previous section, any infringer fails to utilize other counter-retaliation measures to acquire the security and, more importantly, the sense of security. He can only seek another choice, cooperation, which might be the second-rate choice. It is the experience acquired through countless bloody fights.

Another factor for the end of the revenge system is this series of institutions of guaranteeing revenge, especially the institution of retainers and hangers-on has the excessively high demand on the personal characters and training of the avenger. Revenge is originally from the biological instinct of the individual, who seeks survival for himself and close relatives. But when it develops to the level of Cheng Ying and Gongsun Chujiu, it has been completely alienated. Revenge itself is the end, which runs counter to the human survival instinct. But the question doesn't lie in the alienation – perhaps the society of that time demanded such an alienation. Actually, every person influenced by culture can be described as alienated. The key is: How many figures like Cheng Ying and Gongsu Chujiu can we find in society after all? Is it possible for such a group of persons to support an institution and the corresponding ideology?

It is sufficient for us to make a brief analysis of Gongsun Chujiu's words, "Please let me die first,"[40] under the writing brush of Sima Qian.

Superficially, Gongsun Chujiu seemed to pick an easy job and shirk a hard one with these words, but it is precisely because of his words that Sima Qian portrayed the brilliant chivalry and justice, honesty and honor, of Gongsun Chujiu with one word worthy of a thousand pieces of gold. Because if only in terms of two tasks of martyrdom and revenge, death is truly much easier, and to take vengeance for the family of Zhao is more difficult. The question is, first, the death chosen by Gongsun

---

40 Accordingly, in terms of literature, it is reasonable to put the story in *The Grand Scribe's Records* and *The Orphan of Zhao* together for analysis. Even we ignore the fact that *The Grand Scribe's Records* adapted the story of *The Commentary of Zuo*, and only in terms of this story can we totally affirm that the story of *The Grand Scribe's Records* is a literary creation to a certain extent. Otherwise, we can't imagine how Sima Qian could "record" the secrete dialogue between Gongsun Chujiu and Cheng Ying. Therefore, we can also observe that Sima Qian was really a great master in his choice of language for characters and his choice and arrangement of details for action. Sima Qian painstakingly molded two dauntless men worthy of praise in his opinion. It also further proves another viewpoint in this chapter: Although Sima Qian didn't deliberately praise revenge, honor, and other institutions from the ideological perspective, the ideology of that era infiltrated into his writing and consistently played such an institutional function in society from then on.

Chujiu is spot goods, while the revenge promised by Cheng Ying is "futures." The cash value of spot goods and futures is different. Second, after the death of Gongsun Chujiu, Cheng Ying could completely fail his promise to honor the revenge, because there were not any witnesses to prove the existence of such a contract, and there was no power forcing Cheng Ying to honor his promise. If Gongsu Chujiu didn't absolutely trust his friend or he had a smattering of other thoughts, he would definitely vie with Cheng in choosing the heavy burden. In this condition, the so-called "light burden" was actually heavier.

This detail not only exhibits the noble character of Gongsun but also foreshadows the grandeur of Cheng's suicide displayed later. After the successful revenge, Cheng Ying committed suicide in order to honor his promise. Actually, even if Cheng once made such a promise to Gongsun, it was no longer known by others. Henceforth, it was unnecessary for him to honor it – not to mention he hadn't made such a definite promise yet (at least it was not written in *The Grand Scribe's Records*), not to mention the fact that Zhao the Orphan earnestly urged him not to commit suicide at this moment. His death only serves to honor a unilateral promise, only accounts for his friend, only proves to the world that his original survival was not to stay alive at all costs, and his choice to live was not out of the fear of death. Such a personality is so profoundly moving!

But such a type of person is so rare! Even the training and moralizing of revenge ideology can turn out such type of persons, but it is impossible to cultivate them in a large quantity, because the training and moralizing can't fundamentally change the biological instinct of humans. Or, even if this personality is presumed to be affected by the gene (although there is no evidence to prove it, yet theoretically speaking, it can't be simply excluded), the human group carrying this gene is destined to gradually decline in number in terms of biological evolution. The ratio of inheriting this gene will be greatly lowered because those with such a gene are too obsessed with risks. The previous analysis has proved that this institution can't be continued without such a type of person.

The third reason is cruelty, non-restriction, and social destruction of revenge itself. Although for avengers, revenge "tastes good," yet for the whole society, the social cost of this institution is too high. In the story of Zhao the Orphan, 600 persons of the families of Zhao and Tu'an were sacrificed in succession, nearly all of whom were innocent.

Please note it that revenge is usually undertaken by the victim himself or his close relatives (in this sense, they are still the victims). With the revenge passion, the victim is the adjudicator and executioner. Except for occasional mercy for the revenge target, the avenger acts without other restrictions. Therefore, his revenge very easily transcends the condign limitation or the limitation of restoring balance in our opinion of today. Once revenge is above the limitation, it surely ushers in the revenge of the opponent in a new round, especially in a society with institutionalized revenge. Therefore, unrestricted or barely contained revenge inevitably results in a blood vendetta for generations, especially in a community with very low mobility of the population in ancient times. It will enable the development of civilization in a broad sense to lack the necessary premise of expectedly social stability. This institution is arguably unacceptable for those who hope for security; they all demand change of the revenge system.

It is this bitter experience that results in the reform and perfection of the revenge system. One of them with far-reaching influence is "the principle of legality" and "the principle of suiting punishment to crime." Many jurists mistakenly – out of their ignorance or because of ideology – link them to Cesare Beccaria, namely the principle of "an eye for an eye, and a tooth for a tooth," the principle of "repaying hatred with uprightness" such that "if you kill a person's father, that person may also kill your father; if you kill a person's older brother, that person may also kill your older brother."[41] This principle actually resorts to such a physical symmetry to restrictively limit the target and extent of revenge. In the meanwhile, it also implies the limitation of a blood vendetta, the principle of "the unguilty revenge for justice"[42] appears. Because of the social utility of this principle, revenge is further legitimated and institutionalized accordingly.

The fourth reason, and the most important in my opinion, is that a new institution is generated in the enlargement of the group as mentioned earlier. This institution is more efficient accordingly in terms of the lower cost of acquiring peace and security. The premise of replacing the old institution is not because the regime has more or less weaknesses, but whether it can be replaced by the more efficient one or not. If not, any faulted institution can't be abolished at all. Now, this new institution is close at hand though seemingly far away; it is organization, disciplining, and sanctioning within the group that guarantee the realization of the revenge system.

Initially, "there is strength in numbers" – it is one of the benefits of enlarging the group. Theoretically speaking, it is beneficial for external revenge as a result. But with the enlargement of the group, the blood relations within the group are gradually weakened and lack the biological impulse of taking vengeance for others even more. At this moment, if there weren't the strong internal organization mechanism, it wouldn't guarantee that people unswervingly advanced wave upon wave taking vengeance at any cost. The revenge system was in danger of collapse. In the meanwhile, the lack of internal organization mechanism might not prevent the conflict surely occurring within any group. In order to prevent the case that some individuals' careless actions result in the revenge from other groups and others are involved, the group also needs an organization agency to forcefully implement the internal rules and reinforce the internal restriction. In the end, any group action is in need of internal organization, mobilization, and coordination. It is the motivation of these demands that the organization within the groups is increasingly reinforced and the demand for public power is increasingly strong.

---

41 Bloom, Irene, trans. *Mencius* (New York: Columbia University Press, 2009), 158. It should be noted that these words of Mencius are more likely the description of social revenge in those days, which might not be the regulation. Therefore, it could be inferred that people had formed such a norm or "culture" of revenge through the practice of revenge at that time.

42 *Zhouli qiuguan chaoshi* 周礼·秋官·朝士.

Since the internal and external peace caused by the enlargement of a group facilitates and promotes the development of social productivity, which will bring more surplus products and make the further social division of labor possible, the efficiency caused by the division of labor will also further promote the development of social civilization. At this moment, social surplus products acquired through various means, including plunder, will enable some people to acquire daily necessities not through physical labor, but by spending all of or part of their time in undertaking official activities benefitting the whole group in exchange for social surplus products with others. A small-scale public power is possible, and a new centralized governance method thus emerges within the group, namely, to ensure the internal peace with internal discipline, rules, and sanctions. This institution originally might be mainly for the support and assurance of the revenge system and is the assisting institution for revenge. But once it is shaped and accompanied by the enlargement of the group, it will prove to be more effective and secure than the revenge system, and it can secure peace more effectively. Although it is just the internal institution of the group, because of its efficiency of maintaining peace and order, there will be no reason that it can't extend and expand to be a more universal system, which replaces the revenge system for originally the dispersed individual or small group. The defender of the revenge system becomes the gravedigger of this institution, just like the sayings go "taking the initiative into one's own hands" and "substituting this for that."

Thus, a new centralized governance system with public power as the center emerges. Even if the revenge system still exists, it has no chance of contending with such a new system in various aspects. It is destined to be yesterday's newspaper!

Actually, until the Spring and Autumn and the Warring States periods, this situation had existed. The feudalism had begun to be gradually replaced by the centralized polity, with the emphasis on "the reverence for the sovereign," and "states" consistently emerged, and the unification of political power in China has become the basic trend. In this sense, the revenge of Zhao the Orphan can be described as the large-scale successful practice before the death of revenge *as the institution*. Revenge will soon be banned, or at least it will not receive commendations and praises any more like it did in the Spring and Autumn Period. Ideology begins to undergo some changes.

Legalists who advocated for the supremacy of public power were against revenge at the very beginning. In the political reforms introduced by Shang Yang, one of the important contents was to regulate that "whoever engaged in a private feud would receive punishment according to its gravity,"[43] with the purpose of enabling the commoners of the Qin State to be "brave in battles for the state but cowardly in private feuds."[44] Han Feizi then reinforced this statement further and held that "the knights with their military prowess violate the prohibitions," which was

---

43 Ch'en. *The Grand Scribe's Records*, Revised vol. 7, 159.
44 Ch'en. *The Grand Scribe's Records*, Revised vol. 7, 161.

one of the most fundamental factors whereby the state "had the disorder."[45] There-fore, the sovereign power must deal a severe blow and forbid it. Confucianists who consistently acknowledged, praised, or even advocated revenge in the past[46] began to revise their stands on revenge as well and added some restrictive conditions. Just as Professor Zhang Guohua concludes in his research, "the opinion on revenge in Confucian classics . . . the more lately composed, the more restrictions."[47] The revenge figures such as Cheng Ying and Gongsun Chujiu would soon become out-dated historical figures. The professional "chivalrous swordsmen" derived from those with chivalrous spirits who hadn't chosen the sword as their profession, and even assassins and killers, had a price and could be purchased, and the trading mar-ket emerged.[48] The first emperor of the Qin Dynasty was about to unify China soon, who not only held the "service" competition[49] with the private revenge through the centralized violence but also confiscated the civilian weapons and materially deprived the possibility of the civilian private revenge further. Through this "un-fair" competition, the "justice" was provided for those victims in society by virtue of monopoly in the end. Those who were not covered by the public power of the state and still remained in society only became "wandering gallants." After the Han Dynasty, even the profession of wandering gallant diminished.[50]

Once the stage background is changed, a serious drama might become a farce, a tragedy might become a comedy. Afterward, we have no chance of reading vigorous

---

45 Watson, Burton, trans. *Han Feizi: Basic Writings* (New York: Columbia University Press, 2003), 106.
46 See Note 28, 30.
47 Zhang, Guohua 张国华. *Zhongguo falv sixiangshi xinbian* 中国法律思想史新编 (Beijing: Peking University Press, 1998), 195.
48 Therefore, Gongsun Chujiu and Cheng Ying should not be simply identified with the wandering knights of the later generations, although their action was gallant. Their main identity was still "the retainer," which was the predecessor of the knight. They were also engaged in the assassination for revenge, but they were not the assassins who were hired or engaged by others. Thus, it is very reasonable for Sima Qian not to put Gongsun Chujiu and Cheng Ying into "The Assassin-Retainers, Memoir," "The Wandering Gallants, Memoir." See Wang, Qi 王齐. *Zhongguo gudai de youxia* 中国古代的游侠. Chapter 2 and Chapter 5. However, this development is almost inevitable. Because to keep retainers, it seems to emphasize the debt of gratitude for appreciation and recognition of talents ("both treated me as an ordinary man. Thus I repaid them as an ordinary man would . . . he treated me as one of the distinguished knights of his state. Thus I repaid him as a distinguished knight of the state would), and what is emphasized seems to be at the spiritual level "a knight will die for the one who recognizes his worth." However, it actually had implied a trading relationship within, although it was the non-monetized trading. This non-monetized trading would easily trans-form to be the monetized one.
49 "First, the state trades a group of services, which we shall call protection and justice, for revenue. Since there are economies of scale in providing these services, total income in the society is higher as a result of an organization specializing in these services than it would be if each individual in society protected his own property. Second, the state attempts to act like a discriminating monopo-list. . . . Third, the state is constrained by the opportunity cost of its constituents since there always exist potential rivals to provide the same set of services. The rivals are other states, as well as indi-viduals within the existing political-economic unit who are potential rulers." North. *Structure and Change in Economic History*, 23–24.
50 Wang 王齐. *Zhongguo gudai de youxia* 中国古代的游侠, 3.

and stirring revenge stories like Zhao the Orphan any more[51] (only the revenge stories for beloved ones). Actually, even in Sima Qian, we can observe the changing times. In "The Wandering Gallants" of *The Grand Scribe's Records*, Sima Qian praised those wandering gallants who violated the prohibitions with military techniques because "they certainly keep their word, they always follow through with their actions." But first, he still believed that "their actions do *not follow the track of proper righteousness.*" (The righteousness here should be comprehended as the statutory law of state, or royal sovereignty, and the accompanying ideology of politics and law.) He also classified the gallants of the Han Dynasty into "the gallants among the ordinary men," "the gallants of the gates and alleys," and "the gallants of hamlets and villages," who were not exactly like "the plain-clothed gallants of *former* times," and severely condemned "the gallants of hamlets and villages."[52] If Sima Qian only rested with the ideology, the attitude in Ban Gu's *Chronicles of the Han Dynasty* was totally changed. Although Ban Gu kept the memories of wandering gallants, he described their actions as "the *stealing* of the power that decided one's life or death." The power of deciding one's life or death dispersedly applied by people through revenge in the past now has been centralized, materialized, and solidly defined as one part of royal sovereignty. The private application is to steal the state property. After Ban Gu, there is no longer a place for wandering gallants in official history books.[53] The orthodox ideology supporting the revenge system has been completely crumbled.

Not only revenge, this social phenomenon, and its corresponding social ideology but also the story of Zhao the Orphan (and the story of Wu Zixu) is not appropriate. It was once so desolate and fervent, which received great admiration and praise of Sima Qian without the involvement of morality.[54] But after such a social change, it gradually became inscrutable for later generations. One important evidence is about 500 years after the revenge of Zhao the Orphan, and only 60 years

---

51 Perhaps the revenge story of Gan Jiang and Mo Ye, "The Wonderful Swordsmith," compiled or written by Gan Bao of the Jin Dynasty in *In Search of Supernatural* might be an exception, but the background for this story was still in the Warring States Period.

52 Ch'en, Ssu-ma. *The Grand Scribe's Records*, vol. 11, ed. William H. Nienhauser Jr. (Bloomington: Indiana University Press, 2019), 105–111.

53 Chen, Pingyuan 陈平原. *Wenxueshi de xingcheng yu jiangou* 文学史的形成与建构 (Nanning: Guangxi Education, 1998), 201.

54 Since the story of Zhao the Orphan was just part of history of the Hereditary House of Zhao, Sima Qian didn't air comments on Zhao the Orphan. But in "Wu Tzu-hsü, Memoir," Sima Qian highly praised the revenge of Wu ("a stalwart fellow"), but it was only limited to revenge, and he hadn't considered the rights and wrongs in the background story of revenge at all. "How terrible is hatred and resentment in a person! Those who are kings cannot give cause for it among his vassals and subordinates, how much more is this so for men of the same rank! If Wu Tzu-hsü had accompanied his father She to die together, how would he differ from an ant or mole-cricket? Casting aside a lesser duty, he wiped clean a great disgrace, and his name has endured through later generations, how sad! As Tzu Hsü was trapped on the bank of the Chiang and begged for food by the roadside, was Ying for single moment not on his mind? Therefore, through bearing his grievance patiently he achieved merit and fame; if not a stalwart fellow, who could attain this?" Ch'en. *The Grand Scribe's Records*, Revised vol. 7, 107–108.

since the period of Sima Qian (but it had gone through the period of Emperor Wu, the central power had been further reinforced), Liu Xiang praised in *New Prefaces*, "Cheng Ying and Gongsun Chujiu can be described as the loyal and trustworthy friends." But it was impossible for him to understand why Cheng Ying was determined to commit suicide after the successful revenge, and he accordingly commented, "It goes too far for Cheng Ying to commit suicide in order to report it to the deceased."[55] As for this point, I will give a detailed analysis in Chapter 6.

The Extinction of Revenge?

I only state that revenge as an *institution* has been crumbled; the phenomena or events of revenge haven't died out, and likely won't. I will demonstrate that it is also impossible for it to completely disappear in society.

Attentive readers will observe that my earlier-mentioned analytical narrative seems to have a loophole. The most prominent is that the story of Zhao the Orphan took place in the Jin state, where a certain public power had been exercised (although it might not be so perfect), not in the primitive society where the power was highly dispersed. Consequently, my analysis seems problematic.

This loophole is deliberately reserved. On the one hand, it is for the simplification of an analytical pattern – simplicity is where the theoretical power lies. But on the other hand, the revenge story of Zhao the Orphan does point out another social factor causing revenge to happen. That is, within a group, or a society, or a state where centralized public power exists, revenge will still appear in the following cases: If this public power can't effectively go deep among the masses because of various reasons and can't solve the disputes and conflicts (for example, law and government are far from here) of internal members in a fair way (to meet the human biological demands), or because of the human-induced reason, those who are wronged and treated unfairly fail to resort to this public power for the justice (for example, the corrupt officials). Even when the party concerned fails to resort to this right because of *his or her own* reason, he or she will pursue the justice in his or her view through revenge. For instance, consider the conflict between members of gangs. Since they can't resort to public power, revenge will usually be more popular and crueler. Another case is in the society and the specific group where adultery is not deemed a crime, many people will choose "self-help" because of the adultery of their spouses. In a society where the adultery is deemed a crime or illegal act, some people will still choose the "self-help" method instead of going to court for their own reputations. The appearance of public power as a sign is not sufficient to automatically and completely dispel the biological instinct ushering in the revenge impulse. People abandon personal retaliation or revenge only because to utilize public power might more securely, conveniently, and effectively fulfill their own revenge instinct.

55 Liu, Xiang, ed. 刘向. *Xinxu xiangzhu* 新序详注, annotated by Zhao Zhongyi 赵仲邑 (Beijing: Zhonghua Book Company, 1999), 229.

In view of this dimension, *The Orphan of Zhao* implies such a type of revenge. In the story, there was not really public power at all, but Duke Ling of the Jin state, the symbol of public power, seemed to be unable or simply unwilling to sanction Tu'an Gu, or even what was behind the action of Tu'an Gu was just the shadow of Duke Ling.[56] Zhao the Orphan couldn't employ public power that replaced the revenge system; he could only return to the revenge system that was more primitive and barbarian from our perspective.

If viewed from this perspective, although revenge is consistently suppressed by the statutory law of the state from the Qin and Han dynasties onwards, and even is strictly forbidden, yet "the atmosphere of private revenge is still popular." The jurisprudential dispute concerning revenge is invariably on even within the establishment.[57] The reason is there isn't a universal public power with true effects and great strengths in many areas yet.

Even the revenge stories of *The White-Haired Girl*, *Red Detachment of Women* in the Cultural Revolution period, and many stories concerning the Chinese revolution can be classified as the revenge story, with *The Orphan of Zhao* as the prototype. As for the white-haired girl, her father committed suicide (or he was beaten to death, depending on the version of the performance script), she herself was raped, and her beloved Dachun was forced to flee; as for Dachun, his beloved was seized, and he was forced to leave his home town; this injustice even had no place to be redressed, and no strong public power could justly deal with it. Naturally, Xi'er made appeals: "I am water that can't be scooped dry and fire that can't be extinguished! I don't want to die; I want to live for revenge!" and "the hatred of thousand years will be revenged, and the injustice of ten thousand years will be redressed." She realized the revenge on the reliance of the power of the Communist Party of China and the Eighth Army. Certainly, there is also the main line of love in *The White-Haired Girl*.

The story of *Red Detachment of Women* is slightly different, and its main line of revenge is purer but more deep-seated. The growth of Wu Qionghua (or Wu

---

56 Although this point was not stated explicitly, it could be observed relatively clearly in *The Grand Scribe's Records*. The family of Zhao were the important courtiers of the Jin state for generations and were the royal relatives in the meantime (Zhao Dun was the uncle-in-law of Duke Jing). Since they occupied the pivotal position and had the final say, it most likely threatened the power of Duke Jing. (Actually, Zhao Dun once dethroned the Duke of Jin; many years later, the family of Zhao was one of three families to divide up the Jin state). Therefore, Duke Jing was fully likely to let Tu'an Gu or even encourage Tu'an Gu to kill the whole family of Zhao. Otherwise, it was impossible to understand why after the ignorance of the massacre of the whole family of Zhao for nearly 20 years, the Duke of Jing thought to remove Tu'an Gu and restore the honorary status of the family of Zhao until he was gravely ill, while Tu'an Gu's power was on the steady rise and constituted a new major threat to his royal power. At that time, the power of the family of Zhao was small, which was insufficient to threaten the royal power. It is in this sense that the story of Zhao the Orphan is the struggle for power, not the struggle between the righteous and the evil under the writing brush of Ji Junxiang. Therefore, the weakness of the revenge system is more obvious.

57 See Qu 瞿同祖. *Zhongguo falv yu zhongg shehui* 中国法律与中国社会, 75. Zhang 张国华. *Zhongg falv sixiangshi xinbian* 中国法律思想史新编, 196–200.

Qinghua, which is up to the version of performance script) is how to connect the personal revenge with the revolutionary cause in the revolutionary terms and how to suppress the burning personal revenge wish in order to guarantee the success of collective revenge action in the revenge terms, or how to coordinate the relationship between the individual and the group in the revenge issue. In an abstract sense, it is the story in which a revenge action is sublimated because of the cultural restriction, the story emphasizes institutional revenge. But Wu Qionghua's revenge likewise came from the fact that she had no other place to ask for justice.

Why can't the justice be acquired? No matter the story of the white-haired girl or Wu Qionghua, they are all involved in the human-induced and non-human-induced reasons mentioned earlier. In traditional China, because of the limitation of the financial and administrative power of the state, the actual governance power of the central government basically neither went deep to the out-of-the-way area where the white-haired girl lived nor to the frontier with the coconut forest where Wu Qionghua lived. In this sense, they actually lived in the society where nominal public power provided justice, but this justice system was beyond their reach. Consequently, the individualized revenge was surely about to happen. But in another sense, they could be said to live in the society where the mighty villains such as Huang Shiren and Nanbatian (the Tyrant of the South) held public power in hands by hoodwinking the public; they couldn't possibly trust the judicial fairness. They were in an impasse and only resorted to revenge.

Therefore, although revenge as an institution has gone with the history, in plays such as *The Orphan of Zhao*, *The White-Haired Girl*, and *Red Detachment of Women*, we can still observe the importance of judicial public power that is unified, just, and approachable for any victim in terms of social peace and stability. If this condition fails to be fulfilled, then the revenge event will possibly occur. Even in contemporary China, it also has the full possibility to happen.[58] The story of Zhao the Orphan still reminds us of the necessity and urgency of reinforcing the rule of law (not a sign but a practice) in China of today.

Revenge and Criminal Law

The analysis of this chapter has also a certain alarming significance for us to comprehend the legal theory and the system of criminal law of today.

First, my analysis shows that although nowadays people describe the system of modern criminal law as the product of modern civilization and try to sever the connection between it and the disgraceful and "barbarian" revenge history in the opinions of some scholars, no matter from the functional analysis of revenge or

---

58 A famous case is on September 29, 1979, Jiang Aizhen, a nurse in Xinjiang who suffered from all sorts of slanders, took vengeance and killed three persons after she failed to solicit help from public powers. In October 1979, *People's Daily* published the investigation report entitled "Why Did Jiang Aizhen Kill Other?," which raised a great discussion among the readers. Readers universally commiserated with Jiang Aizhen to a large extent and asked to spare her life. In the end, Jiang Aizhen was sentenced to serve 15 years in prison.

viewed from the practical effects of the system of criminal law, criminal law is the outcome of the biological revenge instinct of humans after all. This instinct is so staunch and steadfast that it still tenaciously exists after thousands of years or even more, which has gone through the packaging, diluting, or squeezing of various cultures. No matter how human rationality or culture manages to suppress and mold it in various ways, it still breaches the "super ego" of civilization from time to time and reveals its original aspect of refusing the cultural disciplining. It is actually the basis of the system of criminal law or even the system of tort. It doesn't "let bygones be bygones," and it has a bloodthirsty and unruly aspect. It reiterates and asserts itself with big words of revenge, retribution, corrective justice, fairness, justice, and righteousness. Just in this sense, Holmes intuitively points out that the tort in criminal and civil laws is rooted in the human revenge instinct through his historical analysis of the common law in quite an early period.[59]

The development and change of the penal system must be restricted by humanity. Actually, all the human systems are subject to restriction from two basic aspects. One is the restriction of social environments and conditions; the other the restriction of human biology. This chapter proves that even if human reason is developed in such basic restrictions, it might be impossible to completely shake them off. Henceforth, in this sense, I can understand that the increasingly mitigated penalty is a humanitarian ideal, but as a practice, it is impossible to be free from the restriction of social environments and "humanity" in our consideration. Only the tort exists, no matter whether it concerns criminal law or civil law (it is the human differentiation by later generations, and it hasn't the materialist importance), people will ask for revenge and compensation in a certain way. If it is flawless, perhaps people can make amends in other ways; if it is out of vicious intent, the desire for revenge will surely exist.

On these grounds, I believe, *in the current technical condition of crime prevention in China*, the claim to abolish the death penalty is invalid. Although *some* developed countries abolish the death penalty in the 20th century, in terms of the human society with a long history, it is just a brief moment after all. We shall wait and see what on earth it will be. Chinese jurists and the criminal justice system shouldn't "swim with the tide" (no matter big or small currents) and shouldn't be eager to abolish the death penalty just because of some foreign scholars' theories and ideals that have no solid foundation of society and humanity. The reform of criminal justice must be the evidence-based research on the penal system and basic restrictions that support this system. In other words, the basis for the reform of criminal justice must be the research, not the enumeration.

Another argument that is against the blindly lenient penalty and the abolition of the death penalty comes from the interactive relations between the centralized justice system and the revenge system dispersedly implemented in the earlier-mentioned analysis. Why do people rely on and resort to the centralized justice system? The vitally important reason is because this system will gratify

59 Holmes, *The Common Law.*

the human revenge instinct more effectively and conveniently than the revenge system. If this system has an undeserved reputation and can't gratify this desire, or is restricted by financial or administrative competence, it fails to fulfill its function and means to deprive people of the possibility of gratifying revenge through the modern justice system in another way. Under this circumstance, it is expected that people will utilize other means to gratify this expectation like Zhao the Orphan, Dachun, the white-haired girl, and Wu Qionghua did. Therefore, the one-sided emphasis on the lenient penalty and the abolition of the death penalty fully result in the possibility of upsetting the function of a centralized (unified) justice system, which actually brings forth or augments the dispersed revenge sanction. It will not only greatly increase the cost of maintaining social peace (twofold cost of containing revenge and maintaining the justice system) and lower or even lose the legitimacy of the justice system,[60] but even if viewed from the very practical perspective of reducing the number of the dead and injured, it will enable the punishment of private revenge to be more unrestrained, crueler, and more uncertain with more numbers of the dead and enable the actual punishment on the criminal acts to be more severe in society, which henceforth is further away from the expectation of jurists and legalists. As Chinese jurists, we must be consciously aware of the exchange of this system and must make a choice. Jurists must have merciful emotions and concurrently a grim heart. Those who only know mercy are not practical scholars, but ideologized moralists or rabble-rousers, or the sentimental narrow-minded women in novels.

Therefore, I am against the simple abolition of the death penalty or one-sided lenient penalty. It is not out of my personal preference not to secure or adhere to tradition, but only strives to point out the complexity of the issues concerned in this question; it points out that the abolition of death penalty and the mitigated penalty are not just the job of revising rules and regulations. Law is a practically social activity, which is subject to the influence of variables or restrictive conditions. Once one of the variables changes, the affected people will most likely use their own actions to change the real forms of law and justice in society. The truly kind-hearted persons are not just concerned with the revision of legal articles but also consider the actual outcome of this change as far as possible. Besides, as the previously mentioned analysis shows, the survival of the system is finally decided through the tough competition of institutions, and it is not established or abolished only by presenting a good wish. The biggest distinction between institution and wish is that the institution must be universally useful and effective for society, while the wish can only be effective to the believer himself.

So, I don't deny that China should perfect the system of the death penalty. The analysis presented earlier shall never be comprehended as the must-be augmentation

---

60 This problem is not that important to the framework of my analysis. The legitimacy of the judicial system is only noteworthy under the premise that the judicial system is acknowledged to better guarantee social welfare than other systems. If the revenge system can better realize social welfare, it is unnecessary to consider the lowering of the legitimacy of the judicial system as a problem.

of a penalty or the increased application of the death penalty. In a certain condition, the conclusion of this chapter might be the opposite. Just as the investigation of the revenge system shows, the effectively deterrent force of the system mainly lies in the punitive certainty, not its cruelty (although it must have a certain cruelty). It is because of the inevitable revenge that the potential infringer will be forced to flinch. In a Chinese saying, this deterrent force is "one may get off today, but not necessarily tomorrow." The son takes vengeance for his father, even if revenge finally ends with a failure. The torture of not knowing when revenge comes will also make the infringer feel that the price is too heavy. This institution is particularly effective in a traditional society; like the Chinese sayings go, "fellow villages see each other every day" and "the monk may run away, but not the temple." In a modern society with a highly mobile population, this institution has been hardly effective. Yet the reason deduced from the analysis of revenge can still be what the penal system of today must and can use for reference. There are many reasons for the rising of crime rates and the unchecked corruption in contemporary China. In view of the investigation of the revenge system, one of the important reasons doesn't lie in the lenient punishments stipulated by the penalty law or the ambiguous stipulation of legal articles. The biggest issue is in a society with an increasingly mobile population and increasing multiplication of privacies, it is too easy for the lawbreakers to escape from punishments, whether from private revenge or public justice. Therefore, we must consider how to realize the effective punishment, not just stipulate punishment. In order to guarantee the certainty of revenge, ancient societies once evolved a series of institutions ranging from organizations to ideologies at the great cost of life. Today, in order to guarantee the effective practice of a penal system, we likewise need to establish a corresponding set of institutions that ensures the certainty as the primary objective. In this point, maybe science and technology will and are playing an important role. If the certainty of the penalty is improved, then the cruelty of penalty can or shall even be lowered.

This analysis might be inspiring even for the research of some concrete judicial issues. For example, some criminal jurists privately believe that nowadays, the statutory penalty in some criminal cases is excessively heavy, which urges the criminal to perpetrate in a crueler way. For instance, "to rob is the death penalty, to rob and murder is also the death penalty." They suggest that the related criminal penalties be mitigated and even the death penalty be abolished to eliminate the crime cruelty, which can avoid the death of victims in the meanwhile. In terms of the example cited earlier, this analysis seems to be very reasonable. There shall be discrimination for both types of crimes in the penalty, which is legislatively stipulated, or especially is judicially decided. The death penalty shall be decided with particular discretion. Because the smaller discrimination of statutory penalty between the robbing, and the robbing and murdering is, the lesser additional penalty the robber might receive after killing the victim. The robber does have the possibility of killing as a result.

However, if viewed as *a general model*, this point of view is not convincing, for which there are at least two reasons. The first is the analysts only consider the cost (death penalty in both cases) understood by lawbreakers in perpetrating crimes, not the benefit (of escaping punishment) conceived by lawbreakers, nor the related ratio. The premise of this analysis seems to presume that in any case, the criminals will be caught and punished in the end. Only in this condition will the criminals will act recklessly in despair and rob and murder later. But in reality, lawbreakers are caught and receive criminal punishment; the probability only matters in this case. The modern judicial system is far from realizing the assumption that "the net of Heaven has large meshes." Because of this probability, for a vicious lawbreaker perpetrating crimes, the premise of considering the issue is not "I must be punished," but "I might not be punished." Therefore, what he pursues is "how I have the less likelihood of being punished," and he tries to lower the probability of being punished. The reason why many ordinary criminal cases (for example, rape or theft) are accompanied by murder in the end is that the criminals believe "to kill an eyewitness" can most efficiently lower the probability of victims' resorting to the justice for revenge, which is the same case with Tu'an Gu's "stamping out the source of trouble" to the family of Zhao.

It is because the objective of killing an eyewitness is to lower the probability of receiving *any* punishments, not just the probability of receiving the death penalty, that even if the penalty is lowered, the robber will likewise kill an eyewitness to escape punishment, and even he has the greater possibility of killing, because the cost of killing now is lowered. The outcome of this action only further lowers the deterrent force of criminal law to robbing and murdering. The analysis concerning revenge shows that the effective deterrent for any offense is to punish with sufficient force. In the face of this situation, the correct criminal policy should be, with the premise of keeping death penalty for the crimes such as robbing and murdering, that we further invest all sorts of resources in breaking the cases of robbing and murdering and improve the probability of actual punishments to this type of criminal, not leaving any illusion for criminals of escaping from penalty by killing an eyewitness.[61]

From this, we can further be clear that the certainty of criminal punishments with high probability, not its cruelty (although it must be with a certain force) is the best effective measure to lower the cruelty of crimes, and henceforth protect the life and property of citizens; in the meanwhile, it is also the most effective measure that has reasons to realize the lenient penalty and even the abolition of death penalty in the end. (I am not opposed to the abolition of the death penalty, but it must be the truly public choice, not the choice of jurists living rather comfortably and enjoying more legally secure protections in the name of people.) It is not the dialectics of thinking, but the dialectics of practice.

---

61 It should be explicated that one presumption in my previously mentioned analysis is that the criminal is "the neutral risk" in economics. Actually, some criminals prefer the risk, others avoid the risk, and some are neutral in terms of risk. Therefore, the more powerful deterrents to these three types of criminals are, respectively, the ratio of punishment, the severity of punishment, and the combination of two factors. For the related analysis, see Becker, Gary S. "Crime and Punishment: An Economic Approach," in *Journal of Political Economy*, vol. 76 (1968), 169–217.

2　Actors in Institutional Changes

Starting With the Tragedy of Liang Shanbo and Zhu Yingtai

In traditional Chinese society, the concept of a legal system is basically limited to criminal law and administrative law. Marriage and land laws are usually regarded by modern scholars as civil law and are actually incorporated into the codes of different dynasties mainly as administrative law; they are more involved with governmental management and treatment of these issues. In this sense, overall, it can be said that there hasn't been civil law as statutory law in ancient China. Since the legal system comprehended in the modern sense has already been not limited to the statutory law,[1] it also includes some more broadly conventionalized laws – which can be accordingly considered as being recognized by the state in this sense – such as social practices or habits. For example, some marriage institutions discussed in this chapter.

　　The marriage and family system of ancient China is automatically formed among the people, which is represented as habits and conventions. As for these conventions, the state usually neither interferes with them nor makes the legislative stipulations; the judicial adjudication respects them.[2] Only when the system has directly important relations with national politics and economic life does the state step in. For example, in the reform of Shang Yang, there was a strict stipulation concerning the family division, and Prince Yue adopted the pronatalist policy and made a strict regulation concerning the marriage age in order to avenge the Wu state.[3] Some legal regulations seem to maintain a certain political ideology or Confucian ethics, such as the prohibition of marriage between couples with the same

---

1　Cf. Hayek, Friedrich A. *Law, Legislation, and Liberty*, vol. 1 (Chicago: University of Chicago Press, 1973). Even the definition of law in the mainstream textbook of legal science in contemporary China generally concludes, "law is the stipulated and *recognized* by the state, and is the sum total of behavioral norms that are ensured by the coercive force of the state to be implemented." Yet there are different explanations for this recognition.

2　Qu 瞿同祖. *Zhongguo falv yu zhongguo shehui* 中国法律与中国社会.

3　"Commoners with two and more adult males in their families who did not found different households would have their military tax doubled"; "ordinances prohibited fathers and sons of elder and younger brothers from resting under one roof." Ch'en. *The Grand Scribe's Records*, Revised vol. 7, 159, 161. "The male at the age of 20, the female 17, if they don't get married, their parents account for this fault." *Guoyu yueyu shang* 国语·越语上. Besides, when Emperor of Hui of the Han Dynasty reigned, there was a regulation, "Fivefold taxation for those unmarried female ranging from the age

DOI: 10.4324/9781003615606-4

surname.[4] However, no matter in view of their texts or their historical evolution, they all show that their pursuit is quite practical and still aims to promote concrete and tangible social interests.[5]

But what kind of marriage habits and conventions among the people can be counted as law after all? Because of the lack of eye-catching signs, it is very hard to demarcate this boundary. This chapter adopts H. L. A. Hart's definition of functional law: The existence of law "means that certain kinds of human conduct are no longer optional, but in some sense obligatory."[6] According to this functional definition of law, the analysis of this chapter can rectify the tendency of research on traditional Chinese law to always emphasize criminal law and guides the research on ancient Chinese law to gradually walk out of the traditional legal definition – "law includes mandates and ordinances that are manifest in the official bureau, and penalties that are definite in the mind of the people"[7] – with statutory law as the center to expand the conceptual connotation of law. But more importantly, to make such an entry will be convenient for us to investigate the close connection between social life and folk habits, conventions that are a part of law from another aspect, and further understand the relations between law and social life.

Even following the path of Hart, we still encounter some theoretical problems in studying the legal system represented with habits and conventions in ancient society. One problem is that since any researcher tends to use the value of his own times to feel the duty implied in historical habits and conventions, the researcher of today might very likely fail to observe or falsify habits and conventions that once had strong duty features in ancient society or in one region of ancient society. For instance, some folk marriage ceremonies or procedures (no matter in ancient times

---

of 15 to 30." Ban, Gu 班固. *Han shu huidi ji* 汉书·惠帝纪 (Beijing: Zhonghua Book Company, 1962), 91.

4 For example, the household and marriage law of *The Law Code of the Tang Dynasty* and *The Criminal Code of the Song Dynasty* stipulated that "those married couple with the same surname will be sentenced to serve two years in prison; those married couple who are cousins and above will be tried as fornicators."

5 From the historical perspective, the marriage between couples with the same surname was strictly prohibited in the Tang, Song, and Yuan dynasties. But in the Ming and Qing dynasties, because of the increased population, *The Statues of the Ming Dynasty* and *The Statues and Regulations of the Qing Dynasty*, respectively, distinguished the same surname with the same clan, and those who had the surname but were from different clans could be married. In the late Qing Dynasty, the prohibition for marriage between a couple with the same surname and the prohibition for marriage between relatives were merged, and only the marriage between a couple of the same clan was prohibited. From a textual perspective, "those married couple who are cousins and above will be tried as fornicators" in *The Law Code of the Tang Dynasty* and *The Criminal Code of the Song Dynasty* also showed that what the state considered was just the close degree of blood relations between unmarried persons with the same surname. All of these manifested that the state was not concerned with "the same surname;" this is an easily ideologized concept itself, but must be more concerned with marriage between close relatives that surely exerted a substantial influence on the population situation of one country.

6 Hart, H. L. A. *The Concept of Law*, 2nd ed. (Oxford: Clarendon Press, 1994), 6.

7 Tzu, Han Fei. *The Complete Works of Han Fei Tzu*, vol. 2, trans. W. K. Liao (London: Arthur Probsthain, 1959), 212.

or in the present day) might have the strong significance of regulation and institution to the local people then, which might be belittled or even unacknowledged by us today. One typical example is engagement, which still has relatively universal existence in the countryside. In view of the statutory law, the engagement has no legal significance, but in many rural communities, it still has very strong regulating significance. However, this problem doesn't constitute a threat to this study, because marriage habits chosen for investigation in this study are some common practices in ancient China, instead of trivial social customs with highly localized features. I only try to remind myself and later researchers who choose to confirm and discuss local habits and conventions from the functional perspective that this choice and this analysis are usually reflected in some cultural prejudices of today.

This chapter analyzes *Liang Shanbo and Zhu Yingtai*, a play known to nearly every household in contemporary China. This story has been literally recorded at least since the Tang Dynasty; afterward it was widespread among the people.[8] Until the Yuan and Ming dynasties, the story had entered drama and other folk arts in large quantity. Not only Bai Pu of the Yuan Dynasty once wrote the play *The Death Marriage of Zhu Yingtai to Liang Shanbo*,[9] but also the characters of other Yuan plays once mentioned Liang Shanbo and Zhu Yingtai.[10] Henceforth, it shows that *Liang Shanbo and Zhu Yingtai* had become a folk classic or popular culture item at that time.

After the foundation of new China, the social reform, especially the change of the marriage system in the 1950s, endows the play with new social meaning in China. Its Shaoxing Opera version was produced as the first color film in new China. Chen Gang and He Zhanhao, composers in the middle of the 1950s, adapted the story and created the violin concerto *Liang Shanbo and Zhu Yingtai* with the tunes of Shaoxing Opera as the source materials. Both modern works add or reinforce the factors of class struggle and anti-feudalism in the play[11] and emphasize the freedom of marriage, which enables this folk story to acquire more modernity in contemporary China no matter in the art expression way or in the political and social meaning. In terms of its popular dissemination in contemporary Chinese society, even *A Dream of Red Mansions* can't match it.

8　See Zhuren, Guqiao et al., eds. 古桥主人. "Bianji dayi" 编辑大意. In *Liangzhu gushi shuochang hebian* 梁祝故事说唱合编 (Taibei: Xiangsheng, 1976), 1–2.

9　See Anonymous Playwright 无名氏. "Ti jie" 题解, *Tongchuang ji* 同窗记. In *Zhongguo xiqu xuan* 中国戏曲选, chiefly ed. Wang Qi 王起 (Beijing: People's Literature, 1998), 604.

10　For example, there is a piece of libretto in *The Itinerant Peddler*《风雨像生货郎旦》of the anonymous playwright, "Nor do I sing the story of Liang Shanbo and Zhu Yingtai." Zang, Jinshu, compiled 臧晋叔. *Yuanqu xuan* 元曲选 (Beijing: Zhonghua Book Company, 1958), 1650. It shows that the story of Liang and Zhu was widely popular in those days.

11　For example, in the film *Liang Shanbo and Zhu Yingtai*, Landlord Ma (the squire) was changed to be Prefect Ma (the official), who thus became one of "the ruling class." His son was characterized as a dandy boy; in the meanwhile, Landlord Zhu was characterized as the person who coveted power and forced Zhu Yingtai to marry the son of Ma regardless of the mutual affection between father and daughter. See Shanghai wenyi chubanshe 上海文艺出版社, ed. "Liang shanbo yu zhu yingtai" 梁山伯与祝英台. In *Yueju congkan 1* 越剧丛刊1 (Shanghai: Shanghai Literary and Art, 1962).

The analysis of this chapter is mainly on the marriage institution of ancient Chinese society, which is only one aspect of the marriage and family system, instead of the pursuit of the "whole" or "overall" aspects. From this play, I first try to observe clearly some pieces of evidence concerning the meticulous marriage institution that occurred and existed in the society of that time and comprehend its "advantages" and "disadvantages." The further move is the integration with this play; I also try to briefly discuss institutional features at the abstract level and the incompetence and utility of individual actors in institutional changes, the problem not yet discussed in the previous chapter. I hope to exhibit the nearly destined tragic situation of human beings through the analysis of conflict between the legal system and individual actors.

Why Is It a Tragedy?

Yingtai, the daughter of the Zhu family, disguised herself as a man and went to study in Hangzhou. On the journey, she encountered Liang Shanbo, who also went out for scholarly pursuits. Both of them became "sworn brothers . . . [clinging] to each other like glue, like attracts like."[12] Being classmate for three years, Zhu Yingtai secretly loved Liang Shanbo, while the latter didn't know the true identity of the former. Upon the moment of parting, Zhu pretended to have a younger sister who would be betrothed to Liang. She repeatedly used "two eight," "three seven," and "four six" days to hint that Liang should make a timely proposal for marriage ten days later. But this communication was frustrated; Liang mistakenly believed that he was suggested to make a proposal 30 days later. Thirty days later, Liang went to the family of Zhu to make a proposal on the time of appointment. Landlord Zhu had betrothed her daughter to the son of local Landlord Ma, and the date of the wedding was fixed. Liang and Zhu met each other, and grief mingled with joy, but the marriage contract couldn't be broken. After leaving Zhu's mansion, Liang fell ill, failed to recover, and passed away with a deep regret. On the journey of bringing Zhu Yingtai to Ma's mansion for the wedding, Zhu insisted on bidding farewell in front of the tomb of Liang and received the approval. She wept bitter tears and held the memorial ceremony for Liang. At this moment, with the wind howling and the rain pouring down, the tomb split open. Zhu Yingtai threw herself into the tomb and died for love.

Because of the brevity of life and the rarely encountered love, the love of life and death always returns to our mind with emotion. The story of *Liang Shanbo and Zhu Yingtai* not only has moved young boys and girls for generations but also brings sentimental feelings to many adults. Nowadays, people are habituated to defining this story as a "tragedy," which is claimed as a Chinese version of *Romeo and Juliet*. But why is it a tragedy after all? Every reader must and can only comprehend it from the experiences and feelings of his own angle. However, if we have a second thought, this kind of thing is not rare in daily life. No matter

---

12 *Tongchuang ji* 同窗记, 607 (hereafter cited parenthetically in the text).

whether young, middle-aged, or even senior people, many of them might elope and even commit suicide together because of the frustrated love due to various reasons. We generally don't describe this type of event as a tragedy. Sometimes, we even disdain such foolishly sentimental suicides and hold them unaccountable to their parents or other relatives and society. Many years ago, there was a couple of adults who committed suicide for love on the Badaling Great Wall in Beijing. Since they had their own families, people even condemned them. Although at least in terms of sentimental sincerity and profundity, their love was in no way inferior to the love between Liang and Zhu. But only because of the sincere feelings between lovers and the unfulfillment of this feeling in the existing marriage system, which even ushers in the death of the couple, they can't form a tragedy. Actually, when the love of the couple doesn't severely affect others, society will acknowledge "the supremacy of love." This premise just proves that society has never acknowledged "the supremacy of love."

Maybe this is a tragedy because they die young and parents see their children die earlier than themselves? The sudden end of a young life usually reinforces the feeling of fragile life among the living. It is indeed regrettable, but it still doesn't form a tragedy. Every day, many young people, ranging from newborn babies to promising youth in their prime, pass away because of unexpected events. As observers, we will be distressed for them, but will not think it is a tragedy.

Some people and variously adapted versions of *Liang Shanbo and Zhu Yingtai* after 1949, including the violin concerto with the particular representation of the refusal of arranged marriage, emphasize more the factors of "class struggle and oppression" in this event, because Zhu Yingtai was betrothed to the family of Ma, which was a locally wealthy (landlord) family. It seemed that Landlord Zhu sacrificed his daughter's happiness because of his "greed for money."[13] However, close reading of this playscript proves that this point doesn't exist. Not just Zhu's and Ma's were landlord families, and they were just "well-matched in social status" without the suspicion of intentional pursuit for a higher social position. Besides, when Liang Shanbo traveled from afar to make a proposal for marriage on the time of the appointment, Landlord Zhu didn't set any obstacle for their meeting. Although the play didn't definitely state the family background of Liang Shanbo, we have no reason to deduce that he was surely born in a poor family; on the contrary, if the inference must be necessary, we might have more reasons to deduce that Liang was also born in a landlord family. At that time, how could a truly poor family have the economic capability of supporting Liang and his attendant to study in a big city? If Liang Shanbo hadn't mistaken the hint of Zhu Yingtai and hadn't arrived on the time of the appointment, Landlord Zhu might not have turned down the proposal of Liang and act counter to his daughter's will only for the wealth of Ma's family, at least from the perspective of the story's foreground and background. Landlord Zhu once allowed his daughter, who was eager to do well in everything, to travel far to Hangzhou to study by herself. If viewed by the

---

13 "Ti jie" 题解, *Tongchuang ji* 同窗记, 604.

social standard of that time, this point sufficiently proves that Zhu Yingtai's parents were liberally minded and made quite a few accommodations to their daughter. They didn't accept the ancient doctrine that "a woman without talent is thereby virtuous."

Besides, in the original play, there was not any show of Ma's family's "abusing their wealth."[14] On the contrary, given that Ma's family allowed Zhu to hold a memorial ceremony for Liang on the journey of bringing her for the wedding, in my opinion and in many people's opinion, Ma's family was rather amiable and tolerant. We can imagine who will tolerate the bride's ceremonial mourning over her former boyfriend on the day of the wedding and on the journey of bringing her for wedding? (Certainly, it also prominently reveals one important problem of the traditional marriage system, which will be discussed later.) Indeed, Ma's family was rich, and perhaps a landlord. But we can't just believe that the son of Ma's family was not entitled to marry and Ma's family should die without issue just because Ma's family was rich! Ma's family had *the right* to choose Zhu Yingtai just like Liang Shanbo did at least. Class struggle and oppression are not the main factors for the occurrence of the tragedy.

Nowadays, more people believe that the tragedy lies in arranged marriage and "cannibalistic feudal ethics."[15] But only from this point, it doesn't necessarily cause the tragedy. I will analyze it later that actually not only in Chinese history but also in human history, the major form of the marriage system before modern times is just arranged marriage. Not all arranged marriages lead to the tragedy like Liang and Zhu. Otherwise, the tragedy is countless.

However, the most important thing is that throughout the play, the words and deeds of Liang and Zhu were consistently not against the marriage institution with the words of a matchmaker and the parental arrangement as main features. All pieces of evidence seem to be contrary to this; they *approved* this institution. For example, although Zhu had already fell for Liang, she still concealed this feeling. They once "slept in one bed with one's leg on top of the other's." If they were truly against arranged marriage and advocated for the freedom of marriage, under the circumstance that "a general at the front may even refuse an emperor's order" and in the place beyond the reach of parental power, they would have all the chances to let "what is done cannot be undone." What is more, if we presume that both of them are the ideal embodiment of fighting against arranged marriage and advocating for the freedom of marriage just as the general opinion of today believes, they would have no reason to refuse to do as they like, because their love was reciprocal, not unrequited. However, Zhu Yingtai was just simply unwilling to tell the truth; she must first go back home, wait for Liang Shanbo to make a proposal for marriage, and reveal the truth upon his proposal. When Liang came to know Zhu was betrothed to Ma's family as the bride, he just expressed *deep regret* and didn't evince his only intention of marrying her (Liang didn't put the love on the top priority).

---

14 "Ti jie" 题解, *Tongchuang ji* 同窗记, 604.
15 "Ti jie" 题解, *Tongchuang ji* 同窗记, 604.

Liang was ready to propose to marry the younger sister fabricated by Zhu upon their parting. Only when he found this hope was dashed was he unwilling to accept it and said, he "shall go to find Yue Lao, and must ask him to make pairs with his red cord." In the meanwhile, he reproached, "firstly, I hate that you don't keep your words (in my opinion, this can be understood as extremist remarks); second, I hate that I am ill-fated; third, I hate that Yue Lao is unfair"(612). Even in this moment, in the face of a consumingly sincere confession of her beloved, Zhu Yingtai still adhered to the marriage contract confirmed by the traditional marriage procedure and system and used the wine as the witness, promising "I can't marry you in this life, I will be destined to be your wife in the next life"(613). Finally, they could only part in melancholy. In the play, there was no evidence of forced actions and pressures exerted by Landlord Zhu or Landlord Ma on Zhu Yingtai, nor did Zhu Yingtai go back on her words.

If terms of the play itself, both Liang or Zhu strove to fulfill their dream through the procedure and institution of arranged marriage and a matchmaker's words. They hoped to be acknowledged by this "procedural justice." In this sense, they were the conscious and firm adherents of an arranged marriage system. For them, what they didn't like was just the very cruel outcome caused by this procedure or institution and other factors, which will be analyzed in the final section. Like any ordinary person, they hope to have "substantive justice" through the procedure. If they allegedly nurse any grievance against arranged marriage, it is just because they receive new information afterward; they have walked out of "the veil of igno-rance" and see the outcome of this series of procedures. But even now, they are still ready to accept this outcome and have no intention of challenging this institution. Only because Liang Shanbo unexpectedly died of illness (it should be noted that the disappointment in love might cause or aggravate illness, but it is not possibly the cause of illness and the death of illness), was Zhu Yingtai overwhelmed by sadness and came to realize her true feeling and then determinedly died for love. Henceforth, the so-called saying that Liang and Zhu sought the freedom of mar-riage actually is a series of chosen and constructed readings by the liberal intelli-gentsia of the modern middle and lower strata and contemporary "petty bourgeois" against the background of modern social change. These readings fit the political demand of the change of Chinese society from the 1950s to the 1960s and also fits the rise of the culture of "petty bourgeois" in China from the 1980s onwards.

The Ages of Liang Shanbo and Zhu Yingtai

But I still believe this play might be a profound tragedy, which indeed implies some institutional and life issues worthy of in-depth thinking not only for ancient people but also for people of today. We only need a new reading. This reading must first be rooted in the social and historical condition where the story happened; it should fully understand the targeted audiences for whom the play was written and performed and their reference frame of social cognition.

I first look at the ages of the two protagonists in the play. In earlier versions of the *Liang Shanbo and Zhu Yingtai* story and play, the ages of Liang and Zhu were not mentioned. But the approximate ages of the protagonists are very important or even indispensable for audiences to understand and appreciate this play. If there weren't an approximate age, the play would become unreasonable. If their ages were too small, for instance, both of them were under the age of ten years, the play would be very absurd and amusing. If their ages were too old, the play would become very boring and melodramatic. Therefore, since the playscript didn't mention the ages, audiences must have an expectation concerning the ages of the protagonists in watching the performance, while this expectation is mainly constructed with the direct daily life experiences of audiences and information concerning the ages of protagonists provided by the playscript.[16] Since life experiences of audiences in different times are diverse, it then can be expected that audiences of different times have distinct or even diametrically different expectations in terms of the ages of the protagonists in watching the performance of this play, which ushers in divergent understandings of this play among audiences.

In modern society, to go out for study, to fall in love, to marry – all of these are basically connected with the youth of 20 years old or more. Therefore, in the eyes of modern audiences, Liang and Zhu are approximately like two "college students," or at least "senior high school students," who return home on vacation after many years of studying away from home. With the subconscious expectation of this age, and because of the liberalist concepts caused and molded by social change in modern times, audiences of today basically accept the concept of freedom of marriage and at least completely consider marriage and love between mature youths as the category of personal choice. Social format or prejudice unconsciously makes up the age of the protagonists. Although it is not a right or wrong issue, it enables audiences to very easily accept the comment that the play is against the feudalism and for the freedom of marriage. But in this way, our understanding might have the major deviation from ancient people's.

For ancient audiences or readers, the ages of Liang and Zhu would be much younger. No matter from the inference of marriage age in ancient times or from the deduction of details in the story itself, when the tragedy happened, they were just teenagers *at most*, approximately ranging from age 14 to 15, or even younger. In ancient China, there had already been a stipulation concerning marriageable age quite early, or the confirmed legal age of marriage.[17] But the same marriageable age has not exactly the same meaning; its meaning is up to what social issue the stipulated marriageable age is targeted at. In the early days, especially after the turmoil of war, the state usually adopted a pronatalist policy and tried to realize population growth by practicing a forced marriageable age, namely those who reached this age must be married. With the development of social peace, the state increasingly

---

16 This is what the reader-response criticism has pointed out, that the reading is the activity of reader in which the reader participates. See Fish, Stanley. *Duzhe fanying lilun piping lilun yu shijian* 读者反应批评: 理论与实践, trans. Wen Chuan 文楚安 (Beijing: Chinese Social Sciences, 1998).

17 For the historical investigation and discrimination of legal marriageable age, see Chen, Guyuan 陈顾远. *Zhongguo hunyin shi* 中国婚姻史 (Beijing: The Commercial Press, 1998), 125–129.

practiced the authorized marriageable age, namely those who only reached this age could be married, or their marriage was legally protected.[18] According to the materials at hand, the former marriageable age is usually stipulated as 20 for the male and 15 for the female, while the latter is stipulated as 15 for the male, 13 for the female in the Middle Ages[19] and 16 for the male and 14 for the female after the Ming and Qing dynasties.[20]

In terms of the common sense exhibited in the playscript, when Liang Shanbo and Zhu Yingtai met each other, their ages were about 11 or 12 at most, and they died for love at the age of about 14 or 15. Because even in ancient times, people would generally not go to study until the age of 16 or 17, accordingly, Liang and Zhu had the least likelihood of being male and female adults of 20 years old on a college campus, just as what we watch on the stage.

Second, generally speaking, when male and female teenagers reach the age of 13 or 15, they become gradually sensitive to the opposite sex. Liang and Zhu were classmates for three years and were in each other's company every day, while Liang was totally unaware of the female identity of Zhu. For this, there will be many explanations. But the simplest and reasonable explanation is that for Zhu Yingtai, she was not into puberty, or at least not completely into puberty; otherwise, no matter the body shape, skin, manners, or voice, they will have gigantic changes, which are difficult to be utterly covered in *the very close association* with the opposite sex. As for Liang Shanbo, he might be more immature and had the very likelihood of not entering puberty. Therefore, Liang didn't exhibit the great sensitivity and curiosity to the opposite sex, which was usually reflected among the young men in the strongest way. Not that Liang was absolutely ignorant of Zhu's strange behaviors and manners, but that Zhu's few words dispelled his suspicions (609). On the parting time after the completion of study, on the road, Zhu Yingtai once used love metaphors such as "two neck-to-neck mandarin ducks," "twin lotus flowers on one stalk," etc., to give a hint, which were very easily understood by educated persons: "my emotion is roused by the scene, and my metaphors fall on your deaf ears" (611) and "shedding petals, the waterside flower pines for love while the heartless brook babbles on" (610). Non-responses and insensitivity to love expressions like these can't and shouldn't only be explained with Zhu Yingtai's being disguised as a man; it should be attributed to the physical and psychological immaturity of Liang to a larger extent. Liang Shanbo was very likely to be the age of a young

---

18 For example, in 627, the decree of the emperor of the Tang Dynasty stipulated the marriageable age for the male was 20, the female 15; 100 years later, in 724, the decree stipulated, "the male at the age of 15, the female 13 and above can be married." Guo, Jian; Yin, Xiaohu; Wang, Zhiqiang 郭建、殷啸虎、王志强. *Zhongguo wenhua tongzhi falv zhi* 中国文化通志·法律志 (Shanghai: Shanghai People's Press, 1998), 101.

19 For example, "From now on, the male at the age of 15, the female 13 and above, if they are not in the widowhood, they can be married." *Zhoushu zhoubenji* 周书·周本纪. From 713, the marriage age for the male was 15 and the female 13 in the Tang Dynasty. The Song Dynasty followed the rule of Tang. *Qingming ji liji juan 7*清明集·立继卷7.

20 Guo et al. 郭建. *Zhongguo wenhua tongzhi falv zhi* 中国文化通志·法律志, 101.

boy who played innocently with a young girl and was in the slow-witted state of "being unaware of the concealed love for me." Zhu Yingtai was just a young girl with the first stirrings of love and had a hazy attachment to Liang, but her physical and psychological states weren't mature yet either. Only when their ages are put in this stage can we make a reasonable explanation for their pure and honest relations, which could be understood by ordinary persons.

In the play, other pieces of information are also used to infer the general age of Liang and Zhu. For example, Zhu Yingtai was betrothed to Ma's family. Although it didn't directly prove the age of Zhu, it could serve as a reference, because in ancient times, the age of a girl being betrothed to others was about 15, as mentioned earlier.[21] Zhu Yingtai died for Liang Shanbo, and this act is generally the action of a young girl with pure love and strong integrity, not of a woman who is older and has more understanding of life.

I am not hereby studying the ages of Liang and Zhu! I know the playscript is not the history and the dramatic characters are not true figures. In this sense, the study of age is doomed to bring no result. Through this study, I only observe the implied imagination concerning the ages of the two protagonists, the related sentiments and judgments, and the social reality as the basis of all these things when the author created this play and audiences watched the performance from the historical perspective. Any play enjoying a widespread popularity and universal recognition must include some realities of that time. Consequently, we have reason to consider the social condition then as a standard in order to understand the ambiguity of this playscript. It is also on the basis of this fact that I believe my inference concerning the ages of Liang and Zhu is roughly valid. This age issue is of important significance to understand the tragic features of their love.

Early Marriage and Arranged Marriage

Once the approximate ages of Liang and Zhu are confirmed, we then find that the affection between them is an unusual "puppy love" according to the standard of today, which is roughly equivalent to the love between junior high school students of today. However, it is inappropriate to use the term "puppy love." Nowadays, people have endowed this term with a certain pejorative meaning, and this phenomenon itself seems to be a problem. But any social phenomenon will not naturally become a problem because of its own existence and might only become a problem when it is connected with specific social persons and their social activities. If viewed historically, our so-called "puppy love" was once regarded as a normal thing for a long time, or even might be the necessity for the existence of human society in the history.

"Normal" or "abnormal," they are not the natural concepts, but a social construction. The standard is not the eternal reason, but the social needs. In ancient farming society for ages, the medical hygiene level was naturally low due to the

---

21 See "I married to you at the age of 14" Li 李白. *Changganxing qiyi* 长干行·其一.

very poor level of productivity and science and technology, the inconvenient communications, and the inconvenient mobility of personnel and information. In such a
social condition, the average life expectancy for humans was inevitably very low.[22]
To ensure the normal reproduction and continuity of life, people must be married
early. The average life expectancy of that time was only presumed to be the age of
40, and if the actually marriageable age then amounts to the actually marriageable
age in the contemporary cities, for example, about the age of 25, when the overwhelming majority of people in this society died, their first-born child was only
more than 10 years old. In agricultural society, although the child of this age could
participate in some works with slight strength, it was insufficient for him to earn his
daily bread, while his youngest siblings were very likely still in swaddling clothes.
Obviously, this marriageable age can't ensure the effective continuity of the human species. Accordingly, early marriage is necessary, which is the best choice for
society to maintain its consistent existence. Only in this sense can we understand
the previously mentioned legal age of marriage with the dutiful feature in ancient
times and understand why early marriage and puppy love in our opinion of today
were quite normal then. If a person is married at the age of 16, even he passes away
about the age of 40, and his eldest son or daughter is already over 20 years old, who
can completely earn his or her bread and get married. The younger siblings can
generally make a living by themselves as well. Even the youngest siblings are still
small; the eldest son or daughter can assume the responsibility of bringing them up.
Therefore, in traditional Chinese society, there are always the sayings and practices
of "the eldest brother is like a father, while his wife is like a mother."[23]

Although the effective continuity of human society demands early marriage, it
must be noted that such early marriage must be limited and receive the biological
support of humans. If it is not based on the physically mature time and extent of
humans that are decided by genes, such social needs can't be fulfilled. In the past, a
son of a wealthy family was less than 10 years old, but he married a mature girl as
his child bride, which was early indeed. But they neither gave birth to children nor
had a son to carry on the family name. The true "consummation" only happened
when the boy reached a certain age. Human institutions, no matter subjective designs or natural evolution, are not beyond the biological limitation of humans. On
the contrary, they must be compatible with such a limitation. Generally speaking,

22 When the P. R. China was newly founded, the average life expectancy for Chinese was about
    35 years. According to the research of family trees of some clans in the middle and lower reaches of
    the Yangtze River area, the life expectancy of Chinese ranged from 35 to 40 when they were born
    from 1400 to 1900. See Tsui-jung, Liu. "The Demographic Dynamics of Some Clans in the Lower
    Yang Tze Area, Ca 1400–1940," in *Academic Economic Papers*, vol. 9, no. 1 (1981), 152–156. It
    should be noted that this area was the most prosperous in China in those days, and generally speak-
    ing, these clans might be the well-to-do families. Therefore, this life expectancy might be higher
    than the average life expectancy of Chinese at that time.
23 This section is roughly based on my paper. Zhu, Suli 朱苏力. "Yujing lun yizhong falv zhidu yan-
    jiu fangfa de goujian" 语境论 一种法律制度研究方法的构建. *Zhongwai faxue* 中外法学, no. 1
    (2000).

owing to such social needs, more of those human species with relatively early mature genes can survive in the long-term competition and elimination of human evolution, while others lacking such genes (no matter if their morality is noble or not or their culture is advanced or not) will be eliminated in the end because of their incapability of ensuring the effective continuity of species. From the perspective of genes, the fertility for the rest of human species is basically at the age of 14 or 15. From the perspective of social biology, humans grow slowly at this age. This physical feature is not accidentally acquired, but the outcome of long-term human survival evolution and the outcome of natural evolution and the choice of non-teleology. In terms of the continuity of human species, the institution of puppy love, early marriage, and early childbirth in ancient society not only have a biological basis but also the rationality of social needs. In the historical conditions at that time, it was a reasonable institution.

However, it is not enough for us to acknowledge the rationality of this institution in society of that time. Humans must find other concrete institutional measures as well in order to ensure the effective realization of early marriage and childbirth in the environment with the slow mobility of personnel in an agricultural society, the narrowness of association, and the inconvenient flow of information. The words of matchmakers and arranged marriages are just developed as an assisting institution to ensure the continuity of humans, which effectively corresponds to such social conditions.

The long-term practices enable humans to realize that "the male and female with the same surname will not give birth to healthy babies."[24] Those married with too close blood relations are extremely bad for the reproduction of offspring. Therefore, humans must choose a marriage spouse among those with relatively distant blood relations. But in ancient agricultural society, the chance of contacting those of the opposite sex who could be spouses was slim (occasionally, there was a male or female cousin) because of the inconvenient communications and the flow of information and the narrow world for humans, who basically grew up together in one village. The opposite sex of similar ages in the village were usually close relatives who couldn't be married. It was very difficult to associate with a marriageable person of the opposite sex of other villages. Because generally speaking, without a specific expectation, you might have no likelihood of tramping over hill and dale more than ten *li* or even decades of *li* to seek a mate for no reason. Even because of such a young age, many teenagers still didn't know much about love and might not fully pay attention to the opposite sex. For example, Liang Shanbo didn't know Zhu Yingtai was girl even though they had been classmates for three years. In this social condition, the effective continuity of the human species will be endangered again if the marriage is formed in the mode of free love, which is taken for granted with moral superiority by the city residents of today; in the meanwhile, the

---

24 *Zuozhuan xigong ershisan nian* 左传·僖公二十三年. "The couple with the same surname are not married, they will be free from the fear of not bearing a baby." *Guoyu jinyu* 国语·晋语.

marriage of close relatives must be excluded; the cost of information and trading will be so high that the marriage is impossible.

Humans still create multiple possibilities to increase the chances of association between young people, which lowers the information cost of finding a mate in order to facilitate marriage – for example, the local markets, all kinds of festivals, spring outings, and temples for worshiping Buddha. In Yuan plays, there are many love stories with festivals as backgrounds. Especially in mountainous areas inhabited by some ethnic minorities, there are activities such as singing of folk songs and racing horses. For many young people, the significance of these activities is to provide a public place to associate with the opposite sex; from the perspective of society, one of the important functions of these reunions is to establish a temporary courting market.

But even so, people of agricultural societies were still bothered with the information cost of finding a mate, because not every one of them could apply these institutions. Actually, the overwhelming majority of them had a strong likelihood of not using them.

The marriage of children is still a great thing with which parents are concerned. Comparatively speaking, parents' social experiences and relations are wider and broader, and they have more ability to find a mate suitable for children in terms of their beliefs. To broaden the possibility and successful rate of choosing a spouse, some parents will also greatly rely on matchmakers. Arranged marriage and words of matchmakers become the main institution of choosing a spouse in a traditional agricultural society, whose function is to increase the information channels and save the information cost. Generally speaking, in an agricultural society, its utility is active (although it is not always so), and it has an irreplaceable institutional legitimacy. Those groups that didn't adopt this institution adopted "the free marriage" and brought forth more marriages of close relatives in agricultural society as a result must gradually die out in terms of biological evolution with historical unconsciousness; what accompanies their disappearance is their marriage system of "free love." Any agricultural society that still exists today basically adopted arranged marriage and words of matchmakers in ancient times.[25] It is absolutely not accidental, but the outcome of biological choice. The institution is not the product of morality, but the product of survival.

There are other social factors that facilitate arranged marriage by parents as well. For example, marriage is not just the issue of sex, but a social institution,[26] in which the mundane issues of reproducing healthy offspring and supporting a family are involved. Although sex is based on biological instinct, marriage is inevitably concerned with various choices of gain and loss. There are many miscellaneous affairs

---

25 "In ancient Rome . . . parents decided the marriage of their children without the need of asking for their opinions." Zhou, Nan 周枬. *Luomafa yuanlun shangce* 罗马法原论上册 (Beijing: The Commercial Press, 1994), 137–138.

26 For the distinction between the sexual love and marriage, see Fei, Xiaotong 费孝通. "Shengyu zhidu" 生育制度. In *Xiangtu zhongguo* 乡土中国 (Beijing: Peking University Press, 1998).

to be coped with. Obviously, there will be many difficulties for a teenager of 14 or 15 years old to deal with them. Comparatively, parents have more competences and experiences to handle them. Besides, in an ancient society, a son would live with his parents for a certain period at least after the marriage, or even provide for the aged parents. Henceforth, parents were generally unwilling to have a stranger in their family whose background was totally unknown to them and whose character was in conflict with theirs. To avoid such a conflict, they naturally interfered with the marriage of their children. Because of the control of financial means of family, maturity, experiences, wide associations, and family status formed in a long run, all of these enable parents to occupy a dominant position in this issue. Arranged marriage henceforth becomes a basic marriage system in traditional agricultural society, a de facto law, and a rule that people are obliged to abide by and ensure its operation through social pressures.[27]

Financial Issues in Arranged Marriages

In choosing a marriage spouse, another basic condition is that the counterpart has the capability of bringing up posterity from the female perspective in addition to the requirement that too close blood relations must be forbidden.

This is also the biological instinct of species generated out of the long-term survival competition. The research of social biology finds that every living thing tends to let its gene reproduce more through copulation, which is the same case for humans. However, because of the different roles of the male and female in giving birth, their standard or strategy of choosing a spouse will be different. Generally speaking, man instinctively "hopes" (not the exact word) to have more spouses, which will have more offspring as a result, but because of the impermissibility of social institutions, financial state, and sometimes physical competence, men will instinctively choose those women with more fertile capability, which is usually manifested as the secondary sexual characteristics, namely "beauty" and "sexiness." Because in comparison with men, the fertile resources of women are more scarce (the short age of fertility and the limited number of ovulations), and women puts more investment in giving birth to each baby, and because she and her offspring need more protections and upbringing than men, especially in agricultural society, woman will be more fastidious in choosing a spouse.[28] Generally speaking, women tends to choose those men who are strong, clever, and capable, and accordingly have the competence of providing this protection and upbringing. This competence is mostly represented as wealth and talent (potential wealth). A talented (or

27 "The birth of a son occasions the wish that he should have a wife; the birth of a daughter occasions the wish that she should have a marital home. As parents, all human beings have this mind. But if, without waiting for the command of parents or the permission of go-betweens, the young people bore holes in a wall in order to catch a glimpse of one another or scale the wall in order to come together, their parents and everyone in the state will hold them in low esteem." Bloom, trans. *Mencius*, 63–64.

28 Posner, Richard A. *Sex and Reason* (Cambridge, MA: Harvard University Press, 1992), 91.

wealthy) man and a beautiful woman, talented scholars and beautiful ladies, why can this mundane happy marriage standard exist for a long time and be praised?[29] It actually has a certain basis in social biology, behind which there is a logical domination of biological competition. No matter if we are willing to accept this standard or not today, we only have to examine our own conscience and will find that it is quite a universal phenomenon among ordinary people. Beautiful girls always win more favors of men, while it is generally hard for the weak and incapable men to find wives.

But because of early marriage, these standards of choosing a spouse usually become inapplicable. Because of early marriage, although a woman might usually have exhibited her beauty, a boy usually is not fully developed, and many manly characteristics (whether he is strong, tall, and healthy) haven't been fully displayed. As a result, it is very hard to judge whether he will be strong in the future. What is more, with the development of society, the upbringing capability of man is not only decided by strength but also is decided, and might be increasingly decided, by personal ability and wisdom, which is hard to distinguish in an arranged marriage and words of matchmakers. Ability and wisdom can only be gradually exhibited in association with others, including the opposite sex. Besides, even if a man has the capability of upbringing, he might not have such a will. The will of upbringing is usually up to whether the woman has a sex appeal to him to a considerable extent. In other words, he loves her or he does not. The will of upbringing based on the sex appeal is hardly distinguished and measured in the system of arranged marriage and words of matchmakers. It is only more easily revealed in the association with the opposite sex, even sometimes if only a momentary association.[30] In Yuan plays and many other ancient plays, there are often episodes of love at first sight between a distressed scholar and a daughter from a family of good social standing.[31] Although it is somewhat a cliché, it exhibits a reason of social biology. These problems can't be avoided by the marriage system, which is caused by early marriage with arranged marriage and words of matchmakers.

To avoid or mitigate these weaknesses of the arranged marriage system, there must be other institutional supplements or replacements as a result. In human history, people gradually form a replacement sign in which the family background, including physical strength, family fortune, education, and moral standards, is used to measure the upbringing capability of the targeted spouse. The research of economics shows that this replacement has a certain rationality.[32] First, gener-

---

29 "Through the ages, the beautiful lady is matched for the talented scholar." Since Dong Jieyuan first expressed this empirical proposition in *The Romance of the West Chamber*《西厢记诸宫调》, it has been used to the full in Yuan plays, such as *Cui Yingying Waiting for the Moon in the Western Wing*《崔莺莺待月西厢记》and *Plum Incense*《㑇梅香翰林风月》.

30 See Becker, Gary S. "Imperfect Information, Marriage, and Divorce," in *A Treatise on the Family* (Cambridge, MA: Harvard University Press, 1981), 327.

31 This point was manifested in Yuan plays such as Wang Shifu's *The Story of the Western Wing* and Zheng Guangzu's *Plum Incense* and many folk stories as well.

32 Becker. "Imperfect Information, Marriage, and Divorce," 326–327.

ally speaking, in an agricultural society, the creation of a family fortune mainly relies on physical strength; even today, we know that physical strength and appearance can be inherited. (Today, in selecting excellent young athletes, the height and physical strength of their parents will be always consulted.) Genetic research and some biological research also show that intelligence will be inherited.[33] Therefore, to assess parents as the replacement sign of measuring future physical strength and intelligence of targeted spouses, although it is not accurate, it is reasonable. Besides, generally speaking, parents with better physical strength and intelligence will accumulate more wealth than other parents, and the financial situation of their family will be relatively good. Even if this measuring has a large error, the existing property is the accumulated and materialized upbringing capability, which at least partially protects the life of their offspring from landing in an excessively awkward predicament.[34] Therefore, in choosing a spouse for children, at least in the situation of the same conditions in all other aspects, all the parents generally tend to choose relatively wealthy families, at least the well-to-do families, at the same level. It reflects the natural wish of parents for their children to have a better life, which does provide a necessary condition for the smooth growth and success of the next generation.[35]

This standard is not simply to despise the poor and curry favor with the rich, but a necessary choice out of living needs. When there are no other signs proving that the targeted marriage spouse has a better capability of upbringing, generally speaking, to use the existing family background, including fortune, as a basic standard of choosing a spouse, for parents who choose a spouse for their children, it might be the most practical, visible, and economical means. Even parents of today might not take into consideration the financial situation of the family after their children are married. Certainly, people of today might attach more importance to the counterpart's record of education etc., and it seemingly has an elevated requirement of the counterpart's "schooling." It seems that as society advances, the extent of civilization is improved, but to put it bluntly, the record of education today is still a sign roughly measuring the future income of a potential spouse, because in general, highly educated persons earn more in comparison with those with low education. Since teenagers are affected by the gene which dominates the standard of choosing a spouse in primitive life, they

---

33 See Steen, R. Grant. *DNA and Destiny: Nature and Nurture in Human Behavior* (Berlin: Springer, 1996), Chapter 8. According to the book, the present research shows that the rate of intelligence inheritance is 60%.

34 Actually, when Chinese investigate the family situation, they will usually consider the moral character of the parents and even their ancestors. It is actually a presumption that the moral character and the behavioral approach might have the factor of inheritance to a certain extent. This point also accords with some of the present biological research. At least some criminology studies prove that there is a factor of inheritance that plays a role in some crimes. See *DNA and Destiny: Nature and Nurture in Human Behavior*, esp. Chapter 10, 11, 13.

35 Gary S. Becker. "Family Background and the Opportunities of Children," in *A Treatise on the Family*, 179.

usually consider appearance and other sexual characteristics more, namely the so-called "human nature of loving beauty," but it is very difficult for them to think seriously of wealth and intelligence, the most important factors in the life of agricultural and commercial civilizations. Therefore, in the arranged marriage system, it seems generally reasonable for parents to set store by the family financial condition and fortune.

We shouldn't forget the problems of the arranged marriage system. The biggest problem lies in its ensured inaccuracy in measuring sex appeal by this replaceable measuring mechanism. Because sex appeal itself is hard to be measured. Although physical strength, height, appearance, and fortune can form sex appeal, sex appeal still has some other factors, some very personalized factors, which can only be truly compared and discovered in their own association with the targeted marriage spouses. It is not always very accurate to predict children from the perspective of parents. (The father is tall; his son might not be.) Then, in words of matchmakers and arranged marriage, it does imply the factor of an unhappy marriage because of the lack of love (sex appeal). As mentioned earlier, on the journey of bringing Zhu Yingtai to the family of Landlord Ma for the wedding, Zhu was allowed to hold a ceremonious memorial to Liang Shanbo, which is not the problem concerning the tolerance of Ma's family at all, and reflects that Zhu had no sufficient sex appeal to the son of Landlord Ma because they had never met and associated with each other. The son of Landlord Ma had no passionate love for Zhu Yingtai, which didn't result in the strong sex jealousy that should be found in men falling in love. Certainly, it doesn't mean that their later marriage must not be happy all along. They have a very high likelihood of nurturing the strong love, namely "marriage first, love later." Actually, it is not a rare case in arranged marriages of a traditional society. But there is also the possibility that both of them will never truly fall in love, and even become enemies. It is impossible to predict the actual scenario.

But the point is not that this measuring mechanism is faulty. First, the point is that in the condition of ancient times or traditional society, if humans can't find a better measuring mechanism, these faults will be inevitable. It is impossible for humans to live in a perfect world forever. Second, if viewed from a non-ideological perspective, even the marriage of free love of today might not solve the problem of long-term sex appeal at all. Many personal characteristics can be changed in social life, for example, the counterpart's appearance, physical shape, health and personalities, and changes in terms of preferences and experiences; the increased association, and the continuous appearance of different types of men or women. All these factors will affect sex appeal. The modern marriage system with free love as the basis only turns this problem to "the accountability for one's own choice," and this problem is then hidden or transferred by the high rate of divorce. Finally, we must bear in mind that, in the condition of ancient society, the marriage system first aimed to solve the problem of effective continuity of humans, "the ceremony of marriage . . . in its retrospective character, to secure the services on the ancestral temple, and in its prospective character, to secure the continuance of the family line."[36] "There are three things that are unfilial, and the greatest of them is to have no posterity."[37] Sex appeal was naturally of less importance than the survival problem of humans.

Factors of Tragedy 1: Nature and Society

The story of *Liang Shanbo and Zhu Yingtai* provides inspiration for us to understand the society and institution, which will be respectively analyzed and expounded.

The first is on the social institutional nature of marriage. Many contemporary intellectuals emphasize the individual freedom, which is manifested as the emphasis on the freedom of marriage and love in sex and marriage, the emphasis on the natural attribute of sexual love, and the so-called natural law. With the social change as a political and social pursuit, these efforts and publicities are obviously good and necessary today. But if there is only this type of explanation, we might be dazzled by these words and lost in the jungle of words. Actually, we shouldn't consider something a noble thing worthy of being pursued just because it is natural. Admittedly, sexual love is a natural instinct of living individuals, without which humans can't reproduce. But it shouldn't receive institutional recognition because of this instinct. For the young boy and girl with a very close blood relation, for example, cousins, they have the likelihood of falling in love on the basis of this instinct as well, yet we might consider that it is correct to not allow them to be married – even the statutory law of each country will not allow it. For another example, some sexual impulses toward the opposite sex, even based on the same human instincts, are still subject to various limitations of customs and laws (for example, sex is not allowed on some occasions), and even sanctioned (for example, rape and statutory rape, even if it is consensual). At least in view of the historical condition of today, the behaviors based on instincts are insufficient to acquire social legitimacy, although they should be given the appropriate consideration. Even it can be stated thus, to a very large extent, that the institution should contain human instinctive impulses and thereby coordinate collective instincts in light of individual instincts. Because when viewed as living things, humans have many obvious weaknesses. They can't run as fast as many animals; they can't fly and are not inborn swimmers. But because every individual human lives in the group and forms a culture and institution together, humans can live and grow up as a result. Many human instincts are better satisfied in social life and the institution, which is formed in social life. It is the same case with sexual love.

Actually, nature is not as beautiful as many intellectuals of today have described. In terms of nature itself, it can't meet our social needs on many occasions. In the violent storm with flashing lightning and rumbling thunder, we will feel scared, and only grouping might assuage this fear. In natural disasters, no matter earthquake

---

36 Legge, James, trans. *The Sacred Book Books of China: The Texts of Confucianism*, Part IV, *The Li Ki* 2 (Oxford: Clarendon Press, 1885), 428.
37 Bloom, trans. *Mencius*, 84.

or tsunami, we will be paralyzed with fear, and only the mutual care from humans can bring some slight consolation to us. Even the previously mentioned analysis concerning the arranged marriage system also shows that the human need of sexual love can't be gratified only by natural instincts. In an area with a very low level of production, sparse population, and inconvenient communications, it is hard to find spouse, or to be frank, there is no chance of reproduction. Needless to say, without the establishment of a marriage system and cultural development, we can only have the impulse of sexual love toward the opposite sex and can't feel the beauty of sexual love. Without the further development of a human system motivated by social changes, we will not have the marriage of free love today and might still rest on arranged marriage.

Yes, passionate love, an ideal place for people in love, and a solemn pledge of love, all will let us feel the beauty of nature. But this nature has become the nature supported by the existing social civilization and the nature with a humanitarian orientation. When love is suppressed by various social systems, including the marriage system, we do want to return to nature and desire to abandon ourselves by removing all the obstacles. But can we really do that? We have entered the modern age and understand a lot, and this can't be retracted. Even if it were possible, are we really willing to do so? Except the romantic carefree moment of illusion without the second thought. Even at that moment, we might not really want to return to ancient times. Today, the natural environment for love activities has been greatly expanded. The communications of modern society and other conditions enable us to be more natural, and our nature has been broadened as well. We get closer to nature in some aspects or on some occasions, instead of being further away, narrower, and more "alienated" in the eyes of some modern scholars. Even owing to the development of modern contraception technology, people of today actually enjoy more sexual love than ancient people without the fear, suppression, and rejection of sexual love, which is caused by many people's concerns of pregnancy and bringing up a child. In general, human life of today is more heart-felt and indulgent than ancient human life. The modern age at least makes our marriage and love more beautiful in more aspects. Society, system, and culture don't *just* suppress us, but support and cultivate our needs and feelings, including love and marriage.

Not just, but it does. When we emphasize the social features of humans and emphasize that generally speaking, human instincts and needs must be better satisfied through social institutions, there are still some instincts and needs of many individuals that have to be adapted to the needs of social life on some occasions and follow the institutional demands. Even the instinct of sexual love becomes a biological resource that is incessantly exploited – for example, the exchange for all kinds of resources for sex in order to maintain one's life and family life. Sex will be institutionalized, which is the family, no matter whether it is monogamy or polygamy. Once the institution is formed, no matter what type of form it is, it must satisfy human instincts through a certain method, while suppressing this or that type of human instinct by another method.

But is it a tragedy? For a specific individual with a limited duration of life, it might be tragic; but for humans, from the perspective of the institution, what we can sigh over might be just the saying "Heaven and Earth are not kind: The ten thousand things are straw dogs to them."

Factors of Tragedy 2: Convention and Exception

To acknowledge the contextualized legitimacy of an institution shouldn't result in the veneration of this institution as eternal and the acceptance and insistence on its absolute rationality. Any social practice, once it becomes an institution, it will have weaknesses because what the institution answers is a type of conventional question in a stable society. Therefore, the institutionalization has the very likelihood of presenting the weaknesses in two aspects. First, the basic premise of establishing an institution is the basically stable social condition, in which this type of question can present the normal state in society. Only at this moment, the institution is effective and useful. But society is never in the normal state of stability. Once the social condition has the intense, radical, or even important change, this type of question in that society will change accordingly, and the targeted usefulness of the institution will fall short of a requirement and even be to no avail. For example, people have always known that in a period of social unrest, it is very hard for people in dispute to apply the justice system, which might be replaced by the revenge system.[38] People once had the saying "severe laws are needed to govern a country when it is in disorder." This shows the institutional limitation. The institution can't always control the situation, even if people try to do so.

It is the same case for the marriage system as well. The change from agricultural society to commercial society brings forth a series of changes of social production and living conditions: the improved transportation and communications, the great mobility of personnel, the development of medical care, the extension of human life expectancy, and the flow of associated counterparts. Such a change causes a fundamental alteration to the series of conventional problems of agricultural society, to which arranged marriage is targeted. The improvement of life expectancy enables the fertility problem to no longer be the main issue of endangering the continuity of human species, and early marriage loses its necessity as a result. Because of the increasingly meticulous and complex modern social division of labor, the demands of each type of work for the education and professional skills of laborers are higher, and people must spend more time acquiring professional skills and educational knowledge. Therefore, generally speaking, the human marriageable age is being put off. Puppy love, early marriage, and early childbirth are not beneficial for the needs of social development. This type of custom has become one of the important problems that the modernizing society must solve. Either through the market competition, or through the intervention of national laws, or through the combination, the actual marriageable age of people in modern society is universally put off, and later marriage and birth control gradually become the reality of modernized society and acquire the social legitimacy as well. It is against this great background

38 Aeschylus. *Agamemnon*, trans. E. D. A. Morshead in *The Complete Greek Drama*, 206.

that we can observe why "puppy love" possesses a derogatory meaning today and has changed from a natural physical attribute of humans to one of the social problems that some modern societies try to solve through various means. It means that the rationality of any institution belongs to a certain social and historical category.

Naturally, with this social change, the legitimacy and actual feasibility of the marriage system with arranged marriage and words of matchmakers as the main forms are greatly lowered. Industrialization, urbanization, and the ensuing mobility of personnel greatly quicken the association with strangers, and generally speaking, the chance of associating with a person of the opposite sex is greatly amplified. The problem of scarce information of marriage spouses in an ancient society or small-scale peasant society undergoes the important or even radical changes as well. The mobility of personnel enables many children to leave families and enter society before marriage. In the marriage system, it is no longer necessary for many people to rely on parental arrangements and words of matchmakers to increase the chance of finding a mate. These old practices can be utilized, people occasionally resort to them indeed. It is through this social change that the parental arrangement and words of matchmakers gradually lose their historical rationality as the component of a marriage system.

The story of *Liang Shanbo and Zhu Yingtai* happened in a period of peace, and there was no major social change in the story as well. Henceforth, their tragedy has nothing to do with such weakness of an institution. The second weakness of the institution is closely related. That is, the institution is targeted at the conventional problem. There is a convention, then there will be an exception. The institution usually fails to cope with the problems outside the convention, and even sometimes fails to know in advance that the encountered problem is either treated as the exception worthy of being granted the special permission, or the lawless act that should be constrained by regulations.

For example, in a traditional agricultural society, the mobility of personnel is rare. Because people have a slim chance of choosing spouses, arranged marriage generally causes no "tragedy" or even losses. Because people have no chance of choosing, they will not and cannot calculate the opportunity costs and gains in choosing a spouse for an individual. Although young boys and girls sometimes will fall in love because of the occasional association, this situation usually easily happens between close relatives. Because it violates every type of marriage taboo, it will thereby be suppressed. For those lovers, this suppression is very cruel; especially in a condition without any or a few alternative choices, the fatal tragedy might be more likely to happen. However, this tragedy is still somewhat reasonable for the society at that time, especially the prevention of marriage among close relatives for the sake of healthy offspring and the prevention of disorder caused by romantic love in a small-scale agricultural community, which results in intense internal division, etc. Many taboos concerning love and marriage aim to avoid the greater tragedies.

The situation of Liang and Zhu is not included in this case. If perceived from the level of scientific development and knowledge of today, this tragedy nearly hasn't any social gains, but only costs. Both of them met on their journey while studying away from home and truly fell in love after having become classmates for three years. To travel a thousand *li* on the time of appointment shows that both of them had not the possibility of sharing close blood relations. Both of them were neither married, nor engaged, which would not affect other families and marriages accordingly. The dislocation of generational hierarchy in family, the radical change of relations, the emotional losses and the redistribution of property, none of the others could encounter all these that affected social stability because of the love and marriage between Liang and Zhu. In light of our knowledge of today, in this condition, to still insist on the operation of the system of arranged marriage and words of matchmakers will have no actual benefit, not to Liang and Zhu, or to society or humans at that time, apart from abstractly supporting and reinforcing the marriage system that is universally effective in ancient society (the insistence on the "rule of law" in form) in general. On the contrary, there are many harms: the deprivation of their personal happiness, the loss of social welfare that might be acquired by the voluntary trading among people, and even the obstruction of realizing the pursued objective (the outbreeding) and gains (healthier offspring) of this marriage system that people initially created and insisted on.

Certainly, we can't always adopt an opportunist attitude toward the institution as a result. At that time, the emphasis on the sacredness of an arranged marriage system might be of some value as well, namely, to stabilize the marriage system then and to prevent people's opportunistic attitude. Because the adopted opportunistic attitude toward the institution not only brings forth the nothingness to an institution but also other institutions in the end.[39] On many occasions, even some irrationally conventional systems should not be violated off-handedly.

However, under some circumstances, the institution could and should be violated because the ultimate goal of establishing it aims to gratify human welfare. If an institution is respected just because it is an institution, regardless of whether it meets or could better meet social welfare and human needs, then this institution will definitely lose its legitimacy and vitality as an institution in the end and will surely suppress the new institutional needs incessantly generated out of human social life. In view of this point, as for the situation like *Liang Shanbo and Zhu Yingtai*, if only it doesn't go to extremes, namely, not denying the general marriage system of that time, society and people should allow them to be treated as an exception and allow them to love freely and be married, although such a marriage exception of free love might not guarantee that they will suit each other perfectly and live together to a ripe old age for the rest of their life.

39 Therefore, it is necessary to keep a firm promise beforehand in law. For this point, see Elster, Jon; Slagstad, Rune, eds. *Constitutionalism and Democracy* (Cambridge: Cambridge University Press, 1993), Chapter 7.

Factors of Tragedy 3: When Will the Institution Be Changed?

However, the tragedy of *Liang Shanbo and Zhu Yingtai* is far beyond the conflict between the institutional convention with the equal legitimacy and the individual case; its lesson might not just lie in the attention to the conflict between the balance rule and the individual case, or the assurance of legal stability and flexibility. Many jurists have pointed out this type of principle; however, the principle only serves to admonish people on many occasions and does not solve real problems, because actors don't know when they should listen to an admonition, nor what kind of admonition. To solve real problems, we must apply the principle in a specific way; yet to apply the principle is not the theoretical problem, but a practical one, which is involved with time, place, and individual cases. Therefore, the tragic features of this story are much more profound.

Although I have analyzed the historical rationality (and irrationality) of the marriage system, including early marriage, early childbirth, parental arrangement, and words of matchmakers in the earlier passages, yet we must notice that the rationality (and irrationality) is unfolded in history and is diachronic, not so concise, logical, and synchronic just as I have analyzed before. Therefore, each person living in a specific time, space, and institution usually doesn't know the rationality or irrationality of this institution. People are just accustomed to this way of doing things and even might not know it is an institution. They can't draw any life guidance from my analysis. In other words, rationality and irrationality constructed in the previous passages are just a belated effort, which is just looking back on history. This belated effort is helpful to understand history yet is not useful for life. As Kierkegaard said, life can only be understood backwards but it must be lived forwards. We can't begin to live by following the prescribed order after we understand history, or even are unwilling to do so because we actually always hope for some unexpected pleasant surprises in life. The life that can be fully foreseen is not only boring but even intolerable. On the other hand, people can't master the future in a relatively precise way through the understanding of history, but only if the future is not the yesterday's repetition. Especially from the previous analysis, we can see that the formation and replacement of systems such as the marriage system actually is not a conscious human creation, but the unconscious outcome of human actions and historical evolution, just as Friedrich Hayek and others emphasized.[40] We can't expect everyone, or most people, to have the capability of reflecting on the institutional function as well. In life, people usually make the immediate responses to the institution on the basis of their own instincts or interests.

Therefore, even if I analyzed the rationality of Liang and Zhu's love in the previous section, this analysis is only made in the condition of today in accordance with the information that the predecessors couldn't have but that we have today after moving past that section of history and witnessing the tragedy of Liang and

---

40 Hayek, F. A. *Individualism and Economic Order* (Chicago: The University of Chicago Press, 2012).

Zhu. It means that only the development of knowledge can't avoid and lower the occurrences of such a tragedy. Undoubtedly, the tragedy of Liang and Zhu happened in ancient times with underdeveloped science and technology, and even institutional knowledge. They didn't know the historical limitation of arranged marriage and their emotional legitimacy, etc. But what results in the tragedy actually does not mainly lie in the amount of possessed knowledge. The most important distinction lies in the fact that ancient people are the persons concerned; we are outsiders. Ancient people made the judgment affecting their own future in the situation of that time, while we today reach the conclusion as spectators of the past events. When we draw a distance from history, we can make this or that judgment; but no matter which judgment it is, it will not generally affect our own existence. But if we are actors of historical progression, not thinkers reviewing the institutional rationality constructed in history, we don't know whether we should adhere to the institution or create an exception on a specific problem, just as Liang and Zhu did. Even we don't know whether society is undergoing a great change or not and whether this change is so great that an existing specific institution can be completely abolished and a brand-new institution is being created. Therefore, humans always make the decision that affects and even decides their own future in the condition of not possessing the complete information of the present and future situations. In this sense, we might affix our own times with any attribute, but because of the non-teleology or the unknown ultimate goal of human history (the actual outcome of this saying is exactly the same with the former one), we are confronted with abundant possibilities of not going back on our words, and we can't see through the consequence of our choice. Actually, we don't really understand either our historical position or our place in the time sequence. We might confidently make a decision, but can't reasonably give the complete explanation for what the basis for it is.

In this sense, each one of us always incessantly encounters this type of problem in life and makes different choices. We can present various reasons and use all kinds of historical facts and the existing knowledge of all disciplines to support our demands of today, yet we might not truly understand the consequence of these demands, especially those consequences that we don't hope for. Although people rely on a certain institution, they don't understand its social function. (For example, Liang and Zhu tried to acquire words of matchmakers and parental arrangement and Landlord Zhu adhered to the traditional institution, but they all didn't know the embedded reason.) Or even if the social function is understood by some persons, it might be gradually forgotten in society with the change of times, since this reasonable knowledge can't be inherited by genes.

It is in this sense, I believe, that the tragedy of *Liang Shanbo and Zhu Yingtai* is no longer limited to be a marriage tragedy in traditional agricultural society, but lies in the fact that it uses the art method to present the contradiction between the institution as a rule and special problems in real life, and it artistically exhibits the insolvable puzzle over the institutional problem confronted by actors in the historical change. This contradiction is the eternal issue of jurisprudence.

Concluding Remarks

The analysis presented here easily leads to a conservatist conclusion: Human cognitive ability and reflective ability are limited; as actors, humans can't reflect on the institutional rationality; therefore, they must respect the institution. Maybe some readers think this is my conclusion. Actually, the meaning of the story of *Liang Shanbo and Zhu Yingtai* might completely run counter to this conclusion. As mentioned earlier, because the institutional rationality is not eternal, the institution must be changed with the social change. We might not judge how the change can be made and fail to prepare for it in advance; the bygone history can't be used to fully foresee the future, and generally speaking, the future is highly uncertain. Therefore, when everything can't be taken as evidence whether the institution needs to change or not and how the change is undertaken, this might only be exhibited in the actions of violating institutions consciously or unconsciously and be gradually completed.

The traditional marriage system might still continue if the tragedy of Liang and Zhu didn't happen, and there weren't the love and marriage that didn't fit the social marriage system then, and even their tragedy among many young boys and girls who occasionally knew or associated with each other for a long time. In this sense, the tragedy of Liang and Zhu is fatally inevitable. Without these tragedies, the institutional irrationality will not be exposed and the institution will not have the possibility of evolutionary change. Therefore, *Liang Shanbo and Zhu Yingtai* seems to be an ancient romantic drama, but it fully reflects the tragic features, "Here . . . lay the tragic clash between the historically necessary postulate and the impossibility of its execution in practice."[41] If this tragedy, or this type of tragedy, didn't happen to Liang and Zhu, it might befall others. Society must pay this price, so that those who come later will be aware of it, although this awareness might not be sufficient to prevent another tragedy waiting for people at another crossing. This is another human tragedy. A fall into the pit, a gain in your wit. But the wit might not avoid the next fall. This is the difference between the legal system and other natural disciplines. Viewed in this sense, the institution can't be prearranged – indeed, only the outcome of human actions. Hence, none of us holds the future truth in our hands, even "We are *obliged* to be satisfied with forging our history blindly, one day at a time, choosing from all the options the one which seems best to us at present. But we can never hold, concerning history, those cavalier views that helped make the fortunes of Taine and Michelet. We are *inside*."[42] We might thereby have more in-depth understanding of the famous words of Holmes: "The *life* of the law has not been logic; it has been experience."[43]

---

41 Marx, Karl; Engels, Frederick. *Collected Works of Marx and Engels*, vol. 40 (New York: International Publishers, 1983), 445.
42 Sartre, Jean-Paul. "The Nationalization of Literature," in *What Is Literature? And Other Essays* (Cambridge, MA: Harvard University Pres, 1988), 278–279.
43 Holmes, Jr. *The Common Law*, 1.

Part II

The System of "Administrating Justice"

3   The Tragedy of Dou E

In Part I, the judicial investigation reflects "an external perspective," namely the investigation on the historical change of law from the macroscopic perspective. In this perspective, we can't see the institutional details. In the meanwhile, just as I have analyzed, in this historical change, what the individual actors did could nearly not be helped; the individuals were carried by history, and only accumulatively "blind" individual actions could push forward the institutional change.

But for ordinary people, law does not move like glaciers, but the solution is based on each concrete dispute, the satisfaction of each specific request, and the vicissitudes of life on each exact occasion. Therefore, it is necessary to investigate law from "an internal perspective," namely the concrete operation of law; literary works also provide this kind of source material. Part II makes such a try. Some "detective playscripts" become the main texts.

Abundant detective plays have been preserved in traditional Chinese society. Among more than 160 existing Yuan plays, there are 22 detective plays.[1] In *Selected Plays from the Yuan Dynasty* compiled by Zang Jinshu of the Ming Dynasty, 100 Yuan plays are collected (it is said that 4 of them are the plays of the early Ming Dynasty), among which there are 10 detective plays with Bao Zheng appearing on the scene, occupying one-tenth a portion of the whole book. If the five other detective plays are added, the proportion is beyond one-seventh.[2]

---

1 Wang, Qi, chiefly ed. 王起. "Tijie" 题解. In *Zhongguo xiju xuan* 中国戏剧选, annotated and compiled by Wang Qi et al. 王起等 (Beijing: People's Literature, 1985), 269.
2 In *Selected Plays from the Yuan Dynasty*, there are following plays in which Bao Zheng appeared: Guan Hanqing's *The Wife-Snatcher* 《包待制智斩鲁斋郎》 and *The Butterfly Dream* 《包待制三勘蝴蝶梦》, Zheng Tingyu's *The Flower of the Back Courtyard* 《包待制智勘后庭花》, Li Xingdao's *The Chalk Circle* 《包待制智赚灰阑记》, Zeng Ruiqing's *Leaving A Shoe* 《王月英元夜留鞋记》, Wu Hanchen's *Bao Zheng Wittily Obtained the Golden Treasure* 《包待制智赚生金阁》, the anonymous playwrights' *Judge Bao Selling Rice in Chenzhou* 《包待制陈州粜米》, *The Contract* 《包待制智赚合同文字》, *The Ghost of the Pot* 《叮叮当当盆儿鬼》 and *Shennuer* 《神奴儿大闹开封府》. Bao Zheng didn't appear in the following five plays: Meng Hanqing's *The Moheluo Doll* 《张孔目智勘魔合罗》, Sun Zhongzhang's *The Case of the Head Scarf* 《河南府张鼎勘头巾》, Guan Hanqing's *The Injustice to Dou E* 《感天动地窦娥冤》, Wang Zhongwen's *The Unidentified Corpse* 《救孝子贤母不认尸》 and the anonymous playwright's *Feng Yulan* 《冯玉兰夜月泣孤舟》.

DOI: 10.4324/9781003615606-6

But detective plays are not all about the drama concerning judicial decisions.[3] Because of the integration of the administration and judiciary in traditional Chinese society, common people in China are accustomed to generally calling the traditional Chinese drama concerning the officials' settlement of lawsuits "the plays of honest officials" or "detective plays," but the most of them are not related to the issue of judicial trials. Since modern times, at least in the institutional setup, the judiciary has been separated from administration and become a special branch and profession. But people are still habituated to identify detective plays with judicial dramas. It should be noted that the classification itself is not right or wrong, and there isn't a so-called "essential" or "correct" classification. The meaning of classification only lies in whether it is convenient to find, comprehend, and analyze questions for the sake of communication. If we continue to follow the traditional classification, it is usually inconvenient to adopt the conceptual system of modern scholarship and the existing research fruits to analyze the related questions.

If viewed from the tradition of modern legal science and political science, these detective plays or plays of honest officials can be roughly divided into two categories. One category is mainly concerned with the issue of law enforcement or administration. In this type of play, when the court decision is announced, the evidence has been confirmed, and the good and evil are clear as daylight. There isn't a thorny question concerning the judgment for who is right or not. Judicial trials only serve to legitimatize politics, and further reinforce the condemnation of the wrongdoers. Therefore, some scholars call this type of detective play one that "suppress[es] the despots and bullies."[4]

The other type of detective play is called as the play of "solving disputed cases and reversing unjust verdicts," which is mainly concerned with the judicial issue in the modern sense. But the concept of this type of detective play and the modern judicial concept do not completely coincide. In some aspects, the former concept is wider and broader. For example, because of the lack of division of labor within the ancient judiciary, the identity of the adjudicator trying a case is not clear in the eyes of modern people. He is not only a judge but also a policeman, a forensic expert,

---

3 See Deng, Shaoji 邓绍基. "Lun yuanzaju sixiang neirong de ruogan tezheng" 论元杂剧思想内容的若干特征. In *Yuanqu tongrong shang* 元曲通融上, chiefly ed. Zhang Yuezhong 张月中 (Taiyuan: Shanxi Ancient Books, 1999), 522; Li, Hanqiu 李汉秋. "Yuandai gonganxi lunlve" 元代公案戏论略. In *Yuanqu tongrong shang* 元曲通融上, 687.

4 For example, Luo, Jintang 罗锦堂. "Xiancun yuanren zaju zhi fenlei" 现存元人杂剧之分类. In *Yuanqu tongrong shang* 元曲通融上, 548. Deng Shaoji also adopts this classification and believes that there is one type of detective play "in which the described cases of litigation themselves are not complex, and even some of them were quite simple and straightforward in rights and wrongs. It is not hard for officials to make the correct judgment if they are honest and upright. . . . The issue with which honest officials are confronted is whether they are willing or bold to enforce the law. . . . This type of detective plays lays emphasis on the praises for the righteousness and uprightness of officials. . . . The second type of detective plays is usually with relatively intriguing plots and even describes some clueless cases, whose truth can only be ascertained after the meticulous analysis and investigation. It needs more wisdom." Deng, Shaoji 邓绍基. "Lun yuanzaju sixiang neirong de ruogan tezheng" 论元杂剧思想内容的若干特征. In *Yuanqu tongrong* shang 元曲通融上, 522.

and a prosecutor. In *Fifteen Strings of Cash*, which I analyze later, it is reflected in the most typical way. But in other aspects, the concept of detective plays is narrower than the concept of the modern judiciary. For instance, an adjudicator trying cases in traditional Chinese society is more focused on the solution to conflicts and disputes through various means, instead of *particularly* abiding by rules, specially establishing or confirming rules.[5] In order to ensure "an internal perspective," in the following two parts, my discussion is focused on the latter category, namely judicial plays in the modern sense.

Another aspect of consideration is involved in such a classification. Generally speaking, since the former category of detective plays doesn't have the knotty questions in trials, even in the cases that occur in which people are unjustly and falsely charged, it is generally because of fraudulent practices for personal gain, perversion of justice for bribes, or ingratiation with the nobility by obsequious flattery among law enforcers. What is needed to reverse an unjust verdict is a brave and just official with sufficient power. This type of detective play basically fails to present the issue of judicial and jurisprudential theories in a general sense (or I fail to observe it). In any society, there are good or bad men, upright or corrupt officials. Accordingly, the story like the detective plays of "suppressing the despots and bullies" will exist forever, which is not the question that can be solved by the judicial decision itself; nor is it even the problem that the judicial system in the modern sense aims to solve. It is the issue of the political institution concerning the selection of officials. Hence, to address attention to the detective plays concerning trials and to investigate the question with more generality, it will be more meaningful for the judiciary of contemporary China.

This chapter mainly discusses the evidence issue related to trial judgments. The analyzed text is the most famous tragedy in ancient China, *The Injustice to Dou E*.

How Did the Tragedy Happen?

> I would ask for a clean mattress to stand on and a long strip of thin white silk to be hung from a lance. If it is true that I have been unjustly condemned, when the sword strikes and my head falls not one drop of my warm blood will be spilled on the ground. The blood will flow up into the strip of white silk. . . . Now is the hottest period of the summer, Your Honor. If it is true that I am unjustly condemned, when I die Heaven will send down a winter snow three feet deep to cover my corpse. . . . It

---

5 The reason why I emphasize "particularly" is this point is hard to be clearly explained. On the one hand, in traditional society, social life was relatively simple and stable with strong social homogenization. Some simple and concise rules went deep into hearts of people, such as "a murderer must pay with his life as a debtor pays with money." Therefore, "the judges" might not violate the rules even if they were unconscious of them. On the other hand, once the exception occurred, "the judges" did "stretch the rule" regardless of regulations. But my analysis might be still problematic, since not "the judges," but "the administrators" tried cases here. To make the decision in the total disregard of laws, such an example is also presented in many Yuan plays, especially for the high-ranking officials such as Bao Zheng (see Chapter 5).

is true I have been unjustly condemned, Your Honor. And for three years to come the county of Chu shall suffer a drought.[6]

Facing the executioner, Dou E was filled with grief and indignation and had no place to redress this injustice; she made such vows that shuddered heaven and earth and ordinary people. Dou E had an ill-fated life. When she was three years old, her mother died; at the age of 7, she was sold by her father to Cai's family as a child daughter-in-law. She grew up and was married, but two years later, her husband passed away. Dou E wholeheartedly served her mother-in-law, Mother Cai, but a great misfortune unexpectedly befell her. Old Zhang and his son Donkey Zhang, two scoundrels, forced her mother-in-law and her to marry them. Dou E resolutely refused to follow. Donkey Zhang originally wanted to poison Mother Cai, but unexpectedly poisoned his father. Donkey used "official settlement" to blackmail Dou E for "private settlement," namely to gratify his lust. Dou E turned it down. When they went to the court, Donkey filed the suit first. Although Dou E herself withstood the torture, she aggrievedly admitted that she poisoned Donkey's father and was sentenced to death in order to protect Mother Cai from torture. In the face of death, the faithful Dou E made these three vows, which were fulfilled one by one afterwards. Two years later, Dou Tianzhang, Dou E's father who was a high official, made an inspection tour of Chuzhou. The wronged ghost of Dou E lodged the complaint, and the injustice was redressed.

This is a tear-jerking tragic story, which has aroused sympathy among audiences and readers for generations. But it is not quite sufficient to explain why it is touching only with the tragic features of the story, the mythological color added by the scholars, or the literariness of the work. If viewed as a literary or dramatic work, *The Injustice to Dou E* is artistically unrefined in accordance with the Westernized dramatic standard generally accepted by us today. It is flawed[7]; it is over-repeated, Dou E's family background and the truth of her injustice have been repeated in each act from Act 2 to Act 4, which is not only lengthy and dilatory but also lacks the artistic change of narratives, although there might be some alterations in the performance.[8] If viewed from the evaluation standard of traditional bitter tragedy,

---

6 Hanqing, Guan. "The Injustice Done to Tou Ngo," in *Six Yuan Plays*, trans. Liu Jung-en (London: Penguin, 1977), 142–143 (hereafter cited parenthetically in the text).

7 For example, as for Dou E's marriage age, in Act 1, according to the words of Madame Cai, Dou E at the age of 20 then was married when she was 15 years old ("Hardly two years had gone by after their marriage when my son died. My daughter-in-law still observes her widowhood. But three years have already passed, and soon she will no longer need to wear her widow's weeds." Guan, 1977: 122). While Dou E herself said, "At seventeen I was married to my husband" (Guan, 1977: 124).

8 It is not "the defect" only in *The Injustice to Dou E* which is found in most of Yuan plays. But the audiences and the performance sites and methods of opera in those days are not accounted for by the playwrights. In an age when audiences couldn't enter the theater to watch performances together on time (there wasn't an exact timepiece) and they could enter and leave the theater at will, each act of the drama must be relatively complete. This feature is the audiences' molding of the plays in the specific times. Only when the drama becomes the "refined" art and must concentratedly accomplish the art appreciation in a space time or the playscript begins to be scrutinized as a literary text, does this feature then become a prominent "defect."

Act 4, in which Dou Tianzhang reversed the unjust verdict on Dou E, might be very dilatory, and many critics believed it superfluous.[9] All the same, the overwhelming majority of readers or audiences will be still moved by Dou E's unyielding call for justice.

However, how did this tragedy happen? Since modern times, many researches on *The Injustice for Dou E* used some details in the play (for example, Prefect Taowu, who tried this case took the litigation cost) and emphasized that the injustice suffered by Dou E and her like was caused by corruption, interrogation by torture, stupidity, and incompetence of officials.[10] In the play, Dou E *seems* to make a similar summarization. Before the execution, Dou E said, "All because you officials have no care to see justice done, and anyone who has a mind to speak is forced to hold his tongue" (Guan, 1977: 144). Yet before the end of play, the ghost of Dou E expected her father: "Again Imperial Sword and Gold Tablet shall reveal their power, to break corrupt officials and abusers of place, to share the sorrows of the Son of Heaven, and to root out evil for the people's sake" (Guan, 1977: 157). Through such a summarization and citation, the image of Dou E is thereby interpreted as the image of a rebel.

However, such a summarization might not be Guan Hanqing's view, just as many researchers have described. It is more likely the conscious or unconscious creation of scholars in the modern context. We must be sufficiently meticulous in distinguishing the views of major characters in the play (even if they are preferred by playwrights) and the view of the playwright himself. Because the words of characters in the play are always connected with their experiences and concrete scenarios, they might not be the mouthpiece of the playwright. If we scrutinize the play itself, we can find that the tragedy of Dou E is actually not much related to "corrupt officials and abusers" who have "no care to see justice done."[11]

First, from the perspective of the plot, the injustice of Dou E is not related to the "corruption" of officials. Admittedly, the entrance poem of Prefect Taowu trying

---

9 I will argue later that if from the perspective of determining the theme of this play and the social function of "literature" in traditional Chinese society, this end is not superfluous.

10 This viewpoint is quite popular, which nearly becomes the final conclusion and extends to today. For example, "if there were an honest official, it would not be an unjust case." Lu, Kanru; Feng, Yuanjun 陆侃如、冯沅君. "Zhongguo wenxue shigao" 中国文学史稿(12). In *Yuanqu tongrong shang* 元曲通融上, 36; "Besides, the officials were corrupt at that time, Dou E was executed unjustly as a result." Zhou, Yibai 周贻白. *Zhongguo xijushi changbian* 中国戏剧史长编 (Shanghai: Shanghai Bookstore, 2004), 187; "The corruption of officials was one of the reasons." Xu, Zhongming 徐忠明. "Dou E yuan yu yuandai fazhi de ruogan wenti shixi" 窦娥冤与元代法制的若干问题试析. In *Zhongshan daxue xuebao shekeban zengkan* 中山大学学报社科版增刊, no. 3 (1996), 191; "Unexpectedly, Prefect Taowu was a corrupt official." Qiu, Shusen 邱树森. "Yuandai de fantan wenhua" 元代的反贪文化. In *Jinan xuebao shekeban* 暨南大学社科版, vol. 23, no. 1 (2001), 118; "Taowu . . . was corrupt and perverted the law for personal gain." Zhou, Chuanjia 周传家. *Zhongguo gudai xiqu* 中国古代戏曲 (Beijing: The Commercial Press, 1996), 61.

11 In recent years, there have been some scholars who try to renew the explanation of *The Injustice to Dou E*. For example, Guo, Yingde 郭英德. "Guanju wenhua yiyun fawei" 关剧文化意蕴发微. In *Yuanqu tongrong xia* 元曲通融下, 1310.

this case goes like this, "I am a magistrate, the best on the bench. My coffers are filled from the cases I hear." And he claimed, "Anyone who brings a case before me is father and mother to me; it is he who clothes and feeds me" (Guan, 1977: 135). Therefore, it is very easy for the later generations to comprehend his words as the representation of corruption.[12] However, to regard the bureaucracy[13] with fixed incomes as an unconditionally universal and necessary institution, which is defined by Max Weber and more connected with modern capitalism, is a historical misunderstanding based on the context of today. According to the investigation of a scholar, at least in the early Yuan Dynasty (even from 1276 onwards), officers and government officials at prefectures and counties had no stipend.[14] To a large extent, government officials could only make a living or even keep the operation of an organization working by collecting the litigation cost from the plaintiff and defendant. This has appeared quite a lot in other Yuan plays, although it was often satirized and ridiculed by playwrights.[15]

What is more, even though the officials' finding their own means of livelihood is defined as "corruption" in the play, no evidence shows, nor even details hint, that Dou E's death penalty was caused by Prefect Taowu's taking money from Donkey Zhang. In the play, it is not stated who paid the litigation cost: Dou E or Donkey Zhang; there is no evidence of collusion between Donkey Zhang and officials before or after. The positive character in the play only repeatedly mentioned "excessive officials," not "corrupt officials." The most important thing is that Dou Tianzhang, who redressed her daughter's injustice, only confirmed that "Prefect Taowu . . . and the Chief of Police, for conspiring to prevent the *administration of justice*" (Guan, 1977: 157–158) made the mistake of applying law in fact-finding, which is just a fault, not the confirmed act of Prefect Taowu in taking bribes and bending the law for personal interests.

Second, Dou E's injustice is hardly attributed to the outcome of the stupidity and incompetence of officials. Indeed, in comparison with other legendary honest and wise officials such as Bao Zheng and Kuang Zhong, Taowu was truly incapable and didn't have an extremely discerning eye. But because of the institutional limitation and the rare existence of genius, the officials with special capabilities such as Bao Zheng are so rare that we can only encounter them by luck[16]; otherwise, it is impossible for Bao Zheng, the artistically portrayed figure in our culture, to exist. We can't and shall not use Bao Zheng as the general evaluation standard of the officials' capability.

---

12 Gu Xuejie held such a view, see Gu, Xuejie 顾学颉. "Qianyan" 前言. In *Yuanren zaju xuan* 元人杂剧选 (Beijing: People's Literature, 1998), 13–14. See also other essays from the page 1532 onwards in *Yuanqu tongrong zhong* 元曲通融中. Li, Xiusheng 李修生. *Yuan zaju shi* 元杂剧史 (Nanjing: Jiangsu Ancient Books, 1996), 144.

13 Weber, Max. *Economy and Society* (Chicago: University of California Press, 1978), 221–222.

14 Zhu, Dongrun 朱东润. "Yuan zaju jiqi shidai" 元杂剧及其时代. In *Mingjia jiedu yuanqu* 名家解读元曲, compiled by Lv Weifen 吕薇芬 (Jinan: Shandong People's Press, 1999), 34.

15 See Chapters 5 and 6.

16 See Chapter 5.

The most important thing is – as the following analysis will prove – even Guan Hanqing consciously or unconsciously (therefore more significantly) presented in the play that Dou Tianzheng is an honest official, the ideal character in the heart of the playwright would deliver the similar verdict on the case of Dou E in terms of evidence just as Taowu did if there were not the wronged ghost of Dou E and its persistence and if Dou E were not his own daughter. In other words, the tragedy will recur likewise. In view of a series of story prototypes around Dou E, we can't find any trace of corruption or evident incompetence as well. Many playwrights only emphasized that the prefects trying the case turned a deaf ear to others' advice or the trial mistakes.[17]

The third is connected with the former two points. Some scholars elevate Dou E's conscience in a far-fetched way and confirm that this tragedy is rooted in the feudal rule. The most often cited passage is:

There the sun and moon hang by day and night, There the spirits and gods dispense life and death. Heaven and Earth! It is for you to distinguish between right and wrong, What confusion makes you mistake a villain for a saint? The good suffer poverty and want, and their lives are cut short; The wicked enjoy wealth and honor, and always live long. . . . Earth! You cannot distinguish good and evil, can you yet be Earth! Heaven! Who mistake the fool for the sage, you are Heaven in vain!

(Guan, 1977: 139–140)

Considering that "Heaven" sometimes or usually is linked with imperial power in traditional Chinese society, many scholars therefore firmly believe that Dou E was against the feudal rule, especially imperial power (Heaven and Earth).[18] If being

---

17 According to the research of Zhu Zhaonian, the prototype of the story of Dou E could be traced back to *Huainanzi* 《淮南子》, Liu Xiang's *Garden of Stories* 《说苑·贵德》 and *The Book of Han* 《汉书·于定国传》. Zhu Zhaonian observes that in the historical evolution of this story, all the previous tales were in favor of the prefect, who remained unconvinced or "the administrator concerned failed to ascertain the truth." That means that the unjust case was not relevant to the corruption of the official who had "no care to see justice done," but it was just a judicial mistake. Zhu holds that only under the writing brush of Guan Hanqing was this image changed, and he recognizes Guan's adaptation. Zhu, Zhaonian 祝肇年. "Dou e yuan gushi yuanliu manshu" 窦娥冤故事源流漫述. In *Zhu zhaonian xiqu lunwen xuan* 祝肇年戏曲论文选 (Beijing: Culture and Art, 1998), 103–114.

18 "Dou E raised doubts towards Heaven and Earth, questioned and negated them . . . it is the direct denunciation of the supreme ruler, because the feudal rulers of all the past self-claimed to be the son of Heaven." Luo, Zheng 骆正. *Zhongguo jingju ershijiang* 中国京剧二十讲 (Guilin: Guangxi Normal University Press, 2004), 119; "To curse Heaven and Earth is to negate the omnipotent and omnipresent supreme authority in the universe; to curse the sun and the moon is to negate the emperor reigning the country." Tu, Shi 涂石. "Panni yu zhixu tan zhongguo gudian wenxue zhong de liangzhong jingshen jian yu xifang wenxue bijiao" 叛逆与秩序 – 谈中国古典文学中的两种精神兼与西方文学比较. In *Xibei shifan daxue xuebao shekeban* 西北师范大学学报社科版, no. 5 (1996). See also Deng, Shaoji chiefly ed. 邓邵基. *Yuandai wenxueshi* 元代文学史 (Beijing: People's Literature, 1998), 78, 79; Ning, Zongyi 宁宗一. "Tan dou e yuan de beiju jingshen" 谈窦娥冤的悲剧精神. In *Yuwen jiaoxue tongxun* 语文教学通讯, no. 2 (1982); Wang, Jinglan 王景兰. "Dou

perceived abstractedly, this explanation is reasonable. But the premise for the validity of this explanation is, in a traditional society, that "heaven" has the specific reference and is a proper noun. In reality, it is not this case. Heaven is always not the taboo word. In many literary works, authors use the word heaven. Such an elevation is absurd. To understand "Heaven" and "Earth" in the words of Dou E, it can only be put into the context of the play and must be connected with Dou E's identity of a humble girl; it must be comprehended with the ordinary people's code of language; otherwise, it will be an excessive interpretation in the phrase of today.

The fourth point is that although many ordinary people tend to think thus, it will be very difficult to say that Dou E's tragedy stems from Donkey Zhang and his like. In any society, there is such a type of villain who hurts and harms others. If it is attributed to this, then the play is difficult to be classified as a tragedy. Besides, Dou E was sentenced to death by Taowu, although Donkey Zhang made a push.

Actually, *The Injustice to Dou E* itself exhibits Dou E's conflicted and inconsistent comprehension as to the root of her own tragedy. In addition to the lines cited earlier, before her execution, Dou E told Mother Cai, "It is only that I, Dou E, was born when *neither season nor fortune were mine*" (Guan, 1977: 142). Afterward, in appealing for redressing her injustice, Dou E openly stated that "*Do not lay plaint to the yamen office, lay plaint to Heaven*; The ethers of enmity within the heart mere words cannot express" (Guan, 1977: 150). Then, she said, "It all started with my feeling of filial piety, Which, however, became the root of all my *troubles*" (Guan, 1977: 156). She seemed to reflect on the consequence of her own action, namely, to wrongly confess the crime in order to prevent her mother-in-law suffering from being tortured.

Three vows of Dou E don't aim to resist the feudal rule, but mainly hope to prove her innocence to *the whole society* through the supernatural phenomena impossibly occurring. Certainly, there are strong condemning and protesting factors, but they are not just or even targeted at the emperor, the government office, or officials, but the whole society. Because those who suffered from the drought of three years due to her curse were not only officials but mainly the local common people of Chuzhou.[19] It is "the joint liability" or "the collective liability" of society. Psychologically speaking, only a person who feels wronged and exiled by the whole society can launch such strong resistance and challenge and can be so cynical.

From the perspective of the art effect, this self-contradiction and conflict don't form a problem. On the contrary, it is just because Dou E cursed officials, nature, and even compatriots that the play has more art appeal and is more real. Because whether corruption or incompetence of officials or others results in this tragedy, we can't and shouldn't expect a weak girl who used to be a child daughter-in-law in old days to consistently keep rationality, soberness, and fraternity to a high degree

---

e xingxiang qianyi" 窦娥形象浅议. In *Liaoning shifan daxue xuebao shekeban* 辽宁师范大学学报社科版, no. 1 (1994).

19 Luo Zheng once pointed it out, and argued for the vows of Dou E. Luo, Zheng 骆正. *Zhongguo jingju ershijiang* 中国京剧二十讲, 120.

at this critical moment, just as Socrates did in facing death, and to analyze and see through the root of her tragedy like an observer of history. In this moment, an ordinary person who was wronged and desperate for life but had no one to turn to was more likely to be affected by popular folk concepts and folk causality then and accused all the other persons and things that should account for her own injustice, including the whole society.

Such a discrimination doesn't lower the significance of *The Injustice to Dou E*. On the contrary, in my opinion, it is just because Guan Hanqing (or the recorder or creator of the story prototype) didn't only ascribe the similar injustice to the corruption and incompetence of officials, just as common men of letters did then. *The Injustice to Dou E* and the story prototype have more profound meaning and acquire a certain sublimity of true tragedy (the tragedy I hereby refer to is in the sense of ancient Greece, namely the inevitable fate regardless of human efforts), which enables it to be extremely prominent among a great number of detective plays in the Yuan Dynasty. Naturally, I didn't say that Guan Hanqing had seen through the social grounding of this tragedy. In various details of the play, he neither saw it through, nor possibly did thus. He more or less tended to attribute the tragedy to the wrongdoing of Donkey Zhang in a moralist way. In terms of the inspiration to legal science, *The Injustice to Dou E* with tragic features and its thought-provoking power is far inferior to the story of the filial daughter-in-law of Donghai, the prototype of Dou E under writing brushes of Liu Xiang and Ban Gu.[20] However, Guan Hanqing neither ascribed the death of Dou E to the corruption and perversion of law among officials after all nor let the criticism of the system of "administrating justice" in traditional Chinese society rest on the level of political morality. Therefore, his play can leave us the space to deeply consider a series of important questions concerning jurisprudential theory and the legal system through access to the legal system, which is thereby more profound, powerful, and vital.

Whose Words Are More Credible?

The injustice of Dou E is a typical tragedy of a *trial*. It is not only because Dou E was sentenced to death by Taowu, who represented the state and justice, but also because the most important thing was that Taowu had no motive of wrongdoing or even wanted to rid people of an evil. From the perspective of jurisprudential theory, the deep question raised in *The Injustice to Dou E* is this: In the social condition with underdeveloped science and technology and poor professional skills, through which and on which could an adjudicator acquire a basically correct judgment in trying cases? Three vows of Dou E moving Heaven and shaking Earth, and each one of them proves her innocence. Therefore, the play shows that in the traditional social condition, it was very difficult for the judiciary to try cases like Dou E's; this type of tragedy is nearly inevitable.

---

20 See the analysis in Chapter 6.

In the case of Dou E, the adjudicator, Prefect Taowu, and his chief of police were completely unaware of the whole process of this event, nor knew the backgrounds and personalities of Donkey Zhang, Dou E, and Mother Cai. Taowu had to try this case because of his liability. The core issue was: Who poisoned the father of Donkey Zhang after all?[21] Donkey Zhang and Dou E filed the charge against each other, but both parties didn't and couldn't provide the reliable and direct evidence demanded by a modern judiciary. In the condition where sufficient information is lacking but the decision involving human life must be made, the adjudicator can only pass his judgment on the basis of human nature and the general logic, namely, whose words are more credible? For the further acquisition of the related evidence, the adjudicator can only have the confession by torture according to the legal procedure, although it is not "undiscriminatingly extorting a confession" like what some scholars indicate today.[22]

If viewed from the position of Taowu or others who didn't go through this event, namely from *the position of a stranger*, evidence and reason provided by Donkey Zhang at the court were more reasonable and valid. The most important thing is that it was his father who died. Generally speaking, although the possibility of a son's poisoning his own father exists (for example, the murder for inheritance, but this thing generally happens in wealthy families, including royal families in modern and ancient times), yet this possibility is much smaller than the possibility of poisoning Old Zhang by Dou E or Mother Cai. Just as Donkey Zhang said, "You say that I, his son, have poisoned my father? Who will believe you?" (Guan, 1977: 134). In the judicial terms of today, "who will believe you?" means "beyond reasonable doubt." Donkey Zhang accurately understood the psychology of ordinary people and knew that all the commoners, including officials trying this case, would first tend to accept his accusation on this point.

This case is arguably detrimental to Dou E and Mother Cai at the beginning. Perhaps because of it, Mother Cai and Dou E first thought not to make a scene. When Old Zhang suddenly died, Dou E didn't immediately propose to lodge the complaint, but "Don't you fear outsiders laughing at your shame?" Therefore, she asked Mother Cai, "Admit it's your bad luck. See he's given a coffin and a few cotton clothes. When everything's ready send him out of the house, and bury him in another's graveyard, not ours." She repeatedly stated, "He was no relation of mine. I haven't a single sad tear to shed" (Guan, 1977: 133). Mother Cai feared that Donkey Zhang's shouts would be heard by all the neighbors, and she unceasingly begged him for "mercy," and even thereby told Dou E, "Do what he says, child." Dou E once considered the possibility of "private settlement," yet she decided to ask for "official settlement" only because she couldn't accept the terms of Donkey Zhang's private settlement, namely, to be married to him. Naturally, all these

21 The presumption here that serves as the premise is that Donkey Zhang's father was poisoned. However, this issue is not naturally valid. Please see the analysis in Chapter 7.
22 For example, Wu, Guoqin 吴国钦. "Guan hanqing he tade zaju dou e yuan" 关汉卿和他的杂剧窦娥冤. In *Yuanqu tongrong* xia 元曲通融下, 1555.

details could be explained in various ways in concrete contexts. But in the eyes of a common outsider who didn't know the truth, the most direct and convenient explanation was that Dou E or Mother Cai deliberately hid something. With the experiences of a scoundrel, Donkey Zhang made full use of the weaknesses of Dou E and Mother Cai and people's common sense; he gained the upper hand in the burden of proof at the beginning.

Second, Donkey Zhang's "court debate" seemed to sound more reasonable to commoners. At the court, Donkey Zhang claimed that Mother Cai was his step-mother (in the play, Mother Cai agreed to be married to Old Zhang at heart, but it was not fulfilled because of Dou E's opposition). Dou E denied it, but it was just a denial without any evidence to support her rebuttal. Donkey Zhang continued, "Your Honor, Their name is Cai. Our name is Zhang. If her mother-in-law had not made my father her husband, why should she entertain us in her home?" (Guan, 1977: 137). This logical inference really makes sense, which is supported by the fact that Dou E couldn't deny it. If the social condition in ancient times is taken into consideration, Donkey Zhang's evidence and argument are more convincing. Even today, if two widowed women keep two strange men at home for a long time, perhaps the first impression of others might be that they voluntarily do this. There might be some "unseemly dealings" between them in the formulae of Yuan plays.

Third, Donkey Zhang claimed, and Dou E admitted, that the soup poisoning of Old Zhang was done by Dou E. Although it didn't prove that Dou E poisoned Old Zhang, it showed that Dou E had a chance to put poison into the soup after all. Donkey Zhang also had the chance to do so, but his chance might be slimmer (the time was more limited). It was also detrimental to Dou E.

Finally, although what Dou E did to save Mother Cai was out of altruism, in this condition, it also became evidence detrimental to her.[23] Dou E first stood the severe torture and insisted that she didn't poison anyone. At this moment, Dou E actually had escaped the threat of the death penalty. Prefect Taowu said, "Since you didn't

---

23 Contemporary jurists will doubt it and believe that it is absurd for me to consider the unbelievable altruist action of Dou E as the *evidence* disadvantageous to Dou E. Because the altruist action of Dou E was manifested in the trial, which was after Old Zhang was poisoned, therefore, it was utterly impossible to serve as the evidence for Dou E's poisoning. This criticism is reasonable, but it is only in the framework of the principles of a contemporary legal system. This point is important because in history, no matter Eastern or Western countries, "interrogation by torture" was once the component of "the legitimate procedure" or "the procedural justice" of the trial at that time. In analyzing the criminal procedure on the European continent before modern times, Foucault once made the marvelous analysis on this point. See Foucault, Michael. *Discipline and Punish: The Birth of the Prison*, trans. Alan Sheridan (New York: Vintage, 1977). Not only in *The Injustice to Dou E* but also in other Yuan plays it shows that there was a basically routine procedure when yamen tried cases. First, the plaintiff was asked to present his grievance and then the defendant was questioned. Both parties were also allowed to argue for themselves. Since there was usually no evidence or a few pieces of evidence, and most of them were just the verbal evidence (including witness), this process then would be very short. As for the homicide cases, because of the lack of sufficient evidence, the restrictive interrogation by torture became one of the measures of acquiring the information related to the accused's actions. In this sense, the unbelievable altruism exhibited in Dou E had reason to serve as the related evidence *in the society of that time*.

do it, someone go and beat the old woman" (Guan, 1977: 137). If Mother Cai could bear the torture, it would be Donkey Zhang's turn to suffer torture according to the law of that time,[24] or Dou E and Mother Cai could only be "bailed out."[25] Just then, Dou E suddenly said, "Stop, stop, stop! Don't beat my mother-in-law. I am willing to confess. It was I who poisoned my *father-in-law*" (Guan, 1977: 137–138). Dou E not only confessed to administering the poison herself but also admitted Old Zhang was her father-in-law, which was diametrically opposed to her former flat refusal.

This sudden change, although it is with a noble motive and matches the logic of Dou E desperately trying to save her mother-in-law, in the eyes of common people, it is very unreasonable. Because the risk of altruism here is too big. In order to free an elder without the direct blood relation from torture (although torture is painful and unbearable, it *generally* doesn't threaten to kill a person because of the legal limitation), Dou E would rather sacrifice her life and *reputation*; it is an understandable but unwise act, which is beyond the reasonable precinct that can be comprehended and accepted by ordinary people even today.[26]

It is under this circumstance that Prefect Taowu concluded that Dou E killed a person by poisoning. This judgment is wrong, but evidently it is not the outcome of officials' corruption. A series of pieces of information that could be considered evidence in this case is detrimental to Dou E, although it is very insufficient and worthy of being refuted according to the standard of today.

Evidence Issue

Therefore, it is necessary to discuss some theoretical problems concerning evidence and the burden of proof.

Ironclad Evidence. In our view, the evidence detrimental to Dou E in this case is not "ironclad evidence" and not "beyond a reasonable doubt" according to the standard of today. For example, Dou E raised a very hard question, namely, "Where

---

24 It has been stipulated that the plaintiff as family members or relatives of the murdered or the robbed would not be subject to interrogation by torture. See Zhangsun, Wuji et al., compiled 长孙无忌, Liu, Junwen annotated 刘俊文. *Tanglv shuyi* 唐律疏议 (Beijing: Zhonghua Book Company, 1983), 554. Dou, Yi et al., compiled 窦仪, Wu, Yiru annotated 吴翊如. *Song xingtong* 宋刑统 (Beijing: Zhonghua Book Company, 1984), 477. However, considering the fact that Dou E ("the daughter-in-law" of the dead) and Mother Cai ("the wife" of the dead) had been interrogated by torture in this case, if only Mother Cai withstood the torture, it might be surely the turn to interrogate Donkey Zhang.

25 *Tanglv shuyi* 唐律疏议, 552; *Song xingtong* 宋刑统, 476–477.

26 This sacrifice might be possible if the direct blood relation or the youngster is involved. It should be noted that Dou E's action even surpasses the sacrifice of some revolutionaries who come to rescue their comrades. She used her own sacrifice to replace the other's being interrogated by torture, not the sacrifice of the other. Revolutionaries who sacrifice themselves are usually supported by intensely political ideology, while Dou E lacked *that* ideology. Certainly, I will analyze later that "the morality" of the traditional Chinese society was actually the mainstream political ideology in the society of that time. Consequently, in this sense, Dou E could be considered the person who made sacrifices for the ideology.

could I get poison, a woman like me?" (Guan, 1977: 137). This question is powerful. But strictly speaking, it is not the evidence refuting the counterpart's evidence, but the demand that the counterpart present more cogent and sufficient evidence to prove she was guilty. In the modern judicial system, it will be a question worthy of being investigated; in ancient society, it might attract attentions of an official with richer trial experiences (in Chapters 4 and 5, I will cite the related examples) and urge him to make an in-depth investigation to acquire more pieces of compelling evidence. But in discussing the judicial system before modern times, there are several points that especially need our attention to the evidence issue.

First of all, when we demand ironclad evidence, we presume that the evidence principle applied in the major criminal cases or cases concerning the death penalty in traditional Chinese society be "ironclad evidence" or "beyond a reasonable doubt." The fact is not like this. If only viewed from legal articles, even some *written* expressions (not equal to practice) concerning basic evidence principle in procedure laws of contemporary China are generalized as "decision based on facts."[27]

Second, the premise of demand for ironclad evidence presumes that ironclad evidence must be collected if only we strive for it. However, for any person with the related actual experiences, including judges, policemen, and prosecutors who are responsible to investigate and break criminal cases, it is the myth created out of a wish. As an ideal, it is worthy of being pursued. But even today, even if the restrictive factor of financial resources is not taken into consideration, in any country and at least in some cases, it might not be possible to acquire "ironclad evidence" no matter how hard the investigators have worked. Sometimes, it is even impossible to completely acquire the related basic evidence.

Third, the most important thing is, owing to the simply materialist and philosophical guidance and the lack of reflection on cognitive condition, contemporaries, including the overwhelming majority of legalists in China of today, will very likely have a misconception: Probative force is the innate feature of witness and evidence. Hence, whether evidence is sufficient, ironclad, "beyond reasonable doubt," or not, it is "the objective fact" or innate feature beyond the social context. As for the same evidence, any person can have a roughly proper judgement no matter what times he lives in. But I want to point out that "ironclad evidence" or "beyond a reasonable doubt" is actually one decision of an adjudicator; its objectivity is more likely a social consensus, neither the correspondence to one objective existence nor the innate feature of "evidence." Admittedly, we often consider some pieces of evidence as indisputably ironclad ones, and others in society will think alike. But this certainty is due to the fact that we share lots of common premises with others to a large extent. Once these premises are not shared, we will have

---

27 Certainly, according to my knowledge about contemporary Chinese judges, the evidence standard adopted by them in the judicial practices varies in light of the different natures of cases. The evidence standard of the criminal cases is actually higher, which demands "the ironclad evidence with the absolute certainty," while civil cases could be generally concluded with sufficient evidence.

different judgments on the same evidence, or even believe some pieces of very cogent evidence in the eyes of others can't become evidence at all.

This argument has a very strong implication of relativism. Yet it is not because I believe in relativism – it is the reality we must face. We can make a thought experiment. If 300 years ago, I lived in a society where everyone believed witchery could cause a person to die, if a dough figurine with my name on it and a needle in its heart was found in one person's family and I was truly ill or even died of disease, then the figurine would be quite possibly accepted as the evidence that the person concerned killed me, and as the evidence of "beyond reasonable doubt" that would be universally accepted by *judges and others in this society at that time*, which was sufficient to sentence this person to death. Even the person concerned himself also believed it was his witchery that caused my death, although he would be depressed at the finding of his "evidence of killing" and might think he didn't deserve the death penalty. Conversely, the DNA test result is considered perfectly safe today; if it appears in the society where no one knows it at all and there isn't any general knowledge of modern biology, judges and common people will doubt whether the tester or the biologist testifying in court is a liar or not. They thereby had the very likelihood of rejecting this evidence.

This thought experiment sufficiently shows that the probative force of evidence is consistently the creation of a social and cultural community. Evidence itself doesn't possess the force of proving any fact, unless we first accept the world outlook on how the world is connected and take this world outlook as the unalterable truth.[28] Consequently, as for the analysis of Dou E's tragedy, when Taowu evaluated the evidence provided by Donkey Zhang as the ironclad one or not, his judgment was not based on our present scientific knowledge and common sense, but on the standard of society where Dou E lived. Just as the previously mentioned analysis shows, if viewed from the position of a stranger, Donkey Zhang at least presented "preponderant evidence" – more sufficient evidence. Because of the limitation of social condition, "preponderant evidence" in our eyes nowadays *might* be considered evidence of "beyond a reasonable doubt" in those days.

Presumption of Guilt. Those who are familiar with modern legal theories might think this case is based on "presumption of guilt," because before making a decision on who was the true criminal, Taowu used torture to interrogate the defendants one by one. I am against interrogation by torture, but I think it is not related to presumption of guilt here.

First of all, although people easily think or understand thus from the present perspective, in ancient society at home and abroad, it is not the case that "the accused will be subject to torture if he doesn't confess."[29] In *The Injustice to Dou E*

---

28 For other examples in which evidence plays or doesn't play its roles and the more meticulous theoretical analyses, see Kuhn, Thomas. The Copernican Revolution (Cambridge, MA: Harvard University Press, 1957), Chapter 6.

29 "In criminal litigations of countries with the absolute feudal monarchy, the presumption of guilt was implemented. Before the defendant was convicted, he was treated as a criminal. The defendant would be interrogated by torture if he didn't confess. If the defendant couldn't prove innocent, he

and other Yuan plays, we can clearly see that Prefect Taowu in charge of the case trial didn't immediately believe in the accusation of Donkey Zhang and initiated interrogation by torture. After he listened to arguments and "evidence" from both parties of Donkey Zhang *and* Dou E, he believed in the evidence presented by Donkey Zhang and his reasonable explanation for it. Besides, he was incited by Donkey Zhang's suggestion for torture ("This woman may be young but she is extremely cunning and stubborn. Not even a beating would frighten her"), then he believed, "Human beings are low and cunning worms. Unless you beat them, they never confess" (Guan, 1977: 137). Accordingly, torture followed. We should also note that Donkey Zhang actually was also one of the accused in this case, but he was not subject to torture. Henceforth, even if in ancient China, there was not such an institution that "the accused will be subject to torture if he doesn't confess." Only those who were sufficiently suspected and didn't confess in *major* criminal cases, especially homicide cases, would be interrogated by torture.

Second, although ancient society at home and abroad resorted to interrogation by torture, it was not because the accused was confirmed as the culprit. Interrogation by torture inevitably adds pains, yet it is not used as punishment, but as the method of acquiring evidence in this moment. Although it is very unreasonable nowadays, it fitted the legal procedure then,[30] which was universally accepted by the people of that time.[31] In this sense, interrogation by torture in ancient times is not punishment in nature, but more like various coercive measures (for example, arrest, detention, summons, bailing out for summons, or residing under surveillance) universally adopted for those criminal suspects who might cause major social dangers in the judiciary of each country of today. Generally speaking, it is the procedure that has no alternative but to be applied to prevent greater harms to society. We couldn't and shouldn't thereby consider these coercive measures as punishments before the conviction, as "presumption of guilt" only, because these coercive measures in modern criminal lawsuits just deprive criminal defendants of some valuable things such as freedom to varying extents before the court has reached the guilty verdict. For the defendants, some measures and statutory penalties actually only have a difference in names, such as detention and short term of forced labor under detention, bailing out for summons, and probation.

---

would be sentenced guilty . . . the open verdict is actually the disguised presumption of guilt." See Chen, Guangzhong 陈光中. "Wuzui tuiding" 无罪推定. In *Zhongguo dabaike quanshu faxuejuan* 中国大百科全书·法学卷 (Beijing: Encyclopedia of China, 1984), 625.

30 I haven't found the related law of the Yuan Dynasty. But in the laws of the Tang and Song dynasties, there was the strict regulation for the condition of interrogation by torture, and those violators would be punished accordingly by the criminal law. For example, in the regulation of administrating justice in the Tang Dynasty, "those officials who resort to interrogation by torture without the close examination and the repeated verification will be given 60 strokes of flogging." *Tanglv shuyi* 唐律疏议, 552. In the Song Dynasty, there was a similar regulation, see *Song xingtong* 宋刑统, 474.

31 In other plays concerning honest officials, there was also the saying that "Unless you beat them, they never confess." For example, Bao Zheng in Guan Hanqing's *The Butterfly Dream* (see Chapter 5). It shows that even Guan Hanqing, the playwright of *The Injustice to Dou E*, was not against interrogation by torture as the institution. He was only against the wrong interrogation by torture.

Third, even an open verdict can't be simply considered a presumption of guilt. Research on modern epistemology and modern judicial experiences show that the absolute and ontological objectivity can't be acquired under any circumstance. What the judicial trial can get is only the absolute certainty in the sense of exchange.[32] Just because this certainty is only in the sense of exchange, it also means that different persons usually have no unified judgment for the same evidence or some pieces of evidence; even their judgments might be opposed to each other. It is normal for a more skeptical person to suspect the evidence with irrefutable certainty in the eyes of ordinary people. Besides, even if the absolute certainty in the sense of exchange is acquired, it will not guarantee its correctness. (Please think about the case of killing people with witchery in the earlier passage.) Therefore, in *judicial practices*, none of countries demand to rule out all skepticisms in criminal sentencing.

Even in American criminal justice, which emphasizes presumption of innocence, only demands "beyond reasonable doubt" instead of "beyond all or any doubt." Actually, in any criminal case, there will always be some problems that can't be solved for various reasons or can be suspected; only if they are "beyond reasonable doubt," can and should the judges deliver verdicts. In a general sense, these verdicts can be described as open verdicts. If they are described as presumption of guilt in disguise, then it means the American criminal evidence standard turns out to be the presumption of guilt! Yet many jurists talk about this standard with great relish and consider it the model of presumption of innocence.

We must pay attention to the suspected subject as well, which is the question often neglected in the Chinese community of criminal procedure law. Under the circumstance that there is disagreement in judging evidence, the law doesn't ask all the persons to have absolute certainty, but turns the power of deciding evidence and guilt or innocence over to the specific person who has the right to do so. In civil law, the person is the judge, and the judge's free evaluation of evidence is emphasized.[33] In common law, the decision-maker is the judge and the jury participating in trials of criminal cases.[34] Therefore, "beyond reasonable doubt" is only for the judge or the jury, which neither requires any others to do so, nor even demands the criminal defendant himself or herself to be doubtless. It confirms the insight of Judge Posner: In justice, although there is an epistemological factor in determining evidence, there are other purposes, including the purpose of political legitimacy,

---

32 See Posner, Richard A. *The Problems of Jurisprudence* (Cambridge, MA: Harvard University Press, 1990), 7.

33 France, Italy, Germany, Belgium, the Netherlands, Spain, Austria, Switzerland, and the former USSR adopt the principle of free evaluation of evidence for judges.

34 The judge has the right to decide whether one evidence is adopted or not, while the jury decides whether the person is guilty or not. However, in principle, the judge may not accept the confirmation of the jury, but the judge seldom applies this power. See Abraham, Henry J. *The Judicial Process: An Introductory Analysis of the Courts of the United Sates, England, and France*, 4th ed. (Oxford: Oxford University Press, 1980), 132–133.

as well.[35] Needless to say, such a deployment of power does leave a certain possibility of abusing power for the judge or jury. But if all the persons are demanded to be "beyond reasonable doubt," the principle of the criminal justice system will not work at all.

More importantly (it surely incurs the displeasure of many contemporary jurists), *strictly speaking*, there only exists presumption of guilt and presumption of innocence *in the sense of the institution of transferring the burden of proof* in history, and both are always coexisting, whose function is only to distribute the burden of proof. Presumption of innocence or presumption of guilt, if it is appropriately applied, it can effectively protect the right of the criminal defendant in the same way.[36] In terms of the institution, there never exists the imagined presumption of guilt in history, which suffers the severe criticisms from the jurists of today. If only the defendant is presumed to be guilty beforehand, he or she will surely be sentenced guilty in the end; or if only the defendant fails to provide the compelling evidence that proves him or her innocent, he or she will be uniformly sentenced guilty. Not to mention the existence of the unitary and institutionalized presumption of guilt or innocence.

From Cesare Beccaria on, many legalists at home and abroad speak glibly to aver that the judicial system of each country before modern times or in many countries adopts the system of presumption of guilt. They believe that it surely leads to the violation of criminal defendants' rights. It has become a universal saying, an ideology in contemporary legal science, and an indisputable item of political correctness. Some American jurists even maintain that only common law is based on the presumption of innocence, while a contemporary European judicial system such as France also adopts "presumption of guilt."[37] Some Chinese jurists accuse some methods of solving the burden of proof in the UK and the United States as "presumption of guilt," which is against the sacred eternal truth in their hearts.[38] However, does this type of *judicial system* really exist?

Actually, it is only a scarecrow, a fabricated target. We could only observe a simple and common fact to topple down this ideological myth. The fact is that no matter whether ancient and modern or Chinese and foreign, the *formal* judicial system in each country in each period has set up the appellate system in a certain form.

---

35 Posner. *The Problems of Jurisprudence*, 204–219.

36 See Dershowitz, Alan M. *The Best Defense* (New York: Vintage, 2011). The title of Part 1 of this book is "Guilty until Proven Innocent." Certainly, Dershowitz refers to the defense attorney, not the judge. But all his analyses and cases show that to set such a presumption beforehand will enable lawyers to more carefully and thoughtfully consider the evidence disadvantageous to the defendant and try to find the questions in these pieces of evidence and thereby refute more effectively. Such a presumption is not favorable to the defendant, but instead can more effectively protect the interests of the criminal defendant. Besides, his analysis also shows that the effectiveness of the principle is connected with the specific subject. The presumption of innocence is mainly the demand of judges, not ordinary people.

37 For example, Abraham. *The Judicial Process*, 105, which concludes that the criminal litigation procedure in France follows the presumption of guilt.

38 For example, Chen 陈光中. "Wuzui tuiding" 无罪推定.

The setup of appellate system – if there is any other meaning – aims to examine the criminal facts verified by the subordinate courts in a certain way or to a certain extent. The premise of examination is to admit that the verdicts of subordinate courts might be wrong and those who are sentenced guilty in the first trial might be innocent or not deserve such penalty. In ancient China, the "capital appeals" system, "taking the complaint all the way to the capital" emerged at least from the Sui Dynasty, Jonathan K. Ocko even claimed "the appellate system in general and capital appeals in particular reached their fullest elaboration."[39] It might be exaggerated, but it doesn't affect my viewpoint. With this appellate system, even if the appellant didn't provide new and cogent evidence to prove the defendant innocent, it would usually (although it is not always so) lead to the re-investigation, re-examination, or retrial of the cases from the adjudicators at the higher level, and some cases would be redressed in which people were unjustly, wrongly, or falsely charged or sentenced.[40] If the common saying of today is really valid – the justice before modern times was based on presumption of guilt, and interrogation by torture was practiced if the accused didn't confess, and those who didn't prove themselves innocent would be sentenced guilty – then the appeal might only be conditioned, namely only when *new* evidence was provided to prove themselves innocent could those sentenced guilty in the first trial be allowed to appeal; "capital appeals" couldn't be possible. Or even if the "appeal" was formally allowed, the ultimate result was only the affirmation or confirmation of the guilty verdict in the first trial by the subordinate courts; there would be no re-investigation, re-examination, and retrial initiated only at the appeals. The appeal practice without the change of result would immediately wipe out any appeal, because people would soon know the actual consequence of this appellate system. No one in his right mind will pay extra for an action that will not bring any change of fate. Besides, what is the point of setting up this appellate system?

The *practice* of presumption of guilt exists – to presume someone guilty and then make great efforts to assemble pieces of evidence to prove him or her guilty. But it is actually another expression of "frame-up." But it is impossible for the frame-up to exist as a system which is universally open to anyone. What is more, there never exists such a system. Actually, when we speak of the frame-up, its implication is just that it severely violates the criminal justice system.

There is another way of doing, which is usually considered "presumption of guilt." Someone is sentenced guilty and punished according to his family background or historical experiences. But strictly speaking, it is not the case of presumption of guilt. In the eyes of "adjudicators" then, a person's family background or past "criminal record" was just the sufficient evidence for his "guilt." What

---

39 Ocko, Jonathan K. "I'll Take It All the Way to Beijing: Capital Appeals in the Qing," in *The Journal of Asian Studies*, vol. 47, no. 2 (1988), 291.

40 Even such a trace was left in *The Injustice to Dou E* itself: What urged Dou Tianzhang to redress the injustice to Dou E was just the appeal from the side of Dou E, and those supernatural phenomena that enabled Dou Tianzhang to believe the appeal of Dou E are not accounted as any evidence in the view of today.

is concerned here is still the evidence standards related to social consensus, not the principle of presumption of guilt as I mentioned earlier. This situation recurs many times in history, especially in the period of social turmoil. For example, in Charles Dicken's *A Tale Two Cities*, the masses in the French Revolution put those who were just from noble families or had sex with the nobility to the guillotine, although the principle of presumption of innocence was written in *Declaration of the Rights of Man and of the Citizen* in the French Revolution for the first time in human history.[41]

The extreme form of this implementation has been abandoned today, at least in legal articles. However, the similar implementation exists or is permitted to a certain extent in criminal justice practice of many countries, even including developed countries nowadays. For instance, the "previous criminal record" or some actions of the defendant are allowed to directly or indirectly serve as evidence, which will affect the jury or the judge in order to support the affirmation of crime which the defendant is accused of.[42] Strictly speaking, it is allowed to use a person's previous behavioral posture to affect the affirmation of the accused action. From the perspective of practice, I don't support it in principle out of my prudent consideration after weighing the advantages and disadvantages, since this implementation has such great risks. But from an intellectual perspective, you might find it hard to say that this implementation is groundless at all. People's behaviors do have a stably basic posture; the saying "the child is father to the man" might not always be the ideal apriorism.

If only from the intellectual perspective,[43] the so-called "presumption of guilt" criticized by many jurists of today is actually more concerned with the decision on the evidence, which includes the affirmation of concrete evidence (namely whether evidence itself can serve as evidence or not) and the comprehensive decision on various pieces of evidence (namely whether these pieces of evidence form those "sufficient and beyond reasonable doubt" and sufficiently affirm crimes or not). The controversy that often occurs is, for example, many reliable witnesses saw that the defendant once appeared on the scene before or after the crime took place, and the defendant's fingerprint was found on the scene. Some might think it was sufficient to prove the defendant the culprit, while others might think it insufficient. Their judgment might be out of the same sincerity and unself-interest. Under this circumstance, different judgments are quite normal, which are not related to presumption of guilt or innocence, but personal judgment, temperament and personality (skeptical or credulous), experiences, training, and knowledge that shape the judgment or the well-founded common sense and belief. But if one of them with a certain opinion (or both of them) is very confident of his opinion and believes his

---

41 Qu, Rong, chiefly ed. 曲嵘. *Waiguo fazhishi* 外国法制史 (Beijing: Peking University Press, 1993).

42 Please consult the Federal Rules of Criminal Procedure and Federal Rules of Evidence.

43 What is more, there is no denying that under some special circumstances, the legal professional will accuse the counterpart of practicing the presumption of guilt for the need of the defense strategy. This is the tactic of strategically applying the legal terms and is the rhetoric. Here, we leave this situation aside.

judgment is indisputable, he will easily embark on the road of "exposing others' ulterior motives" and sincerely accuse the counterpart of practicing "presumption of guilt" or "condoning culprits." This saying actually elevates the divergence of concrete judgments to the difference of principles and tries to use the words with more political legitimacy in the current society to augment his discourse power, which aims to overpower the counterpart in ideology (also called the matter of principle). It has become the means of pursuing political correctness.

If correct principles or words surely bring forth good results, it will be no problem. The problem is, they don't improve the rate of correct judgments at all. Even the words and deeds of the same person will be totally opposite. A judge might sincerely accept "presumption of innocence" in principle and considers himself to make efforts to implement it, but he will still be credulous and arbitrary. Therefore, some more skeptical colleagues think that he violates this principle. On the contrary, a person who is always skeptical and circumspect might thereby not firmly believe in "presumption of innocence," and he might be very careful in each detail in terms of the judicial decision. How does the phenomenon of dislocation between principle and practice appear from *the perspective of society*? The reason is the judgment is a practical reason; whether you really have such "knowledge" or capability or not, it must be proven in concrete actions, just like swimming. To understand a term or to clearly and logically analyze a principle in theory, they don't ensure the good implementation in practice. This is what Judge Holmes has pointed out: In the judiciary, a general principle doesn't dictate a specific judgment. This is also the most important lesson drawn from those armchair strategists. Therefore, in terms of the case of Dou E, Taowu might be too credulous, too uncircumspect, who was totally unfit to try cases, at least the case of Dou E. But it is not related to the presumption of guilt or innocence.

Behind the Evidence Issue

Taowu gave ready credence to confession and was uncircumspect. If it has nothing to do with corruption and presumption of guilt, will it only mean that there is something wrong in his temperament and intelligence? Otherwise, why did he interrogate Dou E by torture in haste? And it is interrogation by torture that leads to the tragedy of Dou E. We seemly can only ascribe it to his personal character or intelligence. I can accept such an inference as the explanation to the play of *Injustice to Dou E* and thereby conclude the discussion as the root of this play. For us, such a conclusion is of no avail to more deeply uncover the tragedy of Dou E, but also to understand the universal interrogation by torture in other detective plays of the Yuan Dynasty, because even Bao Zheng, the honest official, publicly claimed, "If you don't beat them, they won't confess."[44] If we don't want to accordingly reach

---

44 Hanqing, Guan. "Rescriptor-in-Waiting Bao Thrice Investigates the Butterfly Dream," in *Monks, Bandits, Lovers, and Immortals: Eleven Early Chinese Plays*, ed. and trans. Stephen H. West and Wilt L. Idema (Indianapolis: Hackett Publishing Company, 2010), 55.

the evidently correct yet quite unconvincing conclusion that "crows are black the world over" and "the ruling class oppresses the broad masses," perhaps we should wonder, is there any other possible explanation? Are there other more important social and institutional factors that urge the officials trying cases to apply interrogation by torture? Therefore, I turn to discuss such a possibility.

People usually believe the judicial issue is mainly concerned with law, but the most important thing in each concrete judicial decision is still "the fact." If we have sufficient understanding of the fact, including the possible consequence of judgment, at least for many conventional cases in which even many ordinary people can make a correct decision, there might not exist the need for judicial professionalization and specialization. "The rule of man" in Plato's words is based on the presumption that we can find or cultivate an omniscient philosopher king. Christians believe that God will deliver the final and just verdict to everything in the end; their reason is based on their presumption (in my opinion) or belief (in the eyes of Christians) in the omniscience, omnipresence, and omnipotence of God. But it is the thought experiment or belief on the basis of impossible presumption. Judicial decisions in reality are all made by common people, although they might have the difference in intelligence, they are limited in rationality and in the finding and understanding of facts. Consequently, all types of legal rules, including procedural rules, are needed to lower the demand for facts in judgment, which is also to lower the cost of acquiring judgment information, and the limited resources must be expended in finding and gathering facts. Even so, the rules still play a limited role in judgment, and the final basis of judgment is still the fact concerning the case, which is constructed with some pieces of evidence and related information. Without this "fact," the judge will be unable to judge and the practical discourse of the justice machine will get stuck.[45]

But before modern times, there was not science and technology especially related to criminal justice, which accordingly can't be used to support the judicial operation; it is extremely difficult to find basic facts and other related information for trials. Except testimonies of witnesses or perpetrators and patently material evidence occasionally found, traditional society had no other basic means of acquiring reliable and credible evidence. There aren't technologies of fingerprint, footprint, and handwriting identifications; other technologies of acquiring or documenting material evidence; chemical testing (such as for poisons); physical testing; and few autopsies. At least in society at the grassroots level, there are basically no such professionals.[46] In such a condition of technologies and talents, even if a large quantity of human resources, material resources, and time are poured into it, it still fails to acquire the sufficient and reliable evidence for guilt or innocence in light of standards of today.

45 Foucault, Michael. "The Dangerous Individual," in *Politics, Philosophy, Culture*, ed. Michael Foucault, trans. Alan Sheridan et al. (London: Routledge, 1990), 125–151.

46 There are still quite a few exceptions. For example, Song, Ci 宋慈. *Xiyuan jilu* 洗冤集录 (Beijing: Chinese Literature and History, 1999).

However, it is impossible for society not to punish crimes because of these difficulties. The legitimacy of one political power ultimately lies in whether it can ensure the most basic social security and order for people to a large extent. If not, other individuals, institutions, and organizations in society can provide the similar "product" at a lower price or provide the better "product" at the same price; then the replacement will partially (for example, clan, family, gangdom) or even completely (dynastic change) follow. It means the weakening or loss of the power of the ruler. Therefore, whatever political power it is, this question can't be avoided: It *must* identify the culprits and punish them as accurately as possible in accordance with existing technologies and other resources.

To cope with this thorny issue, the measure that traditional society might adopt on one hand is to establish the relatively low evidence standard, including what can be counted as evidence – what is sufficient or "beyond reasonable doubt" evidence. We can observe again that the applicable evidence standard in a trial is not always the epistemological standard, but the conventional standard with epochal and local features, which is constructed by society.

On the other hand, traditional society mobilized all the necessary methods that were sanctioned to acquire the related criminal information, including the adjustment of some burdens of proof. In this social condition, when there are no interests involved, credible witness and testimony, and other pieces of obvious evidence (also defined by social conventions), there are only the following methods on which the adjudicator relies to decide whether a defendant is guilty or not or to decide who is the true criminal among some suspects:

The first is the inference on benefits, namely, to infer who might benefit more from the crime according to common sense. For example, in the case of Dou E, Taowu inferred that Dou E was more motivated to poison Old Zhang than Donkey Zhang.

The second is to investigate whether the defendant is normal in his words, behaviors, and manners through the highly spiritual and psychological pressures on the suspect in the trial (including the procedures of pretrial and other similar ones in modern times). The most common practice is the so-called "Five Steps of Psychological Observation for Criminal Trial,"[47] which were adopted in the judiciary of past dynasties to varying degrees and are often manifested in Yuan plays.[48] The judicial "experience" by which we set store today also includes the factor in this

---

47 "Five steps of psychological observation are used to try criminal cases. The first is to hear the words; the second is to observe the complexion; the third is to watch the breath; the fourth is to notice the posture; the fifth is to examine the eyes." *Zhouli qiuguan sikou* 周礼·秋官·司寇.

48 For example, Zhang Ding observed that "Just look at that condemned woman! She must have been wrongly accused! Bearing cangue and lock, her tears continue to stream down. The ancients have said, 'To judge a person, there is nothing better than observing his eyes. The eyes cannot hide his evil.'" It also occurred to him that "Observe his words and examine his conduct. Judge his crime and determine the correction." Zhang Ding didn't personally try this case at this moment. Hanqing, Meng. "The Moheluo Doll," in *The Columbia Anthology of Yuan Drama*, ed. C. T. Hsia, Wai-Yee Li and George Kao, trans. Jonathan Chaves (New York: Columbia University Press, 2014), 166.

aspect to a very large extent. However, its application is positive and negative in the meantime.

The third is that the adjudicator applies some skills that can't be expected by others but are reasonable afterward and makes decisions according to his insight – for example, the method used by Bao Zheng of *The Chalk Circle* and King Solomon in deciding the true birth mother of the child.[49] Besides, under some circumstances, deception and induced confession are included as well. Their function is either positive (if it serves the objective of ascertaining the truth of case) or negative.

The fourth is the strict application of *restrictive but cruel* interrogation by torture to acquire confession under the premise of sufficient suspicions.[50]

All these methods have a certain effect. Actually, they are still used today in each country in altered forms.

Let's first look at the "inference on benefits," which is still a mostly used method. When a homicide occurs today, the police first come up with the questions: Was it done to kill an eyewitness? Who has the feud or discord with the murdered person? Has property or other things been stolen? In one word, did the murderer kill people because of tangible or intangible interests or not?

Undoubtedly, this inference is reasonable, but it has a great weakness as well. It is sufficiently reflected in *The Injustice to Dou E*. Generally speaking, this method is more effective in breaking premeditated crimes. Its premise presumes that premeditated culprits have the whole plan and the full mastery of criminal procedure; therefore, the adjudicators or other detectors can identify culprits according to this logic. It is because of this premise that this logic usually can't be effectively applied to cope with accidental events. The story of *The Injustice to Dou E* is involved with the accidental factor. Donkey Zhang intended to poison Mother Cai and presumed Mother Cai would drink the mutton soup, but Mother Cai suddenly didn't want to drink it, while Old Zhang was so solicitous that he drank the poisoned soup. This accident destroyed the logic of inference on benefits and limited the effectiveness of such analyses. In reality, this logic can't be effectively applied to the impromptu crime, for example, the unexpected crime toward the unspecified target. Therefore, an "unsolved mystery" always occurs. In a nutshell, because of the limitation of human intelligence, the adjudicator or investigator of the case actually has no likelihood of incorporating all the crimes into the analysis and study with the inference

---

49 See Chapter 5.
50 Except the explicit regulations in the laws of the Tang and Song dynasties, some empirical researches of modern history also prove that these laws are not just on paper. At least in the automatic review of cases in the Qing Dynasty, it included whether the criminals were abused in their imprisonment or illegally interrogated by torture. It shows that interrogation by torture is limited. See Ocko, Jonathan K. "I'll Take It All the Way to Beijing: Capital Appeals in the Qing," 292. In his research, American scholar Brian McKnight also discussed a case that happened in 984. Two officials were tried because they beat a suspect to death in the interrogation. They were convicted of the private crime, namely the intentional crime because interrogation by torture was not approved. See McKnight, Brian. "Tang Law and Later Law: The Roots of Continuity," in *Journal of the American Oriental Society*, no. 115 (1995), 415.

on benefits. It is because of this deficiency that the possibility of Donkey Zhang's poisoning Mother Cai was omitted in the vison of Prefect Taowu.

The method of "Five Steps" likewise has a certain effect as well.[51] "A guilty conscience is a self-accuser," which is one of human psychological features that universally exist. Therefore, "Five Steps" is undoubtedly useful through the dignity of the court (a spatial deployment of power relations). Even today, it is still universally applied in different ways within the court in each country, but more probably outside the court (the pretrial room). Not only do the police use various traditional means to deliberately increase psychological pressures in interrogating the suspect, but also there are more scientific methods – the most typical one might be the lie detector.

"Five Steps" likewise has a great weakness. Generally speaking, its utility as evidence (not as the clue to the discovery of evidence) in the formal judicial process is increasingly narrowing, even becoming invalid and extinct. Not only because we have the police specializing in breaking cases and the prosecutor, but also it is basically no longer used in modern courts[52]; even when similar methods are used by the police and the prosecutor, there are many legal limitations – why?

First, as I have mentioned earlier, the basic premise of the "Five Steps" presumes "a guilty conscience is a self-accuser." This presumption is generally correct, but not always so. A criminal with sufficient experience has the full likelihood to cover any sign of a guilty conscience. More importantly, the following scenario can't be ruled out. Some people invariably don't recognize the mainstream morality of this society because of biological or educational reasons, and they thereby will not have the guilty conscience for their behaviors at all. It is not a rare thing to defeat the lie detector. It explains why few countries directly accept the result of lie detection as the evidence of proving the guilt, which is generally used as the evidence to rule out crimes.

Second, even if it is presumed that all the culprits have guilty consciences, others might be likewise nervous. In real life, there are many persons who haven't seen much of the world and feel panic in crowds. To infer the guilty cause from the effect of an uneasy conscience will be the huge error that the modern judiciary can't tolerate. If there aren't other pieces of evidence, it will be very dangerous to only rely on the "Five Steps."

Third, as mentioned earlier, "Five Steps" are usually combined with the dignity of the court, namely the spatial deployment of power relations within the court to

---

51   For the successful cases of "Five Steps" in the traditional Chinese judiciary, there is a relatively systematic compilation and analysis. See Wang, Shirong 汪世荣. *Zhongguo gudai panli yanjiu* 中国古代判例研究 (Beijing: China University of Politics and Law Press, 1997), Chapter 7.

52   He Weifang uses "Five Steps" to analyze the features of modern judiciary and refutes the institution of the judicial committee. See He, Weifang 贺卫方. "Guanyu shenpan weiyuanhui de jidian pinglun" 关于审判委员会的几点评论. In *Beida falv pinglun* 北大法律评论, vol. 1, no. 2 (1999), 368. I don't think his argument is valid, because he neglects the historicity of "Five Steps" and its legitimacy.

play the role. Since ancient times, no matter in the courts or in modern trial rooms or courts, this power technology is produced and applied in a large quantity.

Broadly speaking, I don't think these operative technologies or methods of power should be abolished. I only want to emphasize that the "Five Steps" must be more effective in such a power space and time. In order to fully acquire the effect of the "Five Steps," even this power relation must be reinforced to exert psychological pressure on the suspect. However, this pressure itself has no capability of discriminating culprits, and it functions for the innocent and the true criminals who are all humans. In such a power space, an innocent ordinary person only with common psychological endurance will sometimes look flustered and give an irrelevant answer at times. In such power relations, the adjudicator might get some very precious and correct information, but might or even have more a likelihood of causing the confusion, which leads to the wrong judgment. If the "Five Steps" is allegedly a kind of summarization of judicial technology and knowledge in ancient times as a last resort, it can be accepted since there was not a scientific method of more effectively collecting evidence; then in modern times, the "Five Steps" can only serve as the clue to acquire evidence, at most, and can't be directly used as the evidence.

Fourth, the "Five Steps" raises an extraordinary demand for the case handlers (not only the judges); they must be highly sensitive, meticulous in discrimination, and adept in interpretation. But even if this demand is raised and even if the case handlers have accepted the related professional training, it is very hard to guarantee that different adjudicators make the same or similar interpretations and judgments for the psychological revelations of the same suspect. This capability, technology, or "knowledge" is highly individualized in essence. The ensuing judgments are very subjective on some occasions at least, which can't be repeated or verified. If the "Five Steps" are relied on too much, it will not only leave the excessively wide and even dangerous manipulation space but also the space of abusing power for the adjudicators.

Finally, even if the "Five Steps" is integrated with modern science and technology, such as the lie detector, it is not sufficient to be used widely nowadays at least. The lie detector is only used as a supplementary method right now. As far as I know, although it was invented many years ago, no country uses the result of lie detection as the basic evidence of *conviction* today. Certainly, "to be geared to international standards" is never the reason for accepting or rejecting a certain implementation. Therefore, it can't be the basic reason for rejecting the lie detector. But it shows that the result of lie detection must be faulted at least, and this fault might not be made up for by the improvement of the related technology. In my opinion, the core factor is the lie detector must be based on the voluntary cooperation of the person being tested. You can tie someone to the detector, but if he refuses to cooperate and refuses to answer the sensitive questions raised by you, can you only use this refusal as the evidence of crimes? Or if he tells truth but it is not related to your question, what will you do then?

The judge uses personal wisdom (including the well-meant deception) and makes the unexpected move, which might indeed bring forth very compelling evidence. For instance, in *The Chalk Circle* and *The Holy Bible*, Bao Zheng and King

Solomon, respectively, used their own wisdom to cleverly get the convincing evidence and made the correct decision in the dispute among two women over one child. This method usually wins universal praise among common people and men of letters. As for this question, I will have a special discussion on it in Chapter 5 and don't make a meticulous analysis here. I only want to point out two shortcomings that it might have. The first is that wisdom might not be necessarily linked with justice. Not all corrupt officials are fools. It is not guaranteed that those with wisdom can justly use wisdom. Then the institution is needed. The second is that wisdom is individualized without the possibility of institutionalization. Can we let all the adjudicators act like Bao Zheng by selection or training? Even considering Bao Zheng, can he always find the unique and convincing method in all the cases? Can culprits or lawbreakers be always not as clever as adjudicators? If lots of such wise adjudicators could be found, should we still need the rule of law? If all these demands could be satisfied, I couldn't find any point of not adhering to the rule of man!

This analysis shows that ancient judges had extremely rare methods and channels to have possible evidence. It is in this historical condition, when the case was concerned with homicide or especially important event (at least in Yuan plays and other ancient plays, the cases concerning interrogation by torture are all homicide cases) and there was not sufficient evidence, society permitted that the adjudicator *legally* used different and sometimes even extremely cruel methods of interrogation by torture to get confession *according to the severity of case.*[53] Interrogation by torture thereby becomes the component of judicial procedure in *each* country of ancient world.[54] No society will allow the suspicious criminals to go unpunished just because of the lack of reliable evidence in our present opinion, or let criminals harm the innocent only for "human rights" or "humanity" or some principles of legal concepts.[55] Just as I have demonstrated in Chapter 1, to punish criminals stems from a human revenge instinct and utilitarian consequence, not from any moral consideration, although how to punish has and should have the moral

---

53 In the Tang and Song dynasties, it had been stipulated that "to interrogate prisoners by torture shouldn't exceed three times, and the total number of flogging strokes shouldn't exceed 200; the punishment of flogging should match each crime." "Those who refuse to confess after interrogation by torture can be bailed out." Officials who violated the regulation or applied interrogation by torture outside the legal regulations, or beat people to death by the interrogation would be accordingly punished by flogging or imprisonment. See *Tanglv shuyi* 唐律疏议, 556; *Song xingtong* 宋刑统, 472.

54 See Foucault, Michael. *Discipline and Punish*, 1977. In this sense, it is correct for Beccaria to criticize interrogation by torture. See Beccaria. *On Crimes and Punishments and Other Writings* (Cambridge: Cambridge University Press, 1995), 34–42. However, it is an intellectual mistake to use the argument of the presumption of guilt to launch criticism. He doesn't understand – it is different from his unacceptance – that interrogation by torture was the component of procedure at that time.

55 One important example is the Criminal Justice and Public Order that was promulgated in Britain in 1994, which makes the major restriction of the long-established "right to remain silent." See Long, Zongzhi 龙宗智. "Yingguo xianzhi xingshi chenmoquan de cuoshi" 英国限制刑事沉默权的措施. In *Xiangdui heli zhuyi* 相对合理主义 (Beijing: China University of Politics and Law Press, 1994), 414–424.

consideration. It is impossible for society to allow criminals to get away, and it must use a certain method to crack down on criminals; otherwise, it is not only unjust for victims but also might stimulate more opportunist culprits and crimes.

In *The Injustice to Dou E*, this question is more obvious. Four persons were on the scene, and one of them suddenly died. People believed that he was murdered but lacked sufficient evidence. What should be done? Could society do nothing? Could Prefect Taowu let three go because of the insufficient evidence? In the social condition at that time, society demanded the adjudicator must do something! However, without any method of affirming evidence, what could the adjudicator do then? The generally entitled right (not the right actually entitled by one individual) has never the possibility of surpassing the limitation of an era.[56] It is in this social condition that confession becomes the king of evidence. Even confession becomes the legally indispensable evidence. Although other pieces of evidence are all clearly directed to one result and the case details are clearly infallible, the proof of confession is still needed. It recurs in Yuan plays.[57] Foucault once made the meticulous analysis on the similar practices of Western countries.[58]

However, the cost of this implementation is indeed huge. Evidently, interrogation by torture results in many unreliable confessions, and inevitably some or even many cases in which people were unjustly or wrongly charged, including the tragedy of Dou E, which led Dou E to utter, "Ah, it is true that from olden times, courthouses have faced the south, none inside has not suffered injustice." It also brought forth the fact that people in traditional society reminded themselves from time to time of keeping away from any criminal suspicions. "A gentleman shall take preventive measures, and put himself above any suspicions. Don't bend to pull on your shoes in a melon patch; don't reach to adjust your hat under a plum tree."[59] The poetic line just seems to be moral caution nowadays, yet it can be a life instruction to people at that time, which is the condensation of many bloody lessons.

Supernatural Evidence and the Significance of Ghost

If the tragedy of Dou E is comprehended from this perspective, then we might know that Act 4 of *The Injustice to Dou E* is actually not as superfluous as some modern literary critics believe and doesn't whitewash the traditional society as they think.[60] Besides, its effect doesn't dilute the tragic significance just as some

---

56 Marx, Karl. "Critique of the Gotha Programme," in *Collected Works of Marx and Engels*, vol. 24, ed. Karl Marx and Frederick Engels (New York: International Publishers, 1989), 86–87.

57 For example, in *The Chalk Circle*, and *The Case of the Head Scarf*, the cases had been ascertained and could be concluded. But the adjudicators still needed the confession. It at least explains two problems. One is that in the eyes of both playwrights, "honest officials" strictly abided by the legal procedure; the other is that they should strictly abide by the procedure of interrogation by torture.

58 Foucault. *Discipline and Punish: The Birth of the Prison*.

59 *Yuefu junzixing* 乐府·君子行.

60 For instance, Wu Xiaoru believes that the last act of *The Injustice to Dou E* is "the fault of the play." Wu, Xiaoru 吴小如. *Wu xiaoru xiqu wenlu* 吴小如戏曲文录 (Beijing: Peking University Press,

scholars believe.[61] On the contrary, this act reiterates the tragic features of Dou E and the inevitability of this tragedy from another perspective.

In Act 4, Dou Tianzhang became a high official, "wearing [an] imperial sword and carrying the gold tablet of office" to Chuzhou for the "investigation" of trial records. The ghost of wronged Dou E lodged the complaint, and her injustice was finally redressed. Being different from other ancient Chinese dramas, in this play, the ghost of the wronged Dou E *didn't mainly* wreak vengeance on the enemy (although there is still such a trace) in a direct way, but took vengeance through the state power represented by her father Dou Tianzhang ("to avenge a personal wrong in the name of public interests," which is not in the derogatory sense in this case). Although such an ending can be comprehended as the author's expectation for "the honest official" just as the traditional explanation did, yet another way of comprehension and explanation seems to be more reasonable only in terms of the text. Because if it only emphasizes the contradiction between "honest officials" and "corrupt officials" or "clever officials" and "stupid officials," Guan Hanqing might not necessarily choose Dou E's father to redress this injustice; he could be fully justified in simply selecting a completely signified and almost divinely honest official like Bao Zheng, just as other contemporary playwrights did.

Why did Guan Hanqing select Dou E's father to redress this injustice? Today, we can't reconstruct the intention of the playwright, and this effort also seems unnecessary. However, one explanation that can be more convincing is (or it looks so at least from the dramatic effect) that, according to the existing evidence, no one would believe Dou E was innocent; therefore, even the honest official like Bao Zheng couldn't redress this injustice out of thin air. Or, even if Bao Zheng raised doubts on this case, he might not have a great motivation and will to retry such an unjust and concluded case, and the life of an ordinary person couldn't be brought back.[62] Actually, no living interested party launched an appeal in this case, while some persons in real life pushed Bao Zheng to ascertain the cases in other Yuan plays.

If this circumstance is comprehended, we come to find that in this play, the appeal could be launched only when Dou Tianzhang appeared on the scene and this injustice could be redressed. Only the father is more concerned with the fate of his daughter before and after the death, even if her posthumous reputation. Only the love of the father based on biological instinct can have the great impulse and stimulation (namely the revenge instinct) to redress the daughter's injustice at all costs. Likewise, only the father can more likely believe in the account of his own

---

1995), 18. See also Deng, Shaoji, chiefly ed. 邓邵基. *Yuandai wenxueshi* 元代文学史, 81; Wen, Ling 温凌. *Guan Hanqing* 关汉卿 (Shanghai: Shanghai Ancient Books, 1978), 19.

61 Cheng, Yizhong 程毅中. "Tan guan hanqing zaju de jiewei" 谈关汉卿杂剧的结尾. In *Gudian xiqu xiaoshuo tanyilu* 古典戏曲小说探艺录, ed. Tianjin gudian xiaoshuo xiqu yanjiuhui 天津古典小说戏曲研究会 (Tianjian: Tianjin People's Press, 1982), 140–150.

62 In all the Yuan plays of Bao Zheng, it is the living person whose injustice is redressed. Besides, there is the summary of experiences for "the administration of justice" of the later generations, namely, "to save the living, not the dead." For this point, see Li, Qiao 李乔. *Zhongguo de shiye* 中国的师爷 (Beijing: The Commercial Press International, 1997), 118–119. Although this experience is rather cruel, it might be the best doing in the condition of limited resources.

daughter – the distance of relations will diminish or augment the demonstrating and convincing force of discourse. Besides, if the analysis is undertaken in a more cold-blooded way, only the redressing of this injustice more fitted the personal "interests" of Dou Tianzhang. In those days, Dou Tianzhang sold his own daughter to exchange for travelling fees and went to the capital to take the imperial examination for the sake of his own future. Now, he was old, successful, and famous; he naturally often felt deeply guilty for his daughter.[63] He was more eager to make up for this guilty conscience. Besides, if his daughter really committed one of "the ten most atrocious crimes" and it were once known by others, his official career would be unavoidably implicated.[64] It doesn't mean that this is the main motive of Dou Tianzhang in redressing the injustice of his daughter; it only means that in any case, it will be a subconscious factor which pushes Dou Tianzhang to go all out to reverse the unjust verdict, while all the other honest officials don't have it.

These points have been manifested in the play. At the beginning, when Dou Tianzhang flipped through the case of Dou E, he didn't raise any doubt and believed "this case has already been concluded." No doubt for this ironclad verdict. It was only because of the consistent efforts of the ghost of wronged Dou E that attracted the attention of Dou Tianzhang on this case. When Dou Tianzhang came to know that the ghost of his daughter lodged the complaint, then he fully believed in the appeal of Dou E. The unilateral words of Dou E or the clues provided by her became the foundation of reversing this unjust verdict. In terms of art, only through such a relation between father and daughter, could Guan Hanqing convince audiences that Dou E's account without any support of witnesses and material evidence was *sufficient* for Dou Tianzhang to believe her words. While the same words might not have such a power to any other officials, even Bao Zheng. Certainly, we unnecessarily guess whether Guan Hanqing clear-mindedly or instinctively made

---

63 "When I arrived at the capital I sat for the imperial examination, passed and was made an assistant to the prime minister. Lately, thanks to the special grace of His Majesty, I have been promoted Inspector-General of the Huai River Valley. Wherever I go I pass sentence on prisoners, investigate records, and whenever I discover officials who are corrupt or misuse their authority, I have power to execute them first and report afterwards. I am both happy and sad. Happy because I wear the imperial sword and carry the gold tablet of office; sad for my child Duanyuan. When she was seven, I gave her to become Mother Cai's daughter-in-law. Since my appointment I have sent people to Chuzhou to ask after Mother Cai. But her neighbors say she has moved elsewhere and nobody knows where she has gone. So far there is still no news. I have wept for my child till my eyes have grown dim and my grief has turned my hair white" (Guan, 1977: 145).

64 Please read the following words of Dou Tianzhang to Dou E: "Say no more, wretch! I have cried for you till my eyes have grown dim and grieved till my hair has turned white. You have committed one of the ten most atrocious crimes and suffered the penalty. I am a high official now, whose duty it is to see that justice is done. I have come here to investigate cases and discover corrupt officials. You are my child, but you are guilty of the worst crime of all. If I could not control you, how can I control others? When I gave you to be married into their family, I charged you to observe the Three Duties and the Four Virtues. You did nothing of the kind. For three generations not one male member of the Dou family has violated the law, and for five generations not one female has married again. But now you have disgraced your ancestors and endangered my reputation. Tell me the whole truth this instant" (Guan, 1977: 149).

such an artistic decision. Guan actually conveyed this point; if it were not her father, no other officials would believe in the innocence of Dou E. That is enough.

Once this point is observed, we can find that Guan's art intuition and representation of Dou E's injustice have been beyond the summarization of Dou E's tragedy
that might be given by rationality at that time. Why did Guan Hanqing let Dou E
make three vows that moved Heaven and shook Earth? It is because "Indeed the
wrong I suffer is profound. *If there is no miraculous sign to show the world, then
there is no proof of a clear, blue Heaven*" (Guan, 1977: 143). These three vows
show that Dou E and the playwright Guan Hanqing both believed, in the social
condition of that time, that there would be no any other means to prove the innocence of Dou E or to convince others to accept her account; only the supernatural
evidence brought along with the death of Dou E could shock others and prove Dou
E's innocence and injustice. Actually, the death of Dou E did have such an effect.[65]

In this sense, the image of Dou E created by Guan Hanqing is truly beyond the
images of those humiliated and oppressed characters in traditional Chinese bitter
tragedies and beyond the weeping and heart-rending tragedy with which Chinese
are familiar. Actually, Guan was vaguely free from the moralist tendency that universally existed in traditional Chinese dramas, although he still didn't and couldn't
clearly tell the reason for the tragedy. When Dou E appealed for the supernatural
evidence and when these supernatural phenomena did happen, what we feel is not
just the tragedy of Dou E, but the sublimated consideration of human tragic fates
and the consideration of limited human capability in seeking or reconstructing the
factual truth and the ensuing destiny. *The Injustice to Dou E* does have a shudder-
ing sublimity that is very rarely seen in traditional Chinese dramas.

Modern society has the full possibility of avoiding the tragedy of Dou E only in
terms of the individual case. If our vision is broader, because of the limited human
capability in cognition and reconstruction of the past, what *The Injustice to Dou E*
actually touches on is the eternal limitation and tragic circumstance of humans.
Therefore, the appearance of wronged Dou E's ghost in the last act can't be comprehended as a superstition. Maybe we can accept Li Jianwu's judgment that Guan
Hanqing "wrote the ghosts . . . which is only one dramatic measure"[66]; without it,
the severity and gravity of injustice Dou E suffered can't be sufficiently exhibited;
without it, the limitation of human capability can't be sufficiently displayed.

---

65 After the execution of Dou E, there is a dialogue passage between the prison governor and executor:
Prison Governor: Ah, it is really snowing. Can such a thing be possible!
Executioner: Usually when I cut off a head the ground is covered with fresh blood. But the blood
of Dou E has all flown up into the strip of white silk. Not a single drop has fallen to the ground. I'd
never have believed it!
Prison Governor: There must be injustice in this case. Two of the prophecies have been fulfilled.
Who can say whether the prophecy of three years' drought will not come true? We shall have to see.
(Guan, 1977: 144–145)

66 Li, Jianwu 李健吾. "Cong xingge shang chuxi jianji guan hanqing chuangzao de lixiang xingge" 从
性格上出戏兼及关汉卿创造的理想性格. In *Yuanqu tongrong* xia 元曲通融下, 1349. It must be
pointed out that the patj of Li Jianwu is correct, but he still perceives the issue of Dou E from the
moral, not technical, perspective.

The Injustice to Dou E is a criminal case, but it isn't only in the homicide lawsuit that the problem concerning the evidence and reconstruction of the truth occurs. In other disputes of traditional society, the similar question is raised as well, for example, *The Foe Creditor*,[67] a Yuan play that is involved with the case of a money swindle. A monk entrusted ten silver ingots that he raised in begging alms with Zhang Shanyou's wife for her keeping, but neither the IOU nor other pieces of evidence were preserved. When the monk returned to retrieve the ingots, Zhang's wife refused to do return them and denied such a thing. Many years later, Zhang's wife and two sons died in succession for no reason, and Zhang Shanyou was left alone. Owing to the instruction of the ghost, Zhang came to realize that it was the divine retribution for the evil act of his wife in those days. This story filled with superstitious aspects seems to be absurd nowadays, along with too much moralizing significance. But if viewed from the evidence issue raised in the chapter, *The Foe Creditor* could be the repetition of the question in *The Injustice to Dou E* as for how to find the truth in disputes. Because except the parties concerned, others, including Zhang Shanyou himself, had no chance of knowing the truth. Because there was no evidence and the dispute was not so grave like the homicide case in which interrogation by torture was necessary, then it was actually impossible to solve this case through worldly methods in the social condition of that time. Therefore, it was not presented to the court for trial. (Even today, this case can only be ascertained in the condition with specific technologies.) People can't tolerate this injustice and only resort to the folk ideology of ghosts, divinity, and divine retribution in the art world to settle this dispute.

If we return to the large quantity of ghost plays in traditional drama (not limited to detective plays) from this perspective, we might find that it is neither just "the feudal superstition" nor the simple and patterned art expression "to take a shortcut in solving problems," as modern critics have commented.[68] For the people who lived in the condition lacking modern science and technology, it seemed that they could only heap hopes on it. This is the despaired hope.

If the analysis presented here is valid, then even Prefect Taowu is also a tragic figure at a certain level. His tragedy didn't lie in that he was finally "given a hundred strokes of the lash" and "permanently dismissed from the service" by Dou Tianzhang, but in that he tried to strictly enforce the law to remove a scourge for the people and made the basically reasonable judgment in the possible condition, which still resulted in the tragedy of Dou E. "A hundred strokes of the lash" was only the physical pain, "permanent dismissal from the service" only meant the end of his official career, but the moral pressure caused by his realization that

---

67 *Yuanqu xuan* 元曲选, 1130–1145.
68 Deng, Shaoji 邓绍基. "Lun yuan zaju sixiang neirong de ruogan tezheng" 论元杂剧思想内容的若干特征. In *Yuanqu tongrong shang* 元曲通融上, 522. See also Liu, Shusheng; Zhang, Tao 刘树胜、张涛. "Lun yuan zaju zuopin zhong de meng" 论元杂剧作品中的梦; Zeng, Yongyi 曾永义. "Zaju zhong guishen shijie de yishi xingtai" 杂剧中鬼神世界的意识形态. In *Yuanqu tongrong shang* 元曲通融上, 525, 528–529.

he himself made such an injustice – only he was still an ordinary person with conscience – would oppress the rest of his life.

Preliminary Summary

The analysis of this chapter has further implications. First, the issue raised in this play can even expound some characteristics of traditional Chinese culture – for example, the characteristic of "aversion to litigation" among Chinese common people. Inevitably, it owes to the deficiency of national finance and the failure of providing the convenient litigation mechanism, which I have indicated in other places, but the more important thing might be the lack of measures that are sufficient to accurately and effectively find and gather evidence. In the condition of ancient society, if all the disputes are presented to the judiciary, the mistakes will be surely abundant, and the basic layout of the judiciary must be "from olden times, courthouses have faced the south, none inside has not suffered injustice." Under this circumstance, if it didn't matter life, or it was not a grave affair, people would have no other choice than resort to lawsuits, and they would more likely settle a large quantity of disputes through mediation and other "private settlements" facilitated by other organizations and individuals. Therefore, the game between "private settlement" and "official settlement" is not an accidental case in *The Injustice to Dou E* and many other Yuan plays.[69]

On the other hand, because of the lack of science and technology and other resources, officials do "have no care to see justice done," because the outcome of intervention might result in the wrongful convictions, which is not only to no effect but also vexes themselves and even ends their official careers. Under this circumstance, officials more likely refuse to intervene in those general disputes through various means, for example, to dismiss disputes on the pretext of "an honest official reserves judgement in family quarrels" or to keep abundant lawsuits out of the gate of yamen and take pains to reduce social demands for the formal trials by raising litigation costs, and not just the effort of charging litigation expenses.

Once social demands for formal trials are lowered, there will be no need to improve efficiency through the further social division of labor, and the independent judicial department has no likelihood of evolution and development. Without such a social division of labor, the judiciary has much less chance to develop in turn, and the professional circle of the judiciary can't come into being, the professional knowledge and technologies of the judiciary can't be accumulated; even so, the accumulated knowledge and technologies can't have their deserved positions in the whole knowledge system in those days. Viewed from this perspective, "the

---

69 In addition to *The Injustice to Dou E*, *The Chalk Circle* and *The Moheluo Doll* also have similar plots. It should be noted that in these plays, it was the culprit who first proposed for private settlement, while the victim (for example, Dou E) once considered the possibility of private settlement and turned it down just because private settlement was too disadvantageous to her. It shows that "private settlement" had been universally recognized by people in those days.

aversion to litigation" among Chinese common people, their great attention to "the prized harmony," their emphasis on "tolerance," and their inaction of "fighting for the rights" are not the outcome of whatever "culture" at all and not the voluntary choice out of cultural awareness, but the chosen culture with institutional and technical restrictions.

Second, we can observe that the judicial tragedy is not all attributed to the personal integrity of officials. In an era and society with underdeveloped science and technology, not only was interrogation by torture inevitable but also the tragedy. Nowadays, interrogation by torture is reduced in each country, especially those developed countries; this is because of the development of science and technology and their wide application in the judiciary to a large extent (although it is not the whole reason); the judicial system has more measures that are more convenient and reliable, and thereby more effective to acquire the correct or basically correct judgment on the truth of case. (If I had a simple test to absolutely identify the criminal, why would I resort to interrogation by torture? Or even I would not need the trial before the court.) It is not the outcome of thoughts of modern bourgeois enlightenment legal thinkers such as Cesare Beccaria, and it is not related to the moral standard of judicial officials (who dares to say judges of today are superior to the previous officials in the moral standard? On what grounds?), or even not too much directly related to the increasingly meticulous and complicated "legitimate" procedures. It is only related to the development of science and technology in a positive way.

The influence of science and technology on the judiciary is wide. It brings more information that judicial judges can acquire and thereby reinforces their capability of making correct judgments. Besides, the advanced science and technology make society more prosperous, which can accordingly feed those who don't directly participate in production activities but practice different professions, including judicial professions. The varyingly complicated science and technology also force people to undertake more meticulous division of labor, while the appearance of meticulous division of labor and professionals demands, or even inevitably results in, the more refined and complicated judicial procedure that is deemed "legitimate" in modern society. In the society where the plaintiff and defendant accuse each other and there is no sufficient, solid, and credible evidence and related information provided by other institutions, organizations, or individuals, you can't expect to derive a complex and "legitimate" procedure from it. The complex and rigorous procedure is only the outcome of the social division of labor and accumulated knowledge. If there isn't the basis of the corresponding science and technology, the so-called complex and rigorous procedure might be more confusing, which enables people to walk even further on the wrong road, and even greater wrongful convictions appear.

But the most important thing is that the wide dissemination of science and technology will eliminate those incorrect causalities. The long-term handling with the refined science and technology will enable people to think more precisely, and their judgments will be more focused on evidence and information; they will demand more direct and indirect evidence; they will not be credulous and will be more skeptical. All of these will fundamentally reshape people's viewpoints and opinions concerning evidence and evidence standards in the greater society where the judiciary is seated. It changes "the judicial culture" of society as well.

Third, if science and technology are important, we must be sufficiently clear-minded about the present judicial reform in China. In recent years, the community of legal science is almost unified in the emphasis on the importance of procedure, the burden of proof, the procedural justice, legal or judicial concepts, and the training of legal professional skills. It is completely necessary and legitimate as well. However, in such a unified public opinion, few jurists really analyze the importance of science and technology, especially the fruits of natural sciences or social sciences (not the so-called legal research fruits filled with cliché moralization and originally political correctness) to the judiciary. Almost no legalists emphasize the improvement of technical equipment, the training and staffing of sci-tech personnel in public security organs, procuratorial organs, and people's courts. "Procedural justice," "presumption of innocence," "the right to remain silent," "zero confession" – it seems that all these concepts themselves can guarantee the improvement of the judiciary and the fulfillment of justice. Abundant monographs and papers of legal science attribute the credit to the doctrines of a few Western scholars or the proposition of a certain concept of justice instead of the progress of science and technology *in the first place*.

Consequently, on this issue, I think the demonstration and evidence presented by jurists are not sufficient; some of which are even "fruit of the poisonous tree" (the wrong path at the very beginning), our forensic and discriminating measures are not scientific (although not illegal); hence, our "judgment" is also mistaken. We must emphasize the importance of modern measures of science and technology in contemporary judiciary again, including their importance to the construction of modern judicial procedure; we must take into consideration the force of science and technology as the core and basic institutional variable or perimeter of judicial reform and institutional structure.[70]

In this sense, *The Injustice to Dou E* tells such a human tragedy: In the judicial system lacking the scholastic tradition of powerfully natural science and technology and empirical science and the support of legal professional tradition, even if an adjudicator has a clear conscience and morality, he is destined to not likely deliver justice, but more likely deliver disaster and tragedy. Perhaps this should be the ever-lasting admonition of *The Injustice to Dou E* to us!

---

70 Judge Posner once proposed for the legal development of the developing countries and believed, "As for granting extensive rights to criminals, this is bound to undermine the efficacy of the criminal laws, and by doing so, unsettle property rights. Rights make it harder to convict the guilty as well as the innocent. Sophisticated police forces and prosecutors can apprehend and convict the guilty without trampling on rights; but sophisticated law enforcement is costly. . . . In such countries a strict criminal law and a corresponding de-emphasis on the protection of civil liberties may be an important part of legal reform and an important tool for the protection of property and contract rights." Posner, Richard A. "Creating a Legal Framework for Economic Development," in *The World Bank Research Observer*, vol. 13, no. 1 (1998), 9.

4   Institutional Role and Competence

In Chapter 3, I chose *The Injustice to Dou E* as a judicial case for discussion, which is concentrated on the issue related to evidence. However, people easily forget that Prefect Taowu in charge of the trial was not a professional judge, but a prefect with an attached jurisdiction. To a larger extent, he was an administrator. (Therefore, in the earlier analysis, I consistently use "an adjudicator," whose concept is wider than the judge's.) Actually, before modern times, except the judicial organ with a sole duty in the central government, all the case trials in provinces were tried by local magistrates with the assistance from clerks or secretaries in charge of criminal prosecution or the like. Naturally, the case of Dou E is not an exception.

Will this discrimination affect the trial of Dou E's case? People will wonder. If Taowu were not the prefect but the court judge of Chuzhou, would the tragedy of Dou E have been avoided? Considering the evidence detrimental to Dou E, it perhaps makes no difference. But in this chapter, I still want to discuss if Taowu were a *full-time* judge without administrative liabilities, perhaps (only perhaps) the trial of Dou E's case might be somewhat different. Or in other words, it is because Taowu was the prefect that the possibility of injustice to Dou E was greatly increased. In this sense, the story of *The Injustice to Dou E* actually poses the question concerning a detached and independent judicial system, which can be simplified as the question of judicial independence.

However, this chapter doesn't cut to this question from the perspective of political correctness that is popular in the community of legal science in China of today, but from the perspective of comparative institutional competence and personal institutional role. It is the perspective with more theoretical and practical significance, which is almost never mentioned in the judicial research in China today; hence, the meticulous analysis is needed. Following this theoretical mainline, I will probe into other questions of institutional competence which are related to the judicial system and raised or implicated in the study with other traditional dramas as source materials. Certainly, I am still focused on the judicially *institutional* issue.

Double Institutional Roles of an Adjudicator

Changes of title, rank, identity, or social status do not bring changes of intelligence, moral integrity, and working capacity to anyone indeed. Generally speaking, this

DOI: 10.4324/9781003615606-7

assertion is valid. However, we also often observe that the same person has a tre-
mendous change in his judgments, words, and deeds only because of the change
of his identity and social status. A famous example in the judiciary is the different attitudes of John Marshall on judicial review, the fourth chief justice of the
U.S. Supreme Court, before and after his assumption of the post.[1] Another famous
example is the change of attitudes of Oliver Wendell Holmes Jr. on antitrust law
before and after his becoming a justice on the U.S. Supreme Court.[2] Similar things
can be found everywhere in daily life. The same legalist will have totally different
performances at the court in the capacity of prosecutor or defense counsel and even
will have diametrically opposed judgments and interpretations toward the same evidence and law. A secretary who "promptly obeys the orders" from her boss in the
office might be in charge of everything when she returns home. A boss who stands
by his words in the company might be "henpecked" at home. It is not because they
don't think and act in one and the same way, but because the roles demanded by
environments or institutions change them. The saying "where we stand depends on
where we sit" puts forward such a role theory if satire and sarcasm are discarded
from this black humor of contemporary China: The change of environments and
the restrictive relations of power will affect a person's comprehension of his role
and then his thinking mode, judgment, and action.

Any adjudicator must perform his duty within a certain institutional framework.
Complete independence is neither possible nor expected. With the exception of a
few persons who are totally free from the institutional restriction, therefore, what
any adjudicator does in the case trial shouldn't be just considered the show of his
personal capability, but must be comprehended as a whole set of explicit or implicit
power relations that restrict and support him. The role he plays in the trial is actually an institutional role and a mark or sign of institutional network; the capability
displayed by him reflects the capability of that institution in which he is placed to
an extent, while his limitation might be also the limitation of this institution to an
extent. Accordingly, we can logically infer more or less that Taowu tried the case of
Dou E in the capacity of administrator, or judge, or the administrator with judicial
power. Even as for the same person, because of the different institutional logics that
restrict him, the factors that support, demand, and restrict him will be different, and
his ensuing judgments might vary.

Only the inference is not enough. Let's take a specific investigation of Taowu's
role, the power relations, and the institutional logic that restrict his decision-making.

---

1 When Marshall was the judge of the lower court and lawyer, he was consistently against the judicial
   review. After he became the chief justice of the U.S. Supreme Court, he advocated for and practiced
   judicial review. See Zhu, Suli 朱苏力. "Zhidu shi ruhe xingcheng de" 制度是如何形成的. In *Zhidu
   shi ruhe xingcheng de* 制度是如何形成的 (Guangzhou: Sun Yat-sen University Press, 1999).
2 One of the intentions of American President Theodore Roosevelt in appointing Holmes as the associate justice of the Supreme Court was to expect the latter to render support, while Holmes beforehand
   indicated his support for antitrust initiatives all along. But in the famous case *Standard Oil Company
   of New Jersey v. United States*, 221 U.S. 1 (1911), Holmes voted against the crack-down on Standard
   Oil Company, which greatly enraged Roosevelt as a result.

In the case of Dou E, although Taowu made a trial, his basic role was the administrator, and the case trial was only one part or attached part of his administrative liability. The liability of administrator is mainly characterized with political feature. The so-called political feature refers to the fact that he must account for his superiors in his placement of administrative system, accomplish the entrusted mission by the superiors, and ensure the good order of the region under his jurisdiction. Under the conventional circumstance of traditional China, officials at different levels were all subject to the supervision of imperial power. In *The Injustice to Dou E*, Taowu himself mentioned that "when any inspector comes to check on my files" (Guan, 1977: 135), namely, to examine the issue of his local governance; while one of jobs Dou E's father, Dou Tianzhang, assumed was "Inspector-General of the Huai River Valley"; "wherever I go I pass sentence on prisoners, investigate records, and whenever I discover officials who are corrupt or misuse their authority." (Guan, 1977: 145) It shows that although law and government were far from here and a magistrate nearly monopolized the discretionary power in local affairs, yet his power was still subject to the restriction and supervision of imperial power or the central administrative power. His power was the extension of imperial power.

But ancient officials not only accounted for imperial power; we shouldn't only observe this aspect. Because of our prejudices and arrogances toward history, we often neglect another aspect in investigating ancient institutions, especially ancient Chinese institutions. In my opinion, it might be a more important aspect – namely, a magistrate still tried to basically meet the demands of local people as far as possible in fulfilling the political liability even for the sake of his own interests. Otherwise, when the public complaint was once known by his superior, he might be removed from the post. In this sense, even for an official of traditional society, his power base was still secular not divine and was conditioned, not absolute. Although democracy in a modern sense didn't exist in those days, public opinion still exerted a certain influence on the legitimacy of a magistrate and somewhat restricted his administration. This point is reflected in many ancient dramas, including *The Injustice to Dou E*. For example, Dou Tianzhang once told Dou E, "If I could not control you, how can I control others?" (Guan, 1977: 149). In other detective plays and literary works, we can still observe the pressure of this local public opinion, including the relatives of victim, on the officials' "the administration of justice."

The play *Fifteen Strings of Cash* reflects such a political pressure of community on the magistrate. In its predecessor, *The Unjust Execution of Cui Ning*, the script for storytelling in the Song Dynasty, we can observe it quite clearly:

Turning a deaf ear to his explanations, they searched his shoulder bag and found there fifteen strings of cash, not a penny more, not a penny less. Everyone cried out. One said, "As the saying goes, 'The net of heaven is of large mesh, but it lets nothing through.' You and the young woman committed a murder. You took the money and the woman and tried to fee this place with her, dragging us all into a case in which the guilty parties couldn't be found."

With Mrs. Liu holding Second Sister, Squire Wang holding Cui Ning, and the neighbors as witnesses, the whole crowd marched noisily to the Lin'an prefectural yamen. Upon hearing of a murder, the prefect immediately called a court session to order and had the parties involved brought in for statements on the case.

The young woman was about to protest her innocence again when the neighbors fell to their knees and said to the prefect, "Your Honor, what you said is indeed the truth. . . . We searched the young man and found fifteen strings of cash on him, not a penny less. Isn't it obvious that the two of them are an adulterous couple and they plotted the murder together? With the money as evidence, how can they lie their way out of it?" Quite convinced, the prefect called up the young man.

With Squire Wang, Mrs. Liu, and the neighbors clamoring that those two were the culprits, the prefect could hardly wait to close the case. Unable to hold out against the torture, poor Cui Ning and the young lady confessed to the false charges. . . . After each of the neighbors drew a cross with his finger on the confession by way of signature, the two accused were put in large cangues and sent to death row.[3]

In these passages, the words "they" and "neighbors" appear repeatedly, and we can keenly sense the pressure from the common people. Because of such a pressure from the community and people, if a magistrate practiced corruption and degeneration in total disregard of human lives (sometimes even he was not corrupt and degenerated, only because of his mistreatment of the problem, or untimely treatment, or incompetence) and stirred public grievance, if it was leaked to his superiors, he might be removed from the post. In this sense, the magistrates would always be indirectly swayed by local public opinion. In *The Injustice to Dou E*, when the injustice of Dou E was redressed, although Taowu, who was transferred to a post in another region, and his chief of police didn't practice any corruption or degeneration and didn't bend the law for personal benefit, just because of preventing "the administration of justice" (while this mistake was sometimes inevitable in the ancient social condition just as I have discussed in the previous chapter), "let them each be given a hundred strokes of the lash and be permanently dismissed from the service" (Guan, 1977: 158). On the other side, if a magistrate governed well and earned the reputation of "an honest official" and praise from the public, he would, or at least more likely, get awards and promotion. Many plays and stories have presented such a practice.[4] Under the mixed *political* pressure of such

---

3 Menglong, Feng. *Stories to Awaken the World*, vol. 3, trans. Yang Shuhui and Yang Yunqin (Seattle: University of Washington Press, 2014), 776–777.

4 For example, in *The Moheluo Doll*, because Zhang Ding rectified the possible unjust case and identified the true murder, Prefect Wanyan declared, "I shall amply reward Zhang Ding with my own stipend for the next three months. By imperial decree you will be rewarded and promoted, Inspector Zhang, controller of punishments!" (Meng, 182). In *Fifteen Strings of Cash*, Guo Yuzhi was "always honest and upright, and is accordingly recommended . . . to be promoted as the official in charge of criminal affairs in Changzhou." Guo Yuzhi was then determined to "let the banners and pennants fluttering in the wind, I must redouble my efforts to make great achievements" (Zhu, 220).

informal and formal institutions, many officials hoped to acquire the reputation of "an honest official."

We must fully recognize the legitimacy and rationality of such a political consideration of officials. Officials cared for local public opinion and strove to be accountable for imperial power; therefore, the local public opinion would restrict magistrates to an extent and urge officials to painstakingly fulfill their duties and prevent them from misconducting in their office, slackening their efforts, corrupting, and bending the law for personal benefits regardless of human life. Viewed from this perspective, such a political consideration, even if it serves their own future, not devotedly serves the people, yet it is consistent with their fulfillment of judicial duties.

But under other circumstances, this administrative role is hardly compatible with the adjudicating role, and even a severe conflict occurs. These political considerations will bother officials in terms of fulfilling their adjudicating duties in a better way. Because as for the trial of an individual case,[5] the duty of adjudicator is only to make a *circumspect* and appropriate decision (not the correct decision in the absolute sense) on the basis of evidence of individual case (not the factors outside the case; instead, these outside factors should be ruled out as far as possible) and try not to make a huge mistake or even a wrong verdict as much as possible. As for the individual case to be tried, pressures from social populace, rewards, and punishments from imperial power are some external factors. In terms of the case of Dou E, if Taowu only took the circumspection demanded in trial into consideration and completely undertook the trial in the capacity of judge, perhaps he might think the evidence was not sufficient and set Dou E free as a result or didn't judge this case for the time being. But such a circumspect decision deemed totally correct in terms of judiciary might be incorrect from the political consideration, and it would be very disadvantageous for Taowu himself who was the magistrate first of all.

We can analyze the features of Dou E's case. First, generally speaking, this case must have a murder; otherwise, Donkey Zhang's father would not die for no reason (Is this really so? Please check another possibility provided in Chapter 7.) Therefore, the public must demand severe punishment for the criminal and expect Taowu to identify this culprit. If Taowu failed, then in the eyes of the public, it only exhibited his incompetence. Second, for the public, no matter what the trial result, either Donkey Zhang killed his father, or Dou E poisoned her "father-in-law," or Mother Cai murdered her "husband," this case was one of "the ten most atrocious crimes," which would receive the severest punishment in traditional society. In this sense, it was a "newsworthy" hotspot case in ancient society, which would arouse universal attention from the local public. As we all know, the attention is a pressure; the more attention, the greater the pressure. Third, because of the high homogenization in ancient Chinese society, we can also infer that the public generally demanded a

---

5 The judiciary also has the function of confirming regulations, and making regulations through interpretation, it will bring more political factors into judicature. But this point is not only rare in traditional Chinese judiciary but also in contemporary judiciary. Therefore, we leave it aside.

decisive, definite, and prompt answer. In other words, they demanded "the heavier and quicker punishment." These three points formed a direct and strong social pressure on Taowu, the adjudicator of this case, which might usher in the administrative pressure from the superiors in turn.

The question is: How did Taowu manage to cope with these pressures? From the perspective of legal creeds quite known to people nowadays, it is very easy for us to say that Taowu should do this or that. However, the actors are not the puppets guided by the legal principles. They don't always ponder over the question from the perspective of "should," but more from the perspective of "could." What role a person shall play on earth is not up to the normative role for him, but all kinds of tangible institutional restrictions on him. If he is confronted with several possibilities, he will generally make the choice that seems to be more beneficial to him among multiple choices, except for wrong information. We can analyze different countermeasures Taowu might adopt at that time and analyze all kinds of related consequences to society and himself.

Taowu could choose the role of adjudicator. Then he was very cautious and didn't make a judgment on this case for the time being; instead, he made an in-depth investigation and gathered new information. Maybe he would finally prove the innocence of Dou E; then he himself might not be "given a hundred strokes of the lash and be permanently dismissed from the service" in the end. However, in doing thus, *even if it were successful*, the main benefactor would be Dou E. Since to make a clear distinction between right and wrong, it was the basic liability of the then magistrates, and Taowu would not be commended and awarded because of his identifying the criminal in the first trial. Therefore, he lacked the sufficient encouragement to undertake the in-depth investigation. More importantly, even if Taowu adopted this countermeasure, since he was not Dou Tianzhang, he might not ascertain the case. Just as I have analyzed in Chapter 3, if there were not "snow in the midsummer" and other supernatural evidence after the death of Dou E, if the ghost of wronged Dou E didn't come to lodge a complaint, if Dou E's father Dou Tianzhang didn't come to "investigate the records," and Dou Tianzhang knew that it was his daughter appealing for justice, the mistake of this case would nearly have no chance of being discovered in the technical condition of that time. All these pieces of information and conditions helpful to redress the injustice of Dou E couldn't be accessible to Taowu in charge of the trial, no matter how circumspect and diligent he was. If all his efforts couldn't guarantee the discovery of the truth, then it means Dou E was still likely to be sentenced guilty in the end. All of Taowu's efforts had no substantial meaning.

The fewer the gains, the greater the risks. Because of the extreme limitation of acquiring evidence in ancient society, this case was very likely to be stalled. Therefore, Taowu couldn't quickly appease the public opinion and grievance caused by socially mechanical solidarity because of this case.[6] He would be almost certainly accused of "incompetence" or "misconduct." Even if he were not removed from

---

6 Durkheim, Émile. *The Division of Labor in Society*, ed. Steven Lukes (New York: Free Press, 2014).

the post, it would not be good for his future official career. The probability of this risk will be neither very high nor very low. We can make an underestimation, and the presumed probability is 20%.

Taowu must hope and try to lower the probability of this risk. He knew that if the risk could be transferred to others or be shared by many persons, then the risk that he himself was actually accountable for would be greatly lowered. However, although Taowu had the great power in his jurisdiction and possessed the power of deciding the life of others, yet he had no method of circumventing or lowering his risk through other measures. It is not only because Taowu concurrently assumed double political and judicial liabilities, but also he did not have many institutions to rely on. If he were an administrator in modern times, he would naturally instruct the police and the court to work hard to investigate this case; then he wouldn't be accountable for judicial mistakes. If he were a modern judge, he would use a series of institutions to protect him as well. For example, he could return this case to the police or the procuratorial organ and demanded them to supplement the evidence after investigation. Even if the progress of breaking the case was slow, the sentence was adjourned, which caused the public grievance, when the superiors came to investigate it, the liability was not shouldered by Taowu himself, at least it was shared by others. If it were in the UK and the United States in modern times, he could let the jury affirm whether the evidence was sufficient to prove the guilt of Dou E or not. Therefore, no matter if the final verdict for Dou E was the death penalty or acquittal, no matter if it turned out to be an unjust verdict or it stirred up a flurry of discussion among common people because the murderer was not caught, he could transfer a part of liability to the police, the procuratorial organ, and the jury. The risk he must assume would be greatly lowered, even to zero. But unfortunately, because of the insufficiency of government finances and social division of labor, it was absolutely impossible to form and support such an institution in traditional society. Taowu, the prefect of Chuzhou, concurrently assumed the liabilities of the police, the procuratorial organ, and the judge; he was the jury and the judge as well. He had no other institutions to rely on; he himself *was* the other institutions. He had his hands tied, facing squarely and lonely such a high degree of risk. His power was very great indeed, and it was so great that it couldn't protect and exonerate himself.

By contrast, Taowu would soon find that in this case, more considerations of political factors could lower the probability of punishment even because of the wrong verdict. In this aspect, Taowu would first think about the probability and degree of the mistake of trying the case according to the evidence at hand. Just as I have analyzed in Chapter 3, many pieces of evidence were detrimental to Dou E; therefore, the preponderance of evidence supported the guilty sentence for Dou E at least at the time of the trial. Let me presume that the probability of mistake would be 40%. Correspondingly, the probability of related punishment would be lower.

However, the probability of mistake might not be too important for his judgment of personal interests (except that he had strong altruism; therefore, the interests of Dou E would not become the important part of his own interests in any case), because the probability of a mistake is not equivalent to the probability of punishment. The more important thing might be the probability of appeal to the superiors, which was launched by the person unjustly sentenced or his relatives, the probability of "investigating the records" by the superiors due to the appeal or the dutiful practice, and the probability of finding the verdict truly wrong and thereby reversing it. Consequently, here is the true rate of punishment because of the wrong verdict.

Let's roughly calculate this rate. First, after the execution of Dou E, the probability of Dou E's appeal was zero except for her wronged ghost. The personal interests of Mother Cai were not unjustly infringed. Even if she took pity on Dou E, she hadn't other pieces of cogent evidence except the supernatural evidence of "snow in midsummer"; besides, she was advanced in years, and the probability of her appeal for Dou E would be quite low. Even we presume the higher rate for it, it would be 10%. But the appeal might not bring in the superiors to investigate the records; then the probability might be half to half at most, namely 50%. As for the superiors who voluntarily investigated the records who not only came to Chuzhou but also happened to read the file of Dou E, the probability might be 5% at most. More importantly, no matter the investigation of records owed to the appeal or the voluntary performance of duty by the superiors, only if the investigator was not the father of Dou E, just as I have analyzed in Chapter 3, he might not be much motivated to investigate the case in which none complained and called for redress. Even if the case was investigated, the probability of reversing the verdict on the basis of existing evidence might be very low, nearly zero. Let's still presume the higher rate for it, namely 5%. Therefore, we can find that the probability of punishment because of the misjudgment in this case for Taowu is:

$$40\% \times 10\% \times (50\% \text{ or } 5\%) \times 5\% = 1 \text{ in a } 1,000 \text{ or } 1 \text{ in } 10,000$$

In the face of the probability of 1 in 1,000 or 1 in 10,000 and 20%, we know what Taowu would choose. While the former is being "given a hundred strokes of the lash and be permanently dismissed from the service" because of the consideration of political factor and wrong verdict in this case, the latter is the end of official career because of his inconsideration of political factor and misgovernance.[7]

Under the pressure of such a choice, Taowu was evidently more eager to break this case, to prove his competence and demonstrate that he was an honest official who was perspicacious and impartial in judgment. He was impatient in making a judgment according to the evidence that existed and might be acquired, while the existing evidence was obviously diametrical to Dou E. He might consider more or even first consider the pressure of public opinion, his administrative liability, and his image of an honest official in the hearts of common people. In one word,

7 This analysis doesn't take into consideration the type of risk appetite of Taowu, or it is presumed that he was the risk neutral. For the related analysis, see Becker, Gary S. "Crime and Punishment: An Economic Approach," in *Journal of Political Economy*, vol. 76 (1968), 169–217.

he would consider more his political role, which also means he would more easily make the judgment disadvantageous to Dou E.

It should be noted that it doesn't mean when Taowu made a decision that he must analyze interests in such a cold-blooded way. But in such a conflicted institutional role, an official might well form the instinct, intuition, and behavioral layout of his conduct that can be analyzed according to the previously mentioned logic. It is because his main liability was administrative that even if an official were not partial in the narrow sense, he would very easily integrate these political and legitimate factors into the case trial like Dou E's. He would consciously or unconsciously mix up politics and judgment. It would be impossible for such an adjudicator to first consider the evidence or to only consider the evidence; more or less, he must consider the factors outside the evidence and consider whether the trial of this case was in line with the local public opinion or not in order to avoid the appeal or public grievance, the removal from his post, and the loss of his "good reputation" or all the losses. From this analysis, we can basically foresee that when an official concurrently assumes double liabilities and considerations, not only Taowu, but also other officials in the similar institutional condition, they might make a certain choice and lay a certain type of emphasis. For Taowu, this choice was completely reasonable. But it was beyond Taowu's expectation that it turned out to be Dou E's father who came to investigate the records; the probability of 1 in 1,000 or 1 in 10,000 unexpectedly actualized the reality.

Certainly, it doesn't mean that an official with two roles will have a conflict. Sometimes, and even on more than one occasion, two roles can be unified, for example, the trial that is not only correct, but also wins more universal support of public opinion. Actually, if not being driven by some partial interests, all the officials more hope to make the judgement, which accords with the popular will and proves their competence in keeping people safe for the public and superiors. Even it is out of personal gain in the broad sense (respects from the public and praises from the superiors). At least under some particular circumstances, two roles might have a conflict. The circumspect judgment that accords with the trial might not be difficult to be comprehended or be accepted by the then political institution and popular will for the time being. Under such a circumstance, double institutional roles urged Taowu to actively circumvent personal risks and implement the administrative liability and thereby transferred the greater risk to the party concerned, Dou E. In this sense, Dou E's accusation, "you officials have no care to see justice done" is valid, only it is the accusation in the sense of institution, not the morality.

Since there are neither other institutions serving as the reference frame for reflection nor the institutional theory that we might have today, Guan Hanqing might well not reflect on such an occurrence of Dou E's tragedy in those days. However, it doesn't prevent his play from "accidentally" leaving such a reflective case for later generations, while we latecomers might consider the injustice to Dou E, the issue that seems to have a final conclusion in terms of the comparison of institutional capabilities on the basis of information we might have today.

Evidence of Judicial Independence

The meaning of this issue is great, because it might actually present another stronger jurisprudential argument to judicial independence as the institution in modern times and pose the question concerning some arguments on judicial independence that are popular in the Chinese community of legal science nowadays.

When the issue of judicial independence is discussed in China of today, the following passage of Montesquieu is mostly cited:

> Nor is there liberty if the power of judging is not separate from legislative power and from executive power. If it were joined to legislative power, the power over the life and liberty of the citizens would be arbitrary, for the judge would be the legislator. If it were joined to executive power, the judge could have the force of an oppressor.[8]

However, people always regard this passage as the authoritative quotation and seldom closely investigate whether it is valid or not with actual evidence of experience and logics. Here, Montesquieu actually only raises three assertions, while the latter two assertions are the arguments for the first assertion. These are assertions truly worthy of being cherished. However, even this kind of assertion also needs to be verified and enriched in experiences; it shouldn't be worshiped as the absolute priori truth or doctrine.

For example, consider the second assertion. When the judge is the legislator, why will he exercise arbitrary power over the life and liberty of citizens? Is it inevitable? In terms of logic, if this proposition is valid, it must possess two presumptions at the same time at least. The first is the legislator always wants to exercise arbitrary power over the life and liberty of citizens; the second is the judge doesn't do this because he might have better morality or other reasons. As general propositions, both premises can't be valid. The first premise might be valid in France of Montesquieu's times, because the legislator was the king in France. But today, this premise is hardly valid because the modern legislator is generally set as the parliament. Since the parliament is generated out of the election, theoretically speaking, it is usually considered the institution to protect the life and liberty of citizens, not the other way around, although sometimes there is the so-called issue of tyranny of the majority. Besides, in terms of facts, in the British judicial system extoled by Montesquieu as the paragon of separation of powers, since common law is the law made by judges, the judge himself is one of the legislators, although not the only one. This situation extends to nowadays in the UK and the United States. Therefore, this assertion is questionable, whether viewed from the experimental or logical perspective.

The third assertion has the same problem. From the logical perspective, first, the combination of the judicial power and the executive power – even if it is presumed

---

that Montesquieu is correct in the identification of the executive power – only enables the judge to *possess* the power of oppressor, but it doesn't logically amount that the judge must *become* the oppressor except if the judge wants to be so. Second, in light of two possible forms that such a combination might have, namely the judge with the executive power or the executives with the judicial power, therefore, one of the outcomes is that the administrators (not necessarily judges) have the power of oppressor. The more accurate expression should be the combination of the judicial power and the executive power might let any official who has both powers at the same time possess the power of oppressor. Third, if this proposition is valid, it likewise needs the presumption that the power of executives is naturally the power of oppressor, while the power of judges has such an immunity. All these logical inferences or presumptions are hardly valid as general propositions. In terms of facts, when John Locke, who first put forward the theory of separation of powers in the modern West, expounded his theory, he didn't separately discuss judicial power, but actually regarded it as a special executive power, which was implied in the executive power.[9] The judicial system of Britain, the model of Montesquieu, actually exists thus. The assertion of Montesquieu is absolutely invalid whether looked at logically or experimentally.

When the research of legal science in China of today analyzes and emphasizes judicial independence, it has its own context and implication. Considering the history and reality of China, when contemporary Chinese scholars emphasize judicial independence, they often have in mind the personal power and integrity of judges and seem to believe that only if the judiciary is not influenced by the administration, the legislation and especially powerful figures, and only has liability for the law, can judicial justice be guaranteed. This proposition presumes the naturally moral superiority of judges, but this presumption has already been smashed by some facts of unjust judiciary and judicial corruption in recent years. The reality tells us that an independent judge must not inevitably value the interests of people and protect the lawful rights of the party concerned. An independent judge might well abuse his power for personal gain and bend the law for personal benefit. Therefore, if the checks and balances of power are necessary, then the judge's power must be one of them.

Even if it is presumed that the judge or the adjudicator is independent without any partiality or moral defect in a general sense, the story of *The Injustice to Dou E*, lots of actual events, and the logical analysis all show that the independent judgment might not usher in the correct judgment. In the case of Dou E, Prefect Taowu had the absolute power in Chuzhou, and no more powerful figure could intervene; he didn't deliberately bend the law for the sake of money and personal gain, yet he still passed the wrong verdict. While in the story of the filial daughter-in-law of Donghai, the prototype story of *The Injustice to Dou E*,[10] we even observe that

9 Locke, John. *Two Treatises of Government and a Letter Concerning Toleration*, ed. Ian Shapiro (New Haven: Yale University, 2003), 164–165.
10 Ban, Gu 班固. "Jun shu yu xue ping peng zhuan" 隽疏于薛平彭传. In *Han shu* 汉书, vol. 71.

Clerk Yu once attempted to intervene in the judgment of the prefect, the adjudicator, but "the prefect remained unconvinced" and insisted on the independent implementation of "the judicial power." This prefect didn't have the correct judgment because of his independent decision.

A dogmatist who blindly believes in the doctrine of judicial independence might think these mistakes are all a necessary price. I admit that for any institution, a certain price will be paid, but it doesn't amount that any price actually paid is necessary. This specious rhetoric is not convincing, or is only falsely convincing. Because when "the necessary price" is mentioned, it implies that we *must* actually weigh costs and benefits, not just know this term and speak it out. This saying seemly sounding reasonable actually doesn't provide any proof that can be inferred or demonstrated: The price paid for such an independence is necessary and relatively small. If analyzed logically, the probability of making mistakes is evenly dispersed among different departments of government. We have no reason to believe that the probability will be surely lowered *just because* one department is called as the court or a person is called as the judge.

Perhaps someone might emphasize that because judges receive rigorous professional training, especially in modern times, they thereby make fewer mistakes. Although there is such a possibility, no positive materials could prove it. The unproved presumption is used to answer this question. It is not only because officials at all departments of government in each country, including China, basically receive rigorous professional training in economics, politics, and management, but also in the United States, many officials graduate from law schools at the very least. Strictly speaking, even in China of today, no matter at the beginning of the reform and opening-up or nowadays, the record of education among officials at the administrative departments in various regions is generally higher than that in the court system. Therefore, in terms of professional training, the judges don't come out first. On the other hand, the U.S. Supreme Court, which enjoys the highest authority in the judicial system among all the countries, might make more and greater mistakes of orientation in history than the executive department.[11] It is because of this reason that some of the most famous judges in the United States always advocate for the judicial self-discipline, whose basic presumption is not the respect for democracy, but lies in the skepticism of some judges on personal competence, just as Judge Posner indicated.[12] "The spirit of liberty is the spirit which is not too sure that it is right." This famous sentence of Billings Learned Hand, the greatest judge of the U.S. Court of Appeals in the 20th century, points out that even independent judges couldn't have the basis of ensuring the correct judgment.

"How can you believe that the judiciary should not be independent?" Some people might criticize this analysis of mine. Not so. The practice of judicial independence is the outcome of the long-term historical development of humans and the condensation

---

11 For example, *Dred Sccott v. Sanford*, 19 Howard 393 (1857), this case led to the outbreak of American Civil War.

12 Posner. *The Problems of Jurisprudence*, 140.

of human tragic experiences and lessons, which must be respected. However, the existing argument is insufficient in my opinion at least. In the analysis of *The Injustice to Dou E*, we not only observe the necessity of the judicial organ and other corresponding organic institutions that should be separated from the administration, but more importantly, the possibility of another argument for judicial independence; namely when it is impossible to presume the legislative, administrative, and judicial organs have a certain priori moral superiority, judicial independence is still necessary, whose essence lies in the comparative institutional capacity of judiciary.

At least in the modern society with the emphasis on democracy, the legislative power and the executive power are not born to be more arbitrary and unjust than the judicial power. The shortcoming of the legislative power might lie in its generality; therefore, except for the rarest situations, the legislative power can't and shouldn't deal with concrete disputes and controversies in which it isn't adept as well. Under many circumstances, the implementation of the executive power is linked with the tackling of concrete issues, which is similar to the implementation of the judicial power in this aspect. However, the shortcoming of the implementation of the executive power might be it always seeks to accord with popular will and exhibit political achievements to varying degrees or in different ways. Although it can't be counted as a mistake (how can we hope the administrative department will fail in reflecting popular will and making political achievements?), yet on some occasions, the judgment and implementation of the executive power might well be tarnished by such a political demand. The judicial power/the power of justice might not be more just because it is the same word with "the justice" in English. When the operative capacity of judiciary is deprived and only its judging capacity is emphasized, the judicial judgment might make up for the innate shortcoming of the administrative judgment with the guarantee of other institutions and social conditions, such as the job with safety and stability, no demand for "political achievements," and no demand (not unnecessary) for the response to public feelings.

Certainly, I must also emphasize that the merit of a judiciary under such a circumstance is analyzed here only; we still can't universalize the merit in such a special context and regard it as the necessary and universal one. Actually, under specific circumstances, such a merit of the judiciary might completely become a demerit. For example, because there are not many compulsory institutions that demand the judiciary account for the public or the superiors (except the restrictions of remanding for retrial by superior courts, the financial allocation by the legislative organ, and the stronger enforcement of law by the administrative organ), the modern judicial organ might always avail itself of this position to shirk its liability. In this sense, the more politics-oriented legislative and administrative organs with an emphasis on the respect for popular will and political achievements can make up for the shortcoming of the judiciary.

Hence, although the repetition can't prevent my views from being misunderstood, I still want to emphasize (perhaps futilely) that my analysis here has absolutely no intention of denying the *practice* of judicial independence, but only questions the currently popular *arguments* concerning judicial independence. Besides, I think that the analysis on the basis of *The Injustice to Dou E* actually emphasizes more the importance of judicial independence *as the institution*; it also reinforces the criticism of "the administration of justice" in a traditional society, which is based on our understanding. My argument is the institutionalist path with emphasis on the separately and competently judicial department with the whole set, not the moralist path with the accent on the independent personality and moral integrity of individual judges. What this path shows is that the judiciary appears as a separate department, or the judge becomes an independent professional, which is separated from the traditional officials. It is not because the administrative departments or administrators (in a certain sense, the judge is the official) have innate moral and intelligent flaws; therefore, there is a need for an increasingly perfect judicial department with higher morality and intelligence to educate and supervise them. It is because when the administration is mixed with the judiciary, the political consideration must impair the fulfillment of the judicial function. If a female secretary behaved in the office like "a dutiful housewife" as if in her own home, everyone would think it is absurd and unbelievable. But in many institutional matters, we can't always understand the meaning of "one who holds no official position does not discuss official affairs" from the aspect of the combination of theory and practice and can't understand the meaning of institutional role: "the filial son at home, the loyal subject in the state."

Consequently, although the analysis of *The Injustice to Dou E* is based on the understandable criticism of history, it has relevance to the judicial reform in China of today. Since traditional Chinese society had no other cultures or institutions as a reference in judiciary, Guan Hanqing and other playwrights were destined to fail in reflecting on the related theoretical issue. They always emphasized the decisive utility of personal moral integrity among officials to the correct administration of justice. This path is still the mainstream of the community of legal science in China today. Many discussions concerning the so-called reform of the judicial system are just moralizing with the accent on judicial "fairness" and all sorts of supervision in opposition to judicial "corruption." The occasional mention of institution is still the discussion on some rules that are seemingly strict and have such high costs of trading, supervision, and information that they can't be practically implemented after all. There is neither any analysis of institutional function nor the analysis of the comparison of institutional capacities and their advantages and disadvantages. Therefore, the role of the judicial institution is mixed with other institutional roles. For example, the emphasis that the judiciary serves the reform and opening-up, the prevention of financial risks, and the guarantee of a certain growth of gross domestic product (GDP) – actually all of these completely abandon the institutional role of the judiciary without understanding the institutional capacity of the judiciary including its merits and demerits.

The tragedy of *The Injustice to Dou E* should awaken us to pay attention to and re-understand the institutional role of judiciary.

Institutional Role: The Competence of Officials and Clerks

The earlier analysis of institutional capacity and role is the comparison between the judiciary and the administration. But a judicial organization or system consists of many concrete institutions and many persons playing differently and specifically institutional roles. What I have analyzed is the trial institution within one organization, the local administration of traditional Chinese society. Therefore, to follow the main thread of comparative institutional capacity and role, we can still and should well further the analysis in this train of thought on different types of persons within the trial organization of traditional society. Yet because of historical setup, the organization of the trial function is seated within the administrative organization.

If we are careful, we can find the repeated appearances of incompetent officials such as Prefect Taowu in traditional dramas and other historical materials. Some of them were honest officials without quite evidently personal moral defects and were positive figures in dramas and stories, which reflects the ideal of playwrights that is restricted by the limitation of the times. But in trials, these officials were actually not astute enough with subjective conjecture and biased comprehension, and they were even cheated. Some of them made the wrong judgment, which directly caused or facilitated the unjust verdict. In their stories, playwrights and historians showed that if there were neither the shrewdness and carefulness of other clerks (for example, the assistance of Zhang Ding in *The Case of the Head Scarf* and *The Moheluo Doll* to Wanyan) nor some special conditions (for example, the assistance of the ghost of wronged Dou E to Dou Tianzhang), they might well make wrong judgments. If these officials had something in common, that would be the desperate deficiency of judging knowledge and skills.

Even in some Yuan plays, a spate of very stupid officials who didn't bend the law for personal gain appeared frequently. In the capacity of county magistrate or prefect, they had to try cases, but they hadn't even basic judging knowledge; they accordingly always shirked their judging liability. Consider the following:

County Magistrate in Henan Prefecture: "How can I set it right? Get the clerk for me."[13]

Su Shun, the Magistrate of Zhengzhou: "This woman really knows how to talk. I think she's someone who is long accustomed to court suits. She just keeps blabbering on and I can't understand a thing. Go and ask the clerk to come here."[14]

Prefect of Henan: "He has been blabbering for such a long time, but I have no clue of it. Zhang Qian, bring the clerk to me."[15]

---

13 Hanqing, Meng. "The Moheluo Doll," in *The Columbia Anthology of Yuan Drama*, ed. C. T. Hsia, Wai-Yee Li and George Kao, trans. Jonathan Chaves (New York: Columbia University Press, 2014), 165 (hereafter cited parenthetically in the text).

14 Xingdao, Li. "Rescriptor-in-Waiting Bao's Clever Trick: The Record of the Chalk Circle," in *Monks, Bandits, Lovers and Immortals: Eleven Early Chinese Plays*, ed. and trans. Stephen H. West and Wilt L. Idema (Indianapolis: Hackett Publishing Company, 2010), 260 (hereafter cited parenthetically in the text).

15 Sun, Zhongzhang 孙仲章. *Henan fu zhang ding kan toujin* 河南府张鼎勘头巾. In *Yuanqu xuan* 元曲选, 671 (hereafter cited parenthetically in the text).

Even in *The Chalk Circle*, after Su Shun, the magistrate of Zhengzhou, watched the trial of Clerk Zhao (who consciously created the injustice in fact), he sighed, "This case may be finished, but when I think on it, I realize that I am the chief official, yet it wasn't decided by me. Whether they are beaten or let off was all a decision of Clerk Zhao. I really am a fool!" He thereby said, "In deciding cases from this point on, I'll be less nervous, and right or wrong, be at the plaintiff's service. Caned, beaten, exiled, or banished – the choice is yours to make, all I want is money and goods, a doubled portion mine to take" (Li, 266).

The sharp contrast is that some clerks in these plays actually undertook the work of trying cases and became the main reliance for the local chiefs. These clerks were rather capable, and they thereby were described as "capable clerks." Even many clerks who bent the law for personal gain in plays, such as Clerk Zhao in *The Chalk Circle*, always were well-versed in trial skills.

For example, Zhang Ding, the intelligent and capable judicial inspector who oversaw the Six Bureaus in *The Moheluo Doll* and *The Case of the Head Scarf*, was "the yamen clerk." He could quickly ascertain the problem in the concluded file, reopen the investigation, find new leads, and identify the true criminal. Let me make the case analysis of *The Moheluo Doll*.

Li Dechang, the boss of a small shop, went out on business and fell ill on the journey back home. He was confined to the temple of General of Five Paths and asked Gao Shan, a craftsman of molded clay dolls, namely Moheluo, to carry the message to his home. Gao Shan passed the message to Doctor Li Wendao, Li Dechang's cousin, and Liu Yuniang, Li Dechang's wife. Li Wendao coveted the beauty of Liu Yuniang and his cousin's property for a long time; he stole a march to arrive at the ruined temple, and cheated Li Dechang to take the poison, then left. When Liu Yuniang arrived, Li Dechang was in a coma; upon arriving home, Li passed away immediately. Claiming that Liu Yuniang collaborated with her adulterer to have poisoned the husband, Li Wendao urged Liu to accept a "private settlement" with the threat of "official settlement," then went to court after Liu refused it. The greedy Clerk Xiao extorted Liu Yuniang's confession by torture for the sake of money. After the appeal verdict of this case was confirmed, Clerk Zhang Ding found this case suspicious and strove to persuade Prefect Wanyan to re-investigate this case. Consequently, Zhang Ding spotted the Moheluo doll left by the messenger at that time and found the messenger Gao Shan through the "trademark" at the bottom of the doll. After knowing the process of this event, Zhang Ding finally plotted to ascertain the truth and caught the true criminal, Li Wendao.

The play used quite a lot of lines and plots to emphatically exhibit Zhang Ding's sense of responsibility as a clerk, "When I think about how clerks twist things around to make the crooked seem straight and play around with the letter of the law to pervert rules, it is obvious that this brush has sent many to wrongful deaths" (Meng, 165) and his intelligence and capability. Here is his work report after he finished the official business and returned:

This is a closed case about a robbery; we retrieved and reviewed the loot.
This is a concluded investigation about the illegal trade of tea and salt. All

these are cases that should come under our jurisdiction. This is a newly arrived official tally; This, a case of granary goods to be sent far away. . . . This
one is on building bridges along the Canal. This one is on setting up granaries
in keeping with towns. This one is on Wang Shou and Chen Li owing rent
on their land; This one is Zhang Qian beating Li Wan and wounding him.
Concerned that your Honor may not trust me, I have called them to match
their confessions with the case statements. This one is on Wang, née Zhang,
cursing her neighbors again and again.

(Meng, 167–168)

Bit by bit, the report is quite meticulous and thorough. Especially in the case of
Liu Yuniang, his insights and experiences are more apparent, while his acquired
experience in official circles for years is fully mobilized and applied. For example,
in order to persuade Prefect Wanyan to allow the re-investigation of this case, he
first showed his consideration for the prefect:

Your Honor, just now when I left the yamen, I saw beyond the wall of the
Main Hall a condemned woman bemoaning injustice. Those who know the
case would think that she simply longs for life and fears death, but those who
don't might think that there was a miscarriage of justice in our yamen. Your
Honor, please give this your consideration.

(Meng, 168)

Prefect told Zhang Ding that this case was concluded by the predecessor when
Zhang was on official business. As for this, Zhang Ding immediately raised objec-
tions and insisted on his responsibility: "I am the judicial inspector who oversees
the Six Bureaus. This is a case of life and death – why didn't you tell me about it?"
(Meng, 168). It should be noted here that there is a sharp contrast with the image of
magistrates in the previous citations, who shirked trial-related affairs. Afterwards,
Zhang Ding studied the statement and affirmation in the verdict of the first trial and
put forward a basic judgment: "This deposition is no good. . . . This case is like
a house without supporting walls on four sides. . . . And there are holes all over
the roof" (Meng, 169). In order to support this judgment, he immediately raised a
series of questions to Clerk Xiao, who was specifically in charge of this case. Here
is the dialogue between them:

Zhang Ding: "Her husband, Li Dechang, went on a business trip to Nanchang with
ten ingots of silver as capital." These ten ingots: have they been confiscated by the government? Or by the relatives of the deceased?
Clerk Xiao: They have not.
Zhang: We will let that pass. "For a year after he left there was no news
of him. Then, in the seventh month, a man of unknown surname
brought a message." Your Honor, this man who brought the message:
how old was he? Has he ever been summoned before the court?
Clerk: We have not summoned him.

Zhang:	If he was never summoned, how could you interrogate him? It goes on: "to the effect that he was suffering from illness in the temple of the General of Five Paths and could not move. When Yuniang heard this, she immediately hired a horse, went straight to that temple south of the city, and, supporting him, brought him home. When he entered the gateway, he stopped breathing and fresh blood flowed from the Seven Holes. Yuniang immediately reported this to her brother-in-law, Li Wendao, and he said that Yuniang and a lover had plotted together." Your honor, was this lover named Zhang, Li, Zhao, or Wang? Has he ever been brought before the court?
Clerk:	If there was no lover, then I did it myself!
Zhang:	"To concoct poison to murder her husband." Your Honor, in whose home was this poison concocted? That poison must have been prepared somehow.
Clerk:	If no one concocted that poison, then it must also have been me!
Zhang:	Your Honor, just think: there is no silver, no messenger, no lover, no preparer of the poison, and no collaborator: if all these people are nonexistent, how can you execute this woman?

(Meng, 169–170)

It must be noted that Zhang Ding completely raised the questions from the technical aspect of the trial, mainly the evidence, and he didn't have any big talk, empty formulae, and verbiage. Each question must and can only be answered with yes or no, which can't be palmed off. And these technical questions are all based on the common sense of ordinary people; therefore, even Prefect Wanyan, who was not familiar with the case trial, could understand and know the serious consequence as well. Each question raised by Zhang Ding alone seems to be not very important, but the combination tends to form a general conclusion with strong grounding and a great deal of importance.

However, it is still not sufficient to reverse the concluded verdict, because it will be involved with some institutional limitations. After all, this case is "concluded by the predecessor," which has acquired quite a legitimacy in terms of procedure. If Prefect Wanyan allowed the reinvestigation of this case, it could not only violate the procedure but also might be accused of deliberately "fixing someone" in case the retrial of this case couldn't reverse the original verdict. Considering the limitations of science and technology at that time and the passage of time, it could be expected that the probability of finding new and cogent evidence that could sufficiently reverse the original verdict was quite low.[16] Thus, to retry this case, Prefect Wanyan and Zhang Ding had to run a political risk to a certain extent. Actually, Zhang Ding was under great pressures to reinvestigate and try this case later.[17]

---

16 See Chapter 3.
17 "Giving you three days to get through. You are to examine and interrogate, and on no account from the law deviate! If you settle this well, I will write a memorial on your behalf, send it by post horse

Besides, Zhang Ding had no power to make a decision in the issue whether the case should be retried or not. Prefect Wanyan had such a power, but he didn't quite know the professional questions of trial. And this type of unprofessional official generally tended to avoid trouble wherever possible and valued procedure, ideology, and political correctness more. Thus, to persuade the prefect, Zhang Ding couldn't only mention professional affairs but had to cater to the prefect's likes. He must talk politics and use the political and moral ideology which his superior was familiar with, and usually more likely tried to support his advocacy of retrying this case. However, in order to persuade his superior official, Zhang Ding as a clerk couldn't bluntly give a moral lesson to his superior; he should keep sufficient self-respect for his superior. When the right time arrived, the head would "independently" make the decision. Then, by virtue of his criticism of Clerk Xiao, Zhang Ding uttered the following words with the orthodox ideology in the society of that time to the prefect:

> Clerk Xiao, let me tell you: a human life concerns heaven and earth. It is not a mere trifle. The ancients have said, "For a prisoner in jail, a day is longer than three years." Outside, the body suffers; inside, the heart is tortured. He is beaten or caned, driven away or sent into exile. The official who administers punishment must carefully examine the case. Rewards and punishments represent the authority of the state. Joy and anger are the common emotions of man. Do not, because of joy, increase the reward, nor should you, because of anger, increase the punishment. Even when you increase rewards because of joy, you may regret it later. How much more momentous then if you should increase punishments because of anger! How about the wrongful end of a human life!
>
> (Meng, 170)

These words finally moved Prefect Wanyan, who allowed Zhang Ding to reinvestigate and retry this case.

In the retrial, like other officials and clerks, he told Liu Yuniang, "If you speak truthfully, there will be no further trouble. If you speak falsely . . . prepare the large rod!" But he was more concerned with facts, details, and clues. Here is a series of questions Zhang Ding asked Liu Yuniang:

> I won't ask you anything else, but when you left the city, what was your big idea? When he died on entering the gate, what was the cause?
>
> . . .
>
> (As for the business partner of the deceased) Did he not have some new business partner? . . . Or was there an old friend sharing tea and drinks from time past? How did he send letters home? How did he send news?
>
> . . .

---

to the capital, to the emperor, who will handsomely reward and promote you. But if you fail, you who seem to rival Sui He and Lu Jia in eloquence, as you confront those of eminence overturning old cases, seeing relevance – I'll knock right off that cursed monkey head of yours, and you'll taste the bronze blade of my glinting ordinance sword" (Meng, 171).

(As for the messenger) Was he tall or short? Thin or fat? Was he dark or sallow of complexion? With a beard and mustache or without?

. . .

Does he not live east of the small lane, is his family not west of that broad street? What hamlet is he from, what village? What are his surname and his given name?

. . .

Does he sell fried noodles or festival food? Or cut out bolts of cloth for autumn garments? I ask you: on what account did he leave his home? For what reason did he come to town?

(Meng, 174–175)

Undoubtedly, these words serve the playwright's purpose of achieving the dramatic effect, but they still exhibit Zhang Ding's meticulous and thorough investigation as a clerk. It is in this thorough inquiry that Zhang Ding found the new evidence. Finally, the injustice was redressed and the true criminal was caught. Although in the plot of *The Case of the Head Scarf*, the Yuan play was different, Zhang Ding's behavior in the play was almost the same as in *The Moheluo Doll*.

This is only one example. In Yuan plays, there are many examples of such type of capable clerk (but not necessarily honest and upright),[18] and it is not necessary to list them one by one. (But in order to expound another problem, I will cite a negative example later – the example of a corrupt clerk who bent the law for personal gain but was likewise adept in trying cases.) But by and large, as for the administrative personnel described in Yuan plays, the capability of trying cases among officials and clerks is sharply contrasted. It is thereby inferred that the Yuan playwrights seemed to believe that officials were universally inferior to clerks in the capability of trying cases.

Trial as the Special Technical Knowledge

Such a sharp contrast exhibited in Yuan plays has a certain basis of reality and reflects the transference of the real power of local governance at that time "from the hands of magistrates of prefectures and counties to the hands of clerks,"[19] or "power manipulated by clerks," or even "the equal power among clerks and their superiors," which exerted a huge influence on the local administration in the Yuan Dynasty.[20] However, this situation was not an occasional or unique phenomenon in Yuan, and similar situations were rather common in traditional Chinese society.

---

18 For example, Yue Shou in Yue Baichuan's *Iron Crutch Li*.

19 Zhu, Dongrun 朱东润. "Yuan zaju jiqi shidai" 元杂剧及其时代. In *Mingjia jiedu yuanqu* 名家解读元曲 (Jinan: Shandong People's Press, 1999), 37.

20 See Zhang, Jinxian 张金铣. *Yuandai difang xingzheng zhidu yanjiu* 元代地方行政制度研究 (Hefei: Anhui University Press, 2001), 267–269.

In the Ming and Qing dynasties, the private adviser, whose role was similar to the clerk in Yuan, had quite a portion of real power of government. Historians think that although they allegedly "assist officials in governance," they actually "govern for officials" to a large extent.[21] However, to the researchers of legal history, it is not very important to observe this phenomenon; the important thing is that this phenomenon raises a series of profound questions. For instance, generally speaking, all the people hope to make their power bigger (it is a common phenomenon that "better reign in hell than serve in heaven"), but why did the local magistrates in ancient China consciously or unconsciously abandon their power of "administrating justice" that was a matter of life or death, and therefore result in the actual transference of this power? Why did the magistrates of prefectures and counties have no skills and knowledge of trying cases and therefore exhibit their incompetence and stupidity? Why did the clerks possess such skills? The playwrights of Yuan made such a characterization: What is the meaning of related jurisprudential theory and practice?

Contemporary researches of legal science increasingly show that the knowledge of judicial trials is a practical reason. The so-called practical reason is the multiple inference methods used by people when logic and science are not sufficient to firmly support practical and ethical choices. The acquisition and application of these methods and skills are connected with the circumstances in which concrete practices and operations take place; they are hard or even almost impossible to be conveyed through words and to be instructed through teaching. Therefore, almost without exception, they must be mastered through practices, and only the practices at great pains might not always have a result or achievement.[22] Evidence shows that the playwrights of Yuan had a certain understanding of such features of judicial knowledge and even showed sympathy toward clerks in some plays to a certain degree.[23] The playwright of *The Case of the Head Scarf* once stated the features of a clerk's knowledge through the mouth of Zhang Ding, the main character of the play:

> It is not an easy job for us, the clerks. Generally speaking, there are eight things of legal matters you must know. What are they then? The first is the writing; the second is the abacus; the third is the written complaint; the fourth is the weapon; the fifth is the legal regulations; the sixth is the script; the seventh is the copying, and the eighth is the behaviors. There are two sentences

---

21 Li, Qiao 李乔. *Zhongguo de shiye* 中国的师爷 (Beijing: The Commercial Press International, 1995), 4. Also see Gao, Huanyue 高浣月. *Qingdai xingming muyou yanjiu* 清代刑名幕友研究 (Beijing: China University of Politics and Law Press, 2000), esp. Chapter 2.

22 Posner. *The Problems of Jurisprudence*, Chapter 2, 3. The feature of judicial knowledge also explains why "private advisers" in the Ming and Qing dynasties were from the same origin and formed the network by blood relations, geography, and business, while their utility was similar to the clerks' in the traditional administration of justice.

23 For example, Zhang Gui, the judicial inspector who oversaw the Six Bureaus in *The Wife-Snatcher*, and Yue Shou, the capable clerk in *Iron Crutch Li*.

beside the desk. One step hell, one step heaven. Three thousand romantic poems of Li Bai pale in comparison with two hundred essays of Han Yu!

I used to be in charge of indictment, now a new mission is waiting for me. Running in and out of the office, I diligently attend to my work, and never make an error in public and private affairs. I put the files in the right order. When I invite the new lord to write down his court decision, I firstly present the escort paper, then the arrest paper.

(Sun, 674)

In the Yuan play *Iron Crutch Li*, through the mouth of a capable clerk, Yue Shou, who took bribes, similar words were uttered, which could serve as verification:

How can you know us, the clerks after all? With the low social status and meager income and property, I don't know how to till the land, but just rely on criminal punishments, flogging, imprisonment, forced labor and hanging.

It occurs to me the robber sent here several days ago. His filthy money changes his fate under my writing brush. The deducted stroke of my brush can sever the criminal liability, while the added stroke can let the accessory be the principal criminal. This straight writing brush that dictates the right or wrong is more ferocious than the knife that kills people for money. With more concerns for the private interests, less cares for the justice, it can imprison any innocent person. Has it ever been in light of God's will? They just make the empty promise and restrict the mass's activities to a designated sphere.[24]

There is another anonymous clerk in *The Unidentified Corpse*:

My writing brush can let people die instantly. . . . My writing brush is sharper than the knife.

In these words, playwrights at least summarized three features of the work of clerks, although this summarization might not be complete. First, their work was very negligible, yet hardly done well without long-term practice or special training. Second, their work had the great importance of practice, which affected other people's life and property, and decided whether others went up to heaven or dropped down to hell: "The deducted stroke of my brush can sever the criminal responsibility, while the added stroke can let the accessory be the principal criminal." Third, their work had quite a low status in the political system of traditional Chinese society, which was usually affiliated with officials and just the work of running errands.

Because of the first and the third features, the knowledge and skills concerning trials not only had no status in traditional Chinese society but also were hard to

---

24 Yue, Baichuan 岳佰川. "Lv Dongbin du tieguaili yue" 吕洞宾度铁拐李岳. In *Yuanqu xuan* 元曲选, 491.

accumulate. No one would specifically impart them, and the intellectuals would not study them unless they had no alternative choice,[25] because these capabilities were so-called skills of "official pettifogger" and "insignificant skills despised by the heroic men" without great prospects. In the meantime, these skills were not taught in the traditional education system, and they couldn't be taught as well. To acquire such a skill through other means, a long-term investment must be needed. As for the second feature, since this skill was involved with "one step hell, one step heaven" and affected other people's life and property, it might be possible to accordingly pervert the justice for personal gain in this work. The reason why there were so few truly corrupt officials in Yuan plays but always stupid or excessive officials and lots of corrupt clerks might not be accidental.

This phenomenon can be interpreted from sociology and economics. On the one hand, as mentioned earlier, to become a clerk proficient in judicial affairs, one needs a large quantity of personal investment, but the clerk has a low position and social status even without a fixed income and expectations for personal promotion. If clerks want to increase returns on their investment, they can only resort to fraudulent practices for personal gain. Since they are in a position of great responsibility, their knowledge and skills enable them to have the chance, the possibility, and the convenient channels to get rich through other means. Since society actually is in great need of this type of knowledge, while there are a few persons with such skills, the real (monopoly) market price (the earning from corruption) of their work is much higher than their nominal market price (income). Because of the features of such knowledge and the lack of efficient supervision in traditional society (being restricted by information and the finance in those days), even if they pervert justice for bribes, it is still very hard to be discovered by others. Even if they are discovered and removed from their posts, the cost is still very low. For them, "permanent dismissal from the service" is not a big deal. Besides, as clerks, they almost will never have a promising future. The social exchange value of their reputation is lower as well. Therefore, in terms of history, for magistrates of prefectures and counties, the possibility of their perverting the law for corruption is much lower than the clerks'.[26] It is not because the former has the higher moral standard, but the opportunity cost of their corruption is too high in terms of economics. This cost not only includes the fixed income but also the social status, the reputation of the clan

---

25 "After the imperial examination was prevalent in the Tang Dynasty, the status of low-ranking clerks in prefectures and counties was much lower. . . . This traditional idea dissuaded some Confucian scholars from taking the post of clerk in the Yuan Dynasty." See Deng, Shaoji, chiefly ed. 邓绍基. *Yuandai wenxue shi* 元代文学史, 11–12. This point is also manifested in Yuan plays. For example, in *The Unidentified Corpse*, Yang Xiezu had to study with clerks, yet his mother said, "Never study with those clerks. You should redouble your efforts in study to acquire an official rank. If you succeed, you will be a high-ranking official; if not, just be a poor scholar." Wang, Zhongwen 王仲文. "Jiu xiaozi xianmu burenshi" 救孝子贤母不认尸. In *Yuanqu xuan* 元曲选, 757.

26 "'If a palace graduate takes bribes, he acts like a fornicator from a good family; if a clerk is honest and upright, he is like a prostitute preserving chastity.' . . . In the eyes of people of that time, this metaphor was quite appropriate." Yan, Changke 颜长珂. "Yuan zaju zhong de liyuan xingxiang" 元杂剧中的吏员形象. In *Yuanqu tongrong shang* 元曲通融上, 710.

family, and official career. In traditional China, "the rich are inferior to the noble" after all. Such a discrimination of status brings forth different trade-off formulae of costs and benefits for officials and clerks.

Despite this, scholars generally will not choose to become clerks because of low social status, low monetary income, and unpromising political future; but the most important thing is that even if the income obtained by fraud for personal gain is high, it is riddled with uncertainty and many risks. If there are other avenues of acquiring official position and wealth, which are comparatively convenient with greater benefits, intellectuals will choose them.

Even at that time, there were other avenues of acquiring official position and wealth. In traditional Chinese society, the mainstream ideology consistently emphasized politics,[27] and the moral essays of that time were "romantic poems." The selection and examination of officials were mainly based on such a political standard. In the Yuan Dynasty, it was even said to "use song writing to assess the merit of scholars," probably for the sake of winning over the intellectuals of the Han nationality.[28] Although this saying is controversial,[29] at least in the Tang Dynasty, there was the practice of selecting scholars by their poems and essays.[30]

To use "romantic poems" as the standard of selecting and examining officials is not only because of political correctness but also other reasons. One of the important reasons is the judicial knowledge and skills of practical reason are hard to be examined (please remember that the practical reason is not expressed by written words, but the actions).[31] If the examination is truly necessary, the cost will be very high and hard to standardize (therefore, the examiner can easily cheat). The examination of "romantic poems" has a relatively lower cost and is more standardized, which *seems* to be fairer. However, once the standard of selecting officials is established, it has the orientation utility; it will naturally stimulate those seeking official positions (not in the derogatory sense) to pay attention to "the scholarship," "the politics," the capability of expression in utterance and written words, and how to utter abundant words and propositions with political correctness such as "loving common people," "honesty and uprightness," "diligence," and "justice" in a proper way, while those concrete and trivial trial skills and knowledge are neglected. It will usher in two guiding utilities for officials in two aspects. On the one hand, generally speaking, a large number of persons with relatively higher intelligence in society tend to participate in the competition for moral essays; as a result, consequently, in the intelligent quality, those concretely handling judicial affairs are generally inferior to the officials

27 See Chapter 6.

28 Zang, Jinshu 臧晋叔. "Yuanqu xuanxu" 元曲选序; "Xu er" 序二. In *Yuanqu xuan* 元曲选, 3.

29 For example, Zhou, Miaozhong 周妙中. "He tan zhengbi xiansheng shangque yuandai shifou yiququshi de wenti" 和谭正壁先生商榷元代是否以曲取士的问题. In *Yuanqu tongrong* shang 元曲通融上, 420.

30 Quoted in Lu, Xun 鲁迅. *Qiejieting zawen erji* 且介亭杂文二集 (Beijing: People's Literature, 1995), 106.

31 Posner. *The Problems of Jurisprudence*, esp. Chapter 2, 3.

selected from scholars. On the other hand, the winners of the competition for moral essays, namely the future governmental officials, usually severely lack trial knowledge and skills. Because they haven't gone through the professional training or practice and lack the capability of effectively trying cases in reality, even if these officials themselves believe in the political ideology of that time and practice what is preached to love common people through diligent work and enforce the law strictly, they can't do that. Once they encounter a slightly complex case, they can't fulfill their promises at the practical level. It is not that they don't want to do it, but they really can't do it. This point is evidently reflected in Yuan plays. Many stupid or excessive officials who are criticized in plays or other officials who do not have the capability of trying criminal and civil cases are mostly "passing the palace examination in the early age, and being promoted repeatedly," or "studying Confucian classics in the young age," or "studying books from my youth."[32]

Some persons with relatively weak intelligent competence have to become clerks at the government and handle a large quantity of concrete routine affairs. Although these clerks haven't read many classic books, because of the long-term engagement with "the administration of justice," they actually master the specific knowledge and skills of such social governance. Because such persons possess the actual competence and affect the actual role and power layout of officials and clerks in the system of "the administration of justice," officials have to rely on clerks, which reflects the change of clerks from "assisting officials to govern" to "governing for officials" and even "the equal power among clerks and their superiors."[33]

If we return to investigate the previously mentioned stories, plays, characters, and dialogues from this perspective, we can more patently observe this issue. It not only existed in the Yuan Dynasty but also existed in ancient Chinese society. For example, in the story of the filial daughter-in-law of Donghai in the Han Dynasty, the prison clerk Mr. Yu doubted the case and persuaded the prefect. Mr. Yu reached the judgement that proved to be correct later from such a fact that "this woman had provided for her mother-in-law for ten years," not from the concept of "filial piety." Although the essay didn't mention why the prefect didn't follow the advice of Mr. Yu (perhaps for the sake of judicial independence, or at least it looks to be so), one probable explanation is that the prefect *started with the Confucian doctrines*, which was the fundamental principle of "constitution," and wanted to defend "the filial piety." He was the good official living in a world that consisted of concepts, legal articles, doctrines, and principles; however, to govern a state or prefecture, principles and doctrines are needed, while the more important thing is to understand the facts.

---

32 For example, Dou Tianzhang in *The Injustice to Dou E*, Wanyan in *The Case of the Head Scarf*, and *The Moheluo Doll*, and Han Qi (he wrongly blamed Yue Shou to a certain extent) in *Iron Crutch Li*.

33 Zhang. 张金铣. *Yuandai difang xingzheng zhidu yanjiu* 元代地方行政制度研究, 268–269.

It is also exhibited in Guo Yuzhi, who was "determined to be an honest official" in *Fifteen Strings of Cash*, and Wanyan, the prefect in *The Case of the Head Scarf*, and *The Moheluo Doll* as well. The opening remark of Guo Yuzhi is as follows:

> The painstaking study for ten years is completed; in my early years, the honorary success at the palace examination is accomplished. The spring scenery of Heyang is at my command, the official rank of thousands of *li* is unfolded before my view.
>
> I am Guo Yuzhi, the Magistrate of Shanyang County. Ten years of hardship are rewarded by the grace and glory. I swear not to take any bribe, and vow not to practice any favoritism. Upon my assumption of the post, I demand the antithetical couplet nailed on the columns of the Hall, which reads "Love the Common People, Enforce the Law Strictly." . . . I am determined to be an honest official. Whenever there is a litigation, I will be indiscriminately level-handed in dispensing justice. After the completion of three-year tenure, I am happy to be commended and promoted to be the official in charge of criminal affairs in Changzhou.
>
> (Zhu, 41)

He was not only bent on being honest and upright with lofty aspirations but also made the marvelous political achievements in the past; however, he was tripped down in the case of 15 strings of cash.

In *The Case of the Head Scarf*, the opening remark of Wanyan is as follows:

> I am a Jurchen of Wanyan lineage. The Wanyans became Wangs, the Puchas became Lis.
>
> I became one of the Top Three Palace Graduates in my early years, and have been repeatedly promoted with quite a good political reputation. Now, I am Prefect of Henan Prefecture. Here in Henan the officials are corrupt and the clerks are crooks, the common people are thickheaded. Our sage emperor bestowed me with the ordinance sword and the golden tablet, so that I can execute first and report to the throne later. I am sent to investigate the records here, and accordingly deal with the affairs. My only purpose is to eliminate excessive officials and corrupt clerks, and strictly govern those stubborn and stupid commoners.
>
> (Sun, 673)

He not only had the wish and ideal to uphold justice for the common people but also knew the corruption of officials at that time, therefore he claimed:

> Legal articles eliminate excessive officials, explicit punishments remove the corruption. If my authority is questioned, try my ordinance sword and golden tablet.
>
> (Sun, 683)

However, the core of the judicial trial as a practical activity doesn't lie in whether you could memorize "legal articles" and "explicit punishments" (all of them could be found in the related formulae of legal ordinances); the problem is to which cases these "legal articles" are applied and on whom these "explicit punishments" are inflicted. The latter point might not be done well even for those who read more classic books with more education and better personal integrity. The first thing when trying a case is that you must understand facts, find facts, and have the wish and capability of knowing facts. It is because of this point that Prefect Wanyan nearly fell into the snare set by corrupt Clerk Xiao if there were not the earnest persuasion and assistance from Clerk Zhang Ding.

Even Dou Tianzhang, who redressed the injustice for his daughter, was not an exception. After selling Dou E to Mother Cai as the child daughter-in-law, Dou Tianzhang "arrived at the capital" and passed the imperial examination. But when he read the file of Dou E, his first response is:

> The first record I read the prisoner happens to *have the same name as mine.* To poison one's father-in-law is one of *the ten unpardonable crimes.* So there are people bearing the same name as me who have no respect for the law. *This case has already been concluded,* I am not going to read any more.
>
> (Guan, 1977: 146)

What did he observe? He first observed that the accused had "the same name" as his; second, to poison one's father-in-law was one of "the ten unpardonable crimes"; third, this case had already been "concluded." All of these were the facts concerning ethics (the same name), morality (ten unpardonable crimes), and politics (the concluded case), and he didn't investigate the facts and evidence in the case. Only if we recall the facts Zhang Ding observed in *The Moheluo Doll* in the verdict concerning Liu Yuniang and the questions he raised can we notice the diametrical difference of questions with which officials and clerks were concerned in trial. The different concerns might bring forth quite divergent results to the defendant and plaintiff in each type of cases.

Maybe someone will criticize me for this unfair comparison, because they are two works with different playwrights. I admit that Guan Hanqing's description of Dou Tianzhang had no likelihood of willingly indicating Dou's incompetence, but more likely used these words to present Dou's integrity, his moral personality, and his "awareness of the rule of law," since he didn't show consideration for the person with the same name and abominated "the ten unpardonable crimes" and respected the concluded case. But the question just lies here. Because Dou Tianzhang is "an honest official," a good official that Guan Hanqing strove to portray, we could more clearly observe what question the honest official (in the eyes of Guan Hanqing and even ordinary people at that time) was really concerned with (if Guan Hanqing used Dou Tianzhang to "represent" the honest officials) or what question the honest official should be concerned with (if Guan Hanqing used Dou Tianzhang to convey his own ideals). Therefore, this point sufficiently helps us to understand the state of mind of officials or society regarding trials at that time.

If this point is valid, then these playscripts have other meanings that playwrights unlikely harbored, but in our eyes, they are implied. That is, at least in the society of the Yuan Dynasty, people (by virtue of the playwrights' expression) had intuitively sensed the necessity of professional trials and the related knowledge; they had sensed that the administrators at the middle and low levels directly governing Chinese society then were in desperate need of such professionally technical knowledge that must be rooted in "the practice of administrating justice"; therefore, these officials couldn't effectively fulfill the governing liability of case trials; they had felt the personal pains because of the deficiency of this skill. Besides, through artistic images, these playwrights unconsciously showed that in the society of that time, there were no such practical knowledge and skills at all, and the practical knowledge of case trials had been generated out of social life. But this knowledge was more in the hands of some clerks at the lower level who often specifically tried the cases. They had acquired judicial knowledge in the relatively professionalized activity of "trial" practice. Hence, these plays also reflect the uniqueness of knowledge production of trial technology and the demand for the social division of labor from such knowledge production. Certainly, these playwrights didn't present, and even had no likelihood of presenting, the proposition of a political institution that a detached, independent judicial department and the related institutions in the whole set be established. Even if this proposition is presented, on the whole, the condition of social material life and the development of standards of science and technology in those days might not possess the possibility and necessity of establishing them. However, in presenting such a real predicament, these playwrights still leave some source materials for the jurisprudential theory for the later generations to reflect on. These plays enable us to observe that when there wasn't a detached, independent, and professionalized judicial organization, when a society only emphasized the political ideology of "romantic poems" and "moral essays," what kind of pains people in this society endured and what kind of miserable life they had! Being ruled by such a knowledge system and hegemony, how incompetent officials were! Besides, such incompetence isn't mainly a problem concerning the personal moral integrity of officials, but more reflects the major flaw of this institution.

"The Magistrate Is Pure as Water, the Clerk Is White as Dough"[34]

There is an indication that in some Yuan plays, playwrights have touched on the conclusion of the previous section, namely, that because of the lack of trial skills, officials not only fail to fulfil their responsibilities but also fail to effectively supervise clerks, which thereby result in the overt abuse of power and bending the law for personal gain among some clerks. In the meantime, these plays even touch on some deeper questions, such as whether reason is sufficient to guarantee its proper

---

34 Hanqing, Meng. "The Moheluo Doll," in *The Columbia Anthology of Yuan Drama*, ed. C. T. Hsia, Wai-Yee Li and George Kao, 162.

application and whether the understanding of trial skills and knowledge is sufficient to guarantee a fair trial.

As mentioned earlier, in Yuan plays, not only capable clerks like Zhang Ding had remarkable trial competence and technologies, but also some greedy and evil clerks likewise possessed the marvelous trial competence; more astonishingly, the number of the latter was not small.[35] It is totally out of the expectation of many contemporary jurists who believe that morality rules or professionalization can prevent judicial corruption. Some clerks could turn a wrong verdict into the make-believe administration of justice; officials in charge and ordinary people failed to spot its inherent flaws. Therefore, through their artistic images, these plays show that even the possession of such practical trial knowledge and skills is insufficient to guarantee the fairness of the verdict. On the contrary, if being manipulated, the mastery of such knowledge and skills can even cause the greater unjust case. The most prominent instance is *The Chalk Circle*, and here is the outline of the story.

Being a prostitute because of family poverty, Zhang Haitang was married to Magnate Ma as a concubine after leaving prostitution and gave birth to a son. The wife of Magnate Ma committed adultery with Clerk Zhao, and they worked together to poison Ma in order to have the chance of marrying publicly and seizing the family property. The wife framed Zhang Haitang for killing Magnate Ma with the adulterer. In order to take the whole family property and prevent the son of Zhang Haitang from inheriting, the wife falsely claimed that this son was born by her and bribed neighbors and the midwife as her witnesses. Su Shu, the prefect of Zhengzhou, was not versed in the trial and transferred the case to Clerk Zhao for trial, the adulterer of Ma's wife. Naturally, Zhang Haitang confessed to false charges under torture and was convicted as the criminal. The appeal was presented to Bao Zheng. Bao raised suspicions on this case and then ordered a circle with lime powder be sprinkled, inside which the son stayed; Bao Zheng ordered Zhang Haitang and the wife to hold each arm of the boy in opposite directions and waited to see who could pull the boy out of the circle. Zhang Haitang dearly loved her son and didn't want to break his arm by force. In accordance with human nature, Bao Zheng judged that Zhang Haitang was the boy's own mother. He made a further meticulous investigation and identified the true criminals who received severe punishments.

I will discuss the trial methods of Bao Zheng in the next chapter. I hereby only intend to analyze the trial procedure of Clerk Zhao in the play. At the very beginning, Clerk Zhao intended to frame Zhang Haitang; yet in the eyes of those who

---

35 A scholar once pointed out that there were two features of "corrupt officials" in Yuan plays: the first was their greed, the second was their incompetence, and "nearly behind each corrupt official was there a capable clerk who was likewise mean but more astute." The author didn't make the explicit statement, which might be paraphrased from the research of foreign scholars. See Sun, Ge; Chen, Yangu; Li, Yijin 孙歌、陈燕谷、李益津. *Guowai zhongguo gudian xiqu yanjiu* 国外中国古典戏曲研究 (Nanjing: Jiangsu Education, 1999), 226. It should be pointed out that this summarization is not accurate; it is somewhat exaggerated to describe these officials as corrupt ones, yet their incompetence is absolutely certain.

didn't know the inside story, Clerk Zhao was not only familiar with the law and procedure but also fair-minded. Clerk Zhao first asked who was the defendant and the plaintiff. After the plaintiff, the wife of Ma, presented the lawsuit, he threatened the defendant with torture as the routine practice of trial. But Clerk Zhao didn't immediately resort to torture, yet allowed the defendant to "reply," which seemed quite fair, reasonable, and composed. In the reply of Zhang Haitang, Clerk Zhao insinuated and guided people to reach the wrong conclusion with a series of digressions. Here are the questions raised by Clerk Zhao to Zhang Haitang:

> "Speak, speak."
>
> . . .
>
> "You poisoned your husband. This is one of the Ten Repugnant Crimes."
>
> . . .
>
> "What kind of family do you come from? How did you marry that Magnate Ma? Explain it to me."
>
> . . .
>
> "So, it turns out that you were a whore and not a fine person at all. Even if you were taken into Magnate Ma's house, did you ever have a son or daughter?"
>
> . . .
>
> "Who else is in your family? Do you still have any contact with them?"
>
> (Li, 260–261)

Quite similar to Zhang Ding, Clerk Zhao raised all these questions in a careful way, which showed his concerns with details, and were not in a vicious tone. In asking about the family members of Zhang Haitang, Clerk Zhao seemed to show a certain kindness. However, in his questions, he emphasized Zhang Haitang's record of being a prostitute and unconsciously belittled the personality of the defendant, which also hinted that such a woman did have the likelihood of "adultery."

Zhang Haitang then proceeded to bring up witnesses to prove the boy was her own; Clerk Zhao presently brought up all the witnesses mentioned by Zhang and asked them to serve as a witness at court. The first witness Zhang mentioned was the neighbors. Zhao allowed them to be witnesses, but their testimony was disadvantageous to Zhang. Zhang thereby turned to accuse the witnesses she herself proposed. Zhang then asked to let the midwife and the shaver of the fetal hair serve as witnesses at court. Zhao also allowed it; their testimony was still not favorable to Zhang. Zhang turned to accuse the witnesses she herself proposed again. The repeated "self-contradiction" easily reinforced the people's suspicions of Zhang Haitang step by step. Finally, Zhang Haitang proposed to let the boy of five years old make the identification at court. Clerk Zhao didn't turn it down. The boy identified Zhang as his own mother; since the boy was too small after all, his testimony was evidently hard to be accepted as a whole. Clerk Zhao then maintained that the boy's testimony was invalid: "we should take this group of people as the main witnesses" (Li, 264). Today, the evidence detrimental to Zhang Haitang would be quite sufficient; hence, even if Clerk Zhao abandoned this evidence, it would be very hard for ordinary people to doubt what a "tricky deal" Clerk Zhao had made.

The application of two trial technologies must be indicated here. The first is that Clerk Zhao let witnesses proposed by Zhang Haitang to appear at court one by one. Clerk Zhao might well let all the witnesses appear at court at the same time and make the testimony at one go. But he didn't. Why? Because in doing thus, it would not only reinforce the claim of Ma's wife twice, but also result in the impression of Zhang Haitang's *consistent* self-contradiction. People will easily link this impression with Zhang's record of being a prostitute and fundamentally suspect Zhang's personality and moral character. Therefore, although the number of witnesses appearing at court is not added, the demonstration effects achieved by the witnesses at court at one go or either one by one will be very different. Especially considering the boy's appearance at court as the witness later, such a sequence arrangement will be more necessary for Clerk Zhao.

The second is that Clerk Zhao gratified all the requests concerning witnesses proposed by Zhang Haitang, including approval to let the boy appear at court as the witness. The appearance of the boy at court was evidently disadvantageous to Ma's wife and Clerk Zhao. But in terms of trial procedure, to let the boy appear at court would be more beneficial for Clerk Zhao to fulfill his purpose than not to do so. Because if Zhao didn't let the boy appear at court, in the eyes of his superior and common people, it was Zhao who violated the litigation procedure, which was unreasonable, and even probably aroused suspicions regarding Zhao's tricky deals. Zhang Haitang could use it as a reason to lodge the appeal as well, which would more easily attract the attention of the superiors. Therefore, the malpractice of Clerk Zhao would be easily exposed. To let the boy appear at court and reject the evidence in light of "the principle of preponderance of evidence" exhibited Clerk Zhao's impartiality of handling the case and his utmost tolerance and patience and achieved his purpose as well. More importantly, at this time, Clerk Zhao could legally and silently utilize fraudulent practices for personal gain, bring the extralegal malpractices inside the procedure, and fully use the discretionary power of officials allowed in the legal procedure to more effectively make a falsification. Both two points are not observed and used by ordinary people; only those who are quite familiar with the trial procedure and see through the loophole of the law and the procedure can effectively exploit such legal advantages.

Until all pieces of evidence were adduced, interrogation by torture could begin according to the procedure. Naturally, Zhang Haitang confessed to false charges under torture. In the whole course of the trial, Clerk Zhao behaved composedly and seemed to have no impartiality and fully perform the duty in a strict way. The reason he could do this lay in his proficient mastery and adroit application of trial knowledge and skills.

Evidently, the playwright didn't think the trial with a professional and procedural orientation was sufficient to guarantee a fair trial, which has already been an important inspiration for us. However, from the perspective of the whole play, the playwright didn't only tell us a moral conclusion and didn't make the prescription to dissolve "judicial corruption" just as many jurists in China of today have done in journals and newspapers: the riddance of corrupt officials, the reinforcement of supervision and education, and the improvement of ideological awareness, etc. On the contrary, when the playwright put Prefect Su Shun and Clerk Zhao together – the former was called by the local common people "Equivocal Su" since "Even though I hold office, I know nothing of the law" (Li, 258) but was not corrupt; the latter was proficient in laws and decrees but bent the law for corruption; he had raised a more in-depth question: How could Clerk Zhao still make such an unjust case on the scene with meticulous care under the circumstance that Prefect Su Shun presently supervised the trial? In this sense, the play reiterates the conclusion of the previous section, namely, that even if an honest magistrate lacks basic trial knowledge and skills, he himself not only fails in trying cases justly, reasonably, and effectively, but also fails in effectively supervising and managing his subordinate clerks; on the contrary, he can create the greater possibility for his clerks to bend the law for personal benefit and even unconsciously become the shield for their malpractices and corruptions.

This is not just my summarization; actually, a passage of doggerel that repeatedly appears in several Yuan plays has clearly pointed out the crux of the problem:

> The magistrate is pure as water,
> The clerk is white as dough.
> Mix water and dough into batter:
> Result, a lump of messy glue!
> (Meng, 162)

Perhaps, it should give greater admonition to us!

5   Honest Officials and the Mode of Rule by Man in Judicature

From two dimensions of science and technology and the institutional division of labor, Chapters 3 and 4 analyze the trial institution of "administrating justice" in ancient China, in which the variable of humans (judges) isn't taken into consideration; instead the limitation of human capability caused by material factor is more emphasized. This analysis is obviously inconsistent with the path of judicial reform in the China of to-day that emphasizes the improvement of judges' personal qualities and capabilities,[1] and it is also against the political tradition that accentuates the importance of humans in China: "Let there be the men and the government will flourish; but without the men, their government decays and ceases."[2] Traditional detective plays or the plays of honest officials always characterize some moral paragons of officials with integrity and principles. The redressing of injustice is usually connected with an incorruptible, diligent, clever, and wise official. For example, the opening remark of Bao Zheng, the honest and upright rescriptor-in-waiting in *The Chalk Circle*, claimed:

> Because I keep a mind of purity and uprightness and hold firm and fast to integrity, I have always busied myself with the state's affairs, never sham-ing myself by grubbing after profit or personal gain. I keep company only with the loyal and filial and never mix with slandering toadies. . . . I seek out excessive officials and corrupt clerks, alleviate injustice to the hundred surnames and right their wrongs.
>
> (Li, 273–274)

This type of line frequently appears in Yuan plays concerning Bao Zheng and other detective plays concerning honest officials. Such mindset that the hope of a wise trial is heaped on the incorruptible officials is passed down today, no matter in the comments on Yuan plays[3] or in the daily life of common people, even in popu-lar literary works or films and television shows of today.

---

1 I have made a meticulous analysis in other articles, and I present "an institutional path" for this point. See Zhu, Suli 朱苏力. "Panjueshu de beihou" 判决书的背后. *Faxue yanjiu* 法学研究, no. 3 (2001).
2 Legge, James, trans. *The Chinese Classics: The Doctrine of the Mean*, vol. 1 (Hong Kong: Hong Kong University Press, 1960), 405.
3 For example, the comments on *The Injustice to Dou E*; see Note 10 of Chapter 3.

DOI: 10.4324/9781003615606-8

Undoubtedly, the honesty of officials is very important for a fair trial, especially strict law enforcement. But the question is: How great is the utility of honest officials after all? To what extent can a judicial system rely on honest officials? Besides, what is the meaning of "honesty" for honest officials? If it is not treated well, we will return to the moral path of criticizing the judiciary in two previous chapters again and mainly attribute some problems in trials to the issue of the personal moral character of officials. It is a vicious circular argument into which people easily fall, but it is not inevitable. Therefore, it is necessary to have a further discussion on the role of an individual, especially an honest official, in the traditional "administration of justice" and other related issues.

Two Types of Honest Officials

At the beginning of Part II, I distinguish two types of detective plays in the Yuan Dynasty. One type is more about law enforcement, namely the detective plays of "suppressing the despots and bullies." In these plays, the so-called conflict between honest and corrupt officials is actually mainly the issue of political force or power balance. In facing the power, are you courageous to fairly try the case and strictly enforce the law in accordance with definite rules? Will you play the jackal to the tiger, or uphold the justice for common people? Will you make a compromise like a conformist hypocrite, or keep to principles and not yield to pressure? In this sphere, the personal moral character of officials undoubtedly works, and even often plays a decisive role. But there is another type of detective play, namely the so-called plays "solving disputed cases and reversing unjust verdicts." The main issue in these plays is the trial of a difficult case or the redressing of injustice. In the latter type of plays, villains, evildoers, and scoundrels also appear, and "excessive officials and corrupt clerks" are often mentioned in the scripts; the honest officials in the plays are morally courageous, upright, diligent, and exceptionally wise and care about the common people. It seems that the personal morality of officials is very important for the judgment. The reason why honest officials successfully tried the difficult cases, in the impression of audiences, is often because of their sense of justice. But is it really so?

Sometimes, impressions are not reliable, because a rather broad concept usually blurs some important distinctions and thereby reinforces a certain existing impression of humans. We need to make more meticulous analysis of the image of honest officials and clerks in Yuan plays.

Let me first presume that any good trial requires the adjudicator's personal qualities in two most basic dimensions: morality (fairness, integrity, uprightness, caring for the common people, and diligent governance on the basis of liability) and competence (wisdom, sensitivity, incisiveness, and adeptness at fraternizing with others under some circumstances). If the permutation and combination are made in accordance with two dimensions, a matrix is formed. Then in light of the deeds of officials and clerks in Yuan plays and *Fifteen Strings of Cash*, I classify them as follows (Table 5.1).

Table 5.1 The Classification of Officials and Clerks in "the Administration of Justice" in Ancient China

	Honest	*Greedy*
astute	Bao Zheng (*The Chalk Circle*, etc.), Zhang Ding (*The Moheluo Doll, The Case of the Head Scarf*), Wang Xiuran (*The Unidentified Corpse*), Kuang Zhong (*Fifteen Strings of Cash*)	Clerk Zhao (*The Chalk Circle*) Clerk Xiao (*The Moheluo Doll*) Anonymous Clerk (*The Unidentified Corpse*) Zhao Zhongxian (? *The Case of the Head Scarf*)
mediocre	Taowu, Dou Tianzhang (*The Injustice to Dou E*), Wanyan (*The Moheluo Doll, The Case of the Head Scarf*), Su Shun (*The Chalk Circle*), Gong Dezhong (*The Unidentified Corpse*), County Magistrate of Henan Prefecture (*The Moheluo Doll*), Henan Prefect (*The Case of the Head Scarf*), Guo Yuzhi, Zhou Chen (*Fifteen Strings of Cash*)	

This classification is highly formalized, and people may have different opinions as for the classification of some officials and clerks. It is estimated that there will be no dispute for two columns, namely the column of "honest and astute" with Bao Zheng as the representative and the column of "greedy and astute" with Clerk Zhao as the representative. But there will be relatively more controversies on the column of "honest but mediocre" with Prefect Taowu who sentenced Dou E to death in *The Injustice to Dou E*.[4] Dou Tianzhang appeared on the stage with the image of an honest official; a similar character is Prefect Wanyan in *The Case of the Head Scarf* and *The Moheluo Doll*. Prefect Taowu in Chuzhou and Prefect Su Shun in Zhengzhou of *The Chalk Circle* are obviously presented as stupid officials and are negative characters.[5] Besides, because Taowu, Su Shun, and others regarded the complainants as the people on whom they relied for living and were eager to charge

4 For the literature as far as I know, only Huang Ke once incisively pointed out that there was not a big difference between Dou Tianzhang and Taowu from a certain perspective. Huang, Ke 黄克. *Guan hanqing xiju renwu lun* 关汉卿戏剧人物论 (Beijing: People's Literature, 1984), 53–70. Yet his viewpoint was criticized. Hua, Shizhong 华世忠. "Dou e yuan disizhe xiyi" 窦娥冤第四折析疑. *Fuyang shiyuan xuebao* 阜阳师院学报, no. 1 (1986).

5 It should be noted that it is not my summarization which has been manifested in the classification of roles in the playscript. In the play, these characters are indicated as the "jing" role; but it is impossible for them to be the upright and vigorous role with "a darkish painted face" – they belong to the "chou" role. This point also applies to Dou Tianzhang and Wanyan.

"the litigation cost," in the hearts of contemporary Chinese audiences or readers, they seem to be the officials with moral flaws. Therefore, it seems unreasonable to classify Prefect Taowu and Dou Tianzhang who redressed the injustice of Dou E into the same column.[6]

I must explain this classification away. It is true that Dou Tianzhang and Wanyan really appeared as honest officials in the plays and were positive characters. But it is mainly because the final trial results can be accepted by us; the reason why they didn't make wrong verdicts and instead became "the honest officials" of redressing the unjust cases is mainly not *because* they were honest and upright, nor even because they were superbly intelligent, but because of a series of external conditions and factors. Dou Tianzhang could redress the unjust case of Dou E; this was because of the information provided by the ghost of wronged Dou E (including supernatural evidence after the death of Dou E) and the father-and-daughter relationship between them (this relationship enabled him to more easily believe in Dou E's words and regard it as the evidence for the case trial). The so-called stupid official Taowu had no likelihood of possessing such information and condition in deciding the case of Dou E. If he had, Taowu would certainly not make the wrong verdict. (How could Taowu sentence his daughter to death as a criminal in haste like this? If he sentenced his daughter to death, even if it was a wrong verdict, Taowu would perhaps be considered "the honest official" who placed righteousness above family loyalty.) The successes of Wanyan in *The Case of the Head Scarf* and *The Moheluo Doll* owed to the exceptional intelligence and competence of the capable clerk, Zhang Ding. Without these additional conditions, Dou Tianzhang and Wanyan would repeat the wrong verdicts made by their subordinate or predecessor. It is reasonable to classify Dou Tianzhang and Wanyan as honest but mediocre officials.

On the other hand, although Taowu and Guo Yuzhi of *Fifteen Strings of Cash* appeared on the stage as "negative characters," they didn't show the defect of personal morality in the strict sense, but some characteristics (weaknesses) of ordinary people at least in the plays. Truly, they made the wrong verdicts, but this mistake was not related to corruption in terms of the play plot; they didn't deliberately make these unjust cases, which were mainly caused by the lack of evidence, the incompetence of the trial, and overconfidence.[7] Strictly speaking, Su Shun, the prefect of Zhengzhou in *The Chalk Circle*, should be classified into this category. He didn't resort to fraudulent practices for personal gain and even "supervised" the trial of Clerk Zhao on the scene. His problem lies in the fact that he knew nothing

---

6 But a foreign scholar once made a similar summarization to mine. For example, Peng Jingxi had quite a low opinion of honest officials, including Bao Zheng, and believed that the difference between honest and corrupt officials only lay in a certain moral value that the former claimed to possess. He held that the common ground between the two types of officials was far greater than their difference; for example, both of them heavily relied on their intuitions and resorted to interrogation by torture. See Sun, Ge; Chen, Yangu; Li, Yijin 孙歌、陈燕谷、李益津. *Guowai zhongguo gudian xiqu yanjiu* 国外中国古典戏曲研究 (Nanjing: Jiangsu Education, 1999), 226.

7 Sun, Ge et al. 孙歌等. *Guowai zhongguo gudian xiqu yanjiu* 国外中国古典戏曲研究.

about the trial and appointed and trusted the corrupt clerk. Therefore, if viewed from two dimensions of form in a strict way, my merging of similar items is valid.

If such a classification is valid, this table then verifies some findings of Chapter 4 and exhibits a series of findings that are different or even opposite to popular opinions or our impression of traditional drama. First, in the trial, although there are the factors of corrupt clerks in the unjust cases, the plays more reflect that it is the mediocre judges who lack intelligence and competence and the ensuing manipulation of power by clerks that bring forth these injustices.

Second, although according to each play, the unjust cases are often summarized as the fight between honest and corrupt or excessive officials, the fight between good and evil, what Yuan plays reflect as a whole seems that the unjust cases *basically* had no direct relations to the personal moral characters of officials as adjudicators, but more direct relations to the intelligence and competence of officials. Therefore, if we still insist on the term "honest officials," then "honesty" here should not only be, or even not mainly be, understood as "morally honest" or "upright," but as intelligently and competently "clear" or "sober."

Third, it also shows, although the playwrights of Yuan used to apply the terms of honest and corrupt officials or other moral terms to discuss and analyze the case trial, the layout exhibited in these plays proves that the playwrights were *actually* more concerned with the administration and trial competence of officials. However, they neither applied these concepts nor explicitly put forward such propositions. These artistic images in plays are actually beyond the traditional binary classification of honest and corrupt officials and actually refuse to use the moral dimension (namely the political dimension of that time) as the scale of classifying "good" or "bad" officials and clerks. In terms of the plot, as for the issue of case trials, the correct verdict naturally demands the basic moral character of officials, but the more important thing is their trial competence. In this sense, we can add the dimension of result as well and make the further discrimination for officials within the category of "honest but mediocre" (Table 5.2).

Fourth, if these traditional dramas are used as the sign to measure Chinese folk ideas,[8] we can still observe that the trope of honest officials with moral significance among Chinese people is mainly focused on law enforcement, not for the judicial judgment. Since the good or bad result usually affects playwrights' appraisal of officials and clerks, these plays further reflect that what playwrights (and common

Table 5.2 The Classification of Honest But Mediocre Officials

Honest But Mediocre	Good Result	Dou Tianzhang, Wanyan
	Bad Result	Tao Wu, Su Shun, Gong Dezhong, County Magistrate of Henan Prefecture, Henan Prefect, Guo Yuzhi, Zhou Chen

8 To what extent the traditional drama reflects the ideas of ordinary people is discussed in Chapter 6.

people represented by them) truly care for is the trial result, not the personal integrity of judges. They stress the personal integrity of judges only for the sake of the trial result. This point is totally consistent with their attitudes of not objecting to interrogation by torture by honest officials, yet criticizing the same practice by stupid officials. Hence, we can reach the conclusion that although detective plays have the tendency of strong and rich moralism and intentionalism in the *expression* of ideas, their contents reveal the philosophical tendency of consequentialism and pragmatism.[9]

Fifth, in these plays, the question concerning the trial competence of officials is raised as a general question concerning personal character. It is a mistake of cognition or expression in my opinion, yet such a conversion might still have this meaning, namely, since the consequence of officials' fulfilling their duties affects others, their competence is involved with special ethics of political liability. Accordingly, to regard it as "morality," it has positive significance and legitimacy in terms of a social function.[10] Such a conversion reflects that society has higher moral demands for officials than it does for ordinary people. Even if officials neither take bribes nor make malpractices, only if the consequence of fulfilling the duty is bad, society will unleash a certain moral lash, including the fictional or/and exaggerated moral defects of officials. Hence, although all the local magistrates cared for the collection of litigation costs in those days, only the same deeds of Taowu became "greedy" and only because he wrongly killed Dou E. Although all the officials laid stress on official ranks, yet only Guo Yuzhi's pursuit for official ranks was ridiculed and only because he misjudged the innocent. Although all the officials set up the posts of assistants, only Su Shun's doing so ushered in the fall of "judicial power" into others' hands because of his incompetence, and only because his assistant was a corrupt clerk. This is not a question concerning reason or fairness; it is just social psychology and demand. As a result, if both aspects of morality and competence are classified in triplex, the result is Table 5.3.

The previous analysis and Table 5.3 show the conclusion again, namely, in the issue of trying difficult cases, the morality of officials in ancient society actually is not the biggest question – their competence and judgment matter more. Or, to be more exact, the core issue of "administrating justice" that actually existed in society then and was exhibited in Yuan plays is in comparison with common people's demand for the substantive justice of judiciary, and the trial competence of officials is too weak. As for this issue, the solution provided by common people (through the expression of playwrights) is that their competence is expected to be

---

9 This point is consistent with the conclusion of Posner's research in *The Problems of Jurisprudence* that makes an entry from the perspective of judicial personnel. See Posner. *The Problems of Jurisprudence*, esp. Chapter 15. Posner further expounds "the everyday pragmatism," which is non-philosophized and shared by American people. See Posner, Richard A. *Law, Pragmatism, and Democracy* (Cambridge, MA: Harvard University Press, 2003), Chapter 1.

10 It might be the foundation of social psychology for the establishment of "the institution of taking the blame and resigning" for administrators. See Feng, Xiang 冯象. *Zhengfa biji* 政法笔记 (Nanjing: Jiangsu People's Press, 2004), 134–137.

Table 5.3 The Subdivision of Officials

	Honest	Ordinary	Greedy
Astute	Bao Zheng (*The Chalk Circle*, etc.) Zhang Ding (*The Moheluo Doll, The Case of the Head Scarf*) Wang Xiuran (*The Unidentified Corpse*) Kuang Zhong (*Fifteen Strings of Cash*)		Clerk Zhao (*The Chalk Circle*) Clerk Xiao (*The Moheluo Doll*) Anonymous Clerk (*The Unidentified Corpse*) Zhao Zhongxian (? *The Case of the Head Scarf*)
Ordinary (Good Result)	Dou Tianzhang (*The Injustice to Dou E*), Wanyan (*The Moheluo Doll, The Case of the Head Scarf*)		
Mediocre (Bad Result)		Taowu (*The Injustice to Dou E*) Su Shun (*The Chalk Circle*) Gong Dezhong (*The Unidentified Corpse*) County Magistrate of Henan Prefecture (*The Moheluo Doll*) Henan Prefect (*The Case of the Head Scarf*) Guo Yuzhi, Zhou Chen (*Fifteen Strings of Cash*)	

improved through the elevation of the personal moral standard of officials – whether by selecting more honest officials or by improving the personal cultivation of officials – in order to fulfill their responsibility of political governance.

Social expectation always has its own legitimacy and then exerts a pressure on officials. The question is: Can this social expectation and pressure improve officials' competence of judicial trials? Is this pressure really beneficial to the whole judiciary? This chapter attempts to prove that the expectation is insufficiently self-fulfilling on the whole because, basically speaking, the personal trial competence of officials will not be substantially improved because of social expectation or pressure, but will have a marginal improvement at most. Since the talented or outstanding persons are always few and it is hard to have an institutionalized selection with accuracy, even the best judicial system is mainly operated by those with a medium standard of intelligence and morality. Even if there is a gifted talent or moral paragon, he can't play his role in an institutionalized way in the social and historical condition of that time, because any reliable and effective system can only accept (accommodate) a few of them. Even the social expectation and institutionalized pressure of improving officials' personal competence instead would cause the impairment of the overall ability of the whole system if there were not a complete set of refined technologies and institutions (this is the reality of traditional society).

Officials' competence of trying cases, especially those difficult cases, is restricted by social factors (such as the level of science and technology and the standard of social wealth) and institutional factors (such as social division of labor, professionalization, etc.) to a large extent, just as Chapters 3 and 4 have analyzed. In these given social, technical, and institutional conditions, personal factors will also work and even sometimes play a decisive role. Honest officials such as Bao Zheng and Kuang Zhong characterized in plays are the important examples, and personal wisdom or a diligent government seems to function greatly. However, the analysis of the playscripts and the reflection on them will soon prove that such an impression is unreliable.

The specific plays I analyze are *The Chalk Circle* and *Fifteen Strings of Cash*.[11] The choice of these two plays is not only because they all recount the story of an honest official who redresses the injustice, but more importantly, the conduct of the two protagonists of the plays, Bao Zheng and Kuang Zhong, mainly exhibit wisdom and diligent governance, although they have their limitations, with which I am more concerned.

The Limitations of Wisdom

In *The Chalk Circle*, Zhang Haitang was framed and confessed to false charges under torture in the first trial. She was not only sentenced to death, but also her son was taken away by Ma's wife, one of the murderers. The appeal was presented to Bao Zheng, who was sensitive and insightful and held that "An evil woman who has poisoned her husband – that's no rare affair. But to steal a child from the primary wife? Is the child so wonderful that she had to steal him? And there's no lover concretely pointed out. Perhaps there is some injustice in this case" (Li, 274). Bao Zheng thought the first thing was to identify who really gave birth to this boy. He ordered a circle sprinkled with lime powder, inside which the son stayed; Bao Zheng ordered Zhang Haitang and the wife to hold each arm of the boy in the opposite directions and waited to see who could pull the boy out of the circle. Zhang Haitang dearly loved her son and didn't want to break his arm by force. In accordance with human nature, Bao Zheng judged that Zhang Haitang was the boy's own mother. He made a further meticulous investigation and identified the true criminals. Zhang Haitang's injustice was then redressed.

---

11 Zhu, Suchen 朱素臣. *Shiwuguan jiaozhu* 十五贯校注, ed. and annotated by Zhang Yanjin 张燕瑾 and Mi Songyi 弥松颐 (Shanghai: Shanghai Ancient Books, 1983). In 1956, Kunsu Troupe of Zhejiang Province went to Beijing and performed the adapted version of *The Fifteen Strings of Cash*, which made a great stir. For contemporary Chinese, their understanding of this play mainly comes from the adapted version. See Zhu, Suchen 朱素臣. *Kunqu shiwu guan* 昆曲十五贯, ed. Jing Chen et al. 陈静 (Hong Kong: Joint Publishing Company, 1956).

In this story, Bao Zheng did show his wisdom and insight based on common sense, and thus the similar stories are consistently widespread among the people.[12] *The Holy Bible* also records a similar story,[13] which is quite popular in the West likewise and has become the signature story of a wise adjudicator. The wide popularity of this story reflects that the case trial is truly great. Not only does the adjudicator makes the a right verdict, but the result wins the universal recognition among the people, while the cost of the trial is very low as well. Besides, such type of trial has other merits; for example, it is not the professional trial, whose logic and reasoning can be understood by ordinary people. However, the verdict is hard to be predicted before the announcement; it is not mysterious at all or unexpected, but quite reasonable; it is not a religious marvel, but commands admiration from people. It is quite dramatic as well.

However, we must first observe that if such "administration of justice" becomes an ideal and standard, then it must lead to the non-professionalized, even anti-professionalized, "administration of justice." At least from the perspective of today, it will not be beneficial for the development of the judicial profession or the accumulation of judicial knowledge. Certainly, it is not actually a question for many ordinary people yet, but a question for those who emphasize the judicial profession nowadays (judges, lawyers, and professors of legal science), because it is involved with the legitimacy of their professional existence and service charges in society. Most of the general public actually don't care much about the settlement of disputes in a professionalized or non-professionalized way. They care about how disputes can be solved smoothly, fairly, effectively, and conveniently, which should become the general institution, not an exception.

The real question lies with which more deserves our concern. The wide popularity of the story just reflects the rarity of such a result. Because of its rarity, it can become the subject of a conversation among people and command marvel and admiration. Just imagine it: If someone meets a case like *The Chalk Circle* today, the judge or other similar adjudicator only needs to order a paternity test or DNA test, and it will not be mistaken. People will never marvel at this decision, and the story will be less likely to spread. Just as a popular saying goes in journalism, "when a dog bites a man, that is not news; but if a man bites a dog, that is news." For the same reason, scarcity endows it with the value of circulation. Even if *The Chalk Circle* is not directly or indirectly affected or inspired by the biblical story, in the human history of thousands of years, how many cases are settled in this way or similar ways? How many cases can be settled in this way? As far as we can remember, only about two classic cases (actually one). In my opinion, the wide circulation of the story of *The Chalk Circle* or King Solomon in *The Holy Bible* more reflects

---

12 According to the textual research of a scholar, the earliest original prototype of this story comes from the story of Prime Minister Huang Ba in Ying Shao's *The Annotation of Customs* 《风俗通义》 in the Eastern Han Dynasty, and it also appeared in the related Buddhist story later. Wu, Xiaoling 吴晓铃. "Shijiu gaojiasuo huilanji tansuo santi" 试就高加索灰阑记探索三题. In *Mingjia jiedu yuanqu* 名家解读元曲, 414.

13 1 Kings, 3: 16–27, in *The Holy Bible*.

the difficulty of making the correct judgment as for the issue of paternity testing and other tricky questions in an extended way in traditional society, namely in the society without the institution of birth registration and the modern technology of biological testing.

It should be noted that, in my words, it is difficult, but not impossible. In the social condition at that time, the judge sometimes could use personal wisdom to make the correct judgment in some cases. However, someone can make such a correct judgment, which can't demonstrate that an effective system of "administrating justice" can be accordingly established on this basis. It is just like a person who can make a clean jerk of 200 kilograms; it doesn't mean that others or even most people can do the same thing. Law as a system should more rely on morality and intelligence of ordinary people, not those of supermen. Bao Zheng in dramas or folktales is a fictional character after all and hasn't been replaced by any others for years. Actually, Bao Zheng is a mythicized figure in the folktales, including Yuan plays, while King Solomon is also one of a few "wise kings" of ancient Jews.

Second, this method can't be applied to all the cases, or even the overwhelming majority of cases. It has been indicated in other plays of Bao Zheng in the Yuan Dynasty. In seven other plays of Bao Zheng in *Selected Plays from the Yuan Dynasty*, Bao Zheng (figure of Bao Zheng can be considered as playwrights or society in those days) didn't have any similar brilliant demonstrations in the issue of ascertaining the facts. Actually, the method applied in this case by Bao Zheng can only be used once and can't be repeated, no matter for others or himself. This type of knowledge, method, or wisdom can't be institutionalized. It looks more like a riddle, "punch line," or "trick" at most, and it is not a method in a strict sense.

Third, the probative force of this method is actually rather limited. In *The Chalk Circle*, if Zhang Haitang were anxious to prove her words and spared no efforts to drag her son, she would have the likelihood of dragging the boy to her side in addition to her strength of a youth. If so, then she might be identified as a culprit, while the true criminal instead escaped from punishment accordingly. More importantly, when no one knew what Bao Zheng had got up his sleeve, Zhang Haitang still had a strong motive to do so. She was first concerned with her own life; second, the boy would feel pain in this scramble, but might not be hurt or severely hurt. The most important thing is if viewed in the long run, once Zhang Haitang was executed, her son still had the possibility of being murdered by Ma's wife sooner or later, because when the wife fought with Zhang Haitang for this boy, her aim was set on his inalienable property inheritance, not the boy himself. In ancient China, if the deceased had sons, the property would be generally divided among them in an equal way regardless of whether their mothers were wives or concubines. The wives and concubines had no right of inheritance and had to live with their own sons.[14] The wives and concubines in widowhood and without male offspring could

---

14 *Qingming ji zhengye xia* juan 5 清明集·争业下卷5, quoted in Cheng, Weirong 程维荣. "Lun zhongguo chuantong caichan jicheng zhidu de guyou maodun" 论中国传统财产继承制度的固有矛盾. *Zhengzhi yu falv* 政治与法律, no. 1 (2004), 152.

inherit the husband's property, but they were not allowed to remarry or to sell the property and also had to designate an heir to the deceased husband, and the property would be inherited by the heir after their death.[15] The institution of property inheritance enabled Ma's wife first to contend for this son if she wanted to hold the property; otherwise, even if Zhang Haitang were executed, the property would still belong to the son of Zhang. But once she got the boy and had the property in hand, the wife must get rid of this boy, then designate a person whom she liked and could control as the heir, because the boy only recognized Zhang as his own mother and knew it was the wife who killed his own mother. It would be as easy as pie, since the boy was only five years old. Zhang Haitang actually should have known it. Therefore, if she really had a long-term plan for the boy, she might know that the present contention of injuring the boy would be better than the future murder of her son. The measure adopted by Bao Zheng was rather risky, and his success only lay in Zhang Haitang's mistake.[16]

Because of these reasons, even Bao Zheng would inevitably make a mistake as well. Actually, even in the Yuan Dynasty, there was a play called *Muddle-headed Rescriptor-in-Waiting Bao*,[17] although this playscript has been lost and we don't know what kind of mistake he made. Yet in other Yuan plays concerning Bao Zheng, we can observe that in other difficult cases, Bao Zheng was not very different from other officials except in his defiance of power. In trying those homicide cases without evidence, he likewise resorted to or threatened to use quite a lot of interrogation by torture. For example, in *The Butterfly Dream*, three brothers beat Ge Biao from a powerful and influential family to death to avenge the death of their father. Only to identify "Who was first to kill this man?" Bao Zheng ordered to torture three brothers one by one:

Not just hemp-wrapped clubs, head clamps, and finger presses
Are the punishments for intense and unending questions and interrogation.

---

15 *Qingming ji li ji* juan 8 清明集·立继卷8, quoted in Cheng, Weirong 程维荣. "Lun zhongguo chuantong caichan jicheng zhidu de guyou maodun" 论中国传统财产继承制度的固有矛盾, 150.

16 Comparatively speaking, King Solomon seems to be more reasonable in his trying the similar case. First, the disputed parties were two women, and other relations of interests were not involved except for their struggle for the child; second, the decision of Kong Solomon was to split the child into half, which not only directly threatened the life of the child but also easily aroused the mother's pity for the child because of this shocking action. (To drag the child didn't threaten the life of the child.) Under this circumstance, the gain of the mother's abandoning the child (to keep the child alive) is actually greater than the gain of the mother's struggling for the child (the dead half of the child). In *The Annotation of Customs*, Huang Ba's doing was more reasonable than Bao Zheng's in *The Chalk Circle*.

17 In Zang Jinshu's "On Yuan Tune," the list of plays included Wang Zemin's *Muddle-headed Rescriptor-in-Waiting Bao* in the Yuan Dynasty. See Zang, Jinshu 臧晋叔. *Yuanqu xuan* 元曲选 (Beijing: Zhonghua Book Company, 1958), 28. This play has been lost. See Li, Chunxiang 李春祥. "Fulu yuandai baogongxi xintan" 附录:元代包公戏新探. In *Yuandai baogongxi xuanzhu* 元代包公戏选注, compiled and annotated by Li Chunxiang 李春祥 (Zhengzhou: Zhongzhou Calligraphy and Painting, 1983), 301 and Note 16.

What are the categories of your investigation
That call for beating them until they are soaked in blood?
The eldest brother gives voice to wrong, cries, "Injustice!"
But you, sir, make no attempt to hear an explanation.
Second brother endures a living hell on earth,
How can he bear such pain?
And the third brother is beaten most harshly

(Guan, 2010: 56–57)

A similar case could be found in Wang Xiuran, the honest official in *The Unidentified Corpse*, and Zhang Ding, the capable clerk in *The Moheluo Doll*. When the legal procedure couldn't solve the problem, Bao Zheng utilized other extralegal or even overtly illegal methods to achieve the purpose, including deception, falsification of the death verdict, and assumption of the name of a condemned criminal.[18] Although I don't accept it as true, it still reflects some social realities. It shows that in the condition at that time, playwrights (and common people represented by them) even recognized the unscrupulous methods of officials for "the substantive justice"; besides, it also shows that they didn't think this type of episode would impair the image of Bao Zheng and other "honest officials" at all and didn't believe honest officials could see the truth as clearly as a blazing fire and have an extremely discerning eye only by their wisdom. Actually, in commenting on this play, some literary critics of today hold that playwrights had to adopt "the special method and measure . . . it was just the hope heaped by common people on honest officials."[19] In the society lacking the trial skills of acquiring reliable and sufficient evidence, even "honest officials" likewise proved to be incompetent in difficult cases and only resorted to interrogation by torture. Such "incompetence" is not the issue concerning personal wisdom and competence of officials, but the result of social condition and public will as well.

Another aspect of limitation of wisdom is power. Although many audiences or readers highly extol the wisdom of Bao Zheng, it must be noted that in the trial issue, just like in many issues, wisdom and knowledge can't automatically and independently function; they must have the support of power and then can enter the judicial trial.[20] Actually, Bao Zheng was not simply wise and honest, but more importantly, he was "Rescriptor-in-Waiting at Dragon Design Pavilion and Academician-in-Waiting at the Hall of Heaven's Splendor" and the top official of the capital, Kaifeng Prefecture. Without these identities, all the wisdoms of Bao Zheng couldn't work, although audiences always consciously or unconsciously omit it in discussing the honest official Bao Zheng, which thereby covers the

---

18 For example, Bao Zheng in the plays of *The Wife-Snatcher*, *The Butterfly Dream*, *Bao Zheng Wittily Obtained the Golden Treasure* and *Judge Bao Selling Rice in Chenzhou*.

19 Guo, Yuheng, chiefly ed. 郭预衡. *Zhongguo gudai wenxueshi* juan 3 中国古代文学史卷3 (Shanghai: Shanghai Ancient Books, 1998), 355.

20 See Foucault, Michael. *Power/Knowledge: Selected Interviews and Other Writings, 1972–1977*, trans. Colin Gordon et al. (New York: Pantheon Books, 1980).

dimension of power. Actually, in Yuan plays, this point is repeatedly emphasized. When Bao Zheng appeared on the stage in *The Chalk Circle*, he first mentioned that

> I thank the sagely grace that took pity and granted me the position of Rescriptor-in-Waiting at Dragon Design Pavilion and Academician-in-Waiting at the Hall of Heaven's Splendor. I have been given the assignment of Prefect of the Southern Yamen of Kaifeng Superior Prefecture. An imperial order has bestowed on me the Golden Plaque and Sword of Power, and I seek out excessive officials and corrupt clerks, alleviate injustice to the hundred surnames and right their wrongs. I have been allowed "to behead first and memorialize afterward."

> (Li, 274)

A similar saying can be found in other Yuan plays concerning Bao Zheng and honest officials. There are two Yuan plays in which the power of Bao Zheng is not explicitly indicated[21]; since the image of Bao Zheng has been symbolized in Chinese society,[22] people have preset his great power only at the mention of him.

We must investigate the power actually utilized by Bao Zheng in plays as well, because on many occasions, the post doesn't equally match the power. What Bao possessed in plays is absolutely not the ordinary power of academician and prefect. His actual power is far beyond ordinary officials, because he can "investigate the records at will" and can even "behead first and memorialize afterward." The wisdom of Bao Zheng, the honest official, must rely on such power to play its role. It seems that our ancestors, including these playwrights, were ahead of Foucault and us in knowing the relations between knowledge and power.

We should be clearer with the significance of Bao Zheng's power. This power is actually the legitimate power beyond the legal system. He can be beyond the legal jurisdiction institution of that time (to investigate the records at will) and procedure (to behead first and memorialize afterward) to exercise power. Considering the fact that some cases might not be reasonably solved by the institution and procedure and they could appear in any society, nearly all societies would accordingly empower a person in a special position with such power beyond law; for example, in the United States, the president and the state governors have a special pardon power. It is the emergency exit that any institution must have in order to cope with unexpected events or special situations.

However, there are lots of problems with such power. First, I want to stress that only under *extremely limited* circumstances can this power be effective, and even

---

21 In the plays of Judge Bao, *The Contract* and *Shennuer*, the power of Bao Zheng is not explicitly mentioned.

22 Mr. Zhao Jingshen once made a comparative research study between the stories of Bao Zheng and other similar stories of honest officials and concluded that "Bao Zheng was another version of honest officials, and just the person who absorbed the legends." Quoted in Duan, Baolin 段宝林. "Guanyu baogong de renleixue sikao" 关于包公的人类学思考. *Guangming Ribao* 光明日报 (Beijing), May 6, 1999.

be possible, and will always be the supplement (emergency exit) to the institution. Just imagine it, not to mention all the officials, even half of officials or even fewer have such authorization in a society, even if all of them are honest, upright, care for common people, clever, and wise, only when there are digressions among their opinions (it might well happen in trial and often happens), then there will be the fight for the power about who can be *more* at will, take the decisive move, and report it to the superiors afterward. Actually, once such power is excessive, the institution must be chaotic and absolutely not functionable. Such power must be monopolized, or at least in a certain jurisdiction. Such power is not allowed to be shared among two or more persons within one jurisdiction, even the power of wisdom. It also decides the limitation of wisdom and decides that no institution can accommodate many powers of such wisdom. In *The Moheluo Doll* and the story of the filial daughter-in-law of Donghai, we can find that the wisdom of Zhang Ding and Prison Clerk Mr. Yu was contained by power, which even didn't work completely.

Second, it also means that once a greater power or even a power on equal footing appears, the limitation of power is exposed to the full. Other Yuan plays concerning Bao Zheng show this point. In *The Wife-Snatcher*,[23] Bao Zheng could not apply his power to execute Lu Zhailang, the powerful bully who forcibly took away a daughter of ordinary people. All that he could do was report to the emperor for the approval of sentencing a person with a falsified name to death; afterward, he took the liberty of changing the falsified name of the death verdict with the name of Lu Zhailang to achieve his purpose. This doing is not only illegal, but also horrible and unbelievable.

Third, such power is even extremely dangerous, because it is applied outside the conventional legal system. You can seek such power, but you can't guarantee beforehand that only "good persons" acquire it. Think about how horrible it would be if a corrupt official did this![24] It is also impossible to guarantee that the application by "good persons" is correct and wise every time.[25]

Admittedly, they are just plays, but the reason has been definite and general: The power of wisdom is limited.

---

23 Hanqing, Guan. "The Wife-Snatcher," in *Selected Plays of Guan Hanqing*, trans. Yang Xianyi and Gladys Yang (Beijing: Foreign Languages Press, 1979), 38–66.

24 In Yuan plays, some corrupt officials used legitimate power acquired extralegally to bring calamity to the country and people. For example, in *Judge Bao Selling Rice in Chenzhou*, the son of Liu, the high official, acquired the purple gold hammer bestowed by the emperor, with which he was free to kill people.

25 For example, Prefect Wanyan in *The Moheluo Doll* and *The Case of the Head Scarf*, although he was willing to "get rid of the evil and uphold the righteous" and had "the ordinance sword and the golden tablet" with which he could "execute first and report to the throne later," yet he nearly fell into the tricky traps by corrupt clerks all along and made huge mistakes because of his deficiency of wisdom.

The Limitations of Diligent Governance

In addition to the wisdom and the defiance of power, another important quality of the ideally "honest officials" is diligent governance. On the one hand, diligent government is the embodiment of honest officials' character of fraternizing and caring for common people; on the other hand, in a certain condition, it can make up for the deficiency of wisdom indeed. Therefore, if it is impossible for many gifted talents with moral integrity to assume official posts, can the officials with ordinary intelligence guarantee the correct trial through diligent governance? "To bend one's back to a task until one's dying day" is a saying that has won universal admiration among Chinese people, which seems to imply such a judgment. Kuang Zhong of *Fifteen Strings of Cash*, a Ming play, seemed to be a typical example – the official with diligent governance (but he didn't rest with it) who therefore prevented the occurrence of injustice. However, the analysis of *Fifteen Strings of Cash* demonstrates from another aspect that diligent governance still makes a limited contribution to a correct trial.

Because of poverty, Butcher You Hulu borrowed 15 strings of cash from his elder sister and jokingly told his stepdaughter, Su Shujuan, that she was sold by him to others as a concubine. Su was agonized over it and ran away to seek safety with her aunt before the dawn while her father was sound asleep. Lou the Rat, the local gambler, happened to notice the door of You's house ajar and entered the room to steal, which awakened You. In the ensuing struggle, Lou used the meat chopper to kill You in a moment of desperation. The next morning, neighbors found You murdered and came to catch up with Su Shujuan and Xiong Youlan, a young scholar whom Su accidentally met on the road and kept company with. Xiong carried 15 strings of cash on him as well. They were brought back to the county magistrate. Magistrate Guo Yuzhi was "determined to be an honest official" and concluded that Su Shujuan and Xiong Youlan committed the fornication and carried the money to run away after their killing You Hulu. Under torture, Su and Xiong confessed to false charges. This case had gone through "three trials and six interrogations," and the central government sanctioned the execution. Kuang Zhong, the prefect of Suzhou who oversaw the execution, raised many suspicions on this case and urged Governor Zhou Chen to reinvestigate it with the latter's approval. After the field investigation, Kuang Zhong not only affirmed that Su and Xiong were truly wronged but also observed the suspicious acts of Lou the Rat. Disguised as a fortune teller, Kuang Zhong made a hunt everywhere and discovered Lou. He tried to fathom Lou's innermost thoughts and urged Lou to tell the truth. Finally, the truth was brought to light.[26]

---

26 The synopsis here is mainly from the adapted version of Kun Opera *Fifteen Strings of Cash* in 1956. The best benefit of this adapted version is the simplification of the overly complex plot in the original text with the omission that Kuang Zhong was instructed by the deity in his dream. However, this version of 1956 also has its weakness, which reinforces the moral color of the officials themselves in the original text because of the sociopolitical influence at that time. Therefore, the play treats the judicial issue as the political issue, which inundates the significance of this play in terms of

In the original version of this play, the image of Kuang Zhong is far more rounded than Bao Zheng's in any Yuan play; other characters in the play and the plot are quite reasonable. But in my opinion, the most significant aspect is that the play neither takes great pains to describe the exceptionally unique competence of Kuang Zhong nor specially emphasizes the difference between Kuang and other officials in terms of morality and competence. Among the limited traditional playscripts I have ever read, this play can be the most meaningful, which almost exhibits all the problems concerning the rationality of "administrating justice" in ancient society and the rationality of all these problems.

For example, in this play, there is not an image of a corrupt official. Guo Yuzhi, the county magistrate, and Zhou Chen, the governor, who appeared on the stage as negative characters were basically decent officials and only became the opposite of Kuang Zhong in performing their duties. Although County Magistrate Guo Yuzhi made a wrong verdict, and this mistake was undoubtedly embedded with the factor of his pursuit for political achievement as an administrator,[27] overall, it was almost inevitable in the condition at that time; even if Kuang Zhong were in Guo's position, Kuang would likely make a similar verdict. Because all the pieces of evidence are quite disadvantageous to Su and Xiong. Su came with her mother to You's family after her mother's remarriage. Besides, "the stepfather was not a good person, my mother died in a fit of the sulks later. Now, the financial condition of family is hard, and we are poverty-stricken. The stepfather didn't utter comforting words, but beat and cursed me instead."[28] Therefore, to a certain extent, Su Shujuan had the potential motive for revenge. The money on Xiong Youlan was the same amount as the money stolen from You Hulu. More importantly, in the ancient social condition that emphasized "man and woman should not touch each other when giving and receiving something," it was hard to imagine that a couple of male and female strangers travelling at night in company hadn't a secret love. Considering the social condition in those days, and under the circumstance of nonexistence of other suspects, ordinary people would all believe Su and Xiong were the murderers. Actually, the neighbors of You averred that "it must be his daughter, who has affairs with a boy. Knowing her father had fifteen strings of cash, she secretly plotted with her lover to kill the father. Now they run away together" (Zhu, 60). After neighbors and yamen runners caught up with Su and Xiong, they immediately identified Xiong as the fornicator. You Hulu's elder sister, namely Su's aunt, then immediately maintained that Su Shujuan killed her younger brother and testified that the money on Xiong Youlan was just "personally given by me to my brother yesterday." She said, "I will memorize this profound enmity, and hate their guts." Later, she served as a witness at court in the capacity of the victim's relative (Zhu, 66). There was no contrary evidence, or the evidence couldn't be established. For

---

jurisprudential theory. In analyzing the character personality of the story, I will mainly rely on the original text.

27 For a more meticulous theoretical analysis on this point, please see Chapter 4.

28 Zhu 朱素臣. *Shiwuguan jiaozhu* 十五贯校注, 26 (hereafter cited parenthetically in the text).

example, Xiong Youlan named the witness who loaned the money to him. Since the witness changed his travel plans, the yamen runner came to the designated place and didn't find this person (Zhu, 70–71). In the face of such eyewitnesses and material evidence, Guo Yuzhi believed "it is absolutely certain" (Zhu, 71). Even Xiong himself claimed, "*How can I blame the lord?* The injustice to others must have a foe who frames things . . . but my injustice is evidently arranged by Heaven! I just walk on the dead road by myself." He asked Heaven, "How can this tricky case be settled?" (Zhu, 77–78).

But in the play, Kuang Zhong's suspicions on this case were also reasonable and credible. Kung supervised the execution and heard the complaints from Su and Xiong. After reading the file, he raised some doubts. Xiong was a scholar who seemed to have no strength to kill You Hulu with a meat chopper. Besides,

> Xiong's family is in Shanyang, which is a thousand *li* away from Wuxi. Xiong and Su have never met before, how can they have a secret love? What is more, the money is not the sure evidence, how can they be sentenced the execution only because of fifteen strings of cash?
>
> (Zhu, 100)

Such doubts raised by Kuang Zhong may be inevitably connected with his personal temperament, personality, and sensitivity, but it was first connected with his experience, which was obviously different from Guo Yuzhi's. Kuang Zhong used to be a clerk who drew up indictments (Zhu, 84, 108), while Guo Yuzhi was "a successful candidate at the imperial examination in his early years after the study for ten years" (Zhu, 41). Second, but more importantly, he was different from Guo in position, liability, and pursuit. Kuang's liability was to supervise the execution and review the case. His main duty included the assurance of no unjust execution. Naturally, the question he was concerned with would be different, and he would be more sensitive than Guo in the execution liability. The institutional support was available too. "One article of *The Canons of the Law* is, 'the law permits us to listen to condemned people who cry out that they have been wronged and to reconsider their cases'" (Zhu, 108). This allowed the supervisor to make a new response according to new information. The position of supervisor enabled Kuang to acquire such information, while it was impossible for Guo Yuzhi to get it in the first trial. Besides, Kuang's position (the appeal trial) also let him go beyond the political pressure from the local common people and consider the related evidence and information in a more balanced way. Guo Yuzhi was a relatively young administrator and had bigger political ambitions because of his successful career without a hitch: "The spring scenery of Heyang is at my command, the official rank of thousands of *li* is unfolded before my view" (Zhu, 41). Therefore, he was anxious to respond to the local public will and deliberately showed his political achievements, including "loving people as his own children, and upholding the law firmly." All these differences enabled Kuang Zhong to be more sensitive to even the slight doubts; although these doubts were not sufficient to reverse the verdict, they had been sufficient to question this verdict for the relatively elder magistrate who "used to be a clerk, but is never an unlearned person" (Zhu, 108) and believed "contemporaries should not belittle clerks drawing up indictments, they push forward the eternal undertaking of wise officials" (Zhu, 97).[29]

At the risk of a forfeited salary and demoted official position, Kuang Zhong urged Governor Zhou Chen to reinvestigate the case with the latter's approval. A debate ensued between the legalism (Zhou Chen) and the realism (Kuang Zhong), and such a debate is the only one in traditional Chinese dramas as far as I know. Zhou Chen was against the retrial, with the procedural justice as his argument that "three trials and six interrogations" had been concluded, and the sentence must be strictly executed; Kuang Zhong debated with the political realism and pragmatic discourse of moral ideology as his argument that the case was suspicious and it involved human life (Zhu, 107).[30] Kuang Zhong used his own official post and salary as the guarantee and finally persuaded Zhou Chen (this also means Zhou Chen finally succumbed to the realism and abandoned the legalism) to give Kuang the privilege of "administrating justice" in others' jurisdiction (the order arrow, namely the issue of power discussed in the previous section). Kuang went to the crime scene to investigate (Zhu, 109). At the crime scene, he found pieces of evidence that challenged the original verdict. He found some scattered copper coins on the ground of You Hulu's house, while You didn't know "where his next meal was coming from." He guessed the coins were scattered in the fight between You Hulu and the murderer, while there wasn't a single coin missing from the 15 strings Xiong Youlan carried. He found the dice in You's house, which was left by Lou the Rat, while You never gambled. All of these attracted Kuang Zhong's attention to Lou, and the investigation was conducted. Since there was no evidence to show that Lou killed someone, and it was impossible to arrest him and much less to torture him (interrogation by torture must be initiated only with relatively sufficient evidence), Kuang Zhong thereby disguised himself as a fortune teller and used a series of explanations like "rats like stealing oil" (in the Chinese, the pronunciations of oil 油 and You 游 are the same) to finally elicit Lou the Rat to tell the truth.

It is a very brilliant case indeed. In terms of the reflection of social reality and the institutional reality of "administrating justice," it is more profound than any detective play in the Yuan Dynasty. In particular, the revised version of this play deletes the episode of the appearance of a deity in a dream to make a revelation, and it fully shows Kuang Zhong's wisdom, his carefulness and sensitivity to facts, and his strong sense of responsibility to the parties concerned in the case. What is more, it shows his effort of going deep into the realities, his emphasis on the

---

29 It verifies the issue of the institutional role that I have discussed. See Chapter 4.
30 The significant meaning of jurisprudential theory in this debate lies in the following: In the specific condition, an adjudicator can use the moralist discourse of ideology for the purpose of pragmatism; in the other condition, he can also apply the formalist discourse of procedural justice. It seems to exhibit that all kinds of jurisprudential theories have the wide applicability, which also shows that all these theories only possess the limited effectivity and persuasiveness. Therefore, there isn't a legal theory that can ensure the forever correctness. The important thing is to first know what shall be done and how to mobilize these theories to legitimize "what shall be done."

investigation, his diligent governance, his loving the people, his arguing strongly on just grounds instead of fawning on his superior, etc. However, even so, we can still find the limitations of diligent governance in the issue of trial through this case.

For example, the play reflects that because of a lack of special peace officers and professional detectives, even Prefect Kuang Zhong had to make the field investigation by himself. In this sense, Kuang Zhong played the roles of criminal policeman, legal medical expert, and prosecutor in modern society. In the course of investigating whether Lou the Rat was a criminal or not, Kuang Zhong also played the role of modern undercover detective and talked with Lou, which means he must know "the criminal psychology." Just as I have indicated in the previous chapter, these roles are not only in conflict with Kuang Zhong's identity of administrator, but are rather different from the liability of a professional judge in modern society. The main liability of a modern judge is to make a wise and circumspect judgment according to the evidence provided by both parties, while what his judgment relies on is the supportive institutional system and the related personnel, technologies, and funds. Without the reliance on such an institution, Kuang Zhong had to gather and find evidence alone in order to make his judgment. Since different roles need different types of knowledge, while human intelligence and study capability are limited, theoretically speaking, he can and should know all types of knowledge; but even with these types of knowledge, he will only be an official with a general knowledge and can't be an expert in multiple aspects, let alone whether society in those days had these systematic types of knowledge or not.

Just because of these facts, we can observe that the knowledge applied by Kuang Zhong in *Fifteen Strings of Cash* is more of the common sense variety, just like those officials in other plays did, not the knowledge and insight of an expert, not the information provided by the knowledge of modern science and technology. Kuang's measures and the knowledge his measures relied on were totally the same in nature with Bao Zheng's in *The Chalk Circle*. That is to say, in such an institutional condition, officials assuming overall liability of administration and justice found it very hard to become experts in especially trying cases. This means it is very difficult to have a professionalized and specialized force in traditional society and the specialized division of labor and the accumulated specialized knowledge. When these supportive conditions don't exist, even if diligent governance might make up for the defect of knowledge partially, it can't replace specialized knowledge.

It is the same case not only in specialized knowledge but also in human and financial resources. In *Fifteen Strings of Cash*, we find Kuang Zhong who went deep into the investigation, but it is a play after all, and the case involves the lives of two persons, and only a case is presented in this play. All these factors enable Kuang Zhong to have the possibility and motivation to go deep into the investigation and to take half a month to investigate Lou the Rat. These factors don't let audiences watching the play easily sense a problem at least. But in real life, if the number of cases is slightly higher, for example, a case a week; if this case is only involved with the life of one person, or even it is not a homicide case, but a case concerning property or injury; and if Kuang Zhong had other busy administrative affairs, then we can infer that even Kuang Zhong had a greater sense of moral responsibility and higher dedication to work. It might be impossible for him to *always* tackle the cases just as he did in the case of Su and Xiong. Even if Kuang could do thus in individual cases, for other cases, he might have to follow Governor Zhou Chen, respect the trial of Guo Yuzhi, the local magistrate and the result of "three trials and six interrogations," and become a legalist and proceduralist. Besides, when he spent a large quantity of time on making an in-depth investigation on a case that was important in his eyes, would another case involving human life be postponed? These analyses thereby mean that he couldn't play a role of honest official in most of the other cases and couldn't be perspicacious and impartial in judgment. For those plaintiffs and defendants and other stakeholders in such cases who have the same expectation for the official upholding the justice for people, Kuang Zhong would be a mediocre or muddle-headed official.

It should also be indicated that although such a selected in-depth reinvestigation is better than the inaction, since the decision concerning the reinvestigation is totally up to the personal will of officials, it is not a restrictive institution. It has no coercive and binding force for officials, and it is completely up to their sense of personal morality and responsibility. Then, we observe another fundamental limitation of such "a system of administrating justice" that emphasizes the moral constraint and lacks institutional constraint, which is the limitation that can't be breached by wisdom and diligent governance. What is more, we also observe the necessity of emphasizing the personal moral character of officials as for this traditional "administration of justice." I will have an in-depth discussion on the latter issue next.

The Mode of Rule by Man in "Administrating Justice"

To point out the limitations of wisdom and diligent governance doesn't mean to abandon them. When there is no *better* alternative, or there is one alternative that exists in imagination (the imagination is possible for everything) yet fails to be fulfilled in reality, perhaps the only way out is just to cherish the old and preserve the outworn and maintain the status quo, or make some slightly symbolic adjustments at most in order to give people a feasible satisfaction. Although such a statement sounds very "immoral" and "incorrect," it might be an irrefutable truth of life. Therefore, what matters is not to indicate the limitations of wisdom and industry and the limitations of honest officials. It also implies a more important question to "the administration of justice" in traditional Chinese society: When two limitations are combined, it actually presents a mode of rule by man, namely *within the purview that the social condition of science and technology in those days allowed*, the effective operation of a trial is only decided by case adjudicators' personal ingenuity, diligent governance, and their love for the common people.[31]

---

31 It must be noted that what I have discussed here is not about the rule of man and the rule by law in society, but the rule of man and the rule by law in the judiciary.

Certainly, there are lots of problems in the mode of "rule by man" in the judiciary, and scholars have many specific discussions, such as the easy unleashing of the abuse of power, corruption, malpractices, substituting one's words for the law, non-professionalization, etc. Considering so many analytical criticisms of the like, I hereby don't utter more words.

What deserves discussion here is another aspect of the mode of rule by man. It has not been discussed by scholars today, but is often considered by many contemporary Chinese jurists as the characteristic of "rule of law" in traditional China, which is "worthy of learning from." That is, once the official's act of "preventing the administration of justice" is discovered, he will be severely punished no matter if he practices corruption and malpractice for personal gain or such things are not exposed. For example, In *The Injustice to Dou E*, Prefect Taowu, the predecessor who was transferred from Chuzhou to other region, was "given a hundred lashes and permanently dismissed from the service." This situation also recurs in other Yuan plays.[32]

Such an institution with an emphasis on the personal liability of the case adjudicator is in sharp contrast with the popular saying of the modern judicial system and judicial practice of modern Western countries. In the modern judicial system, except for the exposure of perverting the law for personal gain in a judge, generally speaking, the judge will not be severely punished because of a mistake preventing the administration of justice due to his poor intelligence or insufficiently diligent governance[33]; the most likely punishment for such a thing is to return his case for retrial. It is still a punishment as well – at least it is "losing face." A judge will be exempt from his mistake in trying a case (even it turns out to be an unjust one), only if no evidence shows that he has the malpractices. His mistake will be considered an institutional one. Certainly, for the modern judicial system, such a way of dealing with judicial mistakes is reasonable, because other institutional factors participate in the judge's adjudication – for example, the conviction from the jury, or the accusation of the prosecutor, or the error of evidence, or the honesty and error of witnesses, etc. Therefore, the personal liability of a judge in the modern judicial system is actually greatly reduced. It is not just like some contemporary jurists in China who suggest more emphasis be on the personal liability of a judge, such as accountability for misjudged cases. It is also in this sense that I emphasize what in the Chinese tradition, even the system of "administrating justice" adopts is a mode with the orientation of rule by man and the rule by morality, not the mode of rule of law.[34]

---

32 Su Shun, prefect of Zhengzhou in *The Chalk Circle*, and the local officials in *Shennuer*, *The Unidentified Corpse*, and *The Moheluo Doll* were all subject to the same punishment.

33 Considering the institutional condition of the United States, Judge Posner even thought judges should be "somewhat lazy." See Posner, Richard A. *Overcoming Law* (Cambridge, MA: Harvard University Press, 1995), Chapter 3.

34 Certainly, there must be some restrictions on my comparison. First, the case adjudicator in traditional Chinese society is not the judge in the modern sense; what is more, although the event that leads to his punishment is in the nature of "administrating justice," he is not punished in the capacity of the judge,

Many people question the truthfulness of the punishment to officials exhibited in these plays. I don't consider these plays to be reality. But as for these questions, I think there will not be much difference between these plays and reality. In addition to some substantial evidence, my main base is the logical inference of economics and sociology. First, it is actually "the strict liability" of the modern legal system practiced toward officials, not "the fault liability." Because in a traditional society (no matter in China or in the West), information was hard to come by, so the strict liability was generally practiced in each legal department except for some specific cases where the related information could be easily acquired.[35] The ancient "administrative law" is naturally impossible to be estranged from this logic. Actually, only from modern times onward, the does fault liability begin to be popular in legal theory, especially in many departments.

From the perspective of the institution, it is also reasonable to adopt strict liability for the management and supervision of officials at that time. The most important reason is it can greatly reduce the information cost needed to supervise, examine, and punish local officials for the central government. Therefore, once the practice of "preventing the administration of justice" is discovered, the official concerned will be punished and "given a hundred lashes and permanently dismissed from the service" without the need of investigating whether the official in charge of a trial is corrupted, bribed, or resorts to fraudulent practices for personal gain. The probability of such a threat is enlarged. Once such an official is demanded to be punished, an investigation is undertaken to check whether he does this on purpose or by mistake; he perverts the law for personal gain or takes the bribe; it is because of the deficiency of related knowledge or his moral defect. If the related evidence is required to be presented for demonstration, the institutional cost of managing officials in ancient China would be greatly augmented, which might even cripple the whole system. Therefore, in the historical condition of that time, only viewed from this perspective, to emphasize personal liability of officials and to adopt the strict liability would be the management and governance institution with the lower cost in comparison with the fault liability.

Another factor contributes to the strict and severe aspects of this liability, which is linked with the excessively high information cost. Because the information cost was excessively high, lots of officials actually had no likelihood of being discovered even if they did prevent the administration of justice because

---

but the administrator. Second, the mitigation of personal liability of the judge in the modern judiciary is a result of the institutional development, which includes the separation of the judiciary as the independent department from other political organizations. The mitigation of the personal liability of the judge is allegedly for the sake of maintaining judicial independence. In a traditional society, since the judiciary and the administration were integrated and there weren't other departments that supported the operation of the judicial department, there would be no reason to mitigate the liability of the case adjudicator. Naturally, it is one of the reasons why ancient society emphasized the personal liability of the case adjudicator.

35 See Posner, Richard A. *Economic of Justice* (Cambridge, MA: Harvard University Press, 1981), esp. Chapter 6.

of their faults. In Chapter 4, I analyzed that the probability of redressing the in-justice of Dou E's case was very low. If it were not Dou Tianzhang who came to investigate the records or it were not the persistence of the ghost of wronged Dou E, her injustice would not be redressed at all. In terms of reality, the probability of punishing these officials was also very low. It means that even if the strict li-ability is adopted, the real threat of this institution to officials will be rather small. In order to augment the real threat of such strict liability, it will inevitably in-crease the legal punishment, which thereby ushers in a stricter personal liability.[36]

The strict liability of a modern society generally doesn't make a moral evalua-tion of perpetrators. However, in traditional society, the strict liability practiced on officials was always accompanied by moral evaluation. Hence, from the perspec-tive of the whole society, the sanction of this strict liability includes the condem-nation of public opinion. For those officials who might have faults but definitely no sins, such as Taowu, society will inflict the additional punishment through the medium such as plays. Why is there such a difference between ancient and modern strict liabilities? As I have indicated in the previous passage, Yuan plays and other traditional plays altogether show many questions proved to be more caused by information, knowledge, and technologies in the analysis of today, and they were usually considered a question of officials' personal morality at that time. Why? The previously mentioned reduction of the information cost of managing and supervis-ing officials doesn't seem to fully explain this phenomenon. Consequently, this moral condemnation must have a certain function for the whole traditional society and social psychology.

It can still be explained with the information cost. Because of the excessively high information cost, and under the circumstances of untimely understanding of actual truth, ordinary people (not the government) first tend to make a moral judgment for the intolerable acts, because it might be the most advantageous to self-protection. If a person hurts me and I don't know his intention, I will gener-ally assume that he harbors evil thoughts to me *in the first place*. In doing so, I can immediately raise my vigilance and reinforce self-protection. It has almost become one human instinct and is more likely the convenient and effective defense mechanism that is formed in the biological evolution of humans. If a person is hurt, he first assumes that the perpetrator inadvertently does it, or he does not make any judgment but patiently gathers all the related information and makes an impartial judgment afterward; then he will be easily hurt. It should be noted that although we often say there are many misunderstandings in the world, yet if we only make an observation, nearly all the misunderstandings are as follows: The good intention is misunderstood as the vicious intention, and its converse doesn't seem to occur.

---

36 The logic here is the same as the logic of punishment by criminal law. It is presumed that the punish-ment forcing officials to work honestly and diligently is X. $X = pS$, p here is the ratio of discovering the officials who don't work honestly and diligently, and S is the legally stipulated punishment. When the ratio p is lowered because of the excessively high cost of information in order to guarantee the sufficient X, it will surely augment S, namely the legally stipulated punishment. It is also one of the factors that enable the criminal punishment to be universally severe before modern times.

From the perspective of human nature, it might be roughly summarized that the human heart is sinister indeed. "Public opinion is the best judge." This saying is definitely wrong and is just self-comforting words for some persons. This point is also meaningful for the understanding of the feature of public opinion around the judicial trial, which thereby effectively prevents the influence of public opinion on the judiciary.

Second, the strict liability of modern law is a *legal* system whose purpose is to lower the operation cost of legal system; accordingly the subjective mentality of law-breakers is not considered as a result. Its purpose also emphasizes the actual relief to the victim, and generally the victim might receive such a relief; therefore the moral judgment toward the perpetrator will be dispensable. What we analyze here is not the formally government punishment, but social evaluation of ordinary people in a traditional society (by virtue of playwrights) toward the mistakes and faults of officials. Social evaluation can neither inflict sanctions through other means nor grant any actual relief to the victims, and therefore only augments the moral condemnation to officials. Besides, once the consequences of officials' misjudgment are typically severe, not only can officials themselves not afford to provide compensation (it might be unfair to these officials) but also the state has no financial power to provide substantial relief such as state compensation. Under such a circumstance, to remove officials who have made mistakes from their posts or to give them 300 lashes seems to be insufficient and doesn't diminish the anger. From the perspective of a social function, society will naturally augment such an informal sanction of morality and opinion to supplement and reinforce the formal sanction of law. It is involved with the issue of a basic strategic layout, which is the mutual cooperation and support between morality and law in a traditional society. This will be the subject of Chapter 6.

The Effectiveness of Strict Liability: A Theoretical Analysis

How should we evaluate such a rule by man and the concomitant severe, strict liability? Roughly speaking, contemporary jurists in China may have two types of evaluation. One starts from the humanitarian philosophy of criminal law and the legal philosophy of intentionalism and holds the critical attitude towards strict liability that such a sanction is excessively severe. The other starts from the political philosophy of "democracy" and holds that the strict liability should be implemented, in which the liability of officials is severely ascertained in order to ensure political integrity and a fair trial and prevent officials' disregard of human lives and their corruption and malpractices.

I think both paths are wrong, which try to start from a priori "correct" political idea or tenet or principle without care for the actual effect of this institution, namely whether this institution fulfills its pursuit: to improve the sense of responsibility in officials, to reduce the occurrence of preventing the administration of justice that most likely happens, and thereby to augment the welfare of the whole society. It is mainly a question concerning the facts, which can't be solved by the analysis of a concept or doctrine.

Owing to the lack of data in this aspect, this book can't make such an empirical analysis. However, we can still build up a theoretical model totally different in nature from the ordinary jurisprudential analysis (the analysis of concepts or doctrines) in order to understand how many main variables can influence the judgment of officials and how many variables will be affected by the strict liability for officials. Accordingly, we can make a preliminary prediction whether the mode of rule by man in "the administration of justice" is effective for the improvement of judicial decisions and provide a basic analytical framework for future empirical verification.

First, we admit that the general experiences and theories also tell us that a change in the motivation mechanism will surely change human behaviors. The strict liability is a motivation mechanism; therefore, when its severity is augmented, logically speaking, it must bring forth a change of behaviors of officials trying cases, who strive to lessen the likelihood of misjudgment for their own interests. In this sense, we can maintain that the strict liability will urge officials to take pains to improve the quality of trials and prevent misjudgment.

But the question is: Are there multiple variables affecting the occurrence of unjust cases?[37] The previously mentioned analysis has stated that under normal circumstances and overall, two main factors affect the incidence rate of unjust cases. The first is the social and historical factor, such as science and technology, and professional division of labor (namely institutions). In the condition of a traditional society, both variables were basically stable in the long run. In the long-term traditional Chinese society, people basically didn't see any important progress of science and technology related to judicial adjudication. Until the end of the Qing Dynasty, there was not even a separate judicial department and a batch of highly specialized professionals with division of labor related to judicial adjudication. Although there were para-professionals like secretaries in legal affairs, their number was quite a few without the support of other professionals as well. Hence, the strict liability allegedly has no influence on two important factors affecting the judiciary. No matter if the adjudicator of unjust cases adopted strict liability or not, it had no likelihood of facilitating the rapid change of social technologies and urging or quickening the division of labor in judicial adjudication.

Another factor affecting the occurrence of unjust cases is related to the adjudicator himself, namely his wisdom, morality, and diligence. We can examine all these factors one by one for analysis and investigate whether strict liability as a motivation can affect them or not and to what extent. But such an analysis is very hard. Totally talented factor plays a role in personal intelligence, which will surely not be influenced by a change in motivation. However, the judicial wisdom in the popular saying has other factors, such as logical thinking, imagination, sympathy, and sensitivity. All of these are concerned with the imaginary reconstruction of the case

---

37 The unjust cases here refer to the severe ones caused by various reasons, but not intentionally caused by officials. Because the mistake of judgment in the general sense is inevitable, this can be accepted by society as well.

and human behaviors in specific circumstances. These factors are talented issues, while some of them might be reinforced with increased practices, which is accordingly connected with the subjectively acquired efforts of individuals. Actually, the moral factor and personal efforts are usually connected with factors in both aspects, not completely the outcome of acquired education. For instance, the sympathy and the loyalty that are often connected with morality, and some personal preferences that are linked with painstaking efforts in appearance, yet can't be explained well by researchers all along, all of these have the innate element, which is proved in the research of today. Therefore, I still classify all these factors as the innate and acquired factors needed to avoid the excessive elaboration of analyzing them one by one.

When making such an abstract summarization, we can observe that the strict liability exerts no influence on the innate factors at all, no matter what type they are. Even in the face of death, I couldn't become Einstein, or Bao Zheng, or Holmes. What can work among the rest is only the so-called personally acquired efforts. In terms of officials, we can describe this factor as "diligent governance," which not only includes a certain moral factor but also the factor of personal efforts and the factor of improved skills and knowledge through practices.

This analysis seems to invariably make insufficient emphasis on the moral character of officials, which might be questioned by others accordingly. Therefore, I will dwell on it more. First, the personal moral factor mentioned earlier also has the acquired element, which is always recognized in Chinese tradition, especially in ancient times. For example, Confucius's words: "The Master said, Rotten wood can't be carved"[38]; "The Master said, Only the highest among the wise and the lowest among the stupid never change" (120); and "The Master said, Women and petty persons are the hardest to look after." (125) All of these and "three classes of human nature" of later generations imply (although not fully) the recognition of moral talent. But I will not have more discussions on the factor of the moral character of judges, because it is very important to the judicial system in terms of theory but is an unimportant factor in my present analysis. Its unimportance lies in that not everyone is engaged in trials, and the analytical model only needs to be focused on those specifically trying cases. Because of the political importance of case trials in society, and just because of the importance of personal morality to the case trial, therefore, no matter which society it is, it will carefully screen this type of officials and select those who at least possess the basic moral quality. Because of the great influence of personal morality on the case trial, even those with low moral standards worm their way into the ranks of officials and will more easily make unjust cases overall. With strict liability, they will be more easily eliminated by this system than other officials with the ordinary moral standard. The rest of the selected officials, although they have varying moral characters, the difference will not be too big from the macroscopic perspective. Actually, from the macroscopic perspective, the basic human moral standard hasn't witnessed

---

38 Confucius. *The Analects of Confucius*, 37 (hereafter cited parenthetically in the text).

any progress for thousands of years.[39] So, if it is not the deliberately moral corruption or malpractices, the moral factor hasn't much influence on the incidence rate of unjust cases. The matrix table in the first section of this chapter and the related analyses verify this point as well. In this analytical model, it is reasonable to neglect the influence of strict liability on the improvement of the moral standard of officials that leads to the reduction of unjust cases.

After such a sorting out, we can observe that strict liability might have the following influences on the officials' trial result:

The greatest benefit of strict liability is to indiscriminately investigate and accordingly punish all officials who are exposed to have made great mistakes in trying cases by actually broadening the scope of punishment. Admittedly, it is disadvantageous to many officials who unwittingly but actually misjudge cases, but is greatly advantageous to the investigation and punishment of unjust and false cases caused by malpractices for personal gain, perversion of justice for bribes, and moral turpitude among officials. The advantage not only lies in the fact that this system reduces the information cost needed to investigate and accordingly punish this type of official but also that there is a great benefit for the central government to cope with these officials and eliminate them from the management ranks, since these cases more easily arouse intense public grievance and endanger the political legitimacy of the rule.

However, the cost of this system is huge as well. First, it is not much help to reduce unjust cases caused by all the other objective factors including "the prevention of the administration of justice." Even if strict liability can urge officials to work diligently to avoid punishment and diligent governance makes a certain contribution to the correct judgment, since diligent governance is just one of the factors affecting the incidence rate of unjust cases, it has no likelihood of being the most important factor; therefore, the augmentation of diligent governance has no likelihood of exerting a great influence on the reduction of unjust cases.

Two factors restrict the increasing augmentation of diligent governance. First, diligent governance needs the investment of energy and attention, on the one hand, but usually needs the investment of additional time, on the other hand. Even if the former augmentation is unlimited (actually it is impossibly unlimited), the investment of time must be limited. A day just has 24 hours, a year just 365 days. No matter how diligently officials work, this reality doesn't change. Any strict liability has no likelihood of urging officials' diligent governance to surpass this limitation. Second, the benefit of any investment will have diminishing marginal utility, which means the effect of diligent governance caused by the strict liability and its ensuing effect on the reduction of unjust cases is definitely limited. When this limit is surpassed, the actual effect of diligent governance is even negative with increasingly severe and strict liability.

---

39 See, Posner, Richard A. *The Problematics of Moral and Legal Theory* (Cambridge, MA: Harvard University Press, 2009), esp. Chapter 1.

This means that excessively strict liability *might* urge many officials to work less diligently and even show more disregard of human life. This logical inference seems to contravene intuition. However, "when the water is too clear, there are no fish." There is such a case in history; indeed, strict administration didn't usher in the long-term incorruptibly local administration desired by the designer of this institution.[40]

We can use an arithmetic problem to prove it. It is presumed that the contribution rate of the variable of diligent governance affected by strict liability to the reduction of misjudged cases is 20%; it is also presumed that an official generally makes a misjudged case per year under normal circumstances during his 20 years of trying cases. This means that in his whole life of trying cases, the contrast of the numbers of misjudged cases because of undiligent governance and diligent governance is 20 versus 16. Because of various reasons, in traditional society, for misjudged cases, the probability of incurring the investigation and the probability of being investigated as unjust cases are generally quite low due to the excessively high information cost. If the probability of being actually investigated and punished because of each misjudged case is presumed to be 1%, then if I don't work hard, the accumulated probability will be 20%. If I work diligently, the accumulated probability will be 16%. The difference between the two rates is only 4%. This means that no matter if an official works diligently or not, the probability of being tracked by the strict liability for misjudged cases in two scenarios will be quite close. If the loss due to the punishment for misjudged cases is the monetarized benefits of all sorts, including economic income, personal reputation, official career, family reputation, etc., then its total amount is 20 thousand taels, the benefit of diligent governance, and that of undiligent governance is 800 taels.

But in order to improve this probability and get 800 taels, you must work diligently for 20 years and must overwork in the long run, because you don't know when and where and in which case you might make a mistake. If what you paid for was just one hour of additional work per day, then for 20 years, you would have extra work for 912 working days, while the benefit of each working day is no more than 1 tael. The contrast between payouts and earnings is quite disproportionate. Such a benefit is insufficient to motivate officials to work diligently. Because only when there is a diametrically different benefit between diligence and lack of diligence and such a benefit is roughly proportionate to the investment (diligent governance) will officials work hard.

Diligent governance also has an opportunity cost. Therefore, officials must unconsciously analyze the comparative benefit as well. They will consider whether the time and energy for diligent governance should be used for investment in the establishment of a social network. "You will have a bright official career, if you have powerful backing in the government." It can not only reduce the probability of punishment for the prevention of the administration of justice but also have

---

40 Ge, Jianxiong 葛剑雄. "Chongdu mingshi hairui zhuan" 重读明史海瑞传. *Zhongguo ai sixiang wang* 中国爱思想网, 2023. www.aisixiang.com/data/174.html.

other benefits. Or, officials spend time and energy on leisure pursuits, such as reading, writing, painting, and traveling; it seems not to have monetary benefit but many nonmonetary benefits, while these benefits will be much greater than those from diligent governance. Actually, according to this formula, if the establishment of a social network could lower the 5% probability of punishment for misjudged cases, then the probability for those officials who are not diligent will be lower than the probability of diligent officials. What is more, the benefit of setting up a social network is far greater than these. Under this circumstance, it is easier for bureaucrats to shield one another.

Viewed from another aspect, such a practice has become the pursuit of governance that is not diligent at the expense of resources. But it is not the whole countermeasure. Some officials might deliberately adopt some completely legal measures to further lower the probability of punishment for their misjudged cases. One of them is to try cases as little as possible and to try cases only when it is absolutely necessary. Non-involvement naturally begets fewer misjudged cases, which lowers the probability of punishment. If it is originally presumed that there will be generally one misjudged case per ten, the error rate is 10%. In the past, if I tried ten cases per year, there would be one misjudged case; now, I only try five cases per year, and the error rate is just 10%, but the number of misjudged cases is only 0.5. Fewer misjudged cases, even if the probability of being tracked and investigated remains the same, means that my probability of being investigated and punished for misjudged cases is still lowered to 50%.[41]

For an individual official, such a utilization of resources is beneficial. But for society, there are no benefits, but too much expenses instead. In terms of a normal society, it should encourage people to invest their time and energy in activities beneficial to themselves and society as well, not those beneficial to themselves and detrimental to society. Such a utilization of resources will be not efficient. If officials intentionally try fewer cases, some cases will be forced only to return to the folk, which are originally tried by officials in a more efficient way. These cases will seek an informal adjudicating mechanism or other methods for disputes and seek a solution with higher costs. Moreover, it will thereby be harder for "the administration of justice" to make progress, and the judicial knowledge is more difficult to be accumulated. As a result, social elites who have better ways out are naturally unwilling to study legal affairs. Therefore, in addition to the analysis of traditional judicial system in China in Chapters 3 and 4, we can have a new perspective to understand why the judiciary was not developed in traditional China.

This analysis has no intention of denying strict liability. Although this institution has various problems, we must observe that the most principal and perhaps the most important problem for which this institution is targeted is how to investigate and deal with those corrupt officials accordingly in a convenient way. The elimination of officials who are most harmful to the state power might not only strengthen

---

41 The analysis of this section still presumes that these officials were risk neutral; actually, their attitudes toward the risk will be different from each other, but it will not impact this analysis.

the legitimacy of political power but also prevent these officials from plundering state-owned resources. For the state, this might be the greatest benefit. Perhaps, to acquire this benefit brought by strict liability, society paid the price to have those nonchalant, indolent and ordinary officials whose number is yet huge, and to bear the institutional cost that was totally invisible in those days, namely the underdevelopment of judicial system and the non-existence of legal profession.

However, it doesn't mean that we should neglect it nowadays. Certainly, it is only an analysis in principle, although it is logically valid; the verification needs more experimental materials.

Preliminary Summary

I believe the earlier analysis has reiterated the theme of this chapter from different perspectives and aspects, namely the limitation of honest officials in the judiciary and the issue of the mode of rule by man in such "administration of justice." I haven't looked at this from the moral perspective, but from the perspective where people usually find no problems. Therefore, my analysis criticizes and does not just morally condemn the mode of honest officials in "the administration of justice" in traditional Chinese society in a more profound way. Considering the change of some important social variables at present, this analysis can be said to pass the death sentence to the traditional system of "administrating justice" in terms of theory, which is helpful to dispel some myths about traditional "justice" that might still be left over in society or among some scholars. It explains that although traditional Chinese society inflicted much severe sanctions on officials who misjudged cases than modern countries do and emphasized the personal strict liability, why did it still fail to effectively motivate officials? Hence, it also explains why the system of "administrating justice" in traditional Chinese society fall into a strange-looking cycle. This argument is even somewhat inspiring to some institutional reforms of today – the prospect of these reforms and the points worthy of being perfected can be predicted. For instance, consider the accountability system for misjudged cases generally adopted in the judicial sector and some "accountability system" for governmental officials in recent years. To varying degrees, these measures actually try to repeat the strict liability for officials in ancient China. Although it may be helpful for a certain period, the long-term effects may be negative.

Along with Chapters 3 and 4, this chapter actually emphasizes the utility of science and technology and the social division of labor again. These factors will not only greatly reduce the information cost and facilitate the trial and the handling of other administrative affairs in a better way but also enable those with general qualities and competences to assume the trial post without relying on the mode of rule by man in "administrating justice" that emphasizes personal morality and wisdom of adjudicators. Accordingly, the whole social governance turns to the modern rule of law that more relies on science and technology, professional division of labor, and greatly improved efficiency as a result. In such a system, the personal liability of adjudicators and decision-makers is greatly lessened, and the social expectation and moral pressure that they assume are weakened as well, but it will not usher in more corruption or slacking-off among officials. Even if the moral standard of officials has not been improved, yet because of all the support and restriction of professional division of labor and the reduction of the supervision fee caused by the lowering of information costs, the deeds of officials will be forced to accord with the code of ethics. In this sense, although science and technology can't change the moral conviction of people, they can indirectly influence (but not decide) the moral standard reflected in the deeds of public officials in society through a series of factors.

Part III
Legal "Culture"

6 The Political and Legal System in the Spirit of "Morality Given Priority Over Penalty"

When considering the factors of the underdevelopment of science and technology, the deficiency of professional division of labor and professional knowledge, and the expensive information cost, the system of "administrating justice" in traditional China has various disadvantages in which the case trial easily can be mishandled, and it is very difficult to supervise and examine officials. In this condition, to guarantee social governance in an effective and economic way and to prevent officials from corrupting and abusing power, other control measures must be mobilized. Hence, the ideological education as an institution becomes particularly important. From the perspective of this social function, the moral doctrines such as the Confucianist "Three Cardinal Guides and Five Constant Virtues"[1] are not just a "culture" but also the important component of the political and social governance system in traditional China; not just the foundation for a person to settle down in his life and career but also the necessity of "establishing peace for all future generations."

The ideological education is not just initiatively assumed by Confucianist intellectuals at the imperial court; the social popular opinion is inevitably affected by ideology; all sorts of literature and art, including the popular literature, also fulfill such a function to a certain extent. Chapter 1 mentioned the rise and decline of revenge ideology along with the revenge institution in the period before the Qin Dynasty, although it was not rolled out. The similar phenomenon that "literature is a vehicle of the Confucian ideas" has consistently existed in China since then, and even continues in China today. In this sense, because of its utility of social control, literature therefore can be described as a certain "law," while it is the blind spot of contemporary American law and literature movement – literature as law.

This part puts such a phenomenon into the productivity level of traditional Chinese society and the corresponding sociopolitical organization structure for investigation, examines the ideological function of literature to society, and tries to present an explanation. My basic proposition is that in a traditional big country, because of the insufficient competence of the national political governance of society through law or the excessively high costs of information and

---

1 The three guides are ruler guides subject, father guides son, and husband guides wife; the five virtues are benevolence, righteousness, propriety, wisdom, and fidelity.

DOI: 10.4324/9781003615606-10

supervision, the state has to resort to the moral ideology and usually reinforces social control through the expressive forms of literature and art. This chapter will investigate the ideological utility of traditional Chinese drama overall and the basic layout of social control in traditional Chinese society jointly constructed by literature and law in a more general sense in order to investigate the influence of such a layout on the literary conveyance of some stories. The related criticisms of dramatists and the historical evolution of stories and opinions around Zhao the Orphan and Dou E's injustice provide the source materials for analysis. Chapter 7 then investigates traditional Chinese drama from a specific aspect, especially the influence of its narrative method and art performance method on the formation of the justice value among ordinary people in traditional Chinese society.

We must define "the ideology." There have been abundant analyses and discussions on it.[2] I adopt the definition in *The Blackwell Encyclopedia of Political Thought*: "Ideologies are patterns of symbolically-charged beliefs and expressions that present, interpret and evaluate the world in a way designed to shape, mobilize, direct, organize and justify certain modes or courses of action and to anathematize others."[3] When the ideology is defined and applied thus, what I am concerned with is not whether the expression of ideology itself is right or wrong, true or false, but the ideological function. Because "in ideology men do indeed express, not the relation between them and their conditions of existence, but *the way* they live the relation between them and their conditions of existence: this presupposes both a real relation and an '*imaginary*', '*lived*' relation."[4] Douglass C. North, the institutional economist, also regards ideology from the functional perspective and lays particular emphasis on three features of ideology. First, ideology is an economizing device by which individuals come to terms with their environment and are provided with a "worldview" so that the decision-making process is simplified. Second, ideology is inextricably interwoven with moral and ethical judgments about the fairness of the world perceived by individuals. Third, individuals alter their ideological perspectives when their experiences are inconsistent with their ideology, but inconsistencies between experiences and ideologies must be accumulated before individuals alter their ideology.[5]

Moral World

By reading a few Yuan playscripts, you can get the overwhelming sense of morality. In Chapter 5, I mentioned that the plays concerning "honest officials" are accustomed to turning the issue of officials' competence into the issue of their

---

2 For the general discussion, see McLellan, David. *Ideology*, 2nd ed. (Minneapolis: University of Minnesota Press, 1995).

3 Miller, David, ed. *The Blackwell Encyclopedia of Political Thought* (London: Blackwell, 1987), 235.

4 Althusser, Louis. *For Marx*, trans. Ben Brewster (New York: Verso, 2005), 233.

5 North, Douglass C. *Structure and Change in Economic History* (New York: W. W. Norton, 1981), 49.

personal moral character. Moreover, even in ordinary plays, we can find moral preaching everywhere, which is quite trite in the perspective of today. In detective plays, a moral creed is even used to directly decide the trial outcome.

For example, in *The Butterfly Dream*,[6] three brothers beat Ge Biao from a powerful family to death to take vengeance for their deceased father. Bao Zheng tried this case to find who was the ringleader, then sentenced him a life for a life. Three brothers vied with each other in assuming the liability of killing Ge Biao, while Mother Wang willingly let her own son, Third Wang, give his life in order to save Eldest Wang and Second Wang, who were not born by her. Bao Zheng was quite moved at this: "In this affair, I see that the mother is virtuous and the sons are completely filial" (Guan, 2010: 61) and "Virtue and obedience of this order should be rewarded with title and praise, such ardent chasteness and excelling worthiness is fit for reward" (Guan, 2010: 62). And he thought, "I support the sagely and intelligent ruler of the present day, hoping to spread a pure reputation for all eternity" (Guan, 2010: 63). Then Bao Zheng ordered his subordinate to hang Pigheaded Ass Zhao, a horse thief, and used his body to save the life of Third Wang. What is more, Bao Zheng delivered the verdict in the end:

> You, having been pampered citizens beneath the imperial sleeves,
> Possess the stuff to be stalwart ministers, to requite the state:
> The eldest brother shall go to follow affairs at court,
> The second shall wear regalia and insignia of high status.
> Stone shall become Prefect of Zhongmou,
> And your mother shall be enfeoffed as Lady of Stalwart Virtue.
> The state treasures righteous husbands and wives of integrity,
> And loves those filial children and compliant grandsons.
> The ruler of sagely light has bestowed these ranks in reward –
> Let us all gaze toward the palace gates to thank his beneficence.
>
> (Guan, 2010: 75)

I don't consider the story of this play to be a true event, nor believe that the official appointment in one society could only be decided by morality without the consideration of competence. But if only in terms of the play, at least this playwright thought, which perhaps implied the social idea at that time to a certain extent, although personal deeds violated the law, only if the main principle accorded with "virtue" and "filial piety" in the morality of traditional society, they not only should be exempt from the legal punishment but also should be praised, or even granted official posts. If there was a moral defect in personal character (such as Pigheaded Ass Zhao, the horse thief), even death would be

---

6 Hanqing, Guan. "Rescriptor-in-Waiting Bao Thrice Investigates the Butterfly Dream," in *Monks, Bandits, Lovers, and Immortals: Eleven Early Chinese Plays*, ed. and trans. Stephen H. West and Wilt L. Idema (Indianapolis: Hackett Publishing Company, 2010) (hereafter cited parenthetically in the text).

insufficient punishment for such a lawbreaker. This actually affirms the supreme status of traditional morality in the society of that time, which emphasizes legal obedience to traditional morality; but it is not the empty moral preaching, and it links obedience with the secular official position and wealth. For most of audiences, isn't this play a public education of morality? In the meantime, isn't this play the education in the general knowledge of law?

Even as for *The Injustice to Dou E* that is greatly commended by modern Chinese scholars and believed to reflect the hardships and resistances of laboring people, only a slight removal from the popular perspective from modern times onwards will give you a totally different feeling of "moving Heaven and shaking Earth" by reading the playscript. The play not only characterizes the evil such as Donkey Zhang and "the excessive official" such as Taowu but more importantly characterizes Dou E as a moral paragon growing up in the miserable hardship, which is concentrated on the morality of "Three Obediences and Four Virtues" in traditional society.

In order to avoid her mother-in-law's suffering interrogation by torture, Dou E would rather sacrifice her life and reputation. Although Dou Tianzhang, her father, sold Dou E at age seven years old to Mother Cai for the sake of his own official rank, which accordingly caused a series of tragedies for Dou E, when Dou E met her father, she didn't utter a reproach or grievance at all of this. (Under common circumstances, reproach is usually the flow of emotions. There is a Chinese saying, "sometimes tough love may be the only way.") Such a "filial piety" might be hardly comprehended by contemporaries. Especially at the end of the whole play, Dou E had three extortions in bidding farewell to her father, from which we can more keenly sense the publicity of the orthodox ideology. Dou E first exhorted her father, "Again Imperial Sword and Gold Tablet shall reveal their power, to break corrupt officials and abusers of place, to share the sorrows of the Son of Heaven, and to root out evil for the people's sake" (this reflects Dou E's "loyalty"). Then, she extorted Dou Tianzhang, "My mother-in-law is well advanced in years and there is no one to look after her. Will you take her into your household and for my sake treat her as is her due? Then I shall be able to close my eyes at last beneath the Nine Streams" (this reflects Dou E's unusual "filial piety"). At last, "father, below my name, Dou E, revoke the sentence of conviction that caused my unjust death" (Guan, 1977:157). How could Dou E be an ordinary girl without education? She was actually the embodiment of traditional morality and the ideologist expert practicing what she preached!

Certainly, Dou E didn't comply with every whim of her mother-in-law if Mother Cai contravened the traditional moral doctrines. In the play, Mother Cai, who was in widowhood for years, intended to remarry Donkey Zhang's father. Dou E repeatedly reproached her, "How lamentable! Blush for shame!" and claimed, "Women! How faithless they have ever been, always ready to elope, no will of their own" (Guan, 1977:132). It should be noted that "women" here is the general reference, not the specific reference. Hence, Dou E repeated the ancient Confucian doctrine, "women and petty persons are the hardest to look after."[7] This attitude sufficiently enrages modern feminists.

Actually, although modern literary researchers always tend to elevate the image of Dou E, according to the verification of dramatists, the summary of the original text of Guan Hanqing's *The Injustice to Dou E* compiled in *Ancient and Modern Masters' Zaju* was "Title and Name: An old lady who marries again is too crooked-hearted, *A virtuous girl who guards her chastity* is strong willed; Bucking the wind and braving the snow, a ghost without a head, Moving heaven and shaking earth, the injustice to Dou E." The present "Theme: Holding a mirror and carrying a scale is the way of the Surveillance Commissioner. Title: Moving Heaven Shaking Earh is Dou E's Injustice" was revised by Zang Jinshu, the compiler of *Selected Plays from the Yuan Dynasty*.[8] Therefore, Guan Hanqing's own intention was to mold Dou E as the image of "a virtuous girl guarding her chastity" and might not want to attack the system of "administrating justice" in traditional society or imperial power.

As for this phenomenon, the simplest explanation is that Confucian tradition occupies the dominant position in traditional Chinese society. But this explanation lacks sufficient persuasiveness if only looked at from the perspective of the tradition of Chinese culture, especially the tradition of Confucian culture. Admittedly,

---

7 Certainly, these moral preachings of Dou E *might* not be treated so seriously. There can be another explanation as well. That is, Dou E might not sincerely believe it – her words are the strategic necessity of self-defense. Just as many scholars have indicated, Dou E's "chastity is not the true motive for the behavior of character, but a measure of the self-defense." Zhou, Xiaochi 周晓痴. "Renwu de qinggan guiji yu zuojia de shenmei pingjia" 人物的情感轨迹与作家的审美评价. In *Yuanqu tongrong* xia 元曲通融下, 1581; Zhang, Yimu 张一木. "Moshi dou e zai mengyuan" 莫使窦娥再蒙冤. In *Yuanqu tongrong* xia 元曲通融下, 1593; Zhou, Yueliang 周月亮. "Dui wu xiaoru xiansheng ping dou e yuan de jidian yijian" 对吴小如先生评窦娥冤的几点意见. In *Yuanqu tongrong xia* 元曲通融下, 1599; and Huang, Ke 黄克. *Guan hanqing xiju renwu lun* 关汉卿戏剧人物论 (Beijing: People's Literature, 1984), 50–74. In the meanwhile, these moral preachings are also the strategy of Dou E to ensure that her alliance of resisting the oppression might not be dismantled. Because once Mother Cai agreed to be married to Old Zhang, then Dou E would not have the perimeter defense, and her situation would be accordingly much more dangerous. Considering the restriction of "Three Obediences and Four Virtues," Dou E couldn't explicitly state it to her mother-in-law. It is under this circumstance that Dou E must get away from the image of all obedience for her own safety and rely on the orthodox moral admonition of traditional society for her own interests in order to elevate her legitimacy to challenge the authority of the mother-in-law. This explanation is surely valid and even more reflects the complexity of Dou E. However, even this saying is accepted, and its premise must be that the saying of "being faithful to one's husband to the very end" chosen by Dou E was a priority and indisputable. It is this priority that enables Dou E to be qualified to launch the limited yet direct challenge to the respect for seniority of traditional society in the capacity of younger generation (if the plot reflected the reality in those days), or in the eyes of the playwright, this legitimacy enables Dou E to be qualified to challenge this order (if it was just the creation of Guan Hanqing). No matter which scenario it might be (or if both scenarios are counted), what we can see is the power of the moral ethics of traditional society. Therefore, the argument of this chapter is still valid.
8 Shao, Zengqi 邵曾祺. "Guan hanqing zuopin kao" 关汉卿作品考. In *Yuanqu tongrong* xia 元曲通融下, 1277.

Confucianism, with Confucius as the representative, always emphasizes the rule by virtue, the rule by rites, loyalty and filial piety, officials' love for common people, benevolent government, "the people are of greatest importance; the ruler is of least importance,"[9] and stresses "Let there be the men and the government will flourish; but without the men, their government decays and ceases." In the meantime, it can't be denied that such a cultural tradition provides the path for the people at that time to conveniently comprehend social problems and provides the basic framework for the generalization and classification of these problems, which thereby influences the methods presented by the people to solve problems.

However, no matter what attitude the interpreter holds toward traditional Chinese culture (criticism or praise), this interpretation is rather unconvincing. It presumes that the formation of cultural tradition is just the personal choice of the founder of a theory. It almost means that Confucius made a great mistake at the beginning and then later generations of Chinese would always follow suit accordingly. Or, "If Heaven didn't give birth to Confucius, the world would be at pitch-dark night for eternity." As for which saying you will accept, it is up to your likes or dislikes toward this tradition.

I don't deny the importance of cultural tradition and believe in the reliance on the path of institution and culture as well. But I believe neither that the creation of cultural tradition is completely accidental nor that the cultural tradition will be stable and eternally unchanged upon formation, and it is the deeds of those beyond real life and without any social function. Cultural tradition molds people indeed, yet each generation will not adhere to it just because a certain activity is a tradition. People always receive new information from real life and change their behaviors and expressions in line with new situations, which alters cultural tradition accordingly. Because the overwhelming majority of people – if not all people – are pragmatists in the sense of general knowledge in my opinion, they lay more stress on all sorts of interests and always vie with each other "for fame at court, for gain in market." Moreover, even if the saying of cultural tradition is valid, it can only answer *intellectuals'* claim that "literature is a vehicle of Confucian ideas" (the so-called great tradition) in traditional society at most and can't answer why drama, the more popular entertainment (I will analyze this point later), is still filled with such moral preaching (the so-called small tradition).

It should be noted as well that although the previously mentioned Yuan plays are pervaded with the so-called "Confucian" morality that occupies the orthodox status in traditional society, it is not just Confucian morality. If we read them closely, we can find many plays are pervaded with ideas irrelevant to Confucian orthodoxy. For example, *The Foe Creditor* tells such a story[10]: An unrighteous woman was greedy for money and misappropriated ten silver ingots deposited by a monk from Wutai Mountain for her keeping. Although she succeeded at this, many years later,

---

9 Bloom, Irene, trans. *Mencius* (New York: Columbia University Press, 2009), 159.
10 Zheng, Tingyu 郑廷玉. "Cuifujun duan yuanjia zhaizhu" 崔府君断冤家债主. In *Yuanqu xuan* 元曲选, 1130–1145.

not only she herself but also her two sons passed away for no reason. At the end of the play, a person of moral integrity stated that it was retribution for the greed for others' property. It should be especially pointed out that two sons who received the retribution were totally innocent. When their mother was greedy for money, they were not yet born, let alone knowing the inside story and participating in it. Therefore, this play more publicizes the Buddhist idea, or even folk causality, especially causality concerning posterity.[11] Another example is in *The Vest* 《相国寺公孙汗衫记》 which promotes the plain folk idea of "every good or bad deed has its just reward" and is considered by scholars as "a play encouraging virtue" or "a moral education play of punishing evildoers and encouraging people to do good."[12] From the perspective of social function and in terms of the possible influence on the ideas and deeds of audiences, what these plays promote is only some basic codes of social behaviors such as not to lust for money, to keep promises, and to requite someone for his kindness. The earlier-mentioned execution of Pigheaded Ass Zhao, the horse thief in *The Butterfly Dream*; the revenge conveyed in *The Orphan of Zhao*; and the reproaches to excessive officials and corrupt clerks and the praises for honest officials and capable clerks in many detective plays, although they are all compatible with Confucian morality, not all of them only belong to Confucianism.[13] Just as some scholars have indicated, Taoism and Buddhist ideas also have direct influence on the creation of Yuan plays.[14]

Although it couldn't be stated that Confucian ideas monopolize, yet one thing must be affirmed – that namely in Yuan plays, the combination of story and characters in the play presents a highly moralized world and reinforces one or a series of moral themes.

We must reiterate the phenomenon discussed in Chapter 5. In many detective plays, such as *The Injustice to Dou E*, due to various social conditions or the limitation of personal competences, the trial mistake of adjudicators will usually be transformed to be a criticism on the personal morality of adjudicators. It seems that whether a case could be tried in a fair and proper way, it is basically or even completely a moral problem. Even if some playwrights actually had presented or even perceived the irrelevance between some unjust cases and personal morality of adjudicators, they still looked at from the perspective of morality and promoted the orthodox morality of traditional society. Therefore, we must raise the following

---

11 For the retribution as the concept of punishment among the people, see Posner, Richard A. *Economics of Justice* (Cambridge, MA: Harvard University Press, 1980), esp. Chapter 8.

12 Deng, Shaoji 邓绍基. *Yuandai wenxueshi* 元代文学史 (Beijing: People's Literature, 1998), 220; Zhang, Daxin 张大新. "Nongjia shan e yiliguan de supu xianxian zhang guobin zaju de wenhua yiyun" 农家善恶义利观的素朴显现 – 张国宾杂剧的文化意蕴. *Pingdingshan shizhuan xuebao* 平顶山师专学报, no. 1 (1999), 18.

13 We can't reach the conclusion that Confucian moral ideology dominates traditional drama from the fact that morality exhibited in plays has this or that type of expression in Confucian doctrines. We must be cautious of it. This seemingly valid inference is idealist and exaggerates the influence of political ideology on literature.

14 You, Guoen et al., chiefly eds. 游国恩. *Zhongguo wenxueshi* 中国文学史 (Beijing: People's Literature, 1964), 175.

questions: In traditional Chinese society, why was the issue of officials' "competence" considered the issue of "morality" in the long run? How did this transformation happen?

Certainly, we can *interpret* the questions from the perspective of the mainstream discourse of traditional society: The mainstream moral discourse provides basic concepts, discursive modes, propositions, and theoretical frameworks to understand and discuss this type of question (it hereby has the function of saving the information cost) and easily acquire the legitimacy, which is convenient to enter society, etc. However, all of these are an interpretation limited to the purview of concepts and ideas, not the *explanation*. They neither explain why this phenomenon can exist for a long time nor how this phenomenon happens. Since they only interpret ideas and behaviors in the conceptual sense, such an interpretation actually abandons the investigation of function and utility of this phenomenon in society. We must seek a new perspective for entry.

Ideology as a Governance Institution

In the chapters and sections earlier, I invariably emphasize that in traditional society, the information cost of human association was very high because of quite a low level of social productivity and the underdevelopment of science and technology; even if the ruler had a wish, it would be very hard for him to have quite an in-depth understanding of the grassroots in society, which was therefore difficult for him to acquire the necessary knowledge concerning the governed objects in terms of their governance. In addition to the low level of productivity, the number of various resources that could be mobilized by public power was rather limited. It was still very hard to have sufficient resources to support an effectively profound system of administration, and "the administration of justice," even the desperate "squeezing" of public power itself, would consume resources, need information, and lead to the diminishing marginal utility. Therefore, overall, in comparison with modern society, the state power was always relatively weak in traditional Chinese society in fact.

Yuan plays repeatedly reveal the situation of such resource deficiency of public power. For example, in many Yuan plays, there is the phenomenon that local magistrates extorted "the litigation cost" to maintain local finance and support their own lives. According to the historical records, in the early years of the Yuan Dynasty at least, officers and officials at the levels of prefecture and county had no income.[15] Hence, these officials must rely on the collection of litigation costs from plaintiffs and defendants to maintain their lives.

Lacking financial resources, local governments in all dynasties had no likelihood of maintaining the relatively huge rank of incorruptible, fair-minded, and

---

15 Zhu, Dongrun 朱东润. "Yuan zaju jiqi shidai" 元杂剧及其时代. In *Mingjia jiedu yuanqu* 名家解读元曲, 34.

efficient officials and clerks, let alone effective local governance.[16] The result is not only "law and government are far from here" in the country or remote regions, but in Yuan plays, even in the urban regions, the governance of officials was relatively weak as well. One evidence is that in Yuan plays, even in cities, even if it was a homicide case with the obvious suspect of murder, there would be often the saying concerning "official settlement" or "private settlement" between the disputed parties, and the parties concerned seriously considered "private settlement."[17] Such a private "discretionary power" in homicide cases has no likelihood of existence in any modern society. Why does the bargain over official settlement and private settlement recur in Yuan plays that portrayed civic life? Then, we can accordingly infer the reason; it is impossible to be just the wishful thinking or fabrication of playwrights – it must be quite possible for private settlement indeed.

Similar evidence or examples proving the incompetence of government are not just one or two cases in Yuan plays; on the contrary, it can be described as universal. We can still choose *The Injustice to Dou E* as an example. First, in the broad daylight, Mother Cai, the creditor, in collecting debts was almost strangled to death by Dr. Lu, the debtor. Immediately after this, Donkey Zhang and his father openly threatened to seize Dou E herself and her mother-in-law as their wives and likewise blackmailed Mother Cai by again threatening to strangle her to death. Afterward, Donkey Zhang and his father forced their way in and lived in Dou E's house for several months. Although Dou E was strongly against it, she couldn't turn to the government to kick Donkey Zhang and his father out. Usually, it is impossible for the government to allow these things to happen,[18] because they indirectly threaten the legitimacy of imperial power; besides, such a stark practice of the jungle law in civil life was a challenge to state power. These things are unbelievable in modern society. Hence, all of these factors in *The Injustice to Dou E* and other Yuan plays only show that the official system of administration and "the administration of justice" in the country at that time hardly guaranteed the basic freedom, property, and safety of people – even if regardless of the factor of corrupt officials – if they

16 See Ch'ü, T'ung-tsu. *Local Government in China under the Ch'ing* (Stanford: Stanford University Press, 1962).
17 For example, In *The Injustice to Dou E*, Donkey Zhang told Dou E, "You've poisoned my father. Do you want to settle it in court or out of court?" (Guan, 1977: 134). In *The Chalk Circle*, the murderer Ma's wife also told Zhang Haitang, "You little slut, here's the gate to Kaifeng Prefecture. If the court deals with you, you'll have to suffer each little step of being bound and beaten. It would be better to acknowledge it and settle it privately" (Li, 259). In *The Moheluo Doll*, the murder Li Wendao told his sister-in-law Liu Yuqiang, "My elder brother has died! Do you want an official settlement or a private settlement?" (Meng, 161). In *Shennuer*, there is also the same detail. Although in these four plays, it is the criminal (or the criminal suspect for the sake of political correctness?) who first proposed official settlement or private settlement, yet the victim such as Dou E or Liu Yuniang once considered the possibility of private settlement and just refused it because private settlement was rather disadvantageous to her.
18 In Yuan plays, especially detective plays, one important theme is how officials representing imperial power applied their talents and power to break through multiple obstructions and crack down on and sanction those powerful and high-ranking officials to protect the commoners.

were not fabricated by Guan Hanqing and other playwrights only for the sake of dramatic effects (in my opinion, it is impossible).

At the mention of the system of administration and "the administration of justice," officials and clerks must be observed naturally, because governance is always fulfilled by officials even today. Therefore, any effective governance must be consistently involved with the issue of how to supervise and manage officials. It doesn't mean the ruler is benevolent or he wants to use "the rule of law" to restrict public power; it means, for the supreme ruler, no matter if he is a tyrant or a philosopher king, it is a very practical issue that must be solved. He can't and won't allow officials to use the authority of public posts to seek personal interests as they please. Such a deed will usher in the loss of various resources of the supreme ruler, not only the material resources (wealth) but also other symbolic resources (legitimacy). In the end, there will be great disorder under heaven, even the loss of political power and the ensuing loss of the life of the supreme ruler and his family members. Consequently, if possible, no matter what kind of government it is, it will reinforce the supervision and management of officials as far as possible and not allow officials to exploit common people without regard for human life as they please.

However, to just have a wish is not enough. In traditional society, because of the limitation of science and technology, the low level of productivity, and the rather scarce wealth in the hands of common people, the state couldn't create something out of nothing and extract oil out of stones. Second, even if some common people possessed wealth, there would be a question: how could we make a differentiation to let the haves pay more money, then establish a system of progressive tax just like the practice of modern countries?; it needed the effort of gathering and processing abundant information and a strong rank of law enforcement. But in a traditional society in a great country like China, in the condition of quite underdeveloped science and technology, information, and transportation, it was nearly impossible to effectively gather and process such information only through human labor. At most, only the system of taxes and levies including forced labor of all sorts according to the number of persons, households, and/or lands was adopted; later, with the development of monetary economics, it was possible to adopt "the integrated cash tax," which quantified all the forced labors levied by the state and simplified taxes. From this perspective, many taxation systems in modern times, especially the system of progressive tax, and the concomitant rate and type of tax in the steady flow can possibly be established in society where costs of information and transaction are greatly reduced. If a huge rank of law enforcement were established only to levy taxes, this effort itself would consume lots of fortunes and need the excessively high cost of supervision in the meantime; otherwise, this rank might have the likelihood of embezzling wealth originally levied for the state or misappropriating the power entrusted by the state for the private utility. For the ruler, the loss outweighed the gain in this situation; he would rather conceal wealth among the people and establish a "small government."

Hence, in the condition of traditional society, the central government was nearly doomed to have no likelihood of possessing sufficient wealth to establish an effective system of administration and "the administration of justice." Besides, due to the issue of wealth and information, the central government even couldn't establish the wide, meticulous, and effective supervision mechanism to oversee officials, which created the possibility of corruption or at least malfeasance of officials and enabled the system with the original defaults to effectively operate in a harder way.

The ruler was accordingly confronted with a huge difficult issue in social governance or control: how to effectively mobilize all resources to maintain this political power, not only to "herd people" but also to manage officials. It is from this perspective with the target of such a basic issue that the discursive practice of moral and ethical ideology in traditional society is actually another type of institution and law, which is indispensable in the bureaucratic system of administration and "the administration of justice" with the complementary functions. Viewed from this aspect, the moral discourse in traditional society is targeted at two aspects at least. One aspect is targeted at common people, such as "Three Cardinal Guides and Five Constant Virtues," which stipulates the basic principles of human deeds and thoughts and serves as the most basic social norms. Its utility is like the constitution of today. The general folk norms such as credibility, decency, and non-avarice for money also serve to regulate thoughts and deeds and likewise specify interpersonal associations and trading relations of all sorts. Besides, a social organization structure that is closely linked to traditional society constitutes the power relations within the small group, the community pressure and sanction, which force people to have the self-regulation to dispel the conflicts or to solve the large quantity of conflicts and disputes in daily life at the social level; it accordingly guarantees social peace and basic order. Only on the basis that is preliminarily formatted, and from the perspective of the ruler, they then might relatively, composedly mobilize and apply the rest of limited material and human resources to more directedly and efficiently cope with the relatively large social conflicts which can't be solved by those ideologies and the organization structure of agricultural society itself. From the perspective of ordinary people, they can live in a relatively ordered society and then effectively and meaningfully organize and arrange their daily lives.

The other aspect of such a moral discourse is targeted at officials, such as "loyalty," "rule by virtue," "benevolent government," "care for ordinary people," "the people are of greatest importance, the ruler is of least importance," "people's will may support the ruler, but may cause the ruler to fall from power," etc. Its utility is to use these ideologies to regulate the deeds of officials and internalize them as the self-restraint of officials as far as possible; it also forms a certain pressure of public opinion in the meantime to prevent officials from seeking personal gain through power; it is with a certain restriction and integration function. It emphasizes the importance of personal moral character of officials to governance and asks officials to work diligently, love ordinary people, honestly perform official duties, and care for hardships of the people; it encourages officials to fully utilize their wisdom, competence, and diligence to compensate for a series of problems of governance caused by the insufficiently financial, technical, and talent resources; it fully encourages and forces officials to mobilize the maximum subjective initiative, namely, the so-called "devoted loyalty" to fulfill effective governance.

Therefore, the moral discourse of traditional society is not "the morality" as a discipline discussed at the department of philosophy in universities and is not just concerned with the personal moral cultivation of officials and intellectuals (the candidates for official posts). According to the classification by function, it is actually a type of political science, a governance study and legal science, and the ideology of the ruling class occupying the dominant position in society at that time and is the institutionalized *political* ideology. It is actually one of the most important methods and technologies of governing the state. In this sense, in traditional society, the so-called "rule by virtue" is the politics and rule by law of that time.

"Truly, a Tale Without Moral Teaching, No Matter How Finely Written, Is Useless"[19]

Ideology is one part of the governance system in traditional society (even any society), but it is not material and can't live independently. As a discursive practice and practical discourse, it must be only circulated in society to be manifested. It must resort to carriers of all sorts, and in the meantime only rely on the basic power relations formed by social structure to function. Besides, ideology is not only limited to the official system. As the conceptual culture occupying the dominant position, the mainstream ideology in society is always all-pervasive, like the mercury on the ground, and clings to any place it can pervade. Literature and art are obviously an important form in which ideology can take root. It is only in this big institutional framework that we can understand the utility of literature and art (especially drama) in this mechanism and practice of moral discourse.

Actually, in traditional China, this point was invariably understood by intellectuals, who consciously practiced it. The highest art standard pursued by Confucius is "acme of perfection." The scholars of later generations, including many scholars of the Yuan Dynasty, are clearly aware of it and greatly promote the ideological function of various art forms including drama. For example, Yang Weizhen, the scholar and poet in the Yuan Dynasty, stressed the dramatic functions of "euphemistic remonstrance and admonition" in *On Zhuming's Burlesque Performance* and *Preface to Mr. Shen's Yuefu Poems*.[20] Another scholar from the Yuan Dynasty, Xia Tingzhi, also thought that in the relations of the ruler and subjects, mother and son, brothers and friends, plays "can enrich ethics and beautify morals."[21]

Certainly, what is promoted by some persons doesn't amount to a drama that might inevitably possess and actually fulfill this function in society. Hence, it is necessary to point out the features of drama and the concomitant possibility, reality, and effectivity of receiving and transmitting traditional ideology.

---

19 Ming, Gao. *The Lute: Kao Ming's P'i-p'a chi*, trans. Jean Mulligan (New York: Columbia University Press, 1980), 1.

20 Ye, Changhai 叶长海. *Zhongguo xijuxue shigao* 中国戏剧学史稿 (Shanghai: Shanghai Literature and Art, 1986), 55.

21 Tan, Fan; Lu, Wei 谭帆、陆炜. *Zhongguo gudai xiju lilunshi* 中国古代戏剧理论史 (Beijing: China Social Sciences, 1993), 301.

Drama is one type of literature and art but has its uniqueness in comparison with the former art forms of poetry, prose, and even novels that come into being later. The earliest poetry and prose are probably not for the transmission of personal sentiments, but mainly for the purpose: "Poetry is the expression of earnest thought; singing is the prolonged utterance of that expression"[22]; therefore, it is with much privacy, and not too much "exteriority." Even thus, poetry and prose have specific formatted demands for audiences: readers who can read and must be "intellectuals" and media (paper and writing brush) and the limited copying because of ancient technical levels, which means that audiences are rather limited. What is more, audiences must only utilize the act of reading to accept the idea conveyed in texts. Even novels appear later and are produced mainly for the consumption of audiences but are still limited by the similar technical conditions.

While drama is different from the literary forms noted earlier, it mainly creates the effect through performance and is a comprehensive art. Its demand for the literacy of audiences is relatively low, and it can accordingly be inferred that audiences of drama can be illiterate ordinary people, although it might not be so. Besides, at least in the early period of the emergence of drama, its main audiences were indeed mainly the ordinary city dwellers in Chinese society at that time. It doesn't mean that audiences couldn't be boorish philistines or there wasn't the policy of "disseminating art in the countryside"; it means that the emergence of drama entailed the social labor of division (art production) and consumers who were relatively concentrated (otherwise, there was the need of convenient information exchange and transportation to gather consumers) and had the ability to pay. Actually, some researches also demonstrate this point.[23]

Since drama (and script for storytelling) is more "folk" than traditional elite culture and is "popular literature," "civic literature," or "popular culture" which is aimed for the consumption of others (not for the diversion or the emotional conveyance of one or a few individuals). Hence, it can be expected that traditional drama must be more restricted by social mainstream and orthodox ideology, and it might not be the case that it was less restricted by ideology of traditional society and even was "anti-feudalism," just as some scholars of today[24] think or believe.

---

22 Legge, James, trans. *The Chinese Classics: Shoo-King*, vol. 3, Part 1 (Hong Kong: Hong Kong University Press, 1960), 48.

23 See Liao, Ben 廖奔. "Chongzhou zhuangfu cong washe goulan dao miaohui xitai yuan zaju huodong fangshi kaocha" 冲州撞府: 从瓦舍勾栏到庙会戏台 – 元杂剧活动方式考察. In *Yuanqu tongrong* shang 元曲通融上, 912.

24 As the major representative of the school of Chinese popular literature, Zheng Zhenduo praised popular literature and pointed out its progressive nature, but he explicitly stated that it reflected the conservative nature of the commoners more than orthodox literature. Zheng, Zhenduo 郑振铎. *Zhongguo suwenxue shi* 中国俗文学史 (Beijing: The Commercial Press, 1998). However, some scholars of today usually more emphasize or even exaggerate the feature of "anti-feudalism" or the "rebellious" spirit of popular literature, including Yuan plays, perhaps whose aim is to legitimatize the sphere of their own specialty. For example, Zheng, Chuanyin 郑传寅. *Zhongguo xiqu wenhua gailun xiudingban* 中国戏曲文化概论修订版 (Wuhan: Wuhan University Press, 1998), 328; Xie, Taofang 谢桃坊. *Zhongguo shimin wenxueshi* 中国市民文学史 (Chengdu: Sichuan People's Press,

Because even if for the sake of attracting more audiences to guarantee its survival, drama can't be for the elites, but inevitably suits and caters to the masses and yet in the meantime molds the most generally art, moral, and political taste that audiences have formed. At any time, the bottom line of real popular literature is "not to offend others."[25] Consequently, it can be foretold that aesthetic taste, standards of appreciation, and moral evaluation must and will exert the influence on the creation of playwrights and the performance of drama to an extent.[26]

In works of all sorts, the subjective intention and preference of authors themselves are usually not the decisive factor defining whether the works are "anti-feudalism" or not. Admittedly, literary works always assume the written form through the individuals or first through the personal creation, but it doesn't mean the works mainly reflect the personal thoughts of authors. There have been many researches beforehand indeed, but they usually start from an individual work and the life story of authors in order to investigate the meaning of works of popular and refined literature, and they usually adopt the enumeration method in a large quantity. This method of demonstration is not convincing. Because there is the issue of the analytical unit in the research of social sciences. Because of the number, we can't enumerate the individual case one by one to answer the issue of totality concerning popular and refined literature. Generally speaking, we can only assume, whether popular literature or refined literature, some of their authors are against the tradition and feudalism. But if we want to compare refined literature with popular literature in the general sense, we can only use two methods, or the empirical method of statistical analysis for all the popular and refined literary works. Such a method is obviously inapplicable. The rest is only the theoretical analysis and demonstration, and it must be investigated from the perspective of social and institutional environments in which literary works play a role. In this sense, the proposition "the author is dead" is correct.

It is the analysis from this perspective that leads me to believe, because of the social factor that literary works exert influence on society, the authors of popular literature such as drama (not just the playscript) have less freedom of expression than the authors of refined literature such as poetry, prose, and even novels (but not scripts for storytelling) do overall. However, in traditional society, more of the former authors were "in the wide world" instead of being at court in comparison

---

1997); Ma, Jigao 马积高. "Qingdai yasu liangzhong wenhua de duili shentou he xiquzhong huaya liangbu de shengshuai" 清代雅俗两种文化的对立、渗透和戏曲中花雅两部的盛衰. *Xibei shifan daxue xuebao shehui kexueban* 西北师范大学学报社会科学版, no. 3 (1994); Jin, Danyuan 金丹元. "Shilun yuanqu zhong de minjian yinsu dui chuantong rujia lunli de chongji" 试论元曲中的民间因素对传统儒家伦理的冲击. *Yunnan daxue xuebao shehui kexueban* 云南大学学报社会科学版, no. 5 (2004), 81.

25 See Zhu, Guangrong 朱光荣. "Lun yuan zaju fanrong de yuanyin" 论元杂剧繁荣的原因. In *Yuanqu tongrong shang* 元曲通融上, 383. For the analysis of contemporary popular culture, see Wang, Shuo 王朔. "Wo kan dazhong wenhua gangtai wenhua ji qita" 我看大众文化、港台文化及其他. In *Wuzhizhe wuwei* 无知者无畏 (Shenyang: Chunfeng Literature and Art, 2000).

26 Zhong, Tao 钟涛. *Yuan zaju yishu shengchanlun* 元杂剧艺术生产论 (Beijing: Beijing Broadcasting Institute Press, 2003), 146–151.

with the latter ones. This a paradox, *generally speaking*; the art works created by the elites for reading turn out to have more individualities and more reflect the especially individual experiences and feelings and have more likelihood of breaking through the orthodox ideology; while *generally speaking*, the art works created among the people mainly for mass consumption are more restricted by orthodox ideology.

A quantity of evidence shows that the Yuan plays are concertedly created by playwrights and audiences to quite a large extent and are the outcome of all-around coordination of the playwright, his cultural environment, language customs of that time, and stage skills.[27] It is not only manifested that "the created plays" such as *The Injustice to Dou E*, *The Orphan of Zhao*, and *The Chalk Circle* themselves are borrowed and adapted from historical works or source materials by playwrights but also exhibited in other aspects. For example, many dramatists in the Ming Dynasty doubted that some of the spoken parts in many Yuan plays were not written by original playwrights, but improvised by actors in line with the character formula or the progress of story. Some scholars of later generations hold this view as well.[28] A large number of Yuan plays handed down today are created by anonymous playwrights.[29] Naturally, there are many reasons for this anonymity, but at least quite a lot of them are due to the fact that the works have gone through the long-term creation, adaption, performance, and records by many people, and even the original playwrights are forgotten, or these playwrights become irrelevant to this process. Some researches show that many playscripts went through the alteration of playwrights and compilers in different times.[30] In this process, surely many works are eliminated in the public choice of playwrights, actors, and audiences. In this sense, the Yuan plays seen today as a whole can be basically considered "a social contract," a long-term consensus of secular society condensed in the dramatic form, which is generated out of the interaction between various playwrights, actors, and audiences in a relatively long period and includes secular art, social concepts, and orthodox ideology in society of that time.

27 Xi, Rugu 悉如谷. "Zang maoxun gaixie dou e yuan yanjiu" 臧懋循改写窦娥冤研究. In *Wenxue pinglun* 文学评论, no. 2 (1992).
28 See Gu, Xuejie 顾学颉. *Yuan ming zaju* 元明杂剧 (Shanghai: Shanghai Literature and Art, 1979), 23–25; Renmin wenxue chubanshe bianjibu, ed. 人民文学出版社编辑部编. *Yuan ming qing xiqu yanjiu lunwenji* 元明清戏曲研究论文集 (Beijing: People's Literature, 1958), 53–54; Xu, Shuheng 徐树恒. "Guanyu yuanren zaju de binbai" 关于元人杂剧的宾白. In *Zhongguo gudai xiqu lunji* 中国古代戏曲论集, ed. Wang Jisi et al. 王季思 (Beijing: China Prospect, 1986), 137–138. For the general discussion on the opposite viewpoints, see Zhou, Yibai 周贻白. *Zhongguo xiqushi changbian* 中国戏曲史长编 (Shanghai: Shanghai Bookstore, 2004), 214–215. For the empirical analysis of the specific case (*The Injustice to Dou E* etc.), see Xu, Fuming 徐扶明. *Yuandai zaju yishu* 元代杂剧艺术 (Shanghai: Shanghai Literature and Art, 1981), 202.
29 Nearly one-fourth of 100 plays included in *Selected Plays of the Yuan Dynasty* were written by anonymous playwrights.
30 Xi 悉如谷. "Zang maoxun gaixie dou e yuan yanjiu" 臧懋循改写窦娥冤研究. Deng, Shaoji 邓绍基. "Cong dou e yuan de butong banben yinchu de jige wenti" 从窦娥冤的不同版本引出的几个问题. In *Yuanqu tongrong* xia 元曲通融下, 1583.

There is another aspect reinforcing this argument. In comparison with other literary and art works for reading, drama has the different sphere to present art effects. Poetry, prose, and even novels are generally for reading, while reading (except reading aloud) usually only affects many individuals at most who are separated in time and dispersed in space and in the private space such as the family. However, even the performance of a makeshift troupe would form a temporary "public space" and affect many people at the same time. Such a dramatic feature enables the ruler to invariably pay more attentions to and set more regulations on drama. Actually, some laws of the Yuan Dynasty obviously set limits on the content of plays and "the gathering of the crowd" for plays.[31] It means that the creation and performance of plays are under greater political pressure than the creation and reading of poetry and prose. Even playwrights and actors were subjectively against the mainstream ideology; they might be more scrupulous. Certainly, this pressure is not necessarily obvious or always present, but as a great environment, a background, it must affect the creation and performance of plays at any time. Besides, some troupes were often called up or invited to perform at mansions then[32]; it was unthinkable that the nobility would allow plays to promote characters and events running counter to orthodox ideology.

This is the reality. Just as we have observed, some traditional plays seemed to somewhat challenge traditional society, including the mainstream moral discourse in society, yet overall, this challenge was far inferior to the affirmation and reiteration of such a mainstream discourse. In some traditional plays analyzed in my book, whether *The Injustice to Dou E*, *The Orphan of Zhao*, *The Chalk Circle*, *The Moheluo Doll*, *Fifteen Strings of Cash*, or other plays that are not so well known, all of them condense the mainstream moral discourse of traditional Chinese society, good and evil, loyalty, filial piety, Three Cardinal Guides and Five Constant Virtues, etc. Even *Liang Shanbo and Zhu Yingtai*, the ancient romantic play, never truly questions the rationality of the marriage system in traditional society just as I have analyzed and only exposes the flaw of the system of arranged marriage through artistic images.

When these works were performed on the stage, they would disseminate "general knowledge of law" among the people and undertake "the moral education of political thoughts." If this point is linked with the citizen class, the main consumers in those days, then the function of social control is particularly prominent. Although playwrights, actors, and audiences didn't enter the theater to receive such an education, playwrights and actors only aimed to seek a livelihood, while audiences were there only for entertainment, yet the moral education happened thus.

---

31 See Yan, Dunyi 严敦易. "Lun yuan zaju" 论元杂剧; Fu, Xuancong 傅璇琮. "Du lun yuan zaju" 读论元杂剧; Zhang, Peitian 张培田. "Lun yuan zaju yu yuandai fazhi" 论元杂剧与元代法制. In *Yuanqu tongrong* shang 元曲通融上, 323–324, 330, 409–410.

32 See Liao, Ben 廖奔. "Chongzhou zhuangfu cong washe goulan dao miaohui xitai yuan zaju huodong fangshi kaocha" 冲州撞府: 从瓦舍勾栏到庙会戏台 – 元杂剧活动方式考察, 914, 915.

Besides, we must consider that in the theater as a "public space" mentioned earlier, the performance here served as a special medium of public opinion and played the role of social control from ordinary people to local officials as well. When corrupt and stupid officials were denounced and honest and wise officials were praised, it would surely exert indirect influence on some local officials, although it should not be exaggerated. Hence, there was the saying in the Yuan Dynasty, "officials can't match actors," and it was even shown that the play had "the force of reversing a hopeless situation."[33] Although such an exaggeration of a play's social function might be a unilateral wish of scholars or playwrights and a method of acquiring self-complacency, there is no denying that plays do possess such a function within a certain purview. Therefore, in such a social context, not only the mainstream ideology affirmed by the play itself has the function of social control, but also the production and expressive forms of the play itself all have the function of social control as well.

Consequently, we can reach a judgment: The intensity of moral discourse in traditional Chinese society and Yuan plays might not have such a *great* connection with the cultural choice of creators and founders of traditional Chinese culture, but might be more related to the insufficient competence of political governance in traditional society. It might be a basic layout and strategy of governance that gradually evolves to form and stabilize through the institutional elimination method of trial and error in such constrained conditions.[34] Moral discourse and its dramatic form at least make up for such an insufficiency of national governance competence. It not only verifies Douglass C. North's opinion that ideology as an institution forms

---

33 Yang, Weizhen 杨维桢. *Youxi lu xu* 优戏录序. Quoted in Yao, Wenfang 姚文放. *Zhongguo xiju meixue de wenhua chanshi* 中国戏剧美学的文化阐释 (Beijing: Renmin University of China Press, 1997), 18.

34 In a certain social condition, people live by production and will automatically form various types of social organizational modalities. Some of these organizational modalities are relatively efficient, while some are not. These existing institutions are actually in a state of competition. In the established condition, those institutions that can't effectively guarantee the social order will be gradually eliminated in the long run by the public choice manifested in the action of people because of the inefficiency. In Chapter 1, my explanation concerning the revenge system and the emergence of the centralized system takes this perspective. If viewed from this perspective, the centralized governance of the Qin Dynasty that emphasized "to rule by law" and "to model on officials" could be said to be fatally short-lived at the beginning because the social resources at that time were insufficient to support this system. From this perspective, it was inevitable for the Western Han to uphold the non-interference philosophy of Taoism and the coexistence of the system of enfeoffment and the system of prefectures and counties in the early period. But it was also impossible to endure for a long time, which was nearly fated to bring forth the political split-up and the social chaos. Viewed still from this perspective and beforehand, it was still trial and error to adopt Dong Shuzhong's suggestion of "paying supreme tribute to Confucianism" during the reign of the Emperor of Wu. Only because this experiment proved to be relatively effective through facts (in comparison with the institutions of the Qin and the early Han), the basic layout of ancient China gradually came into being, and the basic strategy of governance "morality given priority over penalty" was formed. In this sense, Confucian doctrine became the orthodox ideology from the Han Dynasty onward in China. It is the outcome of social choice concerning the institution and the corresponding ideology and is the adaptation of the institution to social conditions, which is a feature of historical necessity.

a part of society, the greater institution.[35] What is more, to Chinese, this analysis is of help to profoundly comprehend Feng Xiang's theoretical summary that the legal system of Chinese society in the broad sense (including the present to a certain extent) is the institution of "politics and law."[36] In this institution, politics (namely administration, morality, and the related political ideology) is the main tool of the ruler to exercise social control or governance. Law in the narrow sense must be marginalized. According to the saying of traditional Chinese scholars, "morality is given priority over penalty." Viewed from this perspective, it even helps us to understand the historical origins of some political, art, and legal practices since the foundation of P. R. China, and more importantly, their social origins; it helps us to understand the experiences and lessons of legal construction in China in the non-moralizing orientation and in a broader vision[37] and keep a clear-minded understanding of the construction of the rule of law in contemporary China.

I don't want to politicize literature and art completely and describe their development history as the development history of political ideology. Actually, just as Wang Shuo analyzes, at least in Chinese society of today, many "literary and art works" have become an "entertainment."[38] But in understanding the rule of law in China, we should still not abandon the possible investigation of literature and art

---

35 North. *Structure and Change in Economic History*, esp. Chapter 5.

36 See Feng, Xiang 冯象. "Falv yu wenxue daixu" 法律与文学代序. In *Mutui zhengyi* 木腿正义, 23; Feng, Xiang 冯象. *Zhengfa biji* 政法笔记 (Nanjing: Jiangsu People's Press, 2004). Perhaps I should be hereby clearer with the meaning. Since the foundation of New China in 1949, "zhengfa" (politics and law) has been consistently the general wording, yet it seems to have been outdated in the discourse of "rule of law" of the contemporary community of legal science in China in recent years, and it even has been given a certain derogatory sense and might be discarded. When Feng Xiang discusses the relations between law and literature, he elevates it to the scholastic concept for the first time in contemporary China. With this so-called scholastic concept, I mean to remove the subjective preference in the term bestowed by different persons, peel it off from the dominating political discourse since the foundation of New China, and apply its utility of serving as the foil to the discourse of the rule of law in contemporary China (therefore, in this sense, this discourse of the rule of law is still a political discourse), and to treat it as the concept that describes reality and can serve to analyze reality in the meantime. In my opinion, in this sense, it can even serve as a path of research, a core concept, and a keyword for jurisprudence and legal sociology. As for the scholastic concept, the significance of "politics and law" not only lies in its precise definition of the relations between law and politics in Chinese society (until today) (in this sense, this concept is descriptive); also, it is impossible for any scholar who tries to understand Chinese law to completely leave the political factor of the specific period with which he is concerned outside his analytical framework. But this concept can be further generalized and serve as the general path of investigating law. That is, when we investigate the legal system of any country or society, sometimes even some concrete laws, we should investigate the relations between politics and law at the same time; we shouldn't consider law as completely self-sufficient *only* in accordance with the narration of some Western legalists.

37 One prominent example is *Fifteen Strings of Cash* that was adapted and performed in 1956 and staged again in 1979 and the ensuing stir in society. In addition to other factors, the biggest factor is related to the then politics. See Wang, Shide 王世德. *Shiwuguan yanjiu* 十五贯研究 (Shanghai: Shanghai Literature and Art, 1981), 2; Zhou, Enlai 周恩来. "Guanyu kunqu shiwuguan de liangci jianghua" 关于昆曲十五贯的两次讲话. *Wenyi yanjiu* 文艺研究, no. 1 (1980).

38 Wang 王朔. "Wo kan dazhong wenhua gangtai wenhua ji qita" 我看大众文化、港台文化及其他.

from this perspective. What I try to demonstrate is that there is such a factor in the development of literature and art. If the investigation of this factor is completely abandoned, its outcome might not only be the loss of perspective to possibly investigate and understand literature but also the loss of perspective to deeply investigate and understand politics and law.

Examples: The Reshaping of Drama Materials by Morality

The previous analysis still has too many theoretical analyses and constructions, and even if it is valid logically, it is still easily doubtful. Since the May Fourth Movement, many researchers tend to emphasize the folk aspect of traditional drama, its opposition to the orthodox thinking of traditional society, and the folk identity of playwrights and showcase their deliberate and conscious efforts of "anti-feudalism."[39] These judgments obviously can't coexist with the analysis of the previous section. Hence, in order to support the theoretical analysis of the previous section, it needs an empirical demonstration, namely the creation of ancient plays did draw attention to the orthodox ideology of traditional society and was hard to escape from it.

Truly, some scholars once exhorted that there should not be too intense and direct political intention in the creation of an opera. Wu Mei, the famous opera researcher at the turn of the Qing Dynasty and the Republic of China, once "picked up the common sayings" on the issue of the creation of opera and emphasized "the dispensation of satires." But what he turned against was

> a mean person in the world who acts perversely in a deliberate way, and uses the playscript as the tool to vent his hatred for revenge. As for those he likes, he grants them the male and female roles, as for those he dislikes, the painted and comic roles; he heaps the misconduct with monstrosity unheard for thousands of years on one person.

He believed the occurrence of opera "owes to the stupid people in the world, who are nearly illiterate. There is no way to persuade them to do good, and dissuade them from wrongdoings, then, the words are written down." Therefore, he claimed "to use the lines of actors to let all the audiences know what is the good like or what is the evil for"; "its main purpose is the admonition, and shouldn't be the allusion"; "the satire must be cleansed from the bottom of heart, the sincerity and kindness must be kept in the mind, and the evil things must not be done."[40] He thought "the

---

39 The most typical is Tian Han's drama *Guan Hanqing*. See Tian, Han 田汉. "Guan hanqing" 关汉卿. In *Zhongguo dangdai shida zhengjuji* 中国当代十大正剧集, chiefly ed. Ji Yu 集于 and Wang Jisi 王季思 (Nanjing: Jiangsu Literature and Art, 1993), 273–371. See also Jin, Danyuan 金丹元. "Shilun yuanqu zhong de minjian yinsu dui chuantong rujia lunli de chongji" 试论元曲中的民间因素对传统儒家伦理的冲击, 81.

40 Wu, Mei 吴梅. *Guqu zhutan zhongguo xiqu gailun* 顾曲麈谈·中国戏曲概论 (Shanghai: Shanghai Ancient Books, 2004), 54; Wu, Mei 吴梅. "Quyuan" 曲原. In *Yuanqu tongrong shang* 元曲通融上, 5.

wonder is the lines concerning moral affairs that are moving to tears; they consider the circumstances and judge by common sense in beautiful words, they will move people profoundly, change prevailing customs and habits, and make remarkable achievements."[41]

Since Wu Mei lived in the late Qing Dynasty, we obviously can't use his viewpoints to represent or include the general opinions and practices of playwrights in the Yuan Dynasty or ancient times. However, with these words, we can still observe some problems. First, at least in Wu Mei's view, some playwrights in history used the drama as the medium to vent their hatred for revenge (however, even this phenomenon criticized by Wu Mei had a certain political function in those days). Second, Wu Mei thought that some or even most functions of drama should be "the admonition" and "move people profoundly, change prevailing customs and habits," while the main target of its moral education was the illiterate common people, not intellectuals; therefore, he granted drama quite a high social function and obviously treated the drama as the tool of social control. Third, Wu Mei thought drama should not be moralizing bluntly and be careful with the selected materials ("the wonder is the lines concerning *moral affairs* that are moving to tears"), the sense and literary grace of story ("they consider the circumstances and judge by common sense in beautiful words"), and the dramatic feature ("to use the lines of actors"). Fourth, in the narration of Wu Mei, the most important thing we can observe is the mainstream viewpoints with the long-term stability concerning traditional drama, namely the so-called "common saying." Another example is the words of Gao Ming, the famous playwright of Southern Drama of the Yuan Dynasty, "Truly, a tale without moral teaching, no matter how finely written, is useless." Although it can't still serve as the representative of the playwrights of that time, especially Yuan playwrights,[42] it more or less reflects the creation idea of some playwrights then.

If the viewpoints of Wu Mei are put into the social condition of art progress and appreciation for observation, they will be quite reasonable. However, if this happens then it will be more difficult for drama to be separated from the orthodox ideology of traditional society. It is initially connected with the aesthetics of reception. Especially in the age when Yuan plays were first created and began to thrive, drama must rely on those stories already known by people, the moral norms of society habitually obeyed by people, and the concomitant "natural" habits of art appreciation and tastes acquired by common people through other avenues in order to gradually cultivate and create its own audiences. It is the preformatting of society that an art

---

41 Wu. 吴梅. *Guqu zhutan zhongguo xiqu gailun* 顾曲麈谈·中国戏曲概论, 62; Wu. 吴梅. *Yuanqu tongrong* shang 元曲通融上, 7.

42 A scholar points out in his analysis that Yuan plays have more factors opposed to Confucian ethics than the Southern plays. Since it utilizes the enumeration method, its argument is not quite convincing. See Jin, Danyuan 金丹元. "Shilun yuanqu zhong de minjian yinsu dui chuantong rujia lunli de chongji" 试论元曲中的民间因素对传统儒家伦理的冲击, 84–85.

appreciation must have.[43] Even from the perspective of art appreciation, drama in those days only marginally challenged such an art taste cultivated by traditional society and its political ideology at most. Therefore, the experience of selecting source materials from the touching stories concerning moral affairs in the works of predecessors that was summarized by Wu Mei is not on a whim. In the meantime, it also explains why Yuan plays drew materials from historical stories in a large quantity (such as *The Injustice to Dou E* and *The Orphan of Zhao*) or connected history with the symbolized characters (such as Bao Zheng).

Even if we admit that some playwrights were recalcitrant, just as Guan Hanqing's claim: "I am the resounding bronze bean that cannot be steamed to mush, broiled to pulp, hammered to submission, fried to explosion."[44] Yet in society, the resistance of rebels must often resort to the orthodox ideology in order to achieve effectiveness. Actually, even sociopaths usually have to employ orthodox ideology. Just as the words of Zhuangzi said, "the thief, too, [has] a Way," which points out the consistency between the thief's code of ethics and the mainstream ideology of society in those days.[45] It is allegedly the most profound and sharpest example. In Yuan plays, there were lots of such examples. For instance, in *The Injustice to Dou E*, Dou E redoubled her efforts to utilize the traditional moral norm of "being faithful to her husband to the very end" in order to resist the bullying and insult from Donkey Zhang.[46] Zhang Ding in *The Moheluo Doll* also once applied such a tactic to persuade the magistrate to retry the case in order to revoke the verdict of injustice.[47] Hence, ancient playwrights had no likelihood of completely breaking away from or resisting the orthodox ideology. What they could do at most was only not to consider ideology or pursue the ideological level of plays and only "art for art's sake." Yet it is in this process for art's sake that the orthodox ideology as the natural background of the playwrights' existence silently enters their plays and shapes their works.

Let me return to some specific examples again and analyze how a mainstream moral ideology of society shapes and changes these plays. I still use *The Injustice to Dou E* and *The Orphan of Zhao* and other related art source materials as examples.[48]

Many researchers pointed out that the prototype of Dou E is the story of the filial daughter-in-law of Donghai in *The Garden of Stories* or *Chronicles of the Han*

43 Bourdieu, Pierre. *Distinction: A Social Critique of the Judgment of Taste*, trans. Richard Nice (Cambridge, MA: Harvard University Press, 1984).
44 *Nanlv yizhihua bufulao* 南吕一枝花·不伏老.
45 Watson, Burton, trans. *The Complete Works of Zhuangzi* (New York: Columbia University Press, 2013), 69.
46 See the analysis of Note 7 of this chapter.
47 See the analysis concerning Zhang Ding in the third section of Chapter 4.
48 Song Geng's article also discusses this issue. See Song, Geng 宋耕. "Yuan zaju gaibian yu yishixingtai jiantan hongguan wenxueshi de sikao" 元杂剧改编与意识形态－兼谈宏观文学史的思考. *Ershiyi shiji* 二十一世纪, May 2003.

Dynasty, although Guan Hanqing narrated the wronged Dou E as another story.[49] The close reading of stories recorded by Liu Xiang in *The Garden of Stories* and Ban Gu in *Chronicles of the Han Dynasty* will show that they are not with many mythical and moral colors. Here is the story:

> A filial daughter-in-law lived in Donghai and became a widow at young age; her son died as well. She devotedly provided for her mother-in-law. The mother wanted her daughter-in-law to be remarried, yet her proposal was consistently turned down. The mother told neighbors, "My filial daughter-in-law diligently waits on me, and I pity her loss of son and husband. I am advanced in years, and will be a burden to this young woman for a long time. What shall I do then?" Afterward, the mother committed suicide. Her natural daughter lodged the complaint to the authorities that "the daughter-in-law killed my mother." The clerks arrested the filial woman, who denied the accusation. The clerks resorted to interrogation by torture, and she made a false confession. The concluded verdict was submitted to the prefecture. Mr. Yu held that this daughter-in-law had provided for her mother for more than ten years, and she was noted for her filial piety. She must not be the murderer. The prefect remained unconvinced. Mr. Yu argued in favor of the woman, but failed. Holding the concluded verdict in hands, he cried at the court of prefecture and resigned from his post on the pretext of illness. The prefect finally sentenced the woman to be executed. A drought raged for three years. A new prefect came and consulted the divination by tortoise to find the reason. Mr. Yu told him, "The filial daughter-in-law should never have been executed, and the former prefect made an arbitrary judgment. Our present ill-fortune was brought on by that act." The new prefect then ordered to kill an ox and personally held a memorial ceremony at the tomb of the woman to redress her injustice. The heavy rain fell immediately, and that years' crops were abundant.[50]

Strictly speaking, this story has not many mythical aspects and only *describes* the phenomenal connection between the injustice and the drought, the redressed injustice and the yearly harvest that might be misunderstood as the cause and effect later. Mr. Yu connected social phenomenon with natural phenomenon, which only serves as a wrong interpretation in line with the view of today, or he deliberately did this for the consideration of a certain strategy. Considering the "harmony of man with nature" emphasized by Dong Zhongshu in the early Han Dynasty, Mr. Yu's interpretation was accepted by the successor prefect, while Liu Xiang or Ban Gu made a record or insinuatingly described it, it is not unexpected, or even is an unalterable truth.

---

49 In the play, Dou E once mentioned the story of the filial daughter-in-law of Donghai (Guan, 1977: 144).
50 Ban, Gu 班固. "Jun shu yu xue ping peng zhuan" 隽疏于薛平彭传. In *Han shu* 汉书, vol. 71.

However, such a mistake often creates a possibility for the generation of myth[51] that the injustice is connected with the drought. Until the Jin Dynasty, Gan Bao repeated this story in *In Search of the Supernatural*, the book of folk tales, but the myth of flowing blood appeared.[52]

Until this moment, no matter under the writing brush of Liu Xiang, or Ban Gu, or even Gan Bao, the filial daughter-in-law of Donghai was basically the image of an ordinary person. Although she was filial, she was only a good person with responsibility and sympathy in a general sense. It should be noted that "the mother-in-law" in this story was a good person as well, who sacrificed her life to relieve the burden from her daughter-in-law. This altruism is understandable, which is not only relatively common in daily life (the elders sacrifice themselves for their posterity) but also can be interpreted from biology; that is, the inclusive fitness[53] in social biology aims to be like this: "as long as the green hills are there, one need not worry about firewood." In this story, the filial daughter-in-law refused to be remarried, and her mother-in-law committed suicide; both of acts are likewise respectable and impressive. Even the natural daughter who accused the filial daughter-in-law (just as the role of Donkey Zhang) and the prefect who executed the woman were not "bad" or "evil" persons in the strict sense. Their words and deeds were not a purposeful frame-up. Although their judgments and inferences were wrong and ushered in the tragedy, yet they were not the evildoers in the moral sense.[54] The whole story is concise, yet it is with the vivid images of characters and reasonable logic. It is soul-stirring and touching to the heart. This story has the feature of ancient Greek tragedy: The tragedy is not mainly caused by the acts of villains, but is inevitable because of the specific circumstances. It sufficiently proves that the author is the master of characterization and event narration.

But in *The Injustice to Dou E*, the Yuan play, we can observe that the image of Dou E has already become the traditional moral paragon to the full and is the only one in the play. The image of Mother Cai has no moral color. She was not only greedy for money (practicing usury) but also couldn't be "faithful to her husband to the very end," which accordingly led to the tragedy of Dou E. (Some scholars verified that in the original script of Guan Hanqing, Mother Cai had accepted Donkey Zhang's father as her second husband, and the related trace is also preserved in the present playscript.) The image of natural daughter under the writing brush of Liu Xiang or Ban Gu is changed as well. Originally, the natural daughter deeply loved her mother and then had the reason, or even had the responsibility in a certain

---

51 Sometimes myth results from the textual misinterpretation. See Evans-Prichard, Edward Even. *Theories of Primitive Religion* (Oxford: Clarendon Press, 1965), 21–22.

52 Bao, Gan. *In Search of the Supernatural: The Written Record*, trans. Kenneth J. DeWoskin and J. I. Crump, Jr. (Stanford: Stanford University Press, 1996), 135.

53 Wilson, Edward O. *On Human Nature* (Cambridge, MA: Harvard University Press, 1978).

54 Therefore, in a scholar's comment, he points out that even the prototype of *The Injustice to Dou E* didn't blame the prefect who insisted on the execution of the filial daughter-in-law, and it was Guan Hanqing who changed this image. Zhu, Zhaonian 祝肇年. "Dou E yuan gushi yuanliu manshu" 窦娥冤故事源流漫述. In *Yuanqu tongrong* xia 元曲通融下, 1537.

sense, to doubt the filial daughter-in-law of Donghai. But in the Yuan play, Donkey Zhang, the villain, deliberately framed Dou E only to gratify his lust. The original former prefect was only not persuaded by Mr. Yu and was just stubborn; he also had no name. But in *The Injustice to Dou E*, the prefect became Taowu, a clown character performed by a painted-face role on the stage, and his name itself had a derogatory association.[55] The change of two characters enables audiences to very easily ascribe the death of Dou E even more to Donkey Zhang's evil and Taowu's stupidity and to neglect or forget the social and historical factor, which lets the factor of personal morality and intelligence become important in the destiny of the character. The factor of moral preaching in the play is reinforced, and Dou E seems to more likely face death unflinchingly and be ready to risk her life to completely comply with the will of the protagonist.[56] However, in terms of artistic images of characters, at least in my opinion, Dou E is far inferior to her prototype of the filial daughter-in-law of Donghai and her mother-in-law in the real, vivid, and moving representation. The playwright's demand for moral ideology has overshadowed the image of humans.

The erosion of social mainstream ideology to Zhao the Orphan is even more obvious and invariably continues today. It was the palace revolution that happened in the Jin state in the Spring and Autumn Period at the very beginning and was recorded in *The Commentary of Zuo* and *Discourses of the States*. Sima Qian described this story in an innovative and vivid literary way in *The Great Scribe's Records*.[57] Ji Junxiang of the Yuan Dynasty adapted this story to be the play *The Orphan of Zhao*. Later, Wang Guowei claimed that this play "doesn't pale even among the greatest tragedies in the world."[58] In the period of the European Enlightenment Movement, the play was once translated into many Western languages and introduced to the West. It is said that many Western thinkers at that time liked it.[59] In recent years, after the adaption, *The Orphan of Zhao* is on the stage again in

---

55 Wang, Qi, chiefly ed. 王起主编. *Zhongguo xiquxuan* shang 中国戏曲选上 (Beijing: People's Literature, 1985), 13, Note 34.

56 Wang, Guowei 王国维. "Songyuan xiqushi" 宋元戏曲史. In *Wang Guowei xueshu jingdianji shang* 王国维学术经典集上 (Nanchang: Jiangxi People's Press, 1997), 281–282.

57 "Zhao, The Hereditary House 43," in *The Grand Scribe's Records*, vol. V.2 (Bloomington: Indiana University Press, forthcoming).

58 Wang 王国维. "Songyuan xiqushi" 宋元戏曲史, 282. It should be indicated that because of various restrictions, Wang Guowei's understanding of Western narrative literature, including drama, was actually rather limited, which was mainly based on his Chinese cultural background and prejudice. He put *The Injustice to Dou E* and *The Orphan of Zhao* alongside Western drama and emphasized the will of protagonists (it might originate from the philosophy of Arthur Schopenhauer), who were ready to risk their lives. However, his summarization of Western classic tragedies is obviously wrong. At least four tragedies of Shakespeare are not relevant to the will of protagonists, namely *Hamlet* (hesitation), *King Lear* (betrayal), *Macbeth* (ambition), and *Othello* (jealousy). *Antigone*, the ancient Greek tragedy, is also irrelevant to it.

59 For the translation and dissemination of *The Orphan of Zhao* in the world, see Wang, Lina 王丽娜. "Yuanqu zai guowai" 元曲在国外. In *Shoujie yuanqu guoji xueshu yantaohui lunwenji* 首届元曲国际学术研讨会论文集 (Shijiazhuang: Hebei People's Press, 1994), esp. Section 1, 2, 9. For the general introduction, see Wang, Lina 王丽娜. *Zhongguo gudian xiaoshuo xiqu zai guowai* 中国古

China. Therefore, the investigation of the origin and evolution of this story might be helpful for us to understand the subtle interaction between literature and the change of the revenge institution and the consistent shaping of social mainstream ideology on the dramatic prototype.

We hereby first distinguish two types of change in the narration of the story. One is the deviation from the historical records for the sake of dramatic effect. Viewed from the perspective of dramatic art, this change is necessary and completely legitimate. If the story narrated by Sima Qian and the play are compared from this perspective, I can observe that except for some reasonable changes of names and identities of characters, the only important episode in which this Yuan play reinforces the dramatic effect is that Cheng Ying used his own son to replace Zhao the Orphan (in *The Great Scribe's Records*, it was stated that he "plotted to use the infant of others"), but inscrutably expunged many moving details under the writing brush of Sima Qian: the detail of a secret plot for the division of labor between Gongsun Chujiu and Cheng Ying (such as the previously mentioned episode, "please let me die first") and the episode of Cheng Ying's resolute suicide after Zhao the Orphan restored his family status. Even Cheng Ying and Gongsun Chujiu, who were ready to risk their lives and were fearless with justice on their side, changed their disposition, and many philistine tastes were added. For instance, Ji Junxiang didn't let Cheng Ying commit suicide and molded him as the revolting person who was rather vulgar, utilitarian, and consistently vigilant and calculating.[60] Therefore, such a change of adaption is definitely not out of the consideration of dramatic or literary effect. After the adaption, the whole play falls from the power struggle between "minister and general" under the writing brush of Sima Qian into the conventional pattern filled with Confucianist morality that the treacherous court officials were in power; faithful and upright officials were executed; their posterity finally redressed the injustice and revenged due to the assistance of righteous persons.[61] Such a selection and adaption of the story's details is a truly

---

典小说戏曲在国外 (Beijing: Xuelin, 1988). Such a reception in the cultural dissemination also shows that revenge as an issue is transcultural, although the specific answer to this question is usually colored by the local culture. In other words, it supports the viewpoint that revenge is based on human biological factors from another aspect.

60 The most typical evidence is that in order to prevent the leakage of the news, Cheng Ying showed his great distrust with the loyalty or steadfastness of the insiders concerned, namely the mother of Zhao the Orphan and General Han Jue, who secretly let Cheng Ying stow Zhao the Orphan out of the palace. In the end, he forced the insiders to commit suicide on scene only to state their attitudes. Cheng Ying even doubted whether Gongsun Chujiu could hold out. There is the sharp and strong contrast for Cheng Ying under the writing brushes of Ji Junxiang and Sima Qian.

61 For the introductory analysis of the evolution of this subject matter, see Mao, Dun 茅盾. *Guanyu lishi he lishiju cong woxin changdan de xuduo butong juben shuoqi* 关于历史和历史剧: 从卧薪尝胆的许多不同剧本说起 (Beijing: The Writers, 1962), 80–91. For the development of moral significance of this subject matter, see Chen, Zhongfan 陈中凡. "Cong lishi sucai dao zhaoshi guer zaju" 从历史素材到赵氏孤儿杂剧. In *Xiju Bao* 戏剧报, no. 15, 16 (1961); Wu, Gan 吴敢. "Zhaoshi guer gushi de fazhan yu liuchuan" 赵氏孤儿故事的发展与流传. In *Quhai shuoshan lu* 曲海说山录 (Beijing: Literture and Art, 1996), 1–19; Zhou, Xianshen 周先慎. "Zhaoshi guer dui lishi sucai de gaizao" 赵氏孤儿对历史素材的改造. In *Wenshi zhishi* 文史知识, no. 11 (1992). For the

fault in terms of dramatic and literary effect and is puzzling from the perspective of aesthetic consideration. It seems that we can only sigh over the playwright's deficiency of literary appreciation capability and dramatic sense to the full.

However, this understanding and interpretation *must* be wrong. In Chapter 1, I have already pointed out that in the age of the pre-emergence of public power, revenge is the basic institution of maintaining social order. Accordingly, no matter the revenge of good persons to bad persons or vice versa, it is the liability of the avenger and an honor and morality as well that wins the universal commendations from people. This revenge ideology was quite necessary at that time, because when there was no public power, or the function of public power was not fully developed, or public power couldn't effectively gratify the basic demands of people because of various reasons, revenge was the institutional core and basis maintaining social order and peace. However, since revenge is based on instinct and needs the support of ideology to become institutionalized, it is hard to contain opportunism; many people will give up revenge when it doesn't make up for the loss or it can't be done; the passage of time will weaken the revenge impulse, or revenge is even completely forgotten; as time passes, the revenge institution will completely collapse. Especially in the Spring and Autumn and Warring States periods, the social group was enlarged, the mobility of personnel was augmented, and revenge was more difficult. It was in this social condition that the revenge ideology was reinforced in the Spring and Autumn Period. Although legalists were against revenge and advocated for the prohibition of revenge, this influence was rather limited. Until the age of Sima Qian, revenge was still *nearly* immoral[62] and was greatly admirable under the writing brush of Sima Qian.

But with the gradual formation and perfection of a centralized governance system of the Qin and Han dynasties, especially the establishment and perfection of the centralized system under the reign of Emperor Wu of Han, although public power was still insufficient to meet the demands of people, the former revenge conception, regardless of morality, could no longer serve as the dominant ideology in society. A series of expressions concerning revenge and "knight" showed that the revenge ideology of the whole society was gradually weakened in this period.[63] In order to guarantee the authority of public power and its effective operation, revenge must be suppressed. Gradually, "loyalty" became the top ideology and loyalty nearly became the special concept affiliated to imperial power. Consequently, revenge gradually became the conditioned ideology, and it must be subject

---

technical analysis of Ji Junxiang's molding "the discord between minister and general" as "the contradiction between the loyal and the evil," see Liu, Mengbai 刘萌柏. "Ji junxiang zhaoshi guer jiqi yingxiang" 纪君祥赵氏孤儿及其影响; Deng, Shaoji; Yao, Shuyi 邓绍基、幺书仪. "Ji junxiang de zhaoshi guer" 纪君祥的赵氏孤儿. In *Yuanqu tongrong* 元曲通融, 2187–2189, 2189–2191. Two articles praise such a molding from the traditional Chinese value of justice.

62 To be more exact, it is without the moral significance that we today, or the later Confucianism period, heaps on revenge. That is, revenge is the action of the good to the bad, or the loyal to the evil. But Sima Qian praised revenge; it was the morality accepted by him or the era beforehand.

63 See the analysis in Chapter 1.

to imperial power and can only be exercised in the place where imperial power doesn't reach and only for the benefit of imperial power. We can evidently observe this point just noticing the historical evolution of the revenge discourse.[64]

Only in this historical process can we understand why in the Yuan Dynasty, in the social environment where people had already forgotten the meaning of revenge in the mind of ancient people, Ji Junxiang adapted the story of Zhao the Orphan to the story of a struggle between loyal and treacherous courtiers. The adapted play had new expression concerning the legitimacy of the revenge of Zhao the Orphan. Revenge was no longer only because of the paternal vendetta, but first because his father was loyal and framed by the treacherous courtier. Besides, there was also the factor of filial piety in the revenge of Zhao the Orphan for his father. Third, the deeds of Gongsun Chujiu and Cheng Ying also contained the factor of loyalty to the sovereign and master, but they were no longer duty-bound not to retreat and were fearless with justice on their side. They had more personal considerations. The fervent and tragic story of Zhao the Orphan could only become meaningful now within the macro-narrative of Confucian morality that distinguished the loyal and the treacherous, the good and the evil, and emphasized loyalty to master; even the story could only be preserved in the affiliation to the macro-narrative. The civic culture and the political and legal ideology in the Yuan Dynasty had been deeply engraved on the understanding of history among the playwright and common people.

In this sense, we can say that Ji Junxiang was the playwright who had not the insight into humanity, which instead helps to accomplish our research and understanding of historical evolution of revenge. However, from another perspective, perhaps just because of this point, Ji Junxiang was a playwright who had the insight into social conditions and psychology of audiences. The most fundamental reason might be that only the adapted story on such loyal and treacherous courtiers could be accepted by the popular culture in those days and could be roughly compatible with the ruler and the political and legal ideology in the dominant position.[65] *The Orphan of Zhao* could be staged as well. It is because of this reason that I think Wang Guowei's artistic evaluation of this play is overstated, yet it is somewhat connected with the Confucian ethics that Wang Guowei himself loved and strictly abided by.

The function of social control in literature hasn't completely disappeared today. Actually, there are continuously ideological discourses along with *The Orphan of Zhao*. Since the foundation of P. R. China, although Wang Guowei highly commended the play, and this play was the first one to "go global," and the academic community highly rated the play, yet *A Selection of Yuan Play* compiled and

---

64 "In Confucian classics, the views of revenge . . . are increasingly restricted with the passage of time." Zhang, Guohua 张国华. *Zhongguo falv sixiangshi xinbian* 中国法律思想史新编 (Beijing: Peking University Press, 1998), 195.

65 In the Yuan Dynasty, there was the law that "those who falsely write poems and tunes to make sneering comments will be banished." See *Yuanshi* juan 9元史卷9 (Beijing: Zhonghua Book Company), 2685.

annotated by Gu Xuejie didn't include *The Orphan of Zhao*, the reason was "it is allegedly with revanchist tendency."[66] Considering the special period of political sensitivity at that time, such a scruple was completely understandable. After the Cultural Revolution, although *A Selection of Yuan Plays*, the version of 1998 included *The Orphan of Zhao* again, and the literary and dramatic community granted the high commendation to the play; however, many critics of the play still tried to avoid the most distinct theme of revenge and instead stated that the play reflected "the struggling spirit of those who made self-sacrifice, and advanced wave upon wave fighting unyieldingly"[67] and "exposed the sharp contradiction within the ruling group, and the evildoing that the treacherous courtier persecuted righteous persons."[68] And this play was believed to extol "the lofty and heroic sense of justice" and "the excellent quality of the Chinese nation."[69] Particularly astonishingly, at the end of 2003, Beijing People's Art Theater (BPAT) and National Theater of China (NTC) presented their adaptations *The Orphan of Zhao* on the stage. Both of them claimed to have "the impressive dramatic plot" and still intentionally avoided the issue of revenge. The biggest change in the two versions was the question raised regarding revenge at the end of play. In the BPAT version, Zhao the Orphan questioned, "Why shall I account for the fault of predecessors?" In the NTC version, Zhao the Orphan said, "Yesterday, I had two fathers; from tomorrow, I will be an orphan." According to the report, some audiences thought that such an adaptation not only enabled audiences to understand the charms of original play but also to *appreciate the masterpiece with the viewpoints of today*; and they believed that the altered end of play presented the new proposition of "*the turn of times*."[70] Whether these words were the reflection of audiences after all or they were fabricated by the journalist, it doesn't matter. These words and the adaptation all reflect that "human rights" that are popular today begin to renovate *The Orphan of Zhao* as well!

The rule of law and political ideology of today are reshaping this story.

The Criticism on the Path of Moralism

Although this chapter analyzes the ideological issue more and discusses the general issue of political governance, it helps to deeply understand the analysis of the issue

---

66 Gu, Xuejie, selected and annotated. 顾学颉. "Qianyan" 前言. In *Yuanren zajuxuan* 元人杂剧选 (Beijing: People's Literature, 1998), 11.

67 Zhang, Geng; Guo, Hancheng, chiefly eds. 张庚、郭汉城. *Zhongguo xiju tongshi* 中国戏剧通史 (Beijing: China Theater Press, 1980), 220.

68 Liu, Dajie 刘大杰. *Zhongguo wenxue fazhanshi xiace* 中国文学发展史下册 (Shanghai: Shanghai Ancient Books, 1982), 864; Zhang, Yanjin 张燕瑾. "Zhaoshi guer de jiaose anpai he xiju jiegou" 赵氏孤儿的脚色安排和戏剧结构. *Guangming Ribao* 光明日报 (Beijing), March 1, 1983.

69 Que, Zhen 阙真. "Yuandai sida beiju de shenmei tezheng jiqi jiazhi" 元代四大悲剧的审美特征及其价值. *Guangxi shifan daxue xuebao* 广西师范大学学报, no. 4 (1991); Zhou, Xianshen 周先慎. "Zhaoshi guer de shenmei tezheng" 赵氏孤儿的审美特征. *Wenshi zhishi* 文史知识, no. 7 (1992).

70 He, Lulu 和璐璐. "Sanda wenti zhiyi gebanben zhaoshi guer re" 三大问题质疑各版本赵氏孤儿热. *Zhongguo xinwen wang* 中国新闻网, 2003. www.chinanews.com.cn/n/2003-11-11/26/367359.html.

of "administrating justice" in traditional Chinese society along with the analyses of previous chapters. For example, with the emphasis on the personal moral character of the adjudicator, the moralist path is not effective in *today's view*, so why does it persist for a long time in the condition of traditional society and even still exert a strong influence today?

Nietzsche once presented his profound insight into the interaction between the sense for morality and the sense for causality when he said,

> Sense for morality and sense for causality in conteraction. – In the same measure as the sense for causality increases, the extent of the domain of morality decreases: for each time one has understood the necessary effects and has learned how to segregate them from all the accidental effects and incidental consequences, one has destroyed a countless number of *imaginary causalities* hitherto believed in as the foundations of customs.[71]

Nietzsche's words mean that once people have more comprehensions of the causality based on empirical evidence, the causality based on imagined morality will decline; conversely, when people have little comprehension of causality in the world, they will more likely rely on the fabricated and imagined moral causality to understand and control the world; they usually try to solve problems by reinforcing moral responsibility. Oliver W. Holmes, Jr., the famous American jurisprudent, presented the same insight as Nietzsche's nearly at the same time.[72] It should be inspiring for us to reflect on the strongly moralist path in the traditional Chinese "administration of justice." The key lies in the lack of science, information, special division of labor, and the related special knowledge; the ruler hardly establishes the effective and low-priced supervision institution, and society accordingly only tries to solve the ensuing series of problems through a series of formal institutions (the strict liability) and informal institutions (the improvement of moral standards of officials). But the outcome is still sad.

It must be pointed out that even after science and democracy as concepts were introduced into China, this situation still exists. In the investigation of the moral world in traditional dramas and the tragedy of ancient "administration of justice," whether scholars of humanities or scholars of legal science, generally speaking, they don't seriously investigate the factors of social economics, institutional conditions, and science affecting the occurrence of tragedy. They only make the relatively general introduction to the background of the age in addition to the coarse analysis of class oppression or ethnic oppression, which is always pervaded with a strong moral significance. Owing to the lack of scientific training of empirical evidence and the ineptness of meticulously and carefully discriminating different

---

71 Nietzsche, Friedrich. *Daybreak*, trans. R. J. Hollingdale (Cambridge: Cambridge University Press, 1997), 12.
72 Holmes, Oliver Wendell, Jr. "The Path of the Law," in *10 Harvard Law Review*, (1897), 457, 470–471.

factors, the dramatic research of China from 1949 onward stresses the social analysis in a special or even excessive way, but the analysis on detective plays consistently lacks the spirit of truly scientific evidence at least.

Even democracy that was introduced into China in the May Fourth Movement has also gone through a certain distortion. Under the influence of traditional Chinese culture, democracy is usually transformed to the investigation of public will and feeling and the emphasis that officials should care for public feelings and make a just decision for people. Democracy is still understood as the personal moral issue of the ruler. Although this understanding is somewhat reasonable, in analyzing the issue of the trial in ancient plays, it is very easy to consider the issue of the trial as the issue of personal character of officials. Even because of the unilateral and simplistic emphasis on class struggle, the pre-understanding of traditional moralism to the literary works has been reinforced.[73] The reason for all such tragedies of "the administration of justice" is invariably attributed to class oppression, the sinister local administration, and corrupt officials in a simple way. The class analysis replaces the concrete analysis. Such a moralist path is not just limited to the literary researchers but also widely exists among legal historians and in legal scholars' understanding of ancient laws. Such moral understanding of legal issues in ancient China conversely affects their understanding of the legal and judicial issues in the China of today, these scholars easily or habitually understand the judicial system in the China of today only from the moral (actually, it is often traditionally political) perspective.

If the viewpoint of this chapter is valid, then it not only explains the basic layout of traditional legal culture in China but also presents another path of studying this layout: an institutionalist path, a legal path. It is the legal or institutional interpretation of culture, not the cultural interpretation of law. To understand the basic layout and situation presented by Chinese culture through the analysis of institutional weakness caused by various factors in traditional Chinese society not only explains the long-term system of politics and law in Chinese politics but also explains why the personal moral character of officials is consistently emphasized in trials. The concept of culture or the legal culture is accordingly no longer used as the variable of interpretative force, but the variable that must be interpreted.

It must be stressed that when I mention that the rule by virtue is politics and the moral discourse is ideology, I use the terms in their neutral meaning. Politics and ideology themselves are not necessarily used in a derogatory sense, and moral discourse in traditional society will not naturally suffer from criticism and reproach just because it is a political ideology. It is the same case that no matter what kind of problem it is today, it can't be criticized if it becomes the discourse

---

73 See Xu, Shuofang 徐朔方. "Yuanqu zhong de baogong xi" 元曲中的包公戏. *Wenshizhe* 文史哲, September 1955. Feng, Yuanjun 冯沅君. "Zenyang kandai dou e yuan jiqi gaibianben" 怎样看待窦娥冤及其改编本. In *Wenxue pinglun* 文学评论, no. 4 (1965). Both articles are quoted from *Mingjia jiedu yuanqu* 名家解读元曲, 144–151, 212–226. See Gu, Xuejie, selected and annotated 顾学颉选注. "Qianyan" 前言. In *Yuanren zajuxuan* 元人杂剧选, 12–13.

of rule by law or human rights. Actually, any society must have an ideology as one part of its governance system. In this sense, "the rule of law" advocated by contemporary jurists in the China of today neither transcends ideology nor finds or arrives at "eternal truth" or "ultimate truth," just as we ourselves, the jurists, thought. The important issue is not whether governance needs ideology itself or not, but – to start from the pragmatic perspective, the profession of legal professionals and the easily related practical position – whether this ideology relatively has the more effective function in terms of social stability, economic development, and safety of people's life and property and whether it is compatible with other systems in society or not. If a social ideology can play such a role and is the most effective in the situation such that other conditions remain the same, then it can be described as the tool of safeguarding and creating social welfare in a special sense, and it can be acceptable. If it can't do this, it should be replaced and actually will be replaced in the end. As for the practice and mechanism of moral discourse in traditional Chinese society, seemingly, it should and can only be understood and evaluated thus.

The most important meaning of this chapter doesn't lie in the investigation of ancient times, but in the present. In the investigation of the ancient system of politics and law in China and law and literature, this chapter implicitly presents a research sphere of contemporary legal science that is possible but neglected. This sphere was once disrupted in chaos and nowadays is easily misunderstood, but it must be investigated. That is, we can't just investigate the material and historical condition in which the rule of law occurs but also must investigate the ideological conditions of the "legal system" or "rule of law" in all the concrete social forms and their limits. Just as Feng Xiang has said, even for the investigation of "the rule of law" in modern times, we

> must overpass "the terminal" of market bourgeois ideology, breach the limit of keywords, turn inwards and examine ourselves, and question the historical, ethic and ideological condition of making possible jurisprudence in literature and law as literature. Therefore, we should firstly review the most basic correspondence between literature and law, namely their strategic placement of mutual dependence in the discursive practice of rule of law . . . only when such a question of "archaeology of knowledge" is firstly answered, Law and Literature can have the chance of making the entry into the role of critic that will be seriously treated by people, not identified as rhetorical and self-amusing one.[74]
>
> (Appendix: "Legal Morality" in Chinese and
> Western Contexts of Legal Science)

I must clarify "morality given priority over penalty" mentioned in this chapter and my criticism of it, because it might cause some misunderstandings.

---

74 Feng, Xiang 冯象. *Mutui zhengyi* 木腿正义, 24.

One misunderstanding most likely comes from traditional Chinese thoughts. In this tradition, Confucian "morality given priority over penalty" is usually considered the opposite of legalist "stern laws and severe punishments" and wins praise accordingly. But I don't *evaluate* morality over penalty through the moral path of Chinese tradition, but *analyze* the governance strategy of traditional society through the path of modern political sociology and legal sociology. I strive to *analyze, understand*, and try to *explain* why traditional society laid stress on morality and why the function of morality was not as effective as people imagined or believed. I only analyze the limitation of moral discourse and don't indicate my preference. I have less likelihood of turning against morality.

In the system of "politics and law" in traditional Chinese society presented by me, at least in line with the practice of "administrating justice" in those days presented in Yuan plays, we can observe that there isn't a contradiction between morality over penalty and draconian laws. Both of them are actually targeted at the issue in different aspects. The former is about the basic strategy and policy of national governance or social control and is the issue of "political system" or "constitution," while the latter is only the subordinate policy within the "legal" sphere. It may be likened to the compatibility between the addressing of "people-oriented politics" and the addressing of "severely cracking down on crime" at the meetings of political and legislative affairs. To make morality over penalty and draconian laws opposed, it is the imaginary construction concerning Chinese tradition, which occurs on the basis of our present knowledge system. In terms of the injustice from which Dou E suffered, the problem didn't lie in the draconian laws of ancient times; even the emphasis on morality over penalty couldn't save Dou E and would instead support the draconian laws because the so-called crime committed by Dou E was one of "the ten most atrocious crimes." On the other hand, at the end of *The Injustice to Dou E*, Dou Tianzhang ordered Donkey Zhang to "be quartered then beheaded," I believe no one (or even few people today) in those days thought that such an evildoer should be granted "morality over penalty."

Some scholars have the misunderstanding of Western tradition of natural law or the dispute between natural law and positive law because of their *unawareness of the traditional Chinese context*. These scholars are divided into two groups. One group of them receive the so-called new Western ideas of natural law, especially the ideas of Lon Luvois Fuller, John Rawls, and Ronald Dworkin, and emphasize that law must be based on morality and the morality of law and the basis of natural law. Since there isn't the term of "natural law" in traditional Chinese law or legal thoughts, they then criticize that traditional and contemporary morality of law in China is not sufficient, and they are laws, not *the law*. Scholars of positive law hold the opposite view and advocate for the separation of morality and law. They start from the abstract concepts of morality and law; being guided by the intention of criticizing the Chinese tradition of rule by virtue, they think one of problems of traditional Chinese law is that it is without the discrimination of morality and law; therefore, modern Chinese law should emphasize legal positivism and legalism and strictly distinguish the spheres of law and moral norms. Certainly, such a distinction is only a theoretical construction, because it is not quite strict in the real community of legal science in China. Many jurists keep "two commodities in stock for future specific uses," which is completely decided by the question and the occasion. Therefore, in the trial of an inheritance case of kept women, they might believe the verdict of court is to replace "law with morality," but as for the issue of "regulation on custody and repatriation," they would think it is "a vicious law" because of immorality. Because of unclear concepts and disordered train of thoughts, they will use "each and every one of the 18 weapons by turns" for the same issue.

However, whether natural law or positive law, if it is used to analyze the problem concerning the relationship between traditional Chinese law and morality, it is not very appropriate, and it is to fill the law and legal thoughts in traditional Chinese society in the conceptual system of the West. Such a filling is misleading and can't be effectively analyzed and demonstrated. The discussion on the relationship between morality and law in traditional China is not the discussion of jurisprudence of today, namely, the issue of how law and morality are unified at the philosophical or metaphysical level, but the discussion on politics and sociology. Although it can be included in the legal philosophy in a broad sense, the first question that the latter should answer in those days is in the big country with underdevelopment of agricultural economics and science and technology, what is the basic and possible political strategy? According to this strategy, law is only one part, while moral preaching is primary. As for the judicial issue, one of the questions that morality over penalty should answer is in the condition that there is not an effective and reliable judicial system (including the independently and professionally judicial department and the internal division of labor within the judicial department) and the corresponding science and technology, how can one guarantee a fair trial through the change of other variables except the personal wisdom of the adjudicator? The traditional Chinese answer is to focus on the personal moral character of officials. If we replace the dramatic characters with abstract concepts, we then have Table 6.1.

In this table, we can observe that in traditional China, the personal moral character of an adjudicator is consistently regarded as one of the most basic factors of judicial justice. Personal morality can be said to be invariably one of the basic questions of "judicial theory" or "judicial philosophy" in traditional China. Even today, there will not be much change on this point, which is manifested in almost all aspects of the judiciary. For example, as for the issue of judicial independence, as of today, I haven't noticed any discussion from the perspective of comparative institutional competence, and it is always through the lens of the personal morality of the judge. At the mention of a judge, what people emphasize more is still "the uprightness in justice" and "the hatred towards the evildoings"; then his

Table 6.1 The Classification of Judicial Officials in Traditional China

	Honest	*Greedy*
Astute	Astute and Honest	Astute and Greedy
Mediocre	Mediocre and Honest	Stupid and Greedy

competence will be emphasized. Even in the judicial reform, it starts from the perspective of anti-corruption and anti-injustice in the judiciary as well. Morality enters the traditional Chinese "administration of justice" from this aspect.

This classification is a local knowledge and a local imagination, although the overwhelming majority of jurists in contemporary China who imagine such a judicial issue all believe they are following international practice. However, only singling out two classifications of Western scholars on the judicial issue to make a comparison, we can observe the distinction of such imagination and can find that the so-called issue of legal morality discussed by Western scholars is *totally different*. The issue of legal or judicial morality discussed by Western scholars is totally irrelevant to the personal morality of judges, and their issue of legal morality can be roughly equivalent to the issue concerning heavenly principles (sometimes human feelings) and national law in China. In terms of Western scholastic concepts, it is the issue of the conflict between natural law and positive law. In traditional Chinese society, although this issue has been involved, it is not discussed as the issue of legal philosophy or judicial philosophy.

First, let's check the classification of Max Weber. In *Economy and Society*, Weber used two basic categories,[75] namely formalism and rationality, to classify the types of ruling including the types of judiciaries (see Table 6.2).

Posner, an American judge and jurist, presented a classification which is more easily understood in the American legal community[76] and quite similar to Weber's (Table 6.3).

In both matrixes, the issues of form/substance and natural law/positive law are the question of "whether law is moral or not" in Western legal science, while the issues of rationality/irrationality and formalism/realism are related to the question

Table 6.2 The Classification of Judicial Types of Weber

	Form	*Substance*
Rationality	Formal Rationality	Substantial Rationality
Irrationality	Formal Irrationality	Substantial Irrationality

Table 6.3 Posner's Classification of Judicial Types

	Natural Law	*Positive Law*
Formalism	Natural Law and Formalism	Positive Law and Formalism
Realism	Natural Law and Realism	Positive Law and Realism

75 Weber, Max. *Law in Economy and Society*, trans. Edward Shils and Max Rheinstein (Cambridge, MA: Harvard University Press, 1954).
76 The table is developed in accordance with Posner's table and his related argument. See Posner. *The Problems of Jurisprudence*, 12.

of how the judge applies the law, which roughly amounts to the question of competence and wisdom of judges in Chinese judicial theory. In terms of daily discourse,
the former question is concerned with whether a judge could or should (and to what
extent) set his preferred (and can be recognized by the community) morality (heavenly principles, human feelings) as the legal regulations, especially when the law
itself is faulted or even unjust. The latter problem touches on the fact that, whether
and to what extent we can interpret, or even make "a far-fetched interpretation,"
apply legal regulations so as to achieve the better result in our own opinion in specific ases when the legal source is definitely undoubted.

Only by comparing both tables and the understanding of the fundamental judicial issue in traditional (maybe including the present Chinese society in transition)
Chinese society outlined by me can we find the fundamental distinction. In Western
judicial theory (not only the European continent, but also the UK and the United
States), the *personal* morality of judges has nothing to do with the fundamental
issue of the judiciary. To be more exact, the moral issue of judges is outside the fundamental issue of the judiciary and only indirectly connected. That is the question
of how to select judges, and it is a political question. While in the judicial theory of
China, both questions are mixed.

Several factors might facilitate the difference between Chinese and Western judicial theories. In terms of Western judicial theory, Westerners might think the
personal morality of adjudicators is the issue of *pre*-judiciary and should be solved
by the political procedure (such as selection or appointment) and guaranteed by
the system such as the life tenure of judges. It reflects the institutional division of
labor. In the meantime, it also reflects that society has no impractical demand for
the personal morality of the adjudicator. Those with ordinary moral standards can
become adjudicators, and because of the institutional guarantee, it is presumed that
the adjudicator is basically just. What the judicial theory of China reflects might be
that since there is no independently judicial department in tradition, the independently judicial philosophy will not come into being as a result. The judicial theory
is still mixed with the political philosophy and is even one part of the latter.

Many contemporary jurists in China might question my conclusion. They will
point out that in Westen legal philosophy or judicial philosophy, morality is consistently an important perimeter, and the struggle between natural law and positive
law in legal science of the West for 2,000 years is just the struggle concerning
legal morality,[77] while Lon Fuller even wrote a monograph to discuss the morality of law.[78] How can I say the Western legal philosophy is actually removed from
morality?

Admittedly, natural law and positive law are concerned with the debate of legal
morality, which is different from the morality of *judicial officials or adjudicators*
in traditional Chinese society, although both of them have used the term "morality."

---

77 See Posner. *The Problems of Jurisprudence*. Weinreb, Llyod L. *Natural Law and Justice* (Cambridge, MA: Harvard University Press, 1987).
78 Fuller, Lon. *The Morality of Law*, rev. ed. (New Haven: Yale University Press, 1969).

When Western scholars discuss whether law is moral or not, they don't refer to the personal moral character of judges, but whether the law as regulation itself is moral or more moral. From the perspective of jurisprudence, it is not the moral issue discussed by Chinese jurists and is not related to the personal moral character of the judge himself, but is an issue of legal epistemology: whether we have the competence to find the best or better law as regulation, and it might be indirectly involved with the issue of legal ontology; whether there is a moral law in the world waiting to be discovered by judges. Since the ontology and the epistemology are involved in the Western intellectual tradition, especially in the social condition of the development of modern Western science and technology, such an issue concerning judicial morality might be relatively easy (in comparison with China) to be transformed as the issue of science and technology. Certainly, the personal quality of the judge is also one issue of judiciary and needs to be solved, but it is not discussed in judicial theories.

The issue of judicial morality discussed in traditional Chinese society and even today is irrelevant to the epistemology and the ontology and is basically attributed to the issue of personal character. Once the issue of the judiciary is transformed as the issue of the adjudicator, it is unnecessary and impossible to be transformed as the issue of science and technology for discussion and solution accordingly, and it only and always can be solved by the methods of political control such as moral education, supervision, punishment, and rectification. Thus, it reinforces and reiterates the consistency between politics and law and politics and judiciary again.

In order to clarify this point further, we can make a very simple analysis of the ancient Greek tragedy *Antigone*, which is believed to be the first to put forward the concept of natural law. In summary, one brother of Antigone betrayed the city of Thebes and led the enemy army to attack the city state, yet was killed in the battle. Creon, the usurper of the throne of Thebes, ordered (a positive law) not to bury the traitor as punishment. (Ancient Greeks believed that humans must be buried; otherwise, the soul would have no home to return to. Therefore, it was a punishment.) Defying the political order of Creon, Antigone believed that even as a traitor, he should be buried properly, and the soul should rest in peace after a man died. It was the eternal law of God. The law of Creon that violated the law of God was accordingly immoral. In the Western cultural tradition, this story was believed to be the first to present the very abstract issue of natural law and positive law.[79]

However, among ordinary Chinese, such a question has no likelihood of being posed. Who poses this question will be instead believed to be very boring. If only the characters of this story are changed with fictional Chinese names can it be imagined that in Chinese society people can discuss this issue. Then it can be distinctively observed that there is the diametrical difference of legal "morality"

---

79 For example, Bodenheimer, Edgar. *Jurisprudence: The Philosophy and Method of the Law*, 2nd ed. (Cambridge, MA: Harvard University Press, 1967), 2; Posner. *The Problems of Jurisprudence*, 10; Corwin, Edward S. *The "High Law" Background of American Constitutional Law* (Carmel: Liberty Fund, 2008), 2.

between the expressions of Chinese and Westerners. An ordinary Chinese will first ask, was this traitor a good or bad person? (If he is a good person, even terms such as "traitor" or "betrayal" will not be used.) Was Creon a good or bad person? He didn't allow the traitor to be buried; was his purpose to protect the people of Thebes or maintain his power? Should Antigone put blood relations above "the state"? In this context, the so-called issue of legal morality of Antigone can't allegedly exist absolutely among Chinese.

I don't compare the advantages and disadvantages of Chinese and Western judicial theories. Only from an intellectual perspective, it is impossible to judge which is better. Only when it is connected with a certain issue and will then bring forth some consequences can we make a judgment with our desires as the standard. What is more, since there are many differences between common law and civil law, and even British judiciary and American judiciary,[80] the hasty comparison of the so-called advantages and disadvantages of Chinese and Western judicial theories would be destined to "mix water and dough into a batter; result, a lump of messy glue." I hereby only want to express that the issue of morality in the traditional Chinese theory of "administrating justice" doesn't exist in the framework of Western judicial theory, and vice versa. To distinguish the issue of legal morality in Chinese and Western legal discourses, we can temporarily describe the morality involved in the case trial in traditional Chinese society as the morality of those *who administered the justice*, while the morality that is emphasized in Western jurisprudence, especially natural law, can be temporarily described as *legal or judicial* morality. This point deserves to be observed and distinguished by Chinese scholars who discuss legal morality or morality.

80 For the summarized difference between common law and civil law, British law and American law in jurisprudence, especially judicial philosophy, see Posner, Richard A. *The Problematics of Moral and Legal Theory* (Cambridge, MA: Harvard University Press, 1999), esp. Chapter 2 on the analytical criticism of the jurisprudence of H. L. A. Hart, Ronald Dworkin, and Habermas. See also Posner, Richard A. *Law and Legal Theory in England and America* (Oxford: Oxford University Press, 1996).

7 Dramatic Space and the Shaping of Justice Value

In Chapter 6, I provide a *general* explanation of functionalism on the relationship between law and literature from a macroscopic perspective, which is not related to the concrete literary texts or the forms of literary expressions. Such an analysis and explanation at the macroscopic level must be defined appropriately; otherwise, it will be misleading and create some problems. First, this explanation doesn't meticulously discuss different expressive methods on the relationship between literature and politics, and it easily enables people to identify literature with politics in a simple way. Second, this explanation also neglects different types of literature and art and doesn't point out their divergence, especially the difference of drama discussed in this book, which therefore obstructs full comprehension. Third, this explanation emphasizes the content conveyed in literary works, which might usher in total ignorance of expressive forms of art concerning the conveyed content, and it seems that the form is not important. Fourth, even the concept of drama, if it serves as a unique classification system, will cover some particular expressive methods of all types of drama. To avoid such type of question, more meticulous analysis is needed.

I only present these potential questions, but have no intention of making the related comprehensive analysis. It will be beyond the scope of this monograph, and my professional competence as well. On the basis of understanding the narrative forms, performance features of traditional Chinese drama, and the construction of dramatic space, this chapter tries to discuss how these factors *can* affect the audiences' awareness and understanding of ancient and general trials and create a condition for such social thinking (collective unconsciousness), which transforms the issue of intelligence and technology in trials into the issue of morality. Consequently, my key proposition is as follows: There are various avenues to convey truth in writing; in addition to the efforts of directly publicizing and reiterating the content of orthodox ideology, traditional Chinese drama also constructs the judicial value of justice and the social consensus that are compatible with people's orthodox ideology in those days through the formal factor of dramatic performance and creates the condition of social cognition for the morality oriented judicial justice system in traditional Chinese society.

In a certain sense, this chapter is the rectification of the misunderstanding that might be caused in Chapter 6 and also reinforces the theme of the previous chapter.

DOI: 10.4324/9781003615606-11

The "rectification" is I no longer discuss literature and art in the abstract sense, but strive to investigate the specific social context in which the types of literary and art work, expressive forms of art, and art effect take place. The "reinforcement" is since I observe the influence of expressive forms of literature and art on law and don't emphasize the influence of the literary and art content on law, I bring the issue of art forms into the research sphere of law and literature, which is easily ignored and consistently ignored by people and thereby might create a new perspective for this study.

Narratives of Chinese Drama

As a literary genre, generally speaking, drama has a major difference from mainstream literature in traditional Chinese society. Drama is a narrative work after all and not a sentimental work. Even if the main component of Yuan plays is poetic (tune), the framework linking all these arias is still a story. In this aspect, Yuan plays have more similarities with the scripts for storytelling and novels after the Tang and Song dynasties. In addition to the structural completion, the narrative method really matters. Actually, in recent years, the emphasis on the narrative method is on the rise, and monographs on narratology are increasing[1]; the reason why the works of Latin American writers such as Gabriel García Márquez and Jorge Luis Borges are popular among many Chinese readers from the 1990s onward is the narrative of these works brings a special sense of beauty to readers to a very large extent.

The narrative method of traditional Chinese narrative works is rather simple. Only when readers know traditional Chinese narrative works more and have a knowledge of Western literary works will they patently sense it. Generally speaking,

> Although a few of them adopt the inversion narration . . . a few adopt the first-person narrative and the third-person limited narrative . . . a few adopt the narration with the character or background as the structural center. . . . But in the overall, ancient Chinese novels basically adopt the consistent narration in the narrative time, the omniscient vision in the narrative perspective, and the plot as the structural center in the narrative structure.[2]

What Chen Pingyuan hereby discusses is ancient Chinese novels, but these three features and the ensuing basic layout are also shared by other traditional Chinese

---

1 Pu, Andi 浦安迪. *Zhongguo xushixue* 中国叙事学 (Beijing: Peking University Press, 1996); Shen, Dan 申丹. *Xushuxue yu xiaoshuo wentixue yanjiu* 叙述学与小说文体学研究 (Beijing: Peking University Press, 1998); Zhao, Yiheng 赵毅衡. *Dang shuozhe beishuo de shihou bijiao xushuxue daolun* 当说者被说的时候: 比较叙述学导论 (Beijing: Renmin University of China Press, 1998); Chen, Pingyuan 陈平原. *Zhongguo xiaoshuo xushi moshi de zhuanbian* 中国小说叙事模式的转变 (Beijing: Peking University Press, 2003).
2 Chen 陈平原. *Zhongguo xiaoshuo xushi moshi de zhuanbian* 中国小说叙事模式的转变, 4.

narrative works. In the vernacular literature with more folk aspects, these features are even more prominent.[3] In Yuan plays, such a narrative mode can be unique.

Although traditional Chinese drama belongs to "drama," the internal difference is huge. We can make a rough classification. In the West, there are dramas emphasizing the plot, with the ancient Greek tragedy as the representative, and dramas emphasizing the emotional conveyance, with Italian opera as the representative. Inside the traditional Chinese drama, there is naturally such a difference as well. However, overall, traditional Chinese drama, especially Yuan plays, develops from poetry, *ci* poetry and verse, which lays more stresses on emotional conveyance, not the storytelling. Many scholars therefore usually describe it as "opera" instead of "drama," because it "puts the songs above the story plot and dramatic conflicts," and it is "centered on verse."[4] Some scholars indicate that many Yuan plays lack dramatic elements quite a lot and even believe that Yuan plays were "unmature" in a strict sense.[5] Therefore, to a large extent, in the process of enjoying traditional Chinese drama, the story is only a background, while what audiences appreciate more is actors' "reciting, martial arts performing, acting and singing." Many scripts of Yuan plays at present are only the assembly of librettos without dialogues and cues for the stage performances. Even those playscripts preserved in a relatively "complete" way just have very simple dialogue, acting instructions, and cues, which only have instructions such as "act out."[6] Even so, according to the research of scholars, these elements and other introductions at interludes, acting instructions were all added by the later generations.[7] Librettos in the playscripts are quite similar to traditional poems, which are strongly emotional and subjective. Some arias in Yuan plays often praised by scholars can be completely separated out as poems, such as "A sky azure and clouded, an earth flowered yellow; the western wind is stiff, northern geese fly southward. At dawn what dyes the frosted woods the flush of drunkenness? It will ever be the tears of separated lovers."[8] In all aspects, these arias have nothing different from the poetry of Tang, *ci* poetry of Song, or verses

---

3 Chen Pingyuan's research discovers that some novels in classical Chinese in ancient China, such as *Strange Stories in Oriental Society*, once adopted the inversion narrative, but when the same story was adapted to a novel for storytelling, the time of the novel was rearranged in the proper way. A few novels with simple plots in classical Chinese in ancient China once broke through "the omniscient narrative," but most of the vernacular novels utilized the tone of the omniscient and omnipotent storyteller. *Zhongguo xiaoshuo xushi moshi de zhuanbian* 中国小说叙事模式的转变, 38, 63–65. Certainly, this also further proves my viewpoint in Chapter 6 from another perspective: The factor of reader will enable folk or popular literature and art to be more conservative, even in the forms of artistic expression.

4 Zhong 钟涛. *Yuan zaju yishu shengchanlun* 元杂剧艺术生产论, 4.

5 Luo 洛地. *Xiqu yu zhejiang* 戏曲与浙江. Quoted in Liu, Xiusheng 李修生. *Yuan zajushi* 元杂剧史 (Nanjing: Jiangsu Ancient Books, 1996), 1.

6 See Sui, Shusen, ed. 隋树森. *Yuanqu xuan waibian* 元曲选外编 (Beijing: Zhonghua Book Company, 1959).

7 Gu, Xuejie 顾学颉. *Yuan ming zaju* 元明杂剧 (Shanghai: Shanghai Ancient Books, 1979), 23–25.

8 Shifu, Wang. *The Story of the Western Wing*, trans. Stephen H. West and Wilt L. Idema (Berkeley: University of California Press, 1995), 239.

of Yuan. Owing to these features of traditional Chinese drama, the audiences of today have been more accustomed to appreciating stories, not emotions, because of the modern art training, and they often feel that the rhythm of traditional drama is "too slow." Some scholars have an explanation for it: The rhythm of life in modern society is quickening, and modern audiences demand "the sense of speed." Such a criticism or suggestion is specious. It does not explain why we still appreciate a picture or a photo today or why not all "the shoot 'em up films" and "action films" can capture audiences (some of them are specially presented in slow motion). In my opinion, what the comment of modern audiences reflects is that even for the same traditional plays on the stage, audiences of today and the past have a great change in the dimension of their appreciation. I got carried away with this, but this analysis sufficiently demonstrates that the focus of traditional Chinese *drama* is not on the narrative.

Since the focus is not on the narrative, naturally, traditional drama will not be *concerned* with the structure of story and the narrative method. "Not to be concerned with" doesn't mean "there doesn't exist." "Yuan plays generally have four acts in one book, which has the relatively short length; it is impossible to arrange the complex and intricate plots, and there is often the mutual duplication or copy in the process of opening, developing, changing and concluding of plays in the progress of plot. The fourth act of the play is usually more flawed like 'the arrow at the end of its flight'." "Most of Yuan plays set the main line of plot structure that there are one person and one event, and the thread runs through the play, which creates the art effect of concentration, concision, brevity and clarity."[9] Only according to the standard of narrative works or dramatic structure of today, the structure of traditional Chinese drama seems to be very problematic.

This point is quite obvious in the so-called "compact and tight"[10] structure of *The Injustice to Dou E*. In Act 2 of the play, Dou E repeatedly introduced the process of an event that happened before and was performed on the stage. Besides, such an introduction is completely impersonalized, namely there neither exists the error of understanding caused by personal perspectives, nor the error of personal memory caused by the passage of time, nor the narrator's selective description of the related facts, which naturally happens with the changed circumstances and can thereby be understood by audiences. Dou E narrated the previous facts "truthfully, accurately, and completely" every time. Such a narration and the previous stage performances create the absolute certainty of all facts and indisputable objectivity for audiences/readers.

Perhaps because of the demand for the continuous narrative, and perhaps because of the effect pursued deliberately, the playwrights of Yuan adopted the so-called "scattered perspective" in Chinese painting, namely another method without the

9 Guo, Yingde 郭英德. "Yuan zaju zhongguo gudian xiqu yishu de qipa" 元杂剧: 中国古典戏曲艺术的奇葩. *Guangming Ribao* 光明日报, May 10, 1999.

10 Lu, Kanru; Feng Yuanjun 陆侃如、冯沅君. "Zhongguo wenxueshigao 12" 中国文学史稿 12. In *Yuanqu tongrong* 元曲通融, 36.

concept of the "classical unities" of Western drama. That is, even in the play of one act or a section of play, the stage space is used unrestrainedly or "freely." A scholar once made an analysis of the first section of Act 1 of *The Injustice to Dou E* and found that in just this section, the stage space had been changed five times "as if it were on a merry-go-round."[11] Therefore, even Wang Guowei, who highly praised Yuan plays, had to admit that the structural arrangement of Yuan plays was really bad.[12] Some contemporary scholars have made a similar evaluation.[13]

But carefully reflecting on it, we can find that the implied evaluation standard on dramatic structure in the judgment of Wang Guowei and others is basically Western or for reading. I can't agree on this standard. In my opinion, the pursuit of Yuan plays was the structure that could more clearly show the lyrical dimension of traditional Chinese drama and be more convenient for audiences' appreciation in the *performing environment* in those days. In this sense, the standard of evaluating the dramatic structure of Yuan plays should be the effect of dramatic performances in the condition at that time, not the abstractly essentialist dramatic standard. Relatively speaking, the structure of dramatic text that seems to be lengthy and dilatory in our present view is not "the disadvantage" of *performing* Yuan plays at all, but instead the advantage in comparison with the social environment of appreciating plays in ancient times. Later I will demonstrate it. But at this moment, I temporarily set this comparison aside and put my focus on the features of such a structural method and narrative method of drama in comparison with the structural method, accentuating the dramatic conflict, and the possible influences of these features on audiences' understanding the issue of judicial adjudication.

Pu Andi first described the narrative method of "narrator as an official recorder of history," the whole process of event presented to people is with highly degreed certainty, which creates a purely objective narrative illusion. It is also the all-around or "omniscient" perspective; namely the narrator is not the participator of a specific life and therefore is the person with the inevitable limitation of perceiving and understanding, but seems to be the observer who is always present and thereby clearly understands the whole development process of event, and even the wise person who has insight into the motives of all actors. In this sense, I prefer to describe it as the narration of God.[14] Although there isn't a Western concept of omnipresent, eternal, and omnipotent God in Chinese culture, many narrations in ancient Chinese works

11 Chen, Xiaolu 陈晓鲁. "Xiqu wutai shikong xingshi zai guan hanqing zaju zhong de zuichu biaoxian" 戏曲舞台时空形式在关汉卿杂剧中的最初表现. In *Yuanqu tongrong xia* 元曲通融下, 1362.
12 "It is self-evident that the structural arrangement of Yuan plays is truly poor. It is because this issue had been neglected for years, and playwrights just followed suit since old days, or just rushed through the work." "The best point of Yuan plays doesn't lie in its mind structure." Wang, Guowei 王国维. *Wang guowei xueshu jingdianji shang* 王国维学术经典集上, 282.
13 Yao, Shuyi 幺书仪. *Yuanren zaju yu yuandai shehui* 元人杂剧与元代社会 (Beijing: Peking University Press, 1997), 53.
14 A scholar has also observed this point and accurately described it as "transparency." See Guo, Zhenqin 郭振勤. "Yuan zaju baogongxi faan qingjie touming de gousi yishu" 元杂剧包公戏发案情节透明的构思艺术. In *Yuanqu tongrong* 元曲通融, 708–709. However, "transparency" is actually the effect of this narrative, not the narrative style.

must be premised on such a godly vision – for example, the narration method of Sima Qian in *The Great Scribe's Records* I have mentioned elsewhere. Sima Qian seemed to observe and hear the words and deeds of Cheng Ying, Gongsun Chujiu, Xiang Yu, and Liu Bang on the scene. Actually, Sima Qian had no such likelihood, nor did the authors whose written historical materials were used by Sima. In terms of drama, such a perspective and narrative method can thereby be described as a perspective and narration of audiences, because only audiences in the theater might observe the whole process of the event from the perspective of an observer, who has no direct relations of interests with characters in the play.

Such a narrative method has its own strong points. Its art structure is relatively easy, and the continuous narrative also accords with the daily experiences of common people, and it is then convenient for audiences to enter the dramatic story as quickly as possible; they don't need to spend time and energy focusing on some transient details, and it is easy for them to create a sense of being present on the scene and totally forget the subjective and objective worlds. The art appeal is reinforced. The repetition of the previous section in each act of the play is not only convenient for the performance of the one act play or the one play but also convenient for audiences who missed the previous act because of arriving late.[15] The simple structure and plot are beneficial for audiences or readers to grasp characters and events as the whole and urge them to connect the whole with those prominent details for consideration, which reinforces the sense of details and the mastery of the whole in the meantime. What is more, this structure and narration also "stipulates the tendency of audiences' attention, and channels it into the content purview defined by the playwright,"[16] and lets audiences concentratedly appreciate the actors' reciting, singing, acting, and martial arts performing and emotionally sense the lyrical features of Yuan plays. Viewed from the perspective of seeking the maximum number of audiences – it is just what popular culture seeks – this art structure is completely reasonable. Only from the perspective of readers of today will people feel that the structure is overly dilatory, loose, and excessively repeated.

However, if viewed from the perspective of intelligence – it is more of the perspective of elite culture – this narrative method has some obvious flaws. First, in real life, no one can feel for life and events like this. Each one of us in real life is living in the specific space and time and can only feel for the world from the specific placement in space and time and from a specific perspective. It is impossible for to have the perspective of audiences or the perspective of God. As Mao Zedong stated, "In class society everyone lives as a member of a particular class, and every kind of thinking, without exception, is stamped with the brand of a class."[17] Because of the role limitation defined by various social relations,

---

15 This repetition is important to the non-centralized and non-consecutive performance, and its effect somewhat amounts to the brief summary of the previous episode in the TV series of today.

16 Guo, Zhenqin 郭振勤. "Yuan zaju baogongxi faan qingjie touming de gousi yishu" 元杂剧包公戏发案情节透明的构思艺术. In *Yuanqu tongrong* 元曲通融, 709.

17 Zedong, Mao. *Selected Works of Mao Tse-tung* (Paris: Foreign Languages Press, 2021), 270.

understanding and feeling of other persons and events are affected by social relations and relations of interests. Although each person can share others' experiences to a certain extent because of the biological feature and the competence of social association to acquire a certain mutuality, there are two types of limitations at least. Such a mutual understanding is usually conveyed through language or other symbols; then it is indirect. Any language or symbol has the issue of "Tao called Tao is not Tao. Names can name no lasting name."[18] Language can neither fully convey that "truth" nor completely (although this is not absolutely impossible) convey the feeling of the narrator himself toward the facts. In this sense, intersubjectivity is limited. Each one of us is confined to our own world. Hence, when the narrative method of traditional Chinese drama entrusts people with a vision of God and an omniscient feeling, people forget their own limitation, and it is not easy for them to reflect that they might not know something or couldn't know something.

Second, when drama directs audiences to emotionally feel for the play – it is the feature of traditional Chinese drama – it will suppress them to rationally feel for the play to a certain extent, although theoretically speaking, both of them can be complementary. In terms of judicial adjudication discussed in this chapter, more importantly, this narrative completely suppresses and annihilates the perspective of adjudicator and annihilates one of core issues of jurisprudence with which he is confronted, namely for a person who doesn't participate in the whole process of event, how can he surely know the truth of dispute for his adjudication and make the reasonable and fair judgment?[19] I certainly don't demand that drama must make an entry from the perspective of the adjudicator; such a demand is ridiculous and arbitrary. I only want to say that in the performing space of drama, the narrative method of traditional Chinese drama is to exclude the perspective of the adjudicator. Within such a specific space, this narrative method provides the perspective that can't be acquired in real life for audiences and lets them share the vision of God, which accordingly enables them to forget or even repel the perspectivism, or perspectivist narrative; it enables audiences to sense and face the issues presented by perspectivism in an in-depth way and understand the dilemma and thorny issues of adjudicator in the play.

Third, from the perspective of the judiciary, this narrative easily leads to the fair sense of substantive justice. One scholar who studies the plays concerning Bao Zheng in the Yuan Dynasty once pointed out that since the case had been fully presented on the stage beforehand, "audiences have a fair scale in mind before Bao Zheng judged the case. It arouses their great interests to observe how the adjudicator judged and concluded the case. When Bao Zheng finally made the fair or relatively fair verdict, punished evildoers and encouraged people to do good, and upheld justice, the clean, honest and just image of Bao Zheng is convincingly

---

18 Addiss; Lombardo, trans. *Tao Te Ching*, 1.
19 Posner. *The Problems of Jurisprudence*, 7.

erected."[20] It is certainly right. But this researcher didn't point out that due to the limitation of perspective and information, another official failed to make a fair or relatively fair verdict just as Bao Zheng did, so what kind of image could be erected in the mind of audiences?

We can use *The Injustice to Dou E* to understand this issue. When we observe Donkey Zhang's bulling, threatening, and framing Dou E in the capacity of audiences or readers, we have made the moral judgment that Donkey Zhang deserved the 10,000 deaths, and we naturally hope the official in charge of the trial makes the same judgment. However, at this moment, we have forgotten that we are audiences, the God in the theatrical seats. We will use the omniscient vision and the corresponding expectation that the theater creates for us to make a demand for the adjudicator in the play. When the prefect of Chuzhou, Taowu, failed to fulfill this expectation and made a mistake, the problem popped up. Certainly, if the consequence of this mistake is not severe, we might remain indifferent, and even will give an understanding smile to feel for the humor in life due to the superior perspective of audiences. However, this feeling is only that of the observer, while the actors are under great pressure, and are at the critical moment. Once this mistake or misunderstanding causes a severe consequence, we will not only be disappointed and consternated but also will have the moral indignation. Although theoretically speaking, moral judgment is only involved with the subjective intention of actors, in practice, the moral response instead is the outcome of consequence (but not always so).[21] In *The Injustice to Dou E*, the mistake made by the prefect of Chuzhou just brought forth the severe consequence. Under ordinary circumstances, we can tolerate some weaknesses and flaws usually found in humans, such as selfishness, weakness, prejudices, stubbornness, and lasciviousness, but once these weaknesses cause or even only bring forth severe consequences, they will usually not be brooked by people. Besides, the better the dramatic effect, the stronger the art appeal (more "real"); the more easily audiences will be controlled by these sentiments, the more uneasily they will investigate and feel for the perspective of adjudicator in a rational and detached way. The strong sentimental and psychological need for social solidarity will push us to seek and find enemies and create evildoers.[22]

"What you have said is only the effect of theater!" Someone might say generally that people would not consider the life represented in literature or drama to be true things like Don Quixote did. Not necessarily. There are many people who consciously or unconsciously identify themselves with fictional characters after reading books and watching plays and films. There are always boys who fall for Lin Daiyu or Xue Baochai or Shi Xiangyun and girls who fall for Jia Baoyu after

20 Guo, Zhenqin 郭振勤. "Yuan zaju baogongxi faan qingjie touming de gousi yishu" 元杂剧包公戏发案情节透明的构思艺术. In *Yuanqu tongrong* 元曲通融, 709.

21 Williams, Bernard. "Moral Luck," in *Moral Luck: Philosophical Papers 1973–1980* 20 (1981), quoted in Posner. *The Problematics of Moral and Legal Theory*, 44.

22 Durkheim, Émile. *The Division of Labor in Society*, ed. Steven Lukes (New York: Free Press, 2014).

they have read *The Dream of Red Mansions*. It is a ubiquitous phenomenon that someone likes an actor or actress after watching the film and considers him or her a dream lover. To consider art as life, it is actually quite a common social phenomenon. After all, literature and art themselves draw the related information from social life and are the important resources that affect the decision of one's own life. Although the adults will not become fans, many people come to understand life from plays, films, and novels and use these to solve problems. Don Quixote is just the outdated ridiculous figure in a Spanish novel. As the animal applying symbols, each one of us is a Don Quixote to a certain extent.

It is because of the factor of Don Quixote that enables us, the audience, to very easily have moral indignation at the adjudicator misjudging cases in the face of tragedies of Dou E, Su Shujuan, and Feng Youlan. This is because ordinary audiences and readers don't understand the thorny problems with which the adjudicator is confronted, and it is generally very hard for them to put themselves in the adjudicator's place to understand the nature of this mistake. Under the circumstances without other reference frames and other possibilities, owing to the concerted efforts of other previously mentioned factors, people are very easily "addicted to morality" and habitually understand, mold, and summarize the problems in life from the path of the personal character of the adjudicator.

This perspective is generally accompanied by theatrical space and atmosphere, yet it is not limited to the theatre. Theatrical effect has a certain molding utility on the thinking mode of audiences and readers and cultivates "the habitus" of thinking, in the words of Pierre Bourdieu, to affect people in terms of understanding and judging problems in social life. In the meantime, since this perspective is usually accompanied by the political and moral evaluation of life and events and characters in plays, it is a cultural education concerning the general knowledge of law. Hence, it will also cultivate the basic path and the reference frame of pondering over and understanding social issues. In this sense, the aesthetic posture might be transformed as the posture of social life.

The narration method of traditional drama can certainly annihilate the perspective of adjudicator, yet the issue of perspectivism is realistic and inevitable. How does traditional drama tackle this issue? Generally speaking, the traditional Chinese detective plays always avoid it. Just as I have analyzed in Chapter 5, among the existing Yuan plays, there is only one play that can be qualified as the application of an adjudicator's wisdom in trying cases. Other detective plays are either focused on the issue of law enforcement or turn the issue of adjudication to the issue of diligent government. As for the former issue, it is sufficiently solved only if there is a high-ranking official who can behead first and memorialize afterward and forcefully enforce law or wisely apply the law; as for the latter issue, the problem of discovering the real truth in trying cases can be cracked only if officials work diligently and carefully in addition to some luck or coincidence.

Once power and diligent government can't solve the problem, the playwrights will resort to ghosts or a "revelation dream" to solve (or more exactly avoid) this epistemological issue. Why did the ghost appear in nearly half of detective plays in

Selected Plays from the Yuan Dynasty? This might be an explanation. The appearance of a ghost indicates the avoidance of this issue on the one hand, but just indicates the severity of this issue on the other hand. When the wisdom of playwrights couldn't solve the issue of adjudicator, their easiest and clumsiest solution was to bring the ghost in.

In this sense, I conclude that traditional Chinese drama has never seriously considered the core jurisprudential issue in the judiciary and indirectly touches on this issue at most. Such ignorance urges the formation of a moralist path.

The Construction of Art Space in Traditional Drama

If narrative allegedly distinguishes dramas, novels, scripts for storytelling, short stories of the Tang and Song dynasties, etc., and lyrical poems, then what distinguishes dramas and others is performance (although storytelling has a certain performing element). The art effect of drama is basically not realized by the reading of audiences (as for the scripts for storytelling, there is a listening element) and mainly actualized by the watching and listening of audiences. Considering this point, although the drama materials that I have analyzed here are the recorded texts, we should notice that in the age when these plays had their art effect, they were not the texts, and even there was no need for texts. Playscripts are only the guide to facilitate the art effect of drama, although it might be the most important guide. Therefore, to investigate law and literature through drama in a meticulous way, researchers should not only read texts but also must imaginarily construct the space where the play is staged and imagine the performance of play and how, to whom, and in what environment the play is functional. Thus, some words and signs that just serve as the reading instruction can become the component of a larger dramatic text. Dramatic knowledge and experiences acquired by a reader in his daily watching performances might become the important supplement to his reading of dramatic texts in a narrow sense.

I would like to cite an example. In the playscript of *The Injustice to Dou E*, when Taowu, the prefect of Chuzhou who tried the case of Dou E, appeared on the stage, there is a line in the bracket (*Jing*-role in-make-up-of official leading attendant enters). If only viewed from the dimension of narrative text, these words are not important for the development of plot in the play and can be fully replaced by the specific character, Taowu. Considering that it is a play, these words have irreplaceably important meaning and are the important component of the dramatic text for the performance, not the playscripts for literary reading. These words are not just the cue for art performance, at least not for me. They remind me of the highly formalized world constructed by other art forms in traditional Chinese drama, and such a formalized art world might imply the political and moral evaluation of playwrights and actors toward this play and their political and moral guidance of audiences or readers.

If we read the texts of traditional drama again from this angle in addition to the investigation of other dramatic factors, we can observe that traditional Chinese drama applies some formal elements to construct and convey a certain political and moral evaluation in society in a large quantity. These formal elements are discussed next.

Names of Main Characters

Through the homophonic hint or literal meaning of names, playwrights construct a world with the opposition of good and evil. For instance, Taowu, the prefect of Chuzhou who sentenced Dou E to death, and Guo Yuzhi, the county magistrate who made the wrong verdict in *Fifteen Strings of Cash*, are the most typical examples. The name of Taowu 桃杌comes from Taowu 梼杌, one of four evildoers in ancient times.[23] While the name of Guo Yuzhi 过于执 is more blunt: "excessively stubborn." Obviously, playwrights used the same name or homophone between characters in plays and ancient figures to hint audiences and readers in advance. In Yuan plays, there are lots of similar examples.

It is the same case with "positive characters" in the eyes of playwrights. For example, Dou Tianzhang 窦天彰, who finally redressed the injustice to Dou E. The Chinese character 彰 has an explicit and evident meaning, and it has the meaning of "extolling" in the meantime. The surname of Tianzhang 天彰 therefore has amply positive implications. The most obvious method is to utilize the morally authoritative figures who have been universally acknowledged or confirmed among the people, such as Bao Zheng, Wang Xiuran, Zhang Ding, et al., and to popularize and symbolize these figures. Therefore, we can understand why among fifteen detective plays in *Selected Plays from the Yuan Dynasty*, there are ten plays of the honest official Bao Zheng, two plays of Wang Xiuran, and two plays of Zhang Ding, while the latter two were also famous figures in history, at least in those days.

The Entrance Poem and the Exit Poem

Admittedly, the name of a character has a hint of its utility, but it usually acts more on readers and hardly works on the stage of traditional drama because it is seldom necessary to call the name directly on the stage. In order to avoid "the invalidity" of this hint, "the entrance poem" and "the exit poem" are more used in traditional drama in order to define the identify or personality of characters in plays. In some plays, even the names of some characters are omitted and only their entrance poems are kept. In light of the empirical research on the entrance poem in Yuan plays, among all of these poems, 80% of them define the identity and 40% define

---

23 "The emperor Chuen-heuh had a descendant devoid of ability and virtue. He would receive no instruction; he would acknowledge no good words. When told, he was obstinate; when left alone, he was stupid. He was an arrogant hater of intelligent virtue, seeking to confound the heavenly rules of society. All the people under heaven called him Block." Legge, James, trans. *The Chinese Classics: The Ch'un Ts'ew with The Tso Chuen*, vol. 5 (Hong Kong: Hong Kong University Press, 1960), 283.

personality. Therefore, the characterization is the most important function of the entrance poem.[24]

For example, the entrance poem of Taowu in *The Injustice to Dou E* is "I am a magistrate, the best on the bench. My coffers are filled from the cases I hear. When any inspector comes to check on my files, I'm to be found at home too sick to appear" (Guan, 1977: 135). It is the most typical example, but these examples are abundant.[25] On the contrary, the entrance poem of positive officials in plays is filled with the justice and heroism. For instance, Bao Zheng: "In years gone by, I personally received the Imperial Commission; My hands grasp the Golden Plaque and the Sword of Power. I exhaust the way of justice in the Southern Yamen; No need for the Soul-frightening Dais at the Eastern Marchmount" (Li, 273). "Dong, dong, sounds the yamen drum, public servants line up on the two sides; Of King Yama, at the Court of Life and Death, of the Spirit of the Eastern Marchmount at the Soul-snatching Terrace" (Guan, 2010: 51). And Wanyan: "Legal articles eliminate excessive officials, explicit punishments remove the corruption. If my authority is questioned, try my ordinance sword and golden tablet" (Sun, 683). Even if positive characters are poverty stricken, they have lofty aspirations. The entrance poem of Dou Tianzhang is: "Having read ten thousand books of great profundity, Sima Xiangru still remained as poor as he could be. When the Emperor summoned him to the court of Han one day, he spoke no more of wine but of his Master Fantasy" (Guan, 1977: 119).

Classification of Roles and Types of Facial Make-Up

Although the entrance poem and the exit poem are important, they only resort to the sense of hearing, which appears once, while drama is the art for multiple senses. Therefore, traditional Chinese drama also lays particular stress on the mobilization

---

24 You, Zongrong 游宗蓉. "Yuan zaju shang xiachangshi tanjiu" 元杂剧上下场诗探究. In *Zhongguo wenxue yanjiu* 中国文学研究, ed. Taiwan daxue zhongwensuo 台湾大学中文所, no. 13 (1999).

25 Here are the examples of the entrance poems of negative officials:

The incompetent magistrate of county in Henan Prefecture in *The Moheluo Doll*, "I am an official who loves only money. Plaintiff and defendant: both must pay! If my superiors should come my cases to review, they'd beat me in the hall till like a pig I squeal!"

(Meng, 161)

Su Shun, Prefect of Zhengzhou in *The Chalk Circle*, "Even though I hold office, I know nothing of the law; All it takes is just a little silver to bring to an end any official matter"

(Li, 258)

Clerk Xiao in *The Moheluo Doll*, "The magistrate is pure as water, the clerk is white as dough. Mix water and dough into batter: Result, a lump of messy glue!"

(Meng, 162)

Clerk Zhao in *The Chalk Circle*, "My job as clerk is only a way to get drunk or bed someone's old lady. And after all, whom shall I love? Any pretty face that's a match for my own."

(Li, 246)

of other senses. One is the special attention to the classification of roles. If we only read Yuan playscripts, we can find that all the major characters in plays enter the stage in the capacity of their role instead of their character.[26] That means they appear on the stage as the type-oriented characters, not the specific characters acted by actors.

It should be noted that such a classification of roles is not only the classification of types of actors, but also the rough classification of dispositions and personalities of characters acted by actors. Although researchers usually attach more attention to the art function of this classification and the organization function within the troupe, in terms of its social function, it may be mainly targeted at audiences, which is convenient for audiences to master the classification of characters.

In accordance with the research of experts, the roles of actors in Yuan plays can be generally divided into four categories: *mo* 末, *dan* 旦, *jing* 净 (including *chou* 丑), and *za* 杂.[27]

Mo is the positive male role; the male lead is *zhengmo* 正末; and there are *waimo* 外末, *fumo* 副末, and *chognmo* 冲末, etc. In terms of Yuan plays, Dou Tianzhang (*chongmo*), Bao Zheng in *The Chalk Circle* and other plays (*chongmo*), and Zhang Ding in *The Moheluo Doll* (*zhengmo*) and Wanyan (*waimo*) are all roles of *mo*. In this sense, the role of *mo* is almost only for positive characters.[28]

Dan is the female role; the female lead is *zhengdan* 正旦; besides, there are *fudan* 副旦, *huadan* 花旦, *laodan* 老旦, *dadan* 大旦, *xiaodan* 小旦, and *chadan* 搽旦. It should be noted that generally speaking, the role of *dan* is the positive or neutral character, and only *chadan* is generally the negative character. Those vicious female roles in Yuan plays are acted by *chadan* – for example, Ma's wife in *The Chalk Circle* who murdered her husband and snatched the son from others.

Jing is the so-called painted face. In the plays of the Yuan, Ming, and Qing dynasties, the distinction between *jing* and *chou* is not clear.[29] *Chou* can't constitute a separate type, and *jing* often includes *chou*. In Yuan plays, although many positive characters are the roles of *jing*, all the officials who are negative characters in the eyes of playwrights are the role of *jing* – for example, Taowu; Donkey Zhang who framed Dou E, and Dr. Lu who attempted to murder someone for money in *The Injustice to Dou E*; Su Shun in *The Chalk Circle*; the county magistrate in Henan

26 A scholar holds that "'The type of role' is the unique thing in the formation of Chinese drama. It is not only the division of labor for actors of a troupe each of whom had his own part while acting in complimentary way, but also the classification of various characters with multiple interactive relations in the play . . . therefore, in traditional Chinese play (playscript), it was 'the type of role,' not 'the character' that went on stage." Luo, Di 洛地. "Zhongguo chuantong xiju yanjiu de quehan" 中国传统戏剧研究的缺憾. *Shehui kexue yanjiu* 社会科学研究, no. 3 (2000), 133, Note 7.
27 For the general introduction to the roles in traditional drama, see Gu 顾学颉. *Yuan ming zaju* 元明杂剧, Chapter 4.
28 Among the plays of Bao Zheng I have consulted, the only exception is that the negative character Lu Zhailang in *The Wife-Snatcher* is played by the role of *chongmo*.
29 Gu 顾学颉. *Yuan ming zaju* 元明杂剧, 29. See Zhao, Jingshen; Hu, Ji, selected and annotated. 赵景深、胡忌. "Daoyan" 导言. In *Ming qing chuanqixuan* 明清传奇选 (Beijing: China Youth, 1957), 10.

Prefecture; Li Wendao who poisoned his brother and harmed his sister-in-law in *The Moheluo Doll*; and the local prefect and Wang Zhiguan, who raped and killed someone, in *The Case of the Head Scarf*. Those clerks designated as *chou* are all corrupt clerks, such as Clerk Xiao in *The Moheluo Doll* and Clerk Zhao in *The Chalk Circle*.

Za refers to the characters outside the previously mentioned three types and without a clear role.

In order to emphasize the classification of roles, traditional drama designs highly visible and intense art expressive methods of various types including arias, tunes, gaits, and postures for different roles. Among them, the most important and the most visible is undoubtedly the facial make-up along with these roles. Hence, types of facial make-up and their basic tone are formed. According to Gu Xuejie,

> Through long usage for years, different colors gradually become the spe-cial measures of make-up to display personalities of characters. For instance, the red face mainly represents those loyal and upright characters; the black face those reckless and courageous characters; the white face those clever and crafty characters; the yellow face those scheming and concealingly hot-tempered characters; the blue face those ferocious and calculating char-acters; the green face those tenacious and irascible characters. There are gold, silver, purple, orcher, pink and grey colors in types of facial make-up. Types of facial make-up of basic red, black and white colors have been adopted in the plays of Yuan and Ming dynasties.[30]

Not only the basic tone but also the composition of many types of facial make-up have symbolic meaning – for example, the facial make-up of Bao Zheng in the early Beijing Opera play *The Execution of the Judge in the Nether World* 《铡判官》, which is kept in the paintings of opera characters from the Administration of Performances for the Qing Imperial Court. The play tells the legendary story that the ghost of Bao Zheng went to the nether world in order to investigate the mis-judged case of Yan Chasan and executed with a guillotine the judge in charge who protected the closest relative and put the blame on others. In this facial make-up, the black and white colors occupy each half with a crescent on the forehead. Even the gauze hat on his head is black and white. In the modern Beijing Opera play *The Case of Executing Chen Shimei* 《铡美案》, the white crescent also appears on the forehead of Bao Zheng, which indicates that Bao Zheng tried the cases of the human world in the daytime and tried the cases of the nether world at nighttime. The two white eyebrows are knitted closely to show his concerns for the country and people day and night. The black face shows the honesty and innocence of the character.[31]

30 Gu 顾学颉. *Yuan ming zaju* 元明杂剧, 32.
31 Fu, Xuebin, ed. 傅学斌. *Lianpu gouqi* 脸谱钩奇 (Beijing: China Bookstore, 2000).

The combination and mutual reinforcement between types of facial make-up and roles creates a highly formalist art system that is set in advance.[32] It should be noted that in comparison with names and the entrance poems, the roles and types of facial make-up have quite a lot of differences. The latter is more visible, and only if characters perform on the stage will be continuously presented and incessantly exert influence on audiences, while the former is easily forgotten by people. With the development of a story plot, the deeds of characters in plays will constantly verify and enrich the information conveyed by roles and types of facial make-up in advance.

Although this system is excessively formalized and simplified and its expressive power is inevitably limited, its function roughly amounts to "the formatting" in advance. On the one hand, it provides the most basic art classification for audiences, a preliminary art reference system, then greatly saves "the cost" needed to understand the personalities, moral conducts of characters in plays, and the basic relations between characters for audiences. On the other hand, in any specific play, the basic layout constructed by characters and types of facial make-up with the supplements of names and entrance poems of characters can immediately construct a relatively complex and symbolic art world and moral world. It is convenient for audiences to apply their most basic art intuition or art experiences accumulated in their previous experiences of watching the dramatic performances to enter a new play plot soon and understand a new story. The process of art appreciation is the reinforcement of art experiences and makes audiences prepared to encounter the play next time.

What are described as art features by people nowadays is neither the regulation on the essence of traditional Chinese drama nor the outcome of art law of its own. If viewed from the perspective of dramatic phylogenetics and genealogy, it is the result of collision, extrusion, and struggling of a series of survival passions, interests, and powers.[33] In those days, drama just emerged as a popular art, and troupes

32 "Types of facial make-up become a standard, and the type of facial make-up for each *jing* role remains the same, which also produces the very potent dramatic effect. All the protagonists in the play are in need of introduction, which will let audiences not only know their personality, but also have an in-depth understanding; not only have the response, but also the strong reaction. However, unlike novelists, playwrights have no much time and a large length to introduce protagonists. With types of facial make-up, audiences will completely understand the known characters at their first sight, and it is unnecessary to make any introduction. Even for a *jing* role unknown to audiences, audiences can roughly know his quality and personality only by observing his whole red face, or his painted face with evil stripes, or green dots, which can save a lot of time in making the introduction. The reason why a *jing* role can have such an effect is that the psychology of audiences has the so-called association utility. After watching the plays of Bao Zheng for dozens of times, it will naturally occur to our mind his righteousness at the sight of his black face. Likewise, audiences observe that those characters with red face or white face have that type of personality, they naturally come up with that reaction in their hearts immediately at the sight of red face or white face." Xu, Yizhi 许逸之. *Huaili ouji* 怀梨偶寄 (Beijing: Baowentang, 1987).

33 See Foucault, Michael. "Nietzsche, Genealogy, History," in *The Foucault Reader*, ed. Paul Rabinow (New York: Pantheon House, 1984), 76–97.

travelled to everywhere for performances; there was usually no routine theater for performances, no accurate timepiece in society, and no unified and set schedule for performances accordingly; audiences could enter the social space of "theater" at any time.[34] It was very hard for drama to survive. Therefore, these formalized art measures have indisputably important significance in keeping the appreciable and understandable features of drama, attracting and molding consumers of drama, creating the market of drama, and thereby guaranteeing the survival and development of actors, playwrights, and dramas. From the perspective of phylogenetics and genealogy, this formal system is destined not only to be artistic but also more social and utilitarian. It is not the art for the sake of art (although the creator, innovator, or researcher of today might think so, and deduct so), but more the art for the sake of life, the art first for the survival of actors and playwrights.[35] Its development and formation are not essentialist but are socially constructed. Certainly, it doesn't deny that this formalist system itself has the significant meaning of art. If we conduct in-depth research, it can completely enrich the dramatic research in China and even might be meaningful for us to study cognitive psychology. In terms of the development of the art itself, it is very hard to explain its origin and evolution.

It must be noted that this formalized system in a highly abstract way also gradually assumes the moral and political function and thereby becomes the moral and political classification system of characters in plays in the process of the long-term development due to the extrusion of political governance analyzed in Chapter 6, which has the greater relations with the research. That is the so-called "as for those he likes, he grants them the male and female roles, as for those he dislikes, the painted and comic roles."[36] Or "those honest and loyal characters are represented with righteous images, while those crafty and evil characters are represented in ugly forms."[37] The art forms with abstract roles and types of facial make-up, etc., not only formalize, standardize, simplify, and categorize the personality of character in the created art world but also highly formalize the moral evaluation system of traditional society to a certain extent, then further formalize, standardize, simplify, and categorize the social life of traditional society, which is closely mixed with art. In the process of dramatic performance, this system not only creates the art expectation on characters but also creates the prediction of the morality or deeds

34 For the performance site of Yuan plays, see Zhou, Yibai 周贻白. *Zhongguo xijushi changbian* 中国戏剧史长编, 228–232; Wang, Jisi 王季思. "Yuan zaju de xingcheng he xingqi" 元杂剧的形成和兴起. In *Yuanqu tongrong shang* 元曲通融上, 341–342; Li, Xiusheng 李修生. *Yuan zajushi* 元杂剧史, 4050; Zhang, Geng; Guo, Hancheng 张庚、郭汉城. *Zhongguo xiqu tongshi shangce* 中国戏曲通史上册, 303–307.
35 See Zhang, Yanjin 张燕瑾. "Tan xiqu zai yuandai fanrong de yuanyin" 谈戏曲在元代繁荣的原因; Zhu, Guangrong 朱光荣. "Lun yuan zaju fanrong de yuanyin" 论元杂剧繁荣的原因. In *Yuanqu rongrong shang* 元曲通融上, 380, 383.
36 Wu, Mei 吴梅. "Quyuan" 曲原. In *Yuanqu tongrong shang* 元曲通融上, 5.
37 *Ducheng jisheng* 都城记胜. Quoted in Wang, Jisi 王季思. "Yuan zaju de xingcheng he xingqi" 元杂剧的形成和兴起. In *Yuanqu tongrong shang* 元曲通融上, 341.

of characters. When an official performed by the *mo* role appears on the stage, we not only see the *mo* role and expect a set of art performances of reciting, singing, and acting that matches this role but also expect the personality of character that we might admire, the morality that we respect, the deeds that deserve the imitation, and the life that we desire to realize. When an official or a clerk performed by the *jing/chou* role appears on the stage, we have a set of art expectations and expect that this is a stupid and ignorant character with a low and boring personality and a dirty and disgusting life. In this set of formalized art system, you can't imagine that Bao Zheng will be performed by the *chou* role or Dou E performed by the *chadan* role. Not only is your art world formatted but also your moral world and your lifeworld. Because the formalized classification of this art world is so simple, the classification in your lifeworld and moral world will be very easily (although not necessarily) simplified and formalized accordingly. The result is the clarity between enemy and ally, loyalty and craftiness, love and hatred.

The simplicity of this formalized classification system of roles and types of facial make-up will at least reinforce the moral world with the opposition of black and white, good and evil, on some occasions. In this art system, since officials who made mistakes (such as Taowu) and villains in terms of morality (such as Donkey Zhang) are all performed by the *jing* role, the art classification of *jing* actually has a suggestive combination function. It groups these people who seemly have evidently different moral and legal liabilities nowadays and forms a team with art roles and moral roles in the meantime, which is opposed to the team of positive characters occupying the *mo* role such as Bao Zheng and the *dan* role such as Dou E.[38] Certainly, careful readers will point out that the world with the opposition of good and evil in plays first and only originates from the opposition of good and evil in life, not vice versa, with which I also agree. I can't prove and don't want to prove which is the cause or the effect after all between the formalized art system and the formalized moral system of people. However, the symbolic world itself has a certain formation or intensification utility, which should not be denied. In daily life, since intellectuals usually wear glasses, when we see a person wearing glasses, the symbol of glasses will enable us to expect that he might be an intellectual. Therefore, in the sense of not pursuing the ultimate causality, it generally can't go wrong if the art world allegedly exerts a certain influence on the formation of moral world of people or has an intensification function. In this sense, we can generally conclude that while this highly formalized art system facilitates the art appreciation and facilitates people's moralized understanding of the lifeworld in drama and the dramatic world in life, it also obstructs people's realistic, rational, and more me-ticulous investigation and understanding of their own lifeworld to a certain extent.

---

38 Certainly, this classification system might be reasonable. As mentioned earlier, because of the issue of the information cost, traditional society adopted a strict liability. Apart from an exception, there was not a strict discrimination between the unintentional or intentional mistakes in punishment, which in our view are obviously different.

The Recalling of *Hamlet*

I hereby want to make a simple investigation of Shakespeare's tragedy *Hamlet* as an example. This play is quite familiar to many readers, who hold various explanations for it; I have no competence to, nor intend to, make an overall review and in-depth analysis. I only want to analyze why Hamlet consistently hesitated on the issue of revenge from the cognitive perspective in accordance with my reading.

At the beginning of the play, Hamlet's father was dead and his mother was remarried to his uncle, the successor king, the murder suspect in the mind of Hamlet. Although Hamlet had this suspicion, he had no any reliable evidence, while the play didn't provide any *direct* representation to audiences. All pieces of evidence were inferred and even covered in the mythical color. From the ghost, Hamlet first knew that his father was killed by his uncle (which can be explained as "what's on your mind during the day goes into your dream at night") and later got a certain verification from the his uncle's response to the dramatized murder plot (but can it sufficiently serve as the evidence?) and found that someone tried to make an attempt on his life (even if it were instructed by his uncle, there would be another explanation, yet it still couldn't be the evidence to prove that the new king killed the old king). Therefore, the issue is could all of these be sufficient to prove the uncle was the murderer who killed his father? For Hamlet, a modern rational person, it was obviously insufficient. Hamlet was the person who needed and desired for a high degree of certainty (not only because of his modernity but also the reason discussed later), and henceforth he was a skeptic who questioned all the unknown things; he questioned because of the desire for the certainty. Many Chinese readers are familiar with his famous words, "To be, or not to be, that is the question," but what is related to my analysis here is the whole passage in the wake of the question he raised, because he didn't know whether the death could relieve the pains of thinking from him, or give him a complete certainty:

> To be, or not to be, that is the question,
> Whether 'tis nobler in the mind to suffer
> The slings and arrows of outrageous fortune,
> Or to take arms against a sea of troubles,
> And by opposing, end them. To die, to sleep –
> No more, and by a sleep to say we end
> The heart-ache, and the thousand natural shocks
> That flesh is heir to; 'tis a consummation
> Devoutly to be wished to die to sleep!
> To sleep, perchance to dream, ay there's the rub,
> For in that sleep of death what dreams may come
> When we have shuffled off this mortal coil
> Must give us pause – there's the respect
> That makes calamity of so long life:
> For who would bear the whips and scorns of time,
> Th'oppressor's wrong, the proud man's contumely,

> The pangs of disprized love, the law's delay,
> The insolence of office, and the spurns
> That patient merit of th'unworthy takes,
> When he himself might his quietus make
> With a bare bodkin; who would fardels bear,
> To grunt and sweat under a weary life,
> But that the dread of something after death,
> The undiscovered country, from whose bourn
> No traveller returns, puzzles the will,
> And makes us rather bear those ills we have,
> Than fly to others that we know not of?
> Thus conscience does make cowards of us all,
> And thus the native hue of resolution
> Is sicklied o'er with the pale cast of thought
> And enterprises of great pitch and moment
> With this regard their currents turn awry,
> And lose the name of action.[39]

As for such a person who doubted the cognitive capability of humans and sought certainty in the meantime, obviously, the information from the ghost and the strange response of the uncle were insufficient for him to reach the judgment "beyond reasonable doubt." It was such a pursuit of certainty that deprived him of acting capably, "thus the native hue of resolution is sicklied o'er with the pale cast of thought."

Many people will say that Hamlet in the play is not the adjudicator of a case; therefore, there isn't a comparison between him and the judicial adjudicator. However, those who raise this question only consider the issue from the name of the institution; in terms of the circumstance of thinking, Hamlet is more like a judicial adjudicator, especially his circumspection. Hamlet had a strong wish for revenge if his father was truly murdered. In those days, or only because Hamlet couldn't resort to public power for revenge, this revenge became a duty for the directly related members of the deceased.[40] But the first mission of the avenger is to judge on whom he shall take vengeance; it is not enough to only have "the native hue of resolution." He must find the target of revenge; then he can implement his judgment. Hamlet was clearly aware that he must directly account for his judgment and the ensuing consequence of revenge. Hamlet's hesitation therefore was no longer the issue of personality, nor the respect for life and the state law (the state law was now in the hands of his possible enemy); it was mainly because his possible target of revenge was his uncle, one of his own relatives, and the present husband of his mother, namely the relative of his dearest relative, while the ghost of his father also admonished him that "Taint not thy mind, nor let thy soul contrive against thy

---

39 Shakespeare, William. *Hamlet*, ed. John Dover Wilson (Cambridge: Cambridge University Press, 2009), 60–61 (hereafter cited parenthetically in the text).
40 See Chapter 1.

mother aught" (29). Under this circumstance, Hamlet must have a high degree of certainty for his revenge act. If he made a mistake in taking vengeance on others, he might be guilty and even somewhat distressed. But this distress would not be severe, nor last long, since time heals all wounds. But if he made a mistake toward his mother and uncle, this mistake couldn't be remedied, and he must take vengeance on the murder of his mother and uncle in the capacity of avenger for them, namely revenge on himself.[41] If he lived, it would be impossible for him to be relieved from this huge distress. Hamlet's hesitation actually displayed his accountability for his revenge act. The complicated relations of relatives made him particularly careful and circumspect in terms of his judgment and deeds.

Even Hamlet doubted the ghost of his father that he saw, and at that time it was the only direct evidence (the testimony of the victim) of the uncle murdering his father in his view. He doubted:

> The spirit that I have seen
> May be a devil, and the devil hath power
> T'assume a pleasing shape, yea, and perhaps
> Out of my weakness and my melancholy,
> As he is very potent with such spirits,
> Abuses me to damn me
>
> (57)

Therefore, Hamlet reached the conclusion that "I'll have grounds more relative than this" (57) and he knew that "Rightly to be great is not to stir without great argument" (97). Even at the end, his evidence was "not beyond reasonable doubt." He only represented the imagined scene in which his father was murdered on the stage and observed the strange response of the uncle to it; he was under tight surveillance and even persecuted by the uncle. But the former point was still insufficient to prove his father was killed by the uncle; wouldn't the so-called strange response of the uncle be subjective imagination? Just like a person who lost his axe suspiciously observes his neighbor. The latter point could completely have another explanation, namely the uncle's forestallment. In this condition, whether Hamlet chose or abandoned revenge, he couldn't get rid of the puzzle caused by the incomplete and insufficient information, and he would be confronted with the lifelong moral duty, "the unbearable heaviness of being." He was doomed not to be happy for his whole life. Hence, he would ponder over the question that was deemed ridiculous by an ordinary person "in that sleep of death what dreams may come." He hoped for eternal relief with certainty.

It is in this sense that the question encountered by Hamlet is two questions that all adjudicators will meet in trying tricky cases. The first is: Under the circumstance of being absent from the whole process of event and not knowing the real truth, how can we make the judgment and *act accordingly* in light of the existing and

---

41 See Chapter 1, Note 7.

insufficient evidence? The second is: Who will assume or share this moral duty? The former is the unsolvable issue of epistemology; besides, more importantly, it is an important question. That is, the judiciary needs the action and usually acts in the condition of incomplete information, which decides the life and property of others. It is impossible for adjudicators to act after all things are clear (such a day might never come). The purpose of setting up the judicial institution is to let adjudicators make the relatively, not absolutely, correct judgment and act in the existing condition of incomplete information. It is impossible for judges to shirk this mission. Therefore, the next question comes: What should be done if a mistake is made?

By establishing a series of institutions, the modern judiciary resolves or avoids the two questions with which adjudicators are confronted to a certain extent. The first question is resolved by the confirmation of the burden of proof, the shifting of the burden of proof, in addition to the efforts of providing evidence from other institutions and procedures and the ensuing judgments by adjudicators. In the meantime, the second question is resolved as well: Because of the participation of many institutions, the multiple levels of a trial, and the unaccountability of adjudicators for the burden of proof, even if an adjudicator makes a mistake in trial, he can shirk or at least alleviate his liability. For example, the police gather evidence, the prosecutor presses charges, the jury determines crimes (in the UK and the United States); what is more, the superior court reviews the case; the liability of judge is therefore greatly alleviated, and he can nearly shirk all the liabilities only if not violating the regulation of the procedural law. However, this scenario was impossible for Hamlet (and adjudicators in traditional Chinese society to a certain extent). He had no other institutions and procedures to resort to – he himself was all of these. Once revenge is initiated, it must be a final verdict without appeal and can't be remedied afterward. All the liabilities are heaped on Hamlet and demand him to make judgments in accordance with his own cognitive capability.

Hamlet is hereby confronted with two liabilities and laws that are equally paramount yet impossibly compatible: to redress the injustice and take vengeance for his father (this means to kill or murder one or more relatives) and to avoid his innocent relatives' being hurt as far as possible (strictly speaking, this means to abandon revenge). More importantly, Hamlet's liability is different from the judge's. The case decided by a judicial adjudicator is usually not in the directly sentimental or interested relations to him. Because of the avoidance system, the judicial adjudicator is explicitly forbidden to try such a case, while two parties that Hamlet faced were all dear to him. No matter what choice he makes, only if the information is insufficient, his agony will be inevitable, and the inner torture will be forever. In this sense, although the core of *Hamlet* might not be the discussion of the judiciary, it has great inspiration and shock for the straightforward understanding of the key issue of the judiciary, the perspectives of judges and thorny questions. Accordingly, *Hamlet* is a classic work that is related to the judiciary.

We should investigate how such a huge conflict and its implied question of epistemology and morality are presented in *Hamlet* as well. In comparison with traditional Chinese drama, for example, *The Injustice to Dou E* or *Fifteen Strings of Cash*, or similar detective plays, readers can observe that what leads to this question is mainly the narrative method and perspective of *Hamlet*. Shakespeare didn't directly put the death of Hamlet's father on the stage. The play begins in the middle of the event. The narrative method and perspective of Shakespeare enable the audiences to share the position of Hamlet to a certain extent. Since being unaware of the truth of the death of Hamlet's father, audiences (including readers) must and can only make judgments in accordance with evidence that might seem sufficient to some and insufficient to others. Audiences share with Hamlet the limited anxieties and suspicion of humans, which therefore emphasizes the thorny question that is destined to be eternal for humans in terms of judging.

It can be said that the narrative and interrogation method of *Hamlet* is relatively prominent in the judicial culture of Western society. We have observed how different persons reconstruct the truth of cases in their absence in many modern Western dramas, films, and literary works, such as the novels of Edgar Allen Poe, Sherlock Holmes, and the novels of Agatha Christie and the adapted films and televisions of these novels. Some foreign scholars studying Yuan plays have pointed out this feature in the comparison between Chinese detective plays and Western detective novels.[42] Athena, the Western goddess of justice, is blindfolded. This image might only mean the equal application of law regardless of personal features (this is the meaning of substantive law), but perhaps it is not completely just as what contemporary Chinese jurists have thought. This image also has the full likelihood of being the metaphor for the judicial adjudicator's capability of finding the truth.[43] While the god of justice in the mind of people in traditional Chinese society (if it could be termed thus), Heaven, seemly must "have eyes" to see justice done.[44]

It should be stated that I don't compare the good and bad of oriental, occidental judicial justice. Being detached from the specific contexts where the judicial justice takes place, such a comparison is meaningless and is inevitably politically correct nonsense. I hereby only try to emphasize different narrative methods and perspectives of drama (and other literary works with the feature of story) that *might* exert a subtle influence on the justice value of people, mold their expectation on judiciary, affect their understanding of thorny problems of judiciary, and thereby affect their judgments of judicial verdicts. Only in the society where people admit the trial can't completely reconstruct the truth of the past might they somewhat understand the difficulty encountered by the case adjudicator and have appropriate tolerance for the adjudicator's mistake in intelligence and judgment. In a society where people confirm and emphasize that the truth of a case can be completely reconstructed, the mistake of the case adjudicator is hardly tolerable, and the mistake of intelligence or judgment might be more likely considered as the moral flaw.

---

42 Su, Ge et al. 孙歌等. *Guowai zhongguo gudian xiqu yanjiu* 国外中国古典戏曲研究, 218.

43 For the introduction and analysis of the origin and implication of the Western justice goddess, see Feng, Xiang 冯象. "Zhengyi de mengyanbu" 正义的蒙眼布. In *Zhengfa biji* 政法笔记, 144.

44 "There the sun and moon hang by day and night, There the spirits and gods dispense life and death. Heaven and Earth! It is for you to distinguish between right and wrong, What confusion makes you mistake a villain for a saint?" (Guan, 1977: 139–140).

Another Type of *The Injustice to Dou E*

In order to clarify this point further, we might undertake a thought experiment or make an imaginary adaption of *The Injustice to Dou E*, and we can find that the tragedy will repeat itself, and even Donkey Zhang himself might be a tragic character as well.

As far as we know, *The Injustice to Dou E* tells the whole truth of the story to audiences and constantly repeats "the truth" in the play: Donkey Zhang unintentionally poisoned his father and framed Dou E. However, this "fact" was acquired through Guan Hanqing's perspective of a creator. Therefore, when this case was presented to yamen for trial, what Guan Hanqing informed beforehand had made audiences unconsciously raise the question, who should be tried? Who poisoned the victim after all? But the art imagination of Guan Hanqing was obviously limited by the knowledge concerning the sudden death of people in those days. Then, when he presents all the real things on the stage for audiences, we lose the chance of thinking all the possibilities. His narrative method not only defines the problem that officials trying cases must adjudicate and judge but also the trial problem that we can only raise in this way or can only raise like that.

However, if the play begins with the death of Donkey Zhang's father, or even if the structure basically remains unchanged with the only omission of the plot of Donkey Zhang's buying the poison and poisoning that appears on the stage, namely, the playwright and audiences abandon that vision of the omniscient and omnipotent God, this story will be more complicated, and our inference on Dou E, and even Donkey Zhang, will be more complex and thereby have more intricately moral evaluations. Certainly, we can still infer that Donkey Zhang carried out the poisoning. But even we can rule out the possibility of Dou E's poisoning in light of her personality logic manifested in the previous plot, we can't rule out such a possibility: Maybe Donkey Zhang's father died of a sudden cerebral hemorrhage or myocardial infarction, and no one poisoned him. Perhaps to drink the mutton soup is only the accidental coincidence phenomenon with the sudden death of Old Zhang. At least from the perspective of our knowledge of today, this accident has the full likelihood of happening in life. Admittedly, Donkey Zhang was a lascivious scoundrel, but no evidence proved that he must be so shameless that he went so far as to poison Mother Cai. After all, Mother Cai was the person on whom his father had a crush. If Mother Cai lived, it might be easier to control the filial Dou E; at least Dou E would not run away. Once Mother Cai died, Dou E, who was free from worldly cares, might resist more fervently. After all, Donkey Zhang had the glorious history of "having the courage to do what was right" and saved Mother Cai from the hands of Dr. Lu. On the other hand, Old Zhang in the play was more than 60 years old (Mother Cai was already on the wrong side of 60); since he was excessively lecherous, his fawning on others was frustrated at each go, and it was likely for him to die of a sudden cerebral hemorrhage or myocardial infarction because of his obsession with lusty desires.

If my thought experiment is valid, then we, the audience, might understand the difficulty that Taowu in charge of the trial faced. Actually, officials trying cases are always in this position, and even in worse situations. Under this circumstance, the question we consider will first be: Which reason led to the death of Old Zhang after all? Then, it might be: I someone poisoned the victim, who would be the possible murderer after all? Our attention will be first concerned with the first factual question and temporarily suspend the moral judgment in appreciating the play.

Even if no one administered poison, in the technical condition of traditional society, and only Old Zhang died suddenly, it might still lead to the tragedy of Dou E. Because Donkey Zhang had the same impulse to press the charge and had the grounds to doubt Dou E; although he might still want to use the death of his father to threaten Dou E to do as he liked, it might be somewhat shameless, yet he might not necessarily intend to frame Dou E. What people know is only that Old Zhang died after eating the soup made by Dou E and can only infer the relationship between two events in accordance with their sequence. They might feel that it was not entirely impossible for Dou E to resist thus. "The worm turns." Why did Dou E, the virtuous and able girl, have no likelihood of doing an unbelievable thing? Yes, what people in the past observed or what we observe on the stage or in the playscript that Dou E was virtuous and able, but is it *sufficient* to prove that Dou E was innocent? In life, it is not rare that human deeds are unexpected. Don't we often feel that we haven't seen through somebody? Don't we often say that someone is adept at disguising (although some of them are not disguised)? Only if there are not the modern sci-tech measures to ascertain the true reason that caused the death of Donkey Zhang's father, the tragedy of Dou E might still happen.

If this thought experiment can be valid, we even have reasons to doubt, the final execution of Donkey Zhang might be another tragedy. Donkey Zhang was lecherous and shameless and often went out; therefore, he had the chance of buying poison (although it was unnecessary for the play to show that); he once helped Dou E to give the soup and then had the chance to poison; he had the motive and interests to frame Dou E to extricate himself; in addition to Dou Tianzhang's trust in his daughter, Dou E's vows, and the drought of three years in Chuzhou as the verification, in the age when people were firmly convinced that the sudden death must be caused by someone's poisoning. Dou Tianzhang had the full reason or even could only believe Donkey Zhang was the true criminal after the suspicion on Dou E was ruled out. Under the great torture inflicted by Dou Tianzhang (remember, honest officials in Yuan plays resorted to interrogation by torture in a large quantity as well), it was nearly inevitable for Donkey Zhang to make a false confession and finally to be executed. In such a play, Donkey Zhang would be a more complicated character who might not be entirely impossible to exist in real life. Once this imagination is deemed valid, it will be another tragedy that Donkey Zhang was finally executed *as the poisoner*. Our heart will feel very heavy, or even heavier.

This possibility is ruled out only because Guan Hanqing put the plot of Donkey Zhang's buying poison and poisoning on the stage so that we have the perspective of God. One certain fact has changed the space of our rational and moral thinking and the question we might pose; it has annihilated the question, which we actually often meet, but can't make judgments because of the uncertain facts; it has exterminated the question, which we more often meet, and make the decision accordingly because of the self-conceits, then find it too late to repent. Certainty enables us to be no longer tolerant. Only in comparison with the structure, narrative, and perspective of *Hamlet* in the previous section can we observe the influence of such a godly perspective and theatrical effect on our judgment.

Although I hereby use *The Injustice to Dou E* as the analytical paradigm, I don't regard the part as the whole. I have mentioned in this book that actually in all the playscripts of traditional Chinese drama I ever read, the playwrights used such a godly perspective to tell me the ins and outs of the story from beginning to end and usually presented all the related details including the inner feelings of characters to audiences in a definite and undoubted way. In traditional Chinese drama, audiences have never been confronted with the puzzle like Hamlet's and have never felt the thorny problems officials of "administrating justice" always faced. Besides, it is not only the feature of traditional Chinese drama; in other Chinese classic narrative works of literature that I haven't read much, it is nearly narrated from such a godly perspective (including *The Grand Scribe's Records*; remember the dialogue between Cheng Ying and Gongsun Chujiu under the writing brush of Sima Qian?). None of authors narrated the story from the perspective of an ordinary fallible person.

Preliminary Summary

I don't want to hereby make an all-around evaluation on a series of other features of thinking and emotions that might be caused by this narrative method and more unlikely make the simple appraisal of good and bad, which is not only beyond the theme of this book but more beyond my competence. Besides, the most fundamental question is: What should I use as the reference frame? What is the proper narrative method and standard? For instance, why should we use *Hamlet* as the standard? Inadvertently, I might fall into the position that I detest the mostly, namely, "from the point of view of things themselves, each regards itself as noble and other things as mean."[45] I don't want to make a generally summarized assertion as well and state that it is the cultural gene of Chinese tradition eternally unchanged, because many novels in China of today, including the detective stories, have already discontinued this narrative formula. One comment for one fact. I hereby only want to temporarily but solidly say that the narrative method of traditional Chinese drama will affect people's understanding of reality, mold people's cognitive structure, and cultivate a habitus or convenience of thinking and analyzing questions that is not

---

45 Watson, Burton, trans. *The Complete Works of Zhuangzi* (New York: Columbia University Press, 2013), 129.

just restricted to the art appreciation to a certain extent.[46] Besides, because of the deficiency of epistemological skepticism, Chinese more easily turn to use the perspective of substantive justice and moralism to comprehend human mistakes.

This analysis actually cautions us of another dimension of moral evaluation. When the fact is definitely accurate, the moral evaluation might be necessary; while the fact is unclear, the hasty moral evaluation often annihilates the discussion on the fact and might bring more tragedies. This point should be a warning to various hasty statements of political correctness that have been invariably popular for years in the community of legal science of China of today (actually all the disciplines of humanities and social sciences in China), although I don't expect, nor believe to what degree this warning will have the actual effect.

This analysis also promotes the research on the substantive justice. I once briefly discussed why Chinese society consistently lacked the procedural justice and emphasized the substantive justice from the perspective of the production mode of agricultural society and the concomitant organization structure of acquaintance society in other articles.[47] I believe the most important social factor might be the structure of agricultural acquaintance society and the corresponding mechanism of social control; the industrialized stranger society with the frequent mobility of population more tend to be concerned with the procedural justice in judiciary. I still adhere to the analytical train of thought of historical materialism and its conclusion. Despite this, as a supplement, this chapter still reveals the cultural variable in a narrow sense that the substantive justice becomes popular in China from another perspective, which might have a very accidental connection with the performing arts of traditional Chinese drama and the development of drama.

---

46 See Bourdieu, Pierre. *Distinction: A Social Critique of the Judgement of Taste*, trans. Richard Nice (Cambridge, MA: Harvard University Press, 1984). Becker, Gary S. *Accounting for Tastes* (Cambridge, MA: Harvard University Press, 1996).

47 Zhu, Suli 朱苏力. "Yujinglun yizhong falv zhidu yanjiu fangfa de goujian" 语境论 – 一种法律制度研究方法的构建, Section 6.

Bibliography

Playscripts

Anonymous Playwright 无名氏. "Tongchuangji" 同窗记. In *Zhongguo xiju xuan* 中国戏曲选, chiefly edited by Wang Qi 王起, 604–615. Beijing: People's Literature, 1998.

Hanqing, Guan. "The Injustice Done to Tou Ngo." In *Six Yuan Plays*, translated by Liu Jung-en, 115–158. London: Penguin, 1977.

Hanqing, Guan. "The Wife-Snatcher." In *Selected Plays of Guan Hanqing*, translated by Yang Xianyi and Gladys Yang, 38–66. Beijing: Foreign Languages Press, 1979.

Hanqing, Guan. "Rescriptor-in-Waiting Bao Thrice Investigates the Butterfly Dream." In *Monks, Bandits, Lovers, and Immortals: Eleven Early Chinese Plays*, edited and translated by Stephen H. West and Wilt L. Idema, 37–76. Indianapolis: Hackett Publishing Company, 2010.

Hanqing, Meng. "The Moheluo Doll." In *The Columbia Anthology of Yuan Drama*, edited by C. T. Hsia, Wai-Yee Li and George Kao, translated by Jonathan Chaves, 147–188. New York: Columbia University Press, 2014.

Junxiang, Ji. "The Orphan of Zhao Greatly Wreaks Vengeance." In *The Orphan of Zhao and Other Yuan Plays*, translated and introduced by Stephen H. West and Wilt L. Idema, 73–111. New York: Columbia University Press, 2015.

Sun, Zhongzhang 孙仲章. "Henan fu zhang ding kan toujin" 河南府张鼎勘头巾. In *Yuanqu xuan* 元曲选, compiled by Zang Jinshu 臧晋叔, 668–686. Beijing: Zhonghua Book Company, 1958.

Wang, Zhongwen 王仲文. "Jiu xiaozi xianmu burenshi" 救孝子贤母不认尸. In *Yuanqu xuan* 元曲选, 756–776.

Xingdao, Li. "Rescriptor-in-Waiting Bao's Clever Trick: The Record of the Chalk Circle." In *Monks, Bandits, Lovers and Immortals: Eleven Early Chinese Plays*, edited and translated by Stephen H. West and Wilt L. Idema, 237–282. Indianapolis: Hackett Publishing Company, 2010.

Yue, Baichuan 岳佰川. "Lv Dongbin du tieguaili yue" 吕洞宾度铁拐李岳. In *Yuanqu xuan* 元曲选, 490–511.

Zheng, Tingyu 郑廷玉. "Cuifujun duan yuanjia zhaizhu" 崔府君断冤家债主. In *Yuanqu xuan* 元曲选, 1130–1145.

Zhu, Suchen 朱素臣. *Shiwuguan jiaozhu* 十五贯校注. Edited and annotated by Zhang Yanjin 张燕瑾 and Mi Songyi 弥松颐. Shanghai: Shanghai Ancient Books, 1983.

Zhu, Suchen; Chen, Jing et al. eds. 朱素臣、陈静. *Kunqu shiwu guan* 昆曲十五贯. Hong Kong: Joint Publishing (Hong Kong) Company, 1956.

Chinese Classics

Ban, Gu 班固. *Han shu* 汉书. Beijing: Zhonghua Book Company, 1962.

Bloom, Irene trans. *Mencius*. New York: Columbia University Press, 2009.

Chunqiu gongyang zhuan 春秋公羊传. Shenyang: Liaoning Education, 1997.

Han, Fei Tzu. *The Complete Works of Han Fei Tzu*, vol. 2. Translated by W. K. Liao. London: Arthur Probsthain, 1959.

Lao-Tzu. *Tao Te Ching*. Translated by Stephen Addiss and Stanley Lombardo. New York: Hackett Publishing Company, 1993.

Legge, James trans. *The Sacred Book Books of China: The Texts of Confucianism*, Part 3 *The Li Ki*. Oxford: Clarendon Press, 1885.

Legge, James. *The Sacred Book Books of China: The Texts of Confucianism*, Part 4 *The Li Ki* 2. Oxford: Clarendon Press, 1885.

Legge, James. *The Chinese Classics: The Doctrine of the Mean*, vol. 1. Hong Kong: Hong Kong University Press, 1960.

Legge, James. *The Chinese Classics: Shoo-King*, vol. 3, Part 1. Hong Kong: Hong Kong University Press, 1960.

Legge, James. *The Chinese Classics*, vol. 5: *The Ch'un Ts'ew with the Tso Chuen*. Hong Kong: Hong Kong University Press, 1960.

Watson, Burton trans. *Han Feizi: Basic Writings*. New York: Columbia University Press, 2003.

Watson, Burton. *The Analects of Confucius*. New York: Columbia University Press, 2007.

Watson, Burton. *The Complete Works of Zhuangzi*. New York: Columbia University Press, 2013.

Chinese Monographs

Chen, Guyuan 陈顾远. *Zhongguo hunyin shi* 中国婚姻史. Beijing: The Commercial Press, 1998.

Chen, Hongguo 谌洪果. *Falv ren de jiushu* 法律人的救赎. Beijing: China Democratic and Legal Press, 2011.

Chen, Pingyuan 陈平原. *Wenxueshi de xingcheng yu jiangou* 文学史的形成与建构. Nanning: Guangxi Education, 1998.

Chen, Pingyuan 陈平原. *Zhongguo xiaoshuo xushi moshi de zhuanbian* 中国小说叙事模式的转变. Beijing: Peking University Press, 2003.

Chen, Shan 陈山. *Zhongguo wuxia shi* 中国武侠史. Shanghai: Sanlian Book, 1992.

Deng, Shaoji chiefly ed. 邓邵基. *Yuandai wenxueshi* 元代文学史. Beijing: People's Literature, 1998.

Dou, Yi et al. compiled 窦仪; Wu, Yiru annotated 吴翊如. *Song xingtong* 宋刑统. Beijing: Zhonghua Book Company, 1984.

Fei, Xiaotong 费孝通. *Xiangtu zhongguo* 乡土中国. Beijing: Peking University Press, 1998.

Feng, Xiang 冯象. *Mutui zhengyi* 木腿正义. Guangzhou: The Sun Yat-ten University Press, 1999.

Feng, Xiang 冯象. *Bolidao yase yu wo sanqiannian* 玻璃岛: 亚瑟与我三千年. Beijing: SDX Joint Publishing Company, 2003.

Feng, Xiang 冯象. *Zhengfa biji* 政法笔记. Nanjing: Jiangsu People's Press, 2004.

Fish, Stanley 斯坦利·费什. *Duzhefanyingpipinglilunyushijian* 读者反应批评: 理论与实践. Translated by Wen Chuan 文楚安. Beijing: Chinese Social Sciences, 1998.

Fu, Xuebin ed. 傅学斌. *Lianpu gouqi* 脸谱钩奇. Beijing: China Bookstore, 2000.

Gao, Huanyue 高浣月. *Qingdai xingming muyou yanjiu* 清代刑名幕友研究. Beijing: China University of Politics and Law (CUPL) Press, 2000.

Gu, Xuejie 顾学颉. *Yuan ming zaju* 元明杂剧. Shanghai: Shanghai Literature and Art, 1979.

Gu, Xuejie 顾学颉. *Yuanren zaju xuan* 元人杂剧选. Beijing: People's Literature, 1998.

Guo, Jian; Yin, Xiaohu; Wang, Zhiqiang 郭建、殷啸虎、王志强. *Zhongguo wenhua tongzhi falv zhi* 中国文化通志·法律志. Shanghai: Shanghai People's Press, 1998.

Guo, Yuheng chiefly ed. 郭预衡. *Zhongguo gudai wenxueshi juan 3* 中国古代文学史卷3. Shanghai: Shanghai Ancient Books, 1998.

Huang, Ke 黄克. *Guan hanqing xiju renwu lun* 关汉卿戏剧人物论. Beijing: People's Literature, 1984.

Jiang, Wen et al. 姜文. *Dansheng* 诞生. Beijing: Huayi, 1997.

Li, Chunxiang compiled and annotated 李春祥. *Yuandai baogongxi xuanzhu*. Zhengzhou: Zhongzhou Calligraphy and Painting, 1983.

Li, Qiao 李乔. *Zhongguo de shiye* 中国的师爷. Beijing: The Commercial Press International, 1997.

Li, Xiusheng 李修生. *Yuan zaju shi* 元杂剧史. Nanjing: Jiangsu Ancient Books, 1996.

Liang, Zhiping 梁治平. *Fayi yu renqing* 法意与人情. Shenzhen: Haitian, 1992.

Liang, Zhiping 梁治平. *Guojia yu shehui qingdai xiguanfa* 国家与社会: 清代习惯法. Beijing: CUPL Press, 1996.

Liu, Dajie 刘大杰. *Zhongguo wenxue fazhanshi* xiace 中国文学发展史下册. Shanghai: Shanghai Ancient Books, 1982.

Liu, Xiang ed. 刘向. *Xinxu xiangzhu* 新序详注. Annotated by Zhao Zhongyi 赵仲邑. Beijing: Zhonghua Book Company, 1999.

Liu, Xing 刘星. *Xichuang fayu* 西窗法语. Guangzhou: Huacheng, 1998.

Liu, Xiusheng 李修生. *Yuan zajushi* 元杂剧史. Nanjing: Jiangsu Ancient Books, 1996.

Long, Zongzhi 龙宗智. *Xiangdui heli zhuyi* 相对合理主义. Beijing: China University of Politics and Law Press, 1994.

Lu, Xun 鲁迅. *Qiejieting zawen erji* 且介亭杂文二集. Beijing: People's Literature, 1995.

Luo, Zheng 骆正. *Zhongguo jingju ershijiang* 中国京剧二十讲. Guilin: Guangxi Normal University Press, 2004.

Mao, Dun 茅盾. *Guanyu lishi he lishiju cong woxin changdan de xuduo butong juben shuoqi* 关于历史和历史剧: 从卧薪尝胆的许多不同剧本说起. Beijing: The Writers, 1962.

Pu, Andi 浦安迪. *Zhongguo xushixue* 中国叙事学. Beijing: Peking University Press, 1996.

Qu, Rong chiefly ed. 曲嵘. *Waiguo fazhishi* 外国法制史. Beijing: Peking University Press, 1993.

Qu, Tongzu 瞿同祖. *Zhongguo falv yu zhongguo shehui* 中国法律与中国社会. Beijing: Zhonghua Book Company, 1984.

Renmin wenxue chubanshe bianjibu ed. 人民文学出版社编辑部编. *Yuan ming qing xiqu yanjiu lunwenji* 元明清戏曲研究论文集. Beijing: People's Literature, 1958.

Shen, Dan 申丹. *Xushuxue yu xiaoshuo wentixue yanjiu* 叙述学与小说文体学研究. Beijing: Peking University Press, 1998.

Song, Ci 宋慈. *Xiyuan jilu* 洗冤集录. Beijing: Chinese Literature and History, 1999.

Sui, Shusen ed. 隋树森. *Yuanqu xuan waibian* 元曲选外编. Beijing: Zhonghua Book Company, 1959.

Sun, Ge; Chen, Yangu; Li, Yijin 孙歌、陈燕谷、李益津. *Guowai zhongguo gudian xiqu yanjiu* 国外中国古典戏曲研究. Nanjing: Jiangsu Education, 1999.

Tan, Fan; Lu, Wei 谭帆、陆炜. *Zhongguo gudai xiju lilunshi* 中国古代戏剧理论史. Beijing: China Social Sciences, 1993.

Tang, Degang 唐德刚. *Shixue yu wenxue* 史学与文学. Shanghai: East China Normal University Press, 1999.

Wang, Guowei 王国维. *Wang Guowei xueshu jingdianji shang* 王国维学术经典集上. Nanchang: Jiangxi People's Press, 1997.

Wang, Lina 王丽娜. *Zhongguo gudian xiaoshuo xiqu zai guowai* 中国古典小说戏曲在国外. Beijing: Xuelin, 1988.

Wang, Qi chief ed. 王起. *Zhongguo xiju xuan* 中国戏剧选. Annotated and compiled by Wang Qi et al. 王起等. Beijing: People's Literature, 1985.

Wang, Qi 王齐. *Zhongguo gudai de youxia* 中国古代的游侠. Beijing: The Commercial Press International, 1997.

Wang, Shide 王世德. *Shiwuguan yanjiu* 十五贯研究. Shanghai: Shanghai Literature and Art, 1981.

Wang, Shirong 汪世荣. *Zhongguo gudai panci yanjiu* 中国古代判词研究. Beijing: CUPL Press, 1997.

Wang, Shuo 王朔. *Wuzhizhe wuwei* 无知者无畏. Shenyang: Chunfeng Literature and Art, 2000.

Wei, Minglun 魏明伦. *Pan jinlian juben he juping* 潘金莲:剧本和剧评. Beijing: SDX Joint Publishing Company, 1988.

Wen, Ling 温凌. *Guan Hanqing* 关汉卿. Shanghai: Shanghai Ancient Books, 1978.

Wu, Gan 吴敢. *Quhai shuoshan lu* 曲海说山录. Beijing: Literture and Art, 1996.

Wu, Mei 吴梅. *Guqu zhutan zhongguo xiqu gailun* 顾曲麈谈·中国戏曲概论. Shanghai: Shanghai Ancient Books, 2004.

Wu, Xiaoru 吴小如. *Wu xiaoru xiqu wenlu* 吴小如戏曲文录. Beijing: Peking University Press, 1995.

Xie, Taofang 谢桃坊. *Zhongguo shimin wenxueshi* 中国市民文学史. Chengdu: Sichuan People's Press, 1997.

Xu, Fuming 徐扶明. *Yuandai zaju yishu* 元代杂剧艺术. Shanghai: Shanghai Literature and Art, 1981.

Xu, Yizhi 许逸之. *Huaili ouji* 怀梨偶寄. Beijing: Baowentang, 1987.

Xu, Zhongming 徐忠明. *Faxue yu wenxue zhijian* 法学与文学之间. Beijing: China University of Political Science and Law (CUPL) Press, 2000.

Xu, Zhongming 徐忠明. *Baogong gushi yige kaocha zhongguo falv wenhua de shijiao* 包公故事: 一个考察中国法律文化的视角. Beijing: CUPL Press, 2002.

Yao, Shuyi 幺书仪. *Yuanren zaju yu yuandai shehui* 元人杂剧与元代社会. Beijing: Peking University Press, 1997.

Yao, Wenfang 姚文放. *Zhongguo xiju meixue de wenhua chanshi* 中国戏剧美学的文化阐释. Beijing: Renmin University of China Press, 1997.

Ye, Changhai 叶长海. *Zhongguo xijuxue shigao* 中国戏剧学史稿. Shanghai: Shanghai Literature and Art, 1986.

You, Guoen et al. chiefly ed. 游国恩. *Zhongguo wenxueshi* 中国文学史. Beijing: People's Literature, 1964.

Yu, Zongqi 余宗其. *Falv yu wenxue de jiaochadi* 法律与文学的交叉地. Shenyang: Chunfeng, 1995.

Yu, Zongqi 余宗其. *Falv yu wenxue manhua* 法律与文学漫话. Beijing: Huayi, 2001.

Yu, Zongqi 余宗其. *Zhongguo wenxue yu zhongguo falv* 中国文学与中国法律. Beijing: CUPL Press, 2002.

Yu, Zongqi 余宗其. *Waiguo wenxue yu waiguo falv* 外国文学与外国法律. Beijing: CUPL Press, 2003.

Zang, Jinshu compiled 臧晋叔. *Yuanqu xuan* 元曲选. Beijing: Zhonghua Book Company, 1958.

Zhang, Geng; Guo, Hancheng chiefly ed. 张庚、郭汉城. *Zhongguo xiju tongshi* 中国戏剧通史. Beijing: China Theater Press, 1980.

Zhang, Guohua 张国华. *Zhongguo falv sixiangshi xinbian* 中国法律思想史新编. Beijing: Peking University Press, 1998.

Zhang, Jinxian 张金铣. *Yuandai difang xingzheng zhidu yanjiu* 元代地方行政制度研究. Hefei: Anhui University Press, 2001.

Zhang, Yuezhong chief ed. 张月中. *Yuanqu tongrong shang* 元曲通融上. Taiyuan: Shanxi Ancient Books, 1999.

Zhangsun, Wuji et al. compiled 长孙无忌; Liu, Junwen annotated 刘俊文. *Tanglv shuyi* 唐律疏议. Beijing: Zhonghua Book Company, 1983.

Zhao, Jingshen; Hu, Ji selected and annotated 赵景深、胡忌. *Ming qing chuanqixuan* 明清传奇选. Beijing: China Youth, 1957.

Zhao, Yiheng 赵毅衡. *Dang shuozhe beishuo de shihou bijiao xushuxue daolun* 当说者被说的时候: 比较叙述学导论. Beijing: Renmin University of China Press, 1998.

Zheng, Chuanyin 郑传寅. *Zhongguo xiqu wenhua gailun xiudingban* 中国戏曲文化概论修订版. Wuhan: Wuhan University Press, 1998.

Zheng, Zhenduo 郑振铎. *Zhongguo suwenxue shi* 中国俗文学史. Beijing: The Commercial Press, 1998.

Zhong, Tao 钟涛. *Yuan zaju yishu shengchanlun* 元杂剧艺术生产论. Beijing: Beijing Broadcasting Institute Press, 2003.

Zhou, Chuanjia 周传家. *Zhongguo gudai xiqu* 中国古代戏曲. Beijing: The Commercial Press, 1996.

Zhou, Nan 周枏. *Luomafa yuanlun shangce* 罗马法原论上册. Beijing: The Commercial Press, 1994.

Zhou, Yibai 周贻白. *Zhongguo xijushi changbian* 中国戏剧史长编. Shanghai: Shanghai Bookstore, 2004.

Zhu, Suli 朱苏力. *Zhidu shi ruhe xingcheng de* 制度是如何形成的. Guangzhou: Sun Yat-sen University Press, 1999.

Zhu, Suli 朱苏力. *Songfa xiaxiang* 送法下乡. Beijing: CUPL Press, 2000.

Zhu, Zhaonian 祝肇年. *Zhu zhaonian xiqu lunwen xuan* 祝肇年戏曲论文选. Beijing: Culture and Art, 1998.

Zhuren, Guqiao et al. ed. 古桥主人. *Liangzhu gushi shuochang hebian* 梁祝故事说唱合编. Taibei: Xiangsheng, 1976.

Chinese Articles

Chen, Guangzhong 陈光中. "Wuzui tuiding" 无罪推定. In *Zhongguo dabaike quanshu faxuejuan* 中国大百科全书·法学卷. Beijing: Encyclopedia of China, 1984.

Cheng, Weirong 程维荣. "Lun zhongguo chuantong caichan jicheng zhidu de guyou maodun" 论中国传统财产继承制度的固有矛盾. *Zhengzhi yu falv* 政治与法律, no. 1 (2004): 149–155.

Cheng, Yizhong 程毅中. "Tan guan hanqing zaju de jiewei" 谈关汉卿杂剧的结尾. In *Gudian xiqu xiaoshuo tanyilu* 古典戏曲小说探艺录, edited by Tianjin gudian xiaoshuo xiqu yanjiuhui 天津古典小说戏曲研究会, 140–150. Tianjian: Tianjin People's Press, 1982.

Feng, Xiang 冯象. "Shenghuo zhong de meihao shiwu yongcun buyi" 生活中的美好事物永存不移. *Dushu*, 读书, no. 2 (1997): 146–148.

Feng, Xiang 冯象. "Qiuju de kunhuo" 秋菊的困惑. *Dushu* 读书, no. 1 (1998): 3–7.

Feng, Xiang 冯象. "Falv yu wenxue" 法律与文学. *Beida falv pinglun* 北大法律评论2, no. 2 (2000): 687–711.

Feng, Yuanjun 冯沅君. "Zenyang kandai dou e yuan jiqi gaibianben" 怎样看待窦娥冤及其改编本. *Wenxue pinglun* 文学评论, no. 4 (1965): 42–50.

Ge, Zhaoguang 葛兆光. "Yiban zhishi sixiang yu Xinyang shijie de lishi sixiangshi de xiefa zhiyi" 一般知识、思想与信仰世界的历史 – 思想史的写法之一. *Dushu* 读书, no. 1 (1998): 102–113.

Gu, Zhengkun 辜正坤. "Wailai shuyu fanyi yu zhongguo xueshu wenti" 外来术语翻译与中国学术问题. *Beijing daxue xuebao shehui kexueban* 北京大学学报社会科学版, no. 4 (1998): 45–52.

He, Weifang 贺卫方. "Zhongguo gudai sifa panjue de fengge yu jingsheng yi songdai wei jiben yiju jianyu yingguo bijiao" 中国古代司法判决的风格与精神 – 以宋代为基本依据兼与英国比较. *Zhongguo shehui kexue* 中国社会科学, no. 6 (1990): 203–219.

He, Weifang 贺卫方. "Guanyu shenpan weiyuanhui de jidian pinglun" 关于审判委员会的几点评论. *Beida falv pinglun* 北大法律评论 1, no. 2 (1999): 365–374.

Hua, Shizhong 华世忠. "Dou e yuan disizhe xiyi" 窦娥冤第四折析疑. *Fuyang shiyuan xuebao* 阜阳师院学报, no. 1 (1986): 53–59.

Jin, Danyuan 金丹元. "Shilun yuanqu zhong de minjian yinsu dui chuantong rujia lunli de chongji" 试论元曲中的民间因素对传统儒家伦理的冲击. *Yunnan daxue xuebao shehui kexueban* 云南大学学报社会科学版, no. 5 (2004): 81–86.

Ling, Bin 凌斌. "Pufa famang yu fazhi" 普法、法盲与法治. *Fazhi yu shehui fazhan* 法制与社会发展, no. 2 (2004): 126–140.

Luo, Di 洛地. "Zhongguo chuantong xiju yanjiu de quehan" 中国传统戏剧研究的缺憾. *Shehui kexue yanjiu* 社会科学研究, no. 3 (2000): 128–133.

Ma, Jigao 马积高. "Qingdai yasu liangzhong wenhua de duili shentou he xiquzhong huaya liangbu de shengshuai" 清代雅俗两种文化的对立、渗透和戏曲中花雅两部的盛衰.

Xibei shifan daxue xuebao shehui kexueban 西北师范大学学报社会科学版, no. 3 (1994): 25–31.

Ning, Zongyi 宁宗一. "Tan dou e yuan de beiju jingshen" 谈窦娥冤的悲剧精神. *Yuwen jiaoxue tongxun* 语文教学通讯, no. 2 (1982): 54–57.

Ouyang, Yuqian 欧阳予倩. "Pan jinlian zixu" 潘金莲自序. In *Ouyang yuqian yanjiu ziliao* 欧阳予倩研究资料, edited by Su Guanxin 苏关鑫, 153–155. Beijing: China Theater Press, 1989.

Qi, Sihe 齐思和. *Zhongguo shi tanyan* 中国史探研. Shijiazhuang: Hebei Education, 2000.

Qiang, Shigong 强世功. "Wenxue zhong de falv anti genie dou e yu baoxiya nvxing zhuyi de falv shijiao ji jiantao" 文学中的法律: 安提戈涅、窦娥与鲍西亚 – 女性主义的法律视角及检讨. *Bijiaofa yanjiu* 比较法研究, no. 2 (1995): 29–43.

Qiu, Shusen 邱树森. "Yuandai de fantan wenhua" 元代的反贪文化. *Jinan xuebao shekeban* 暨南大学学科版 23, no. 1 (2001): 116–123.

Que, Zhen 阙真. "Yuandai sida beiju de shenmei tezheng jiqi jiazhi" 元代四大悲剧的审美特征及其价值. *Guangxi shifan daxue xuebao* 广西师范大学学报, no. 4 (1991): 72–78.

Shanghai wenyi chubanshe ed. 上海文艺出版社. "Liang shanbo yu zhu yingtai" 梁山伯与祝英台. In *Yueju congkan 1* 越剧丛刊1, 1–82. Shanghai: Shanghai Literary and Art, 1962.

Song, Geng 宋耕. "Yuan zaju gaibian yu yishixingtai jiantan hongguan wenxueshi de sikao" 元杂剧改编与意识形态 – 兼谈宏观文学史的思考. *Ershiyi shiji wangluoban* 二十一世纪网络版, edited by The Chinese University of Hong Kong 香港中文大学, no. 14, May (2003).

Tian, Han 田汉. "Guan hanqing" 关汉卿. In *Zhongguo dangdai shida zhengjuji* 中国当代十大正剧集, chiefly edited by Ji Yu 集于 and Wang Jisi 王季思, 273–371. Nanjing: Jiangsu Literature and Art, 1993.

Tu, Shi 涂石. "Panni yu zhixu tan zhongguo gudian wenxue zhong de liangzhong jingshen jian yu xifang wenxue bijiao" 叛逆与秩序 – 谈中国古典文学中的两种精神兼与西方文学比较. *Xibei shifan daxue xuebao shekeban* 西北师范大学学报社科版, no. 5 (1996): 16–20.

Wang, Jinglan 王景兰. "Dou e xingxiang qianyi" 窦娥形象浅议. *Liaoning shifan daxue xuebao shekeban* 辽宁师范大学学报社科版, no. 1 (1994): 37–38.

Wang, Lina 王丽娜. "Yuanqu zai guowai" 元曲在国外. In *Shoujie yuanqu guoji xueshu yantaohui lunwenji* 首届元曲国际学术研讨会论文集, edited by Shoujie yuanqu guoji xueshu yantaohui zuweihui 首届元曲国际学术研讨会组委会. Shijiazhuang: Hebei People's Press, 1994.

Wu, Xiaoling 吴晓铃. "Shijiu gaojiasuo huilanji tansuo santi" 试就高加索灰阑记探索三题. In *Mingjia jiedu yuanqu* 名家解读元曲, compiled by Lv Weifen 吕薇芬, 413–415. Jinan: Shandong People's Press, 1999.

Xi, Rugu 悉如谷. "Zang maoxun gaixie dou e yuan yanjiu" 臧懋循改写窦娥冤研究. *Wenxue pinglun* 文学评论, no. 2 (1992): 73–84.

Xu, Shuheng 徐树恒. "Guanyu yuanren zaju de binbai" 关于元人杂剧的宾白. In *Zhongguo gudai xiqu lunji* 中国古代戏曲论集, edited by Wang Jisi et al. 王季思, 137–149. Beijing: China Prospect, 1986.

Xu, Shuofang 徐朔方. "Yuanqu zhong de baogong xi" 元曲中的包公戏. *Wenshizhe* 文史哲, September (1955): 14–16.

Xu, Zhongming 徐忠明. "Cong xuepan dasi zhangsan mingan kan qingdai xingshi susong zhidu" 从薛蟠打死张三命案看清代刑事诉讼制度. *Faxue wenji 4* 法学文集4, *Zhongshan daxue xuebao congshu* 中山大学学报丛书, 1992.

Xu, Zhongming 徐忠明. "Cong qiaotaishou luandian yuanyangpu kan zhongguo gudai sifa wenhua de tedian" 从乔太守乱点鸳鸯谱看中国古代司法文化的特点. *Lishi daguanyuan* 历史大观园, no. 9 (1994).

Xu, Zhongming 徐忠明. "Wusong mingan yu songdai xingshi susong zhidu qiantan" 武松命案与宋代刑事诉讼制度浅谈. *Lishi daguanyuan* 历史大观园, no. 11 (1994).

Xu, Zhongming 徐忠明. "Huo diyu yu wanqing zhouxian sifa yanjiu" 活地狱与晚清州县司法研究. *Bijiaofa yanjiu* 比较法研究, no. 3 (1995): 240–250.

Xu, Zhongming 徐忠明. "Baogong zaju yu yuandai falv wenhua de chubu yanjiu shang" 包公杂剧与元代法律文化的初步研究上. *Nanjing daxue falv pinglun* 南京大学法律评论, Autumn (1996): 96–105.

Xu, Zhongming 徐忠明. "Cong mingqing xiaoshuo kan zhongguoren de susong guannian" 从明清小说看中国人的诉讼观念. *Zhongshan daxue xuebao shehui kexueban* 中山大学学报社会科学版, no. 4 (1996): 54–61.

Xu, Zhongming 徐忠明. "Dou e yuan yu yuandai fazhi de ruogan wenti shixi" 窦娥冤与元代法制的若干问题试析. *Zhongshan daxue xuebao zengkan* 中山大学学报增刊 (1996): 189–197.

You, Zongrong 游宗蓉. "Yuan zaju shang xiachangshi tanjiu" 元杂剧上下场诗探究. *Zhongguo wenxue yanjiu* 中国文学研究, edited by Taiwan daxue zhongwensuo 台湾大学中文所, no. 13 (1999): 1–26.

Yu, Xiaoming 余晓明. "Wenxue yu falv zhijian yi baimaonv de wenben yanti weili" 文学与法律之间－以白毛女的文本演替为例. *Nanjing shifan daxue wenxueyuan xuebao* 南京师范大学文学院学报, no. 1 (2004): 76–80.

Yu, Zongqi 余宗其. "Liangwei meiguo faxuejia de wenxue lunju de deyushi falixue wenti he meiguo falvshi guankui" 两位美国法学家的文学论据的得与失－法理学问题和美国法律史管窥. *Guowai shehui kexue* 国外社会科学, no. 4 (1998): 64–68.

Zhang, Daxin 张大新. "Nongjia shan e yiliguan de supu xianxian zhang guobin zaju de wenhua yiyun" 农家善恶义利观的素朴显现－张国宾杂剧的文化意蕴. *Pingdingshan shizhuan xuebao* 平顶山师专学报, no. 1 (1999): 17–23.

Zhang, Weiying 张维迎. "Falv yu shehui guifan" 法律与社会规范. *Bijiao* 比较, 11 (2004): 158–194.

Zhang, Weiying; Deng, Feng 张维迎、邓峰. "Xinxi jili yu liandai Zeren dui zhongguo gudai lianzuo baojia zhidu de fa he jingjixue jieshi" 信息、激励与连带责任－对中国古代连坐、保甲制度的法和经济学解释. *Zhongguo shehui kexue* 中国社会科学, no. 3 (2003): 99–112.

Zhao, Xiaoli 赵晓力. "Zhongguo jindai nongcun tudi jiaoyi zhong de qiyue xiguan yu guojiafa" 中国近代农村土地交易中的契约、习惯与国家法. *Beida falv pinglun* 北大法律评论 1, no. 2 (1999): 427–504.

Zhao, Xiaoli 赵晓力. "Yaoming de difang qiuju da guansi zai jiedu" 要命的地方: 秋菊打官司再解读. *Beida falv pinglun* 北大法律评论, Spring (2005): 707–718.

Zhou, Enlai 周恩来. "Guanyu kunqu shiwuguan de liangci jianghua" 关于昆曲十五贯的两次讲话. *Wenyi yanjiu* 文艺研究, no. 1 (1980): 4–7.

Zhou, Xianshen 周先慎. "Zhaoshi guer de shenmei tezheng" 赵氏孤儿的审美特征. *Wenshi zhishi* 文史知识, no. 7 (1992).

Zhou, Xianshen 周先慎. "Zhaoshi guer dui lishi sucai de gaizao" 赵氏孤儿对历史素材的改造. *Wenshi zhishi* 文史知识, no. 11 (1992).

Zhu, Dongrun 朱东润. "Yuan zaju jiqi shidai" 元杂剧及其时代. In *Mingjia jiedu yuanqu* 名家解读元曲, 16–51.

Zhu, Suli 朱苏力. "Xiandai fazhi de helixing he juxianxing" 现代法律的合理性和局限性. *Dongfang* 东方, no. 3 (1996).

Zhu, Suli 朱苏力. "Yujing lun yizhong falv zhidu yanjiu fangfa de goujian" 语境论－种法律制度研究方法的构建. *Zhongwai faxue* 中外法学, no. 1 (2000).

Zhu, Suli 朱苏力. "Panjueshu de beihou" 判决书的背后. *Faxue yanjiu* 法学研究, no. 3 (2001): 3–18.

All the Following Articles are from Zhang Yuezhong Chiefly ed. 张月中.
Yuanqu tongrong 元曲通融. Taiyuan: Shanxi Ancient Books, 1999.

Chen, Xiaolu 陈晓鲁. "Xiqu wutai shikong xingshi zai guan hanqing zaju zhong de zuichu biaoxian" 戏曲舞台时空形式在关汉卿杂剧中的最初表现, 1360–1364.

Deng, Shaoji 邓绍基. "Cong dou e yuan de butong banben yinchu de jige wenti" 从窦娥冤的不同版本引出的几个问题, 1583–1586.

Deng, Shaoji 邓绍基. "Lun yuanzaju sixiang neirong de ruogan tezheng" 论元杂剧思想内容的若干特征, 520–523.

Deng, Shaoji; Yao, Shuyi 邓绍基、幺书仪. "Ji junxiang de zhaoshi guer" 纪君祥的赵氏孤儿, 2189–2193.

Fu, Xuancong 傅璇琮. "Du lun yuan zaju" 读论元杂剧, 329–331.

Guo, Yingde 郭英德. "Guanju wenhua yiyun fawei" 关剧文化意蕴发微, 1310–1313.

Guo, Zhenqin 郭振勤. "Yuan zaju baogongxi faan qingjie touming de gousi yishu" 元杂剧包公戏发案情节透明的构思艺术, 708–709.

Li, Hanqiu 李汉秋. "Yuandai gonganxi lunlve" 元代公案戏论略, 687–690.

Li, Jianwu 李健吾. "Cong xingge shang chuxi jianji guan hanqing chuangzao de lixiang xingge" 从性格上出戏兼及关汉卿创造的理想性格, 1348–1351.

Liao, Ben 廖奔. "Chongzhou zhuangfu cong washe goulan dao miaohui xitai yuan zaju huodong fangshi kaocha" 冲州撞府：从瓦舍勾栏到庙会戏台 – 元杂剧活动方式考察, 912–915.

Liu, Mengbai 刘萌柏. "Ji junxiang zhaoshi guer jiqi yingxiang" 纪君祥赵氏孤儿及其影响, 2187–2189.

Liu, Shusheng; Zhang, Tao 刘树胜、张涛. "Lun yuan zaju zuopin zhong de meng" 论元杂剧作品中的梦, 524–527.

Lu, Kanru; Feng, Yuanjun 陆侃如、冯沅君. "Zhongguo wenxue shigao" 中国文学史稿 vol. 12, 33–36.

Luo, Jintang 罗锦堂. "Xiancun yuanren zaju zhi fenlei" 现存元人杂剧之分类, 547–557.

Shao, Zengqi 邵曾祺. "Guan hanqing zuopin kao" 关汉卿作品考, 1270–1273.

Wang, Jisi 王季思. "Yuan zaju de xingcheng he xingqi" 元杂剧的形成和兴起, 1333–1324.

Wu, Guoqin 吴国钦. "Guan hanqing he tade zaju dou e yuan" 关汉卿和他的杂剧窦娥冤, 1553–1559.

Wu, Mei 吴梅. "Quyuan" 曲原, 1–11.

Yan, Changke 颜长珂. "Yuan zaju zhong de liyuan xingxiang" 元杂剧中的吏员形象, 710–716.

Yan, Dunyi 严敦易. "Lun yuan zaju" 论元杂剧, 323–328.

Zeng, Yongyi 曾永义. "Zaju zhong guishen shijie de yishi xingtai" 杂剧中鬼神世界的意识形态, 528–532.

Zhang, Peitian 张培田. "Lun yuan zaju yu yuandai fazhi" 论元杂剧与元代法制, 406–412.

Zhang, Yanjin 张燕瑾. "Tan xiqu zai yuandai fanrong de yuanyin" 谈戏曲在元代繁荣的原因, 378–381.

Zhang, Yimu 张一木. "Moshi dou e zai mengyuan" 莫使窦娥再蒙冤, 1592–1593.

Zhou, Miaozhong 周妙中. "He tan zhengbi xiansheng shangque yuandai shifou yiququshi de wenti" 和谭正璧先生商榷元代是否以曲取士的问题, 420–421.

Zhou, Xiaochi 周晓痴. "Renwu de qinggan guiji yu zuojia de shenmei pingjia" 人物的情感轨迹与作家的审美评价, 1579–1582.

Zhou, Yueliang 周月亮. "Dui wu xiaoru xiansheng ping dou e yuan de jidian yijian" 对吴小如先生评窦娥冤的几点意见, 1599.

Zhu, Guangrong 朱光荣. "Lun yuan zaju fanrong de yuanyin" 论元杂剧繁荣的原因, 382–386.

Zhu, Zhaonian 祝肇年. "Dou E yuan gushi yuanliu manshu" 窦娥冤故事源流漫述, 1534–1537.

Chinese Newspaper and Internet

Chen, Zhongfan 陈中凡. "Cong lishi sucai dao zhaoshi guer zaju" 从历史素材到赵氏孤儿杂剧. *Xiju Bao* 戏剧报, no. 15, 16 (1961).

Duan, Baolin 段宝林. "Guanyu baogong de renleixue sikao" 关于包公的人类学思考. *Guangming Ribao* 光明日报 (Beijing), May 6, 1999.

Ge, Jianxiong 葛剑雄. "Chongdu mingshi hairui zhuan" 重读明史海瑞传. *Zhongguo ai sixiang wang* 中国爱思想网, 2023. www.aisixiang.com/data/174.html.

Guo, Yingde 郭英德. "Yuan zaju zhongguo gudian xiqu yishu de qipa" 元杂剧: 中国古典戏曲艺术的奇葩. *Guangming Ribao* 光明日报, May 10, 1999.

He, Lulu 和璐璐. "Sanda wenti zhiyi gebanben zhaoshi guer re" 三大问题质疑各版本赵氏孤儿热. *Zhongguo xinwen wang* 中国新闻网, 2003. www.chinanews.com.cn/n/2003-11-11/26/367359.html.

Zhang, Yanjin 张燕瑾. "Zhaoshi guer de jiaose anpai he xiju jiegou" 赵氏孤儿的脚色安排和戏剧结构. *Guangming Ribao* 光明日报 (Beijing), March 1, 1983.

English Monographs

Abraham, Henry J. *The Judicial Process: An Introductory Analysis of the Courts of the United Sates, England, and France*, 4th ed. Oxford: Oxford University Press, 1980.

Althusser, Louis. *For Marx*. Translated by Ben Brewster. New York: Verso, 2005.

Axelrod, Robert M. *The Evolution of Cooperation*. New York: Penguin Books, 1990.

Bao, Gan. *In Search of the Supernatural: The Written Record*. Translated by Kenneth J. DeWoskin and J. I. Crump Jr. Stanford: Stanford University Press, 1996.

Becker, Gary S. *A Treatise on the Family*. Cambridge, MA: Harvard University Press, 1981.

Becker, Gary S. *Accounting for Tastes*. Cambridge, MA: Harvard University Press, 1996.

Bergman, Paul; Asimow, Michael. *Reel Justice: The Courtroom Goes to the Movies*. New York: Andrews McMeel Publishing, 2006.

Bodenheimer, Edgar. *Jurisprudence: The Philosophy and Method of the Law*, 2nd ed. Cambridge, MA: Harvard University Press, 1967.

Bourdieu, Pierre. *Distinction: A Social Critique of the Judgment of Taste*. Translated by Richard Nice. Cambridge, MA: Harvard University Press, 1984.

Brooks, Peter; Gewirtz, Paul. *Law's Stories, Narrative and Rhetoric in the Law*. New Haven: Yale University Press, 1996.

Cardozo, Benjamin N. *Selected Writings of Benjamin Nathan Cardozo*. Edited by Margaret E. Hall. New York: Fallon Publications, 1947.

Ch'en, Ssu-ma. *The Grand Scribe's Records*, vol. 1. Edited by William H. Nienhauser Jr. Bloomington: Indiana University Press, 1994.

Ch'en, Ssu-ma. *The Grand Scribe's Records*, vol. 11. Edited by William H. Nienhauser Jr. Bloomington: Indiana University Press, 2019.

Ch'en, Ssu-ma. *The Grand Scribe's Records*, Revised vol. 7. Bloomington: Indiana University Press, 2021.

Ch'ü, T'ung-tsu. *Local Government in China under the Ch'ing*. Stanford: Stanford University Press, 1962.

Corwin, Edward S. *The "High Law" Background of American Constitutional Law*. Carmel: Liberty Fund, 2008.

Curiae, Amicus ed. *Law in Action, an Anthology of the Law in Literature*. New York: Crown Publishers, 1947.

Dershowitz, Alan M. *The Best Defense*. New York: Vintage, 2011.

Durkheim, Émile. *The Division of Labor in Society*. Edited by Steven Lukes. New York: Free Press, 2014.

Ellickson, Robert C. *Order without Law: How Neighbors Settle Disputes*. Cambridge, MA: Harvard University Press, 1991.

Elster, Jon; Slagstad, Rune eds. *Constitutionalism and Democracy*. Cambridge: Cambridge University Press, 1993.

Evans-Prichard, Edward Even. *Theories of Primitive Religion*. Oxford: Clarendon Press, 1965.

Fish, Stanley. *Is There a Text in This Class?* Cambridge, MA: Harvard University Press, 1980.

Foucault, Michael. *Discipline and Punish: The Birth of the Prison*. Translated by Alan Sheridan. New York: Vintage, 1977.

Foucault, Michael. *Power/Knowledge: Selected Interviews and Other Writings, 1972–1977*. Translated by Colin Gordon et al. New York: Pantheon Books, 1980.

Foucault, Michael. *Politics, Philosophy, Culture*. Translated by Alan Sheridan et al. London: Routledge, 1990.

Fuller, Lon. *The Morality of Law*, rev. ed. New Haven: Yale University Press, 1969.

Hart, H. L. A. *The Concept of Law*, 2nd ed. Oxford: Clarendon Press, 1994.

Hayek, Friedrich A. *Law, Legislation, and Liberty*, vol. 1. Chicago: University of Chicago Press, 1973.

Hayek, Friedrich A. *Individualism and Economic Order*. Chicago: The University of Chicago Press, 2012.

Holmes, Oliver Wendell Jr. *The Common Law*. New York: Little, Brown, and Company, 1948.

The Holy Bible (The King James Version). New York: Ivy Books, 1991.

The Holy Qur'an. Surrey: Islam International Publications Ltd., 2021.

Kuhn, Thomas. *The Copernican Revolution*. Cambridge, MA: Harvard University Press, 1957.

Kuper, Adam. *The Chosen Primate, Human Nature and Cultural Diversity*. Cambridge, MA: Harvard University Press, 1994.

Levinson, Sanford; Mailloux, Steven eds. *Interpreting Law and Literature, a Hermeneutic Reader*. Chicago: Northwestern University Press, 1988.

Locke, John. *Two Treatises of Government and a Letter Concerning Toleration*. Edited by Ian Shapiro. New Haven: Yale University, 2003.

Luis Borges, Jorge. *Obras Completas 1923–1972*. Buenos Aires: Emecé Editores, 1974.

Marx, Karl; Engels, Frederick. *Collected Works*, vol. 5. Translated by Clemens Dutt, W. Lough and C. P. Magill. New York: International Publishers Co, 1976.

Marx, Karl; Engels, Frederick. *Collected Works of Marx and Engels*, vol. 40. New York: International Publishers, 1983.

Mayr, Ernest. *This Is Biology, the Science of the Living World*. Cambridge, MA: Harvard University Press, 1997.

Mclellan, David. *Ideology*, 2nd ed. Minneapolis: University of Minnesota Press, 1995.

Menglong, Feng. *Stories to Awaken the World*, vol. 3. Translated by Yang Shuhui and Yang Yunqin. Seattle: University of Washington Press, 2014.

Miller, David ed. *The Blackwell Encyclopedia of Political Thought*. London: Blackwell, 1987.

Minda, Gary. *Post-Modern Legal Movements, Law and Jurisprudence at Century's End*. New York: New York University Press, 1995.

Ming, Gao. *The Lute: Kao Ming's P'i-p'a chi*. Translated by Jean Mulligan. New York: Columbia University Press, 1980.

Montesquieu. *The Spirit of the Laws*. Cambridge: Cambridge University Press, 1989.

Nietzsche, Friedrich. *Daybreak*. Translated by R. J. Hollingdale. Cambridge: Cambridge University Press, 1997.

North, Douglass C. *Structure and Change in Economic History*. New York: W. W. Norton, 1981.

Oates, Whitney J.; O'Neill, Eugene eds. *The Complete Greek Drama*. New York: Random, 1938.

Olson, Mancur. *The Logic of Collective Action*. Cambridge, MA: Harvard University Press, 1971.

Posner, Eric A. *Law and Social Norms*. Cambridge, MA: Harvard University Press, 2002.

Posner, Richard A. *The Economics of Justice*. Cambridge, MA: Harvard University Press, 1981.

Posner, Richard A. *Law and Literature, a Misunderstood Relation*. Cambridge, MA: Harvard University Press, 1988.

Posner, Richard A. *The Problems of Jurisprudence*. Cambridge, MA: Harvard University Press, 1990.

Posner, Richard A. ed. *The Essential Holmes, Selections from the Letters, Speeches, Judicial Opinions, and Other Writings of Oliver Wendell Holmes, Jr.* Chicago: University of Chicago Press, 1992.

Posner, Richard A. *Sex and Reason*. Cambridge, MA: Harvard University Press, 1992.

Posner, Richard A. *Overcoming Law*. Cambridge, MA: Harvard University Press, 1995.

Posner, Richard A. *Law and Legal Theory in England and America*. Oxford: Oxford University Press, 1996.

Posner, Richard A. *Law and Literature*, 2nd ed. Cambridge, MA: Harvard University Press, 1998.

Posner, Richard A. *The Problematics of Moral and Legal Theory*. Cambridge, MA: Harvard University Press, 1999.

Posner, Richard A. *Law, Pragmatism, and Democracy*. Cambridge, MA: Harvard University Press, 2003.

Posner, Richard A. *The Problematics of Moral and Legal Theory.* Cambridge, MA: Harvard University Press, 2009.

Ridley, Matt. *The Origins of Virtue: Human Instincts and the Evolution of Cooperation*. London: Penguin Books, 1998.

Sartre, Jean-Paul. *What Is Literature? and Other Essays*. Introduced by Steven Ungar. Cambridge, MA: Harvard University Pres, 1988.

Schelling, Thomas C. *The Strategy of Conflict*. Cambridge, MA: Harvard University Press, 1980.

Shakespeare, William. *Hamlet*. Edited by John Dover Wilson. Cambridge: Cambridge University Press, 2009.

Shifu, Wang. *The Story of the Western Wing*. Translated by Stephen H. West and Wilt L. Idema. Berkeley: University of California Press, 1995.

Steen, R. Grant. *DNA and Destiny: Nature and Nurture in Human Behavior*. Berlin: Springer, 1996.

Weber, Max. *Law in Economy and Society*. Translated by Edward Shils and Max Rheinstein. Cambridge, MA: Harvard University Press, 1954.

Weber, Max. *Economy and Society*. Chicago: University of California Press, 1978.

Weinreb, Llyod L. *Natural Law and Justice*. Cambridge, MA: Harvard University Press, 1987.

Wesberg, Richard H. *The Failure of the World: The Lawyer as Protagonist in Modern Fiction*. New Haven: Yale University Press, 1984.

Williams, Patricia J. *The Alchemy of Race and Rights*. Cambridge, MA: Harvard University Press, 1991.

Wilson, Edward O. *On Human Nature*. Cambridge, MA: Harvard University Press, 1978.

Wilson, Edward O. *Sociobiology, the New Synthesis*, 25th Anniversary ed. Cambridge, MA: Harvard University Press, 2000.

Zedong, Mao. *Selected Works of Mao Tse-tung*. Paris: Foreign Languages Press, 2021.

English Articles

Atiyah, Patrick S. "Judicial-Legislative Relations in England." In *Judges and Legislators: Toward Institutional Comity*, edited by Robert A. Katzmann, 129–161. Washington, DC: Brookings Institution, 1988.

Becker, Gary S. "Crime and Punishment: An Economic Approach." *Journal of Political Economy* 76 (1968): 169–217.

Dred Sccott v. Sanford, 19 Howard 393 (1857).

Farber, Daniel A.; Sherry, Suzanna. "Telling Stories Out of School: An Essay on Legal Narratives." *Stanford Law Review* 45 (1993): 807–855.

Foucault, Michael. "Nietzsche, Genealogy, History." In *The Foucault Reader*, edited by Paul Rabinow, 76–97. New York: Pantheon House, 1984.

Holmes, Oliver Wendell Jr. "The Path of the Law." *Harvard Law Review* 10, no. 8 (1897): 457–478.

Idema, Wilt. "Why You Never Have Read a Yuan Drama: The Transformation of *Zaju* at the Ming Court." In *Studi in onore di Lanciello Lanciotti*, edited by S. M. Carletti, M. Sacchetti and P. Santangelo, 765–791. Napoli: Istituto Universiatorio Orientale, Dipartimento di Studi Asiatici, 1996.

Jordan, William S. "Legislative History and Statutory Interpretation: The Relevance of English Practice." *29 University of San Francisco Law Review* 1 (1994): 719–734.

Levinson, Sanford. "Law as Literature." *Texas Law Review* 60 (1982): 373–403.

McKnight, Brian. "Tang Law and Later Law: The Roots of Continuity." *Journal of the American Oriental Society*, no. 115 (1995): 410–420.

Ocko, Jonathan K. "I'll Take It All the Way to Beijing: Capital Appeals in the Qing." *The Journal of Asian Studies* 47, no. 2 (1988): 291–315.

Posner, Richard A. "Creating a Legal Framework for Economic Development." *The World Bank Research Observer* 13, no. 1 (1998): 1–11.

Standard Oil Company of New Jersey v. United States, 221 U. S. 1 (1911).

Tsui-jung, Liu. "The Demographic Dynamics of Some Clans in the Lower Yang Tze Area, Ca 1400–1940." *Academic Economic Papers* 9, no. 1 (1981): 115–160.

Index

For Product Safety Concerns and Information please contact our EU
representative GPSR@taylorandfrancis.com
Taylor & Francis Verlag GmbH, Kaufingerstraße 24, 80331 München, Germany

www.ingramcontent.com/pod-product-compliance
Ingram Content Group UK Ltd.
Pitfield, Milton Keynes, MK11 3LW, UK
UKHW021038090625
459195UK00009B/7

.